FORENSIC ASSESSMENT
of VIOLENCE RISK

FORENSIC ASSESSMENT

of VIOLENCE RISK

A Guide for
Risk Assessment
and
Risk Management

MARY ALICE CONROY   DANIEL C. MURRIE

BICENTENNIAL
1807
WILEY
2007
BICENTENNIAL

John Wiley & Sons, Inc.

Contents

Preface   *vii*

Acknowledgments   *xi*

1   Historical Overview of Risk Assessment   1

2   Introducing a Broad Model for Risk Assessment   16

3   Risk of What? Defining the Referral Question   34

4   What Do We Know Overall? Consider Normative
Data and Population Base Rates   45

5   What Do We Know about Individuals Like
This One? Empirically Supported Risk and
Protective Factors   67

6   What Do We Know about This Individual?
Idiographic Factors and the Need for
Individualized Assessment   83

7   What Can We Say about the Results of a
Risk Assessment? Risk Communication   99

8   From Risk Assessment to Risk Management   135

9   Risk Assessment of Patients with Serious
Mental Illness   153

10   Risk Assessment with Sexual Offenders   179

11 Risk Assessment with Juvenile Offenders 202

12 Risk Assessment of Death Penalty Defendants 235

Epilogue 255

Appendix A Risk Assessment Instruments 259

Appendix B Sample Risk Assessment Reports 269

References 309

Index 353

Preface

For decades, justice systems throughout North America have relied on psychiatrists and psychologists to make predictions regarding future violence. As early as 1981, Saleem Shah identified 16 separate junctures in the legal system that required a determination about an individual's potential dangerousness (Klassen & O'Connor, 1988). Most often, risk for violence becomes an issue in decisions regarding sentencing, parole, disposition in juvenile courts, application of the death penalty, civil commitment (including its application to sexually violent predators), and discharge following findings of insanity or incompetence. Courts often make difficult decisions, attempting to strike some reasonable balance between protecting individual civil liberties and protecting the community from potential harm. In these decisions, the stakes are high.

When a mental health professional agrees to conduct a forensic assessment of violence risk, the professional steps into controversy. Certain disagreements rage within the mental health fields; there are also fundamental differences between the ways that the mental health field and the legal field approach questions of individual risk. To navigate the minefields—while maintaining integrity and providing useful information to the decision maker—requires a broad range of expertise. Proper training, supervised experience, ongoing consultation, and constant review of new literature are essential.

We wrote this text for professionals who are taking the first steps toward developing the necessary expertise to conduct forensic assessments of violence risk. This text introduces an integrated model—broad enough to use across a variety of contexts—for science-based risk assessment. The book begins with a brief historical overview of the field. This is followed by an explanation of the risk assessment model, which begins with clarifying the risk assessment question and concludes with linking the completed risk assessment to strategies for risk management. The risk assessment literature has grown almost exponentially in recent decades, and we describe much of what is known at the time of publication. However, new knowledge becomes available daily, and evaluators will need to seek the most current data to prepare for each risk assessment.

Along with the recent explosion in literature on risk assessment, more risk assessment instruments have become available. We review many of these instruments and describe them in Appendix A. However, we emphasize that no single instrument is essential or even appropriate across all risk assessments and that no instrument alone will *fully* complete the task of risk assessment. Our goal here is to describe the current risk assessment toolbox, with the understanding that it will require expansion as new methods are developed.

Appendix B contains a number of sample reports submitted by mental health professionals experienced in conducting violence risk assessments and communicating results to courts or other decision makers. We offer these reports because they can serve as helpful models. However, there is no *single* approach that is perfect for presenting results across all cases, and evaluators will differ according to their context and even their own personal style.

Because we wrote this book primarily for mental health professionals who anticipate conducting risk assessments, we expect most readers will be psychologists, psychiatrists, social workers, and counselors, as well as graduate students in each of these fields. However, we also recognize that many nonclinicians request, read, and make weighty decisions based on violence risk assessments. Thus, we attempted to write a text that will be helpful to judges, attorneys, jail administrators, probation officers, and others in the criminal justice system. Specifically, the discussion of risk management may have broad relevance. We hope that the text will help *consumers* of risk assessment reports become more discerning and appropriately challenge sloppy work and unsupported clinical opinions. To be of value, our model needs to assist decision makers in making society safer, while at the same time respecting individual liberties and allowing those who are at risk for some type of violent behavior to function in the least restrictive environment at the lowest cost to society.

We wrote this book hoping to bring an emphasis on good science to the real world of practical forensic work. We are both academics; our day jobs involve staying abreast of research and training student clinicians based on the latest empirical developments. However, we both maintain private forensic-clinical practices, through which we conduct risk assessments for courts, attorneys, and state agencies. We also consult with these professionals about implementing risk management and risk assessment on a regular basis. Before joining a university, the first author worked 20 years for the U.S. Bureau of Prisons, participating in over 1,200 risk assessments and often observing their consequences in the courtroom and in the community. As academics, we are delighted with the field's increasing wealth of rigorous risk assessment research and methodology. But we also spend enough time in the field to notice that empirical advances have not always influenced widespread practice as much as we might hope, and that real-world cases rarely fit perfectly into empirical models. We have also encountered cases for which few empirical resources are available (consider, for example, the examinee who comes from a context for which no violence base rate data are available and in which no risk assessment measures have been validated).

Furthermore, we notice that the consumers of risk assessments (e.g., judges, probation officers), though often quite intelligent and professionally competent, have rarely received education in the science and principles that underlie good risk assessment practice. This is an exciting time to study risk assessment, and this book is an effort to help the field keep pace with emerging research and emerging practice standards.

What happens when clinicians fail to keep pace with current research and practice standards? Challenges to unscientific courtroom testimony regarding risk are raised. The American Psychological Association (2005) recently filed an amicus curiae brief with the U.S. Fifth Circuit Court of Appeals challenging problematic risk testimony. Subsequently, the Fifth Circuit essentially ruled that no legal standard for risk assessment at capital sentencing exists at present. At the time of this writing, the Texas Psychological Association was in the process of filing a brief in a similar case, and the outcome of that case is pending. However, these are only the beginning. The field has advanced to the point that poor practice and unsupported, pure opinion testimony are increasingly recognized as such.

The goal of this text is not to provide a rigid formula that must be applied to every single risk assessment. We acknowledge that there may be a few circumstances in which the model that we present does not apply, and some circumstances in which the model will require modifications. Nevertheless, our goal is to present a general model—based on good science and comprising key practice principles essential to most cases—that will be useful and appropriate across *most* risk assessments. We emphasize forensic assessment of violence risk—that is, violence risk assessment conducted to inform specific legal questions—as opposed to all possible consultation regarding violence potential (e.g., addressing employer concerns about workplace violence or performing other forms of *threat assessment*). We offer examples of how clinicians can employ the model and describe relevant techniques. Much like the evidence-based practice model currently extolled by clinical treatment providers (American Psychological Association, 2006), the model we present has three components: grounding in scientific research, careful consideration of the individual in context, and use of the clinician's expertise. It requires the clinician to first access the latest scientific data relative to the task at hand. Then the clinician must consider the individual's historical patterns of behavior and the context in which the person is most likely to function in the future. Clinical expertise will be necessary in knowing what evidence is required, where it can best be found, how to integrate the data for a final conclusion, and how to communicate the conclusion effectively to decision makers. We hope this model is useful to clinicians who strive to conduct thorough risk assessments that are scientifically sound, ethically sound, and of practical use to the systems that request risk assessment.

Acknowledgments

We thank Drs. Linda Berberoglu, David Mrad, Chad Brinkley, and Mark Cunningham for contributing samples of their risk assessment reports. We are also grateful to Amanda McGorty for serving as research assistant for one chapter. Finally, we enthusiastically thank Chelsea Janke, our exceptional student assistant, without whose work the final version of this book might not have made it to press.

1

Historical Overview of Risk Assessment

Societies have always had methods of identifying and containing individuals who appeared to put the community at risk. However, it was not until the nineteenth century that scientists entered the field of assessing dangerousness. In the late 1800s, the Italian positivist school of criminology, led by Cesare Lombroso, developed the theory of atavism. According to Lombroso, violent criminals were really throwbacks to primitive humans and could generally be identified by their physical characteristics. Once identified, the punishment should be designed to fit the criminal, not the crime. Lombroso's expert testimony generally advocated that those he identified as throwbacks be permanently contained, or even executed, because they would forever be a menace to the community.

As the positivist movement grew into the twentieth century, the focus changed from containment to treatment. Perhaps criminals who had been identified could be rehabilitated, authorities conceded, but it would take a lengthy period of time, and sentences needed to be indeterminate. This "rehabilitative/incapacitation model" continued to predominate well into the 1970s (Melton, Petrila, Poythress, & Slobogin, 1997, p. 251).

During the 1930s, society began turning to the medical community for explanations of and solutions to criminality. In 1936, Dr. James Pritchard coined the term "moral insanity" to describe people who had a poorly formed conscience but otherwise appeared to function adequately (Conroy, 2003). Shortly thereafter, Hervey Cleckley (1941) published his first edition of *The Mask of Sanity*, in which he described individuals who ultimately became known as "psychopaths." Although these individuals appeared intelligent and clearly were not psychotic, they also presented severe social problems, in that they appeared to have little empathy for others or remorse for harmful behaviors. These medical explanations for crime quickly influenced the legal system. A prime example was the advent of the sexual psychopath laws. In a rare show of unity, medical professionals, the press, and the anxious public optimistically embraced the idea that psychopaths, at risk for sexually assaulting the innocent, could be easily identified and successfully treated (Lieb, Quinsey, & Berliner, 1998). The sexual psychopath statutes were considered humane and enlightened, and by the mid-1960s, 26 states had enacted such laws (Lieb et al., 1998).

The 1960s, however, began an era of disillusionment with medical solutions to violence. The movement away from indefinite hospitalization of the mentally ill and toward treatment in the community gained strength. Thomas Szasz (1963) offered a series of popular books in which he castigated the medical community for diagnosing and confining individuals who were simply deviant. He declared the concept of mental illness to be a myth and psychiatric treatment to be a hoax. The public became concerned both about unnecessary restrictions on individual civil liberties and unnecessary expenses to the taxpayer.

First-Generation Research on the Prediction of Dangerousness

For more than half a century preceding the 1970s, civil commitment of the mentally ill had become increasingly easy. Civil commitment was understood to be a *parens patriae* action in which the state was fulfilling its obligation to care for citizens who could not care for themselves. In many places, one could be civilly committed simply with the signature of one or two physicians. Even if courts were involved, they generally showed great deference to medical judgment. By 1970, 31 states had statutes allowing physicians to confine people to hospitals simply because they allegedly needed treatment (Melton et al., 1997).

However, in the decade that followed, courts began to take a harder look at commitment laws and generally found that a need for treatment, by itself, was not sufficient to severely curtail one's civil liberties. In *O'Connor v. Donaldson* (1975), the U.S. Supreme Court held that it was unconstitutional to confine a nondangerous person who was capable of self-care. Nonetheless, the court continued to insist on clinical expertise to assess illness and predict danger to self or others, saying that the relevant evidence in such cases "turns on the meaning of the facts which must be interpreted by expert psychiatrists and psychologists" (*Addington v. Texas*, 1979).

Meanwhile, mental health professionals raised questions about the legality and the practical viability of clinical assessments of violence risk. Saleem Shah (1975), a key figure in shaping policy and practice related to law and mental health, initially argued strongly that the law should not ask clinicians to make predictions regarding a psychiatric patient's potential dangerousness. He emphasized that dangerousness was poorly defined, restrictions on patients' freedom were severe, and clinician accuracy was poor.

Yet in this era of controversy, several opportunities fortuitously arose for researchers to assess clinicians' abilities to predict dangerousness. The first followed a U.S. Supreme Court decision (*Baxstrom v. Herald*, 1966) that resulted in the release or transfer of many psychiatric patients whom clinicians had predicted to be dangerous. In a 4-year follow-up study, only 20% of the releasees were found to be assaultive either in a civil hospital or in the community (Steadman & Cocozza, 1974). A similar study followed a group of patients released against medical advice from Bridgewater State Hospital in Massachusetts. Although the assault rate among those predicted to be dangerous was considerably higher than for patients not predicted to be dangerous, the false-positive rate (i.e., those predicted to be dangerous who, given opportunity, were not) still exceeded 65% (Kozol, Boucher, & Garofolo, 1972). In 1976, Cocozza and Steadman followed 257 indicted felony defendants found incompetent and released in New York; they found that 14% of those predicted to be dangerous were rearrested for assault, as compared to 16% of those thought not to be dangerous. A subsequent study of patients released from the Patuxent Institute in Maryland revealed a 58% false-positive rate in terms of patients whom clinicians had predicted to be violent (Steadman, 1977). This finding eventually led the state of Maryland to abolish its Defective Delinquent statute.

Following the case of *Dixon v. Attorney General of the Commonwealth of Pennsylvania* (1971), Thornberry and Jacoby (1979) found a false positive rate of 86% among releasees originally predicted to be dangerous. Investigating a Canadian sample, Quinsey, Warneford, Pruesse, and Link (1975) followed 91 male patients discharged against medical advice from a maximum-security mental health center in Ontario directly to the community. Over a 3-year period, only 17% committed a violent offense.

To examine the process involved in predicting dangerousness, Pfohl (1978) studied 12 teams of mental health professionals at a forensic hospital in Lima, Ohio. These teams used no specific, universal criteria to reach conclusions about dangerousness. Predictions appeared to be influenced by a wide variety of theoretical orientations. Explaining what they considered most important in making their predictions, the clinicians listed factors that ranged from the subject's past criminal record to whether they would be comfortable with the examinee living next door to them.

Taken together, these field studies strongly suggested that clinicians labeled dangerous many people who, given the opportunity, hurt no one. However, methodological problems plagued this research. First, given the large number of people released simultaneously, it is doubtful that those sent directly to the community could be consistently located for long-term follow-up. Second, much of the research was done with patients who were institutionalized and treated for a number of years following the prediction that they would be dangerous (Klassen & O'Connor, 1988). Third, most studies relied on official criminal records that were prone to gross underestimation of actual violence (Douglas & Webster, 1999). Fourth, the operational definition of violence was often unclear and/or inconsistent from one study to another (Monahan, 1981). Finally, it was unclear whether the original predictions of dangerousness were really clinical at all, or whether clinicians had simply endorsed administrative decisions for political reasons (Litwack & Schlesinger, 1999).

Methodological flaws like these made any conclusions about the exact percentage of false positives impossible. However, taken together, the data did support the general conclusion that violence among mentally disordered people was not as common as anticipated and that the predictions of dangerous behavior that mental health professionals offered were not particularly reliable. Prominent scholars in the field concluded that the mental health profession was incapable of predicting dangerousness with any reasonable degree of accuracy (American Psychiatric Association, 1974; American Psychological Association, 1978; Cocozza & Steadman, 1976; Megargee, 1981; Shah, 1975). The situation prompted Monahan (1981, 1984) to call for a new generation of better-focused, better-planned research.

The Courts Speak

As social scientists, mental health professionals, and some legal scholars (e.g., Dershowitz, 1969; Dix, 1977) decried the gross inaccuracy of violence prediction, the courts steadfastly held that the problem was not insurmountable. In 1976, the Supreme Court of California, while acknowledging that prediction of dangerousness was far from perfect, still issued the opinion that clinicians had a "duty to warn" third parties about a potentially dangerous client (*Tarasoff v. The Regents of the University of California*). Their opinion clearly implied that the court assumed clinicians should be able to make reasonable predictions of violence. That same year, the U.S. Supreme Court declared that violence prediction in a death penalty case could be reasonably accomplished (*Jurek v. Texas*, 1976).

The case most directly addressing the issue of mental health professionals predicting dangerousness came before the U.S. Supreme Court in 1983 (*Barefoot v. Estelle*). Based in part on the testimony of a psychiatrist regarding future dangerousness, a Texas defendant convicted of murder received the death penalty. The American Psychiatric Association (1983) went so far as to submit an *amicus curiae* brief to the Court arguing that psychiatric predictions of dangerousness were notoriously inaccurate—in fact, wrong as often as 2 out of 3 times. Although the justices acknowledged the brief, as well as the work done by John Monahan (1981), they were not persuaded. Instead, they explained:

> The suggestion that no psychiatrist's testimony may be presented with respect to a defendant's future dangerousness is somewhat like asking us to disinvent the wheel. In the first place, it is contrary to our cases. If the likelihood of a defendant's committing further crimes is a constitutionally acceptable criterion for imposing the death penalty, which it is, *Jurek v. Texas*, 428 U.S. 262 (1976), and if it is not impossible for even a layperson sensibly to arrive at that conclusion, it makes little sense, if any, to submit that psychiatrists, out of the entire universe of persons who might have an opinion on the issue, would know so little about the subject that they should not be permitted to testify. (*Barefoot v. Estelle*, 1983, p. 897)

In the 2 decades that followed, courts and the criminal justice system continued to rely on mental health professionals to assess risk for violence. In *Schall v. Martin* (1984), a case regarding the detention of a juvenile, the U.S. Supreme Court very specifically rejected the contention that it was impossible to reliably predict future criminal behavior. In 1987, the Court came to a similar conclusion in a case regarding preventive detention of adults (*U.S. v. Salerno*). More recently, the Court ruled that civil commitment of a previously incarcerated sexual offender as a "sexually violent predator" required a prediction of future dangerousness, as well as a finding that the person's control of dangerous behavior was impaired (*Kansas v. Hendricks*, 1997). At the present time, all 50 states incorporate "dangerous to others" into their civil commitment criteria (Douglas & Webster, 1999). Both types of civil commitment typically rely on the testimony of mental health professionals.

A Shift in the Paradigm

In 1954, Meehl composed a thoughtful and highly influential treatise distinguishing clinical from statistical methods of prediction, pointing out the general superiority of the latter. Although a number of researchers in the social sciences agreed with his perspective, they realized that there were few statistical data available on which to base violence risk prediction models (Monahan, 1981). However, the high publicity surrounding the poor reliability of dangerousness predictions, coupled with court demands for such predictions, apparently energized mental health scholars. Even those who had initially argued to abolish dangerousness predictions appeared to accept that the law would continue to demand such predictions, and they went about working toward making such predictions as empirically and ethically rigorous as possible (Shah, 1981; see also Lidz & Mulvey, 1995). In the 2 decades following the *Barefoot v. Estelle* decision, research on violence risk assessment grew exponentially. Individual researchers and research groups began studying factors thought to be predictive of future violence (Douglas & Webster, 1999; Klassen & O'Connor, 1988; Webster, Harris, Rice, Cormier, & Quinsey, 1994). Two long-term research programs to study violence prediction began in the late 1980s. One was funded through a grant from the National Institute of Mental Health to Lidz and Mulvey at the University of Pittsburgh. The second was the MacArthur Risk Study, funded by the John D. and Catherine T. MacArthur Foundation. This effort began with 12 active researchers from the fields of law, psychiatry, psychology, and sociology.

As research progressed, the paradigm began to shift from a dichotomy to a continuum, from the yes/no prediction of a violent act ("dangerousness prediction") to an assessment of risk ("risk assessment"). The latter acknowledged that one could not predict, or eliminate, the possibility of future violent behavior with certainty. Rather, the goal became estimating the degree of risk an individual posed. Research has demonstrated that clinicians generally do not think in absolutes, but in terms of contingent conditions (Mulvey & Lidz, 1988). Risk assessment is a broad decision-making concept that calls for evaluators to combine a complex array of data. It generally implies an ongoing process and not simply a single, one-time definitive conclusion (as had the dangerousness prediction). Thinking in terms of risk allowed for decisions that balanced the seriousness of the outcome with the probability of its occurrence (Steadman et al., 1993). It encouraged evaluators to consider context, nomothetic research data, individual history, anticipated situations, and clinical symptoms. Importantly, the shift from dangerousness prediction to violence risk assessment occurred as scholars began to understand violence as a public health concern (Douglas & Webster, 1999; Mercy & O'Carroll, 1988).

Learning to Measure the Risk

Research over the past 20 years has tended to focus not on whether violent acts can be predicted, but on how to measure degrees of risk. Some scholars accepted the position first developed by Meehl (1954) and later articulated by Grove and Meehl (1996) that actuarial methods were consistently superior to clinical judgment. Some went so far as to say that clinical judgment should be completely eliminated from the process of assessing risk. Recently, Quinsey, Harris, Rice, and Cormier (2006, p. 197) reaffirmed their position:

> We again call on clinicians to do risk appraisal in a new way—a way different from that in which most of us were trained. What we are advising is not the addition of actuarial methods to existing practice, but rather the replacement of existing practice with actuarial methods. . . . Actuarial methods are too good and clinical judgment is too poor to risk contaminating the former with the latter.

Others defended, with equal intensity, the use of clinical judgment:

> It is hard to imagine that the day will ever come when actuarial assessments of dangerousness can properly and completely substitute for clinical assessments. That is because actuarial predictors cannot be validated regarding those subsets of supposedly dangerous individuals who are confined (e.g., emergency civil committees) or not released (e.g., supposedly dangerous insanity acquittees) on the basis of decisions by clinicians or judges. Moreover, as of yet, actuarial schemes for assessing dangerousness have not been proven to be generally superior to clinical assessments. (Litwack, 2001, p. 437)

One prominent study of clinicians working in a psychiatric emergency room seemed to suggest that clinical judgment had been considerably undervalued (Lidz, Mulvey, & Gardner, 1993).

One difficulty in this clinical versus actuarial debate has been the definition of clinical judgment. It is perhaps easier to say what clinical judgment is not: exclusive reliance on an actuarial formula. Beyond that, however, is clinical judgment limited to the interview process? Does it include the addition of collateral information? Does clinical judgment employ psychological testing? Does it rely on research data? What about behavioral observations? Is clinical judgment only that which is "subjective" or "impressionistic" (Grove & Meehl, 1996)? Should making clinical inferences to assign numerical scores to a structured measure (e.g., the Psychopathy Checklist—Revised; Hare, 1991, 2003) be considered clinical judgment? Without a consistent, universally accepted definition of clinical judgment,* efforts to study clinical judgment have suffered.

Over time, several scholars suggested that clinical versus actuarial methods may be not a dichotomy, but a continuum. Hanson (1998), for example, suggested that there may be room between pure actuarial and pure clinical assessments for guided clinical judgment or adjusted actuarial assessments. He described guided clinical judgment as assessments that include "a range of empirically validated risk indicators and then make recidivism estimates on the basis of the offender's rankings on these factors and the expected base rates for similar offenders" (pp. 61–62). Adjusted actuarial assessment was defined as an approach that "begins with actuarial predictions and

---

*One recent line of research in clinical psychology highlights some of the confusion surrounding "clinical judgment." Westen and Weinberger (2004) recently argued that the broad debate regarding clinical versus statistical prediction reveals considerable misunderstanding among those involved. Specifically, they argued, Meehl (1954) was clear and consistent in defining *clinical* as a means of aggregating data by unstructured human judgment (as opposed to actuarial methods, defined as statistically aggregating data, often using algorithms that are refined with continued study). And indeed, actuarial methods of combining data almost always outperform clinical methods of combining data. However, some clinicians have mistakenly come to believe that research shows clinicians themselves (or the observations and inferences that clinicians offer) to be demonstrably inferior to actuarial methods of data collection. In actuality, Westen and Weinberger argued, considerable evidence supports clinicians' ability to make specific inferences and observations; these observations and inferences, then, are best aggregated using a structured measure.

then adjusts these assessments on the basis of other compelling evidence" (p. 65). Conceptualized in this way, clinicians may not need to limit themselves to only one or two narrowly defined methods.

The Development of Instruments

Regardless of their individual positions on the value of clinical judgment, psychologists have concentrated vast energy over the past decades on developing instruments to measure psychological constructs. Lengthy catalogues of psychological tests are available to measure every construct, from eye-hand coordination to delusional thinking. Risk assessment presented an ideal area for test developers, given the measurable criterion variable and the need for defensible approaches to the task.

One of the first psychometric devices that proved to be of significant value in efforts to assess risk was the Psychopathy Checklist (later the Psychopathy Checklist—Revised [PCL-R]), developed by Robert Hare (1991, 2003) and his colleagues. It is important to emphasize that the Psychopathy Checklist was *not* developed as a risk assessment device. Rather, the instrument was designed to measure a specific personality construct that Hare and Hart (1993, p. 104) defined as:

> a cluster of personality traits and socially deviant behaviors: glib and superficial charm; egocentricity; selfishness; lack of empathy, guilt, and remorse; deceitfulness and manipulativeness; lack of enduring attachment to people, principles, or goals; impulsive and irresponsible behavior; and a tendency to violate explicit social norms.

The description was intentionally similar to the personality described by Cleckley in 1941. Perhaps not surprisingly (at least in retrospect), studies found that high scores on the PCL-R were significantly related to future violent acts (Hare, 2003; G. T. Harris, Rice, & Cormier, 1991; Serin & Amos, 1995).

Whereas the PCL-R was a psychometric instrument designed to assess a personality construct, it was followed by a series of measures that were quite specific to measuring the probability of future violent behavior. The Violence Prediction Scheme (Webster et al., 1994) was among the earliest efforts, followed by the Violence Risk Appraisal Guide (VRAG; Quinsey, Harris, & Cormier, 1998; Quinsey et al., 2006).* Almost simultaneously, Webster, Douglas, Eaves, and Hart (1997a) published the Historical, Clinical, Risk Scheme (HCR-20). Although more a guide than an actuarial measure, this measure provided a list of well-researched variables to be used in assessing the probability of future violence. It should be noted that both the VRAG and the HCR-20 rely on PCL-R results as one element. One additional instrument, the Level of Service Inventory (later the Level of Service Inventory—Revised; Andrews & Bonta, 1995), was designed to measure not only risk but also service needs.

Researchers quickly acknowledged that not all forms of violence were alike, nor were the perpetrators of violence. Actuarial instruments soon emerged to address specifically sex offender recidivism (e.g., the Sex Offender Risk Appraisal Guide: Quinsey et al., 2006; the Sexual/Violence/Risk Instrument: Boer, Hart, Kropp, & Webster, 1997; the Rapid Risk Assessment for Sexual Offense Recidivism: Hanson, 1997; the STATIC-99: Hanson & Thornton, 1999; the Minnesota Sex Offender Screening Tool—Revised: Epperson, Kaul, & Hesselton, 1998b), spousal abuse (the Spousal Assault Risk Assessment Guide: Kropp, Hart, Webster, & Eaves, 1995), and forms of violence risk among juveniles (the Youth Level of Service/Case Management Inventory: Hoge & Andrews, 1994; the Juvenile Sex Offender Assessment Protocol: Prentky, Harris, Frizzell, & Righthand, 2000; the Estimate of Risk of Adolescent Sexual Offense Recidivism: Worling, 2004). A youth version of Hare's Psychopathy Checklist also became commercially available recently (Forth, Kosson, & Hare, 2003). Finally, a unique approach using a decision tree methodology (and incorporating a PCL-R score) was developed by the MacArthur group (Steadman et al., 2000) for use with psychiatric patients. This complex methodology resulted in a computer software program called Classification of Violence Risk

---

* All instruments mentioned in this section are described in greater detail in Appendix A. Some are also discussed throughout this text.

(Monahan et al., 2006), now available from Psychological Assessment Resources Inc., to assist the practitioner.

Advances in Methodology and Analysis

As instruments developed, statistical methods used in risk assessment research also improved. Like other fields, risk assessment benefited from the increasing popularity and sophistication of meta-analytic techniques. Meta-analysis allows scholars to combine many small studies of the same issue, yielding large samples and numerous variables for the final analysis. For example, Hanson and Bussiere (1998) investigated 69 potential predictors of sexual recidivism, 38 predictors of other violent recidivism, and 58 predictors of any recidivism, with a total subject pool of 28,972 sexual offenders across 61 studies.

Like other fields that study prediction tasks, the field of risk assessment initially relied on indices of predictive accuracy derived from the 2×2 contingency table. The table allows one to calculate true positives (those predicted to be violent who were subsequently violent), true negatives, false positives (those predicted to be violent who subsequently were not), and false negatives. However, this method is very dependent on sample base rates and so may obscure the real predictive performance (Mossman, 1994).

In an attempt to solve this problem, researchers borrowed a methodology from signal detection theory known as receiver operating characteristic (ROC) analysis. The area under the curve (AUC) in this analysis can provide a way of judging the overall accuracy of the predictor or instrument that is less dependent on base rates. It also provides a convenient metric to compare accuracy across various instruments. The AUC can range from 0 (perfect negative prediction) to .50 (chance) to 1.0 (perfect positive prediction). Using ROC analysis, the particular cutoff point chosen could be based on the relative costs of false negatives versus false positives (Rice & Harris, 1995). Costs could be defined by representatives of the affected community. For example, in the case of predicting whether a juvenile is apt to become involved in a fight in the classroom, one might decide that the consequences of a false negative (having to break up the fight) may not be as serious as a false positive (removing a child from the classroom who would actually be nonviolent). On the other hand, if the issue were preventing homicide in a maximum-security prison, the consequences of a false negative (a homicide) might be of much greater concern than the consequences of a false positive (maintaining an individual in administrative segregation).

Over the past 2 decades many risk assessment researchers have also turned to survival curve analysis (Braun & Zwick, 1993; Greenhouse, Stangl, & Bromberg, 1989). Survival analysis differs from the use of percentages or correlations in that it allows researchers to consider the time at risk. This can be significant, given that some offenders reoffend very quickly, whereas others may be in the community for long periods of time before reoffending. Using survival curves, groups of offenders can be compared to determine which type of offender is apt to offend over what period of time. For example, Serin and Amos (1995) compared psychopaths to nonpsychopaths and mixed offenders to establish the likelihood of reoffense over time.

Risk Management

Researchers have long advocated considering violence risk in context and revising assessments over time (Monahan & Steadman, 1994). In 1997, Heilbrun, in a seminal article, outlined two ways of considering risk: from an assessment perspective and from a management perspective. The goal of the first was to determine the risk or probability of a violent event occurring; the goal of the second was to reduce that probability. Despite the tremendous progress made in violence risk assessment technology in recent years, relatively few scientific data relate directly to managing, that is, reducing risk (Douglas & Skeem, 2005).

In 2000, Skeem, Mulvey, and Lidz characterized risk assessment research to date as "developing and applying a maximally predictive, context free algorithm for combining individually based risk factors" (p. 608). Actuarial instruments usually belie an implicit assumption that the risk for a given individual would be the same regardless of the situation, the environment, or the time frame. Yet research indicates that context does matter. Studies in which mental health professionals were asked to predict violence in an institution on a short-term basis suggest that relying on factors predictive of violence in the community on a longer term basis can lead to high rates of false positives (R. Cooper & Werner, 1990; P. T. Werner, Rose, Yesavage, & Seeman, 1984). Many people appear to behave quite differently in the confines of a secure institution than they would in the community, and different contexts provide different opportunities for violence. However, institution versus community is a crude categorization, and actual situational variability tends to be even more complex. Mulvey and Lidz (1995) stressed the need for a "conditional model" of risk, one that could adjust with changing circumstances.

In addition to context, risk reduction requires that evaluators examine factors that are subject to change and/or receptive to intervention. However, initial research and actuarial instruments (e.g., VRAG, STATIC-99) emphasized factors that were static, or historical. For example, researchers focused on factors such as past history of violence, age at which violent behavior began, history of substance abuse, and characteristics of prior victims (Hanson & Bussiere, 1998; Quinsey et al., 2006). Although these were found to be important in terms of making one-time, long-term predictions, they were of little value in determining the likelihood of violence on a day-to-day basis or deciding what interventions might be effective in altering behavior. The factors that determine risk status (i.e., whether one is generally at higher risk for violence) may be different from the factors that determine risk state (i.e., whether one is at risk for violence in the immediate future; Douglas & Skeem, 2005; Skeem et al., 2006).

Investigation of dynamic risk factors is a relatively recent phenomenon. Canadian researchers began examining dynamic risk factors in relation to sexual offenders and developed an actuarial instrument for assessing them (Hanson, 1998; Hanson & Harris, 2000). Examining violence more generally, the HCR-20 (Webster et al., 1997a) incorporated five dynamic variables into a guide for assessing risk that was based on a model using structured clinical judgment. The Level of Service Inventory—Revised (Andrews & Bonta, 1995) is an instrument for assessing general risk that relies on an actuarial algorithm and assesses dynamic risk factors that may be the targets of interventions.

Although there is much agreement that more concentration on dynamic risk factors is essential in developing methods of risk reduction, the effort is only beginning. Douglas and Skeem (2005), following an extensive review of the literature, generated a list of the variables that show the greatest promise in this regard. More investigation into dynamic factors reviewed in context will undoubtedly follow.

In summary, mental health professionals continue to generate, and the criminal justice system continues to demand, information about the risk of violence in diverse populations of individuals. In the past 3 decades, great strides have been made in improving research methodology and establishing a large database relative to violence risk assessment. A number of solid risk factors have been established for various types of violence, and some helpful instruments have been validated. The database is now large enough and complex enough to require considerable expertise in its application. Less data is available to guide risk management. However, developing and applying specific methods of reducing risk is the next great challenge to the field.

Introducing a Broad Model for Risk Assessment

Rationale for a Risk Assessment Model

Why propose a guide for violence risk assessments? Is it really necessary to offer a *model* for risk assessment, when there is already a wealth of professional and academic literature on the topic? As reviewed in the previous chapter and elsewhere (e.g., Borum, 1996; Hanson, 2005a; McNeil et al., 2002; Monahan, 1996, 2003; Otto, 1992; Simon, 2005), the field of risk assessment has grown almost explosively, and our knowledge base is far beyond the knowledge base available just a few decades ago. New risk assessment research emerges constantly. Likewise, several well-validated instruments (see Appendix A) are available to help clinicians formulate opinions regarding risk. When top scholars and well-funded research programs have addressed violence risk assessment and a search on the psychology research database reveals literally hundreds of entries for risk assessment, what's left to say?

We propose that the growing practice of risk assessment and the wealth of available resources make a coherent model for risk assessment *more*, not less, necessary. Typically, the risk assessment literature addresses a particular narrow population (e.g., sexual offenders, civil psychiatric patients) or one component of the evaluation process (e.g., use of a particular actuarial instrument). This circumscribed focus is entirely appropriate, in that one key function of research literature is to disseminate highly specific, specialized knowledge. Furthermore, as emphasized throughout this text, a key task of risk assessment is identifying relevant data from the research population most similar to the evaluation at hand. In other words, we *need* highly specialized literature and highly specialized instruments. Developments such as the Violence Risk Appraisal Guide (Quinsey, Harris, et al., 1998) and the STATIC-99 (Hanson, 1997), an actuarial instrument specific to risk of sexual recidivism, are quite valuable when used properly. However, it remains essential for evaluators to apply precise data and specific measures within the context of a broader, systematic approach to risk assessment. A broad model for risk assessment helps guide evaluators through the process of collecting and considering relevant data, but also contextualizing this data to form and communicate opinions. It is essential to rely on scientific research in almost every risk assessment and to use formal tests or instruments in some. However, neither consideration of research nor testing is sufficient to constitute a thorough risk assessment *process*.

Risk Assessment Is Increasingly Common

A second reason it becomes important to describe a broad model risk assessment process relates to the increasingly common requests for risk assessments across a variety of criminal justice and mental health contexts (see Heilbrun, Dvoskin, Hart, & McNeil, 1999, for a discussion of the increasing use of risk assessments). Indeed, one legal scholar (Simon, 2005) observed that forensic assessments of violence risk have reached a level of acceptability and popularity that is historically unprecedented. Courts often call on clinicians to provide estimates of violence risk when making sentencing decisions about adult defendants. Parole boards and other criminal justice administrators may request risk assessments when considering an offender facing parole, probation, or early release. Clinicians are also often called on to assess risk of violence among psychiatric patients facing release, sexual offenders facing civil commitment under sexually violent predator statutes, and students who have made threats of violence in school. In the juvenile justice system, to take just one example, risk assessment has become ubiquitous. As of 1990, 33% of state juvenile justice systems relied on some form of formal risk assessment; by 2003, 86% of states did (Griffin & Bozynski, 2003, as cited in Schwalbe, in press).

It is important to note that many of the contexts in which risk assessments are requested are not those contexts that have historically tended to employ forensic mental health professionals, that is, those clinicians with specific training and expertise in conducting evaluations for the legal system. Rather, requests for violence risk assessments are also increasingly common in settings—such as outpatient mental health clinics (Monahan, 1996) and schools (Halikias, 2004)—that have not traditionally employed clinicians with specialized forensic training. Thus, a variety of clinicians may be called on to offer opinions related to an individual's likelihood of committing violence, even though their formal education may not have prepared them to conduct such evaluations.

Of course, even those entities, such as courts, that have traditionally relied on forensic mental health professionals may not always be requesting that risk assessments be performed by evaluators who have relevant education and experience. More than 2 decades ago, Grisso (1987; see also Skeem & Golding, 1998) raised concerns about "occasional experts," or mental health clinicians with no formal psycholegal training who sometimes conduct psycholegal evaluations for the legal system. Since then, the changing medical and mental health marketplace, in which managed care has reduced many of the financial incentives for traditional practice, has led many more clinicians to attempt to diversify their services and pursue new areas of practice, such as forensic assessment (Greenberg & Shuman, 1997), to market their services to new clients, such as courts and attorneys. As a result, many clinicians, who may be quite skilled in traditional clinical practice, tend to apply their clinical skills to psycholegal questions, for which they may not have received sufficient, specialized training.

Consider the following example. In a study of 93 licensed clinical psychologists in Michigan (Tolman & Mullendore, 2003), only 9% considered themselves to be forensic psychologists, yet most (53%) had performed some form of violence risk assessment *for the legal system*. Clearly, forensic assessment of violence risk appeared to be a common task, even within this sample of generalist clinicians. However, when the researchers compared risk assessment practice by these clinicians with risk assessment practice by a group of clinicians who had earned diplomate status (American Board of Professional Psychology) as forensic psychologists, the practice patterns of the general clinicians appeared less than optimal, in that they used few relevant assessment measures and demonstrated little knowledge of relevant scientific literature. The study authors concluded that although risk assessment practice may have been commonplace, common practice appeared poor.

Other research in the real world raises similar concerns. A survey of clinicians in several psychiatric facilities—that is, clinicians expected to regularly offer opinions about patients' risk for violence—revealed that the clinicians tended to prioritize patient behaviors that have no research-demonstrated link to violence over empirically supported risk factors (Elbogen, Calkins Mercado, Scalora, & Tomkins, 2002). A study of civilly committed veterans revealed very little agreement among clinicians in terms of the risk factors they used to make risk appraisals (Odeh, Zeiss, & Huss, 2006). In short, research reveals a need to disseminate risk assessment research into mainstream clinical practice (Elbogen et al., 2002).

We should emphasize that many of the clinicians who provide forensic services do have adequate training, expertise, and psycholegal knowledge. However, the changing landscape of the mental health care marketplace and the increasing requests for violence risk assessments have created a situation in which many clinicians conducting risk assessments may not have sufficient guidance to perform these risk assessments adequately. After all, violence risk assessment is rarely part of a standard clinical training program (Borum, 1996). Conducting a well-informed assessment of violence risk requires more than simply applying the strong interviewing, testing, and diagnostic skills that may serve clinicians well for so many other referral questions. Likewise, a comprehensive violence risk assessment requires more than simply obtaining a risk assessment measure (even a well-validated one) from a test publisher and applying it to the evaluation at hand, without a broader consideration of context and the population to which the instrument is best applied. Rather, a comprehensive assessment of violence risk requires a systematic process of integrating broad normative data about violence with increasingly specific and circumscribed data about the individual under consideration.

A Note for Nonclinicians

Clinicians are not the only group who must understand and critically evaluate the process of violence risk assessment. It has become increasingly important for attorneys and judges to have a basic understanding of what constitutes a reliable and valid assessment of risk. A risk assessment will commonly be judged, not by academic peer review, but by the court. Attorneys often must decide what questions are to be addressed and who the most qualified evaluator is. Judges are given the role of gatekeeper, making the final decisions on the admissibility of evidence and expert testimony (Redding & Murrie, 2007). A clearly articulated model for risk assessments can be valuable in guiding their decisions.

To summarize, a risk assessment model is important to help clinicians perform risk assessments in a systematic manner that is empirically sound and clinically rigorous. However, a risk assessment model is also important for nonclinicians such as judges, attorneys, and probation officers. Thus, our second goal for this text is to help nonclinicians understand the rationale and process underlying violence risk assessments so that they become better informed and more demanding consumers of violence risk assessment reports and related court testimony.

Overview of a Risk Assessment Model

As we emphasize throughout this text, risk assessment is not a unitary construct. The evaluator's task may vary considerably based on the specific referral question and the context in which the evaluation is requested. Nevertheless, nearly every risk assessment must include certain key tasks and certain considerations. We present what we consider to be the key components as a series of six stages (corresponding to six chapters in the text):

- defining the question,
- considering normative data and population base rates,
- considering empirically supported risk and protective factors,
- considering idiographic risk factors,
- communicating risk assessment results, and
- linking risk assessment to risk management.

Nearly every risk assessment task will include the first five of these six steps. Most risk assessments, to be ultimately useful, will also include the sixth step, which involves linking risk assessment findings to a risk management plan. However, it is important to note that there may be some contexts or referral questions in which offering input regarding risk management is beyond the scope of the evaluator's assigned task.

Risk of What? Defining the Question

All risk assessment is context-specific. There is no general assessment of violence risk. Even when the consumers of risk assessments (e.g., courts, attorneys, hospitals, parole boards) do not solicit risk assessments using precise terms, evaluators must help them frame questions of risk very specifically. For example, what is the risk behavior to be assessed, over what time span, and across what settings? The party who requested an assessment probably intends to make some decisions that will be influenced, at least in part, by the results of the risk assessment. Thus, the first task an evaluator faces is to help the referring party articulate a referral question in precise terms. Precise referral questions lead to appropriately precise conclusions and recommendations, thereby increasing the chance that a risk assessment report will be useful to the decision maker. Of course, it is worth emphasizing that not all referral questions can be answered. Consumers may have unrealistic expectations about what an evaluator can offer. Certainly, the long-standing pattern of asking evaluators to make a categorical determination of whether an individual is dangerous—with dangerousness considered a fixed characteristic of a person persisting across contexts and time—is now recognized as an inappropriate referral question, to which evaluators cannot provide an adequate answer. Therefore, clarifying the referral question usually involves educating the referring party about the limits of risk assessment science and the limits to any opinions at which one can arrive.

Of course, this type of communication between evaluator and referring party is not unique to risk assessment; authorities have long emphasized the importance of clarifying the referral question and the forensic evaluator's role (Heilbrun, 2001; Heilbrun, Marczyk, & DeMatteo, 2002). However, as detailed in our chapter on defining the risk assessment question, this process becomes particularly important in risk assessment evaluations.

What Do We Know Overall? Consider Normative Data and Population Base Rates

Once the risk assessment question is appropriately defined, evaluators must begin forming a risk estimate by relying on empirically derived data. For at least the past quarter-century, the field has recognized that an assessment of violence risk must consider relevant base rate data, that is, the known rate of violence for a particular population or subgroup of the population. Monahan (1981, p. 60) emphasized that "knowledge of the appropriate base rate is the most important single piece of information necessary to make an accurate [violence] prediction."

However, in practice, clinicians rely on base rate information much less often than we might expect. One reason is fairly obvious: Base rate information is often unavailable or inaccessible. Although broad base rate data tend to be available from national, governmental sources (e.g., Bureau of Justice Statistics), such data may not always be applicable to the case at hand. We propose that, overall, evaluators probably underutilize what we call *local base rate data* from localized sources such as state departments of corrections or even individual psychiatric hospitals. Yet even local base rate data are not available for all contexts. Nevertheless, a risk assessment should begin with a thorough effort to identify the base rate data most applicable to the evaluation at hand.

What Do We Know about Individuals Like This One? Assess Empirically Demonstrated Risk and Protective Factors

A key development in the field of risk assessment over the past 2 decades has been the rapidly expanding literature detailing factors that correspond with particular types of violence among specific populations (for reviews and quantitative summaries, see Bonta, Law, & Hanson, 1998; Cottle, Lee, & Heilbrun, 2001; Gendreau, Goggin, & Law, 1997; Gendreau, Little, & Goggin, 1996; Hanson & Bussiere, 1998; Hanson & Morton-Bourgon, 2005; Rosenfeld, 2004). Indeed, the state of available knowledge has advanced to the point that any ethically or scientifically sound risk assessment *must* include consideration of these empirically demonstrated risk factors. Such an approach is in keeping with the *Ethical Principles of Psychologists and Code of Conduct* (American Psychological Association, 2002) Standard 2.04 ("Psychologists' work is based upon established scientific and professional knowledge of the discipline") and similar standards in other mental health professions.

A second key development in the field of risk assessment helps clinicians make use of this recently derived knowledge of risk factors. Scholars have documented and combined these empirically identified risk factors into structured instruments or guidelines that facilitate risk assessment. McNeil and colleagues (2002, p. 153) summarized the role of such instruments:

> The clinician's inquiry is guided by a preestablished list of risk (and potentially protective) factors that are selected from the existing research and professional literature. Typically, these instruments have structured scoring schemes for each item, although they are not generally intended to be used as formal tests. The objective of these tools is to focus clinicians on relevant data to gather during interviews and review of records.

An example of this structured clinical assessment model is the Historical, Clinical, Risk Scheme (HCR-20; Webster et al., 1997a), a list of 20 items spanning historical variables, clinical variables, and risk management variables. Similar protocols are available to help evaluators consider in a systematic manner the risk factors for violence among a number of diverse populations (See Appendix A).

Authorities in forensic mental health assessment (Heilbrun, 2001; Heilbrun et al., 2002) urge evaluators to use nomothetic evidence to assess the association between an examinee's clinical condition and the outcome of interest (in this case, risk for violence). Fortunately, the data are available to allow evaluators to consider whether the characteristics an examinee presents (particularly the static, historical characteristics) are empirically associated with violence. Even better, the technology—in the form of structured guides detailing risk factors—is available to help evaluators carry out this process in a more organized and efficient manner. Although assessing for the presence of empirically demonstrated risk and protective factors is one critical element of many risk assessments, it is important to emphasize that this process does *not* constitute the entirety of a risk assessment. Rather, considering empirically demonstrated risk and protective factors—even when completed with a structured assessment guide—is only one step in a broader risk assessment process.

What Do We Know about This Individual? Idiographic Risk Factors and the Need for Individualized Assessment

As should be clear from the earlier discussion, a thorough risk assessment is rooted in research-derived data. However, we maintain that a thorough risk assessment also requires a fine-grained individualized assessment of risk, which *may* include consideration of factors unique to a particular case for which no research is yet available. Admittedly, the suggestion to consider idiographic risk factors is controversial. Some scholars have argued that adjusting an empirically derived risk estimate with additional considerations can only decrease accuracy; indeed, they argue, any clinical adjustments are always poor practice (Quinsey, Harris, et al., 1998; Quinsey et al., 2006).

On the other hand, an alternative approach would allow for clinicians to cautiously consider idiographic data, often alongside an actuarially derived risk estimate. Monahan (2003) summarized the two primary rationales scholars have offered for relying on more than actuarial measures alone. First, the problem of "questionable validity generalization" (p. 535) may require that evaluators use clinical judgment to consider case-specific data when the individual being evaluated differs greatly from the population from whom base rate data or actuarial instruments were derived. To take some admittedly extreme examples, base rates or instrument scores derived from a sample of White Canadian offenders may not adequately (or accurately) inform a risk assessment with a young woman who has recently immigrated from Mexico to Southern California or a Native American man with no documented criminal history who lives on a reservation in Oklahoma.

A second commonly identified circumstance that would demand consideration of idiographic data involves rare risk or protective factors (Hanson, 1998; Monahan, 2003). Unusual risk or protective factors exemplify the rare "broken leg" phenomena that Grove and Meehl (1996; originally Meehl, 1954) discussed in the context of a long-standing debate regarding actuarial versus clinical methods of prediction. Simply put, they acknowledged that some truly unusual circumstances may be so compelling as to require altering an otherwise useful actuarial prediction scheme. Rare risk factors in violence risk assessment might include a direct, specific threat of violence by the individual being evaluated. Or, to take an example from one of our recent cases, consider the individual who was incarcerated for two sexual offenses, then was seriously injured during a fight in prison, to the extent that he became completely blind. When he is referred for an assessment of sexual violence risk, should the evaluator (after a dutiful but fruitless search for scientific data regarding reoffense rates among recently blinded sexual offenders) consider the inmate's blindness as relevant to his risk of sexual reoffense? We maintain that an evaluator should reasonably go out on just such an unempirical limb.

Monahan (2003) offered these two rationales for considering idiographic factors under certain circumstances (i.e., questionable validity generalization, and rare risk or protective factors). To his list, we add a third. Evaluators who are tasked with offering a risk management plan can better inform risk management after a consideration of idiographic factors. Many risk assessment tasks will require offering some degree of input regarding risk management strategies (Heilbrun, 1997). Indeed, Hart (2001, p. 15) explained, "The ultimate goal of violence risk assessment is violence prevention." The evaluator who has examined carefully the past antecedents, nature, frequency, and severity of violence that a particular individual has committed (and also examined incidents in which the individual avoided or refrained from violence) is in a much better position to offer detailed, individualized suggestions for risk management. This type of analysis also allows the evaluator to consider context, thus avoiding the common error of assuming that risk for violence is solely an attribute of the individual.

We hope that, to the clinician engaged in general practice, this model looks at least a bit like the one endorsed by the American Psychological Association (2006) related to evidence-based practice. That model has three components: research evidence, client values, and clinical expertise. Likewise, our model of risk assessment has three components. The evaluator must have a solid grasp of the relevant nomothetic data (research evidence). Then the evaluator must consider idiographic data (client values), including characteristics of the individual, culture or subculture, and context. Finally, there is the issue of clinical expertise. In risk assessment, clinical expertise is *not* another term for clinical intuition. Rather, clinical expertise in risk assessment involves understanding (a) what evidence must be sought, (b) where that evidence can best be found, and (c) how that evidence can be integrated to form a solid opinion that will be most helpful to the decision maker.

What Can We Say about Risk Assessment Results? Risk Communication

A well-conducted and empirically sound risk assessment is useless if evaluators cannot convey findings to consumers (e.g., courts, attorneys, hospitals, agencies) in a precise, honest, and easy-to-understand manner. Fortunately, the literature has increasingly devoted attention to the importance of risk communication (e.g., Grisso & Tomkins, 1996; Schopp, 1996) and offered clinicians guidance for communicating risk estimates (Heilbrun, Dvoskin, et al., 1999). Scholars have documented the influence of various risk communication formats on clinicians (Heilbrun, O'Neill, Strohman, Bowman, & Philipson, 2000; Monahan et al., 2002; Slovic, Monahan, & MacGregor, 2000), mock jurors (Krauss & Lee, 2003; Krauss & Sales, 2001), and judges (Kwartner, Lyons, & Boccaccini, 2006; Monahan & Silver, 2003).

Of course, more than research data guides risk communication. Ethical standards (American Psychological Association, 2002) and guidelines (Committee on Ethical Guidelines for Forensic Psychologists, 1991), legal criteria for the admissibility of expert testimony (*Daubert v. Merrell Dow Pharmaceuticals Inc.*, 1993; *Frye v. United States*, 1923; *Kumho v. Carmichael*, 1999), and professional guidance (e.g., Brodsky, 1991, 1999; Heilbrun, 2001) all bear upon the ways an evaluator should present findings and offer opinions regarding risk. Most generally, the task of risk evaluators is to communicate clearly to the decision maker, while also candidly acknowledging the limits to their assessments and avoiding the pull to speculate beyond what available data can support.

What Next? Risk Management

A thorough risk assessment will assist the decision maker in determining the degree of risk an individual may present in a particular context, over a specific period of time. However, it does nothing to alter that risk. Moving beyond risk assessment to risk management opens the door to developing strategies that actually reduce risk (Heilbrun, 1997). There are instances where risk management planning would make little sense (i.e., death penalty cases). However, in many instances it can be very helpful to decision makers. In particular, whenever an authority is considering a release decision (i.e., hospital discharge, parole, probation, diversion) and has the power to assign conditions to that release, a risk management plan is warranted.

Addressing risk management has a number of specific advantages:

- Risk management acknowledges that some risk is always inevitable and thus allows the decision maker to determine what level is tolerable under what circumstances.
- Risk management provides the opportunity to design the least restrictive environment necessary to protect public safety.

- Risk management carefully considers context and does not assume that risk is a fixed individual trait.
- Risk management goes beyond static variables and considers factors that can be altered through intervention.
- Risk management is dynamic in nature and can be revised over time as circumstances indicate.
- Risk management, done well, can reduce the financial costs associated with protecting society.

In comparison to risk assessment, risk management is a young field. Although considerable data are now available on assessing risk, relatively few studies have addressed risk management. Some legal professionals tend to resist management approaches, insisting that risk is an inherent trait of the individual or preferring to apply uniform risk reduction strategies across populations. Therefore, introducing risk management to some legal authorities may require evaluators to serve as educators or consultants. Solid risk management planning begins with identifying those factors, both static and dynamic, that precipitate risk for a given individual. This is followed by an analysis of what, if any, interventions will ameliorate each factor, and, finally, by identifying a mechanism for ongoing review and follow-up. Done well, risk management can target those factors, both nomothetic and idiographic, that truly exacerbate violence potential and eliminate factors from past clinical lore that, in actuality, are unrelated to violence risk.

The Role of Testing in Risk Assessment

Even a cursory review of our risk assessment model reveals that there is no single stage or step labeled "testing" or "assessment." Is this because we doubt the value of testing or instruments in the risk assessment process? Not at all. Indeed, we argue that an evaluator would be hard-pressed to defend a decision *not* to use formal risk assessment measures whenever the examinee and the referral question are sufficiently similar to the population and outcome on which an empirically supported risk assessment measure was developed. However, the process of completing a formal risk assessment measure should be considered *one step* in the risk assessment process rather than a stand-alone risk assessment. The role of risk assessment measures is best defined as informing one or two of the key risk assessment steps identified earlier: *What are the base rates relevant to this risk assessment?* or *What are the relevant risk factors this examinee manifests?*

The first question, *What are the base rates relevant to this risk assessment?* can often be answered, or at least estimated, using a well-designed actuarial risk assessment instrument. Consider, for example, the STATIC-99 (Hanson, 1997), a 10-item actuarial measure designed to inform estimates of sexual and violent recidivism among men with prior sexual offenses. As detailed in a recent manual (A. Harris, Phenix, Hanson, & Thornton, 2003), the STATIC-99 was based on follow-up studies of 1,301 sexual offenders in Canada and the United Kingdom. It essentially offers base rates for reoffense among subgroups of the normative sample, grouped according to the number of risk factors present. These base rate figures from the instrument development sample may then serve as risk estimates for subsequent evaluations. However, as A. Harris and colleagues emphasize (and encourage evaluators to convey in written reports), "These estimates do not directly correspond to the recidivism risk of an individual offender. The offender's risk may be higher or lower than the probabilities estimated in the STATIC-99 depending on other risk factors not measured by this instrument" (p. 71). In other words, there are often times when an actuarial instrument may yield the most appropriate available base rate data to inform a risk assessment, but, this does not mean that the actuarial instrument alone completes the risk assessment task. Furthermore, it is important to reemphasize that actuarial instruments provide meaningful data only when the individual being evaluated is sufficiently similar to the sample with which the actuarial instrument was developed.

Because most actuarial instruments essentially offer sample base rate data (often subdivided according to the number of risk factors present) or rely on a normative instrument development sample, we discuss actuarial instruments in the chapter on normative data and population base rates.

Formal risk assessment measures are also particularly useful in the third step of risk assessment, answering the question, *What are the relevant risk factors this examinee manifests?* As detailed earlier, a number of structured guides, sometimes called an aide-mémoire, are available to guide evaluators through consideration of empirically identified risk factors that may be present in a particular case. At least some developers of these measures caution that the structured measures are best considered guides, rather than formalized tests that yield cut scores (Webster, Douglas, Eaves, & Hart, 1997b). As Webster, Muller-Isberner, and Fransson (2002, p. 186) emphasized, citing the HCR-20 manual, such guides "should largely be viewed as a first, not a last, step in the assessment process." In other words, the structured guides represent a recent technological development that can become an important part of the risk assessment process; nevertheless, they remain only *one* part of this broader risk assessment process.

A Note about Objectivity
in Risk Assessments

Because violence risk assessments are high-stakes evaluations that balance public safety and individual liberties (Schopp, 1996), it goes without saying that clinicians should conduct these evaluations with methodological rigor and objectivity. In institutional settings (e.g., hospitals, prisons), individuals assigned to conduct risk assessments should be essentially neutral parties. However, it is conceivable that some institutional pressures (e.g., fears of litigation, limited space for patients or inmates, pressures from administrators) could influence opinions in such cases. Thus, it is wise to have policies in place that support staff clinicians tasked with offering an objective opinion.

Objectivity becomes much more difficult to pursue in the context of an adversarial legal proceeding. Shuman and Greenberg (2003) detailed ways the adversary system, in which attorneys are ethically bound to zealously advocate for their clients, can pull mental health professionals who serve as expert witnesses toward a role that advocates, more than it objectively informs. Indeed, they observe, "partisanship is often an implicit condition of expert employment, and it may also result unintentionally from empathy or identification with a party or litigation team loyalty" (p. 219).

Like Shuman and Greenberg (2003), authorities have long warned of the potential for mental health professionals serving as expert witnesses to stray from the role of objective informant. One danger might be what Brodsky (1991) labeled a "pull to affiliate" (pp. 8–10), wherein a clinician might gradually reshape clinical opinions to better align with the party that retained the clinician. Scholars (e.g., Hagen, 1997; Jensen, 1993) lament the likelihood of partisan bias in forensic evaluations, and laypersons expect that at least some forensic mental health professionals are hired guns who predictably reach only opinions that support the party who retained their services (Hans, 1986; Silver, Cirincione, & Steadman, 1994). Indeed, the public appears particularly distrustful of well-paid professional experts (Boccaccini & Brodsky, 2002; J. Cooper & Neuhas, 2000), perhaps assuming that paid work in an adversary system guarantees a biased perspective.

Beyond documenting public skepticism, what does research reveal about the possibility of bias in forensic evaluation? Few studies address the topic, perhaps due to the tremendous logistical challenges that a realistic experimental study would pose. In an early analogue study, Otto (1989) distributed to 32 advanced graduate students vignettes describing a criminal case in which legal sanity was at issue. As expected, students with vignettes indicating that they were defense-retained were more likely to draw conclusions supportive of an insanity defense. The author acknowledged that these results are suggestive but may not necessarily reflect real-world clinical practice.

More specific to risk assessment, one recent study examined the possibility of partisan bias in risk assessments conducted in adversarial legal proceedings (Murrie, Boccaccini, Johnson, & Janke, in press). The study compared Psychopathy Checklist—Revised scores (Hare, 1991, 2003), a measure for which there is ample evidence of strong interrater agreement in *research* settings, as scored by opposing expert witnesses in proceedings addressing the civil commitment of sexual offenders. In research settings, it would be unusual for two raters to score the same offender and arrive at score differences greater than 1 or 2 standard error of measurement (SEM) units. However, in this adversarial context, more than half of the cases revealed PCL-R score differences between opposing expert witnesses that were greater than 2 SEM units (i.e., score differences of more than 6 points on the PCL-R). Furthermore, the substantial differences between scores from opposing expert witnesses were always in a direction that supported the party who retained their services. That is, defense-retained evaluators assigned lower PCL-R scores to the offenders than did prosecution-retained evaluators. Statistically, the intraclass correlation coefficient for absolute agreement for the PCL-R total score ($ICC_{1,A} = .39$) was well below levels of agreement observed for the PCL-R in research contexts (usually greater than .85). Although it was impossible to rule out all other explanatory factors in this naturalistic study, the results strongly suggested a pull for evaluators to form risk opinions—and even to score ostensibly objective assessment measures—in a manner biased toward the party that retained their services.

To summarize, observations from authorities in clinical psychology (Brodsky, 1991; Rogers, 1987), as well as some research evidence (e.g., Murrie et al., in press; Otto, 1989), suggest that at least some evaluators, on at least some occasions, may be vulnerable to the temptation to stray from strict objectivity. Perhaps recognizing this vulnerability, the authors of *Specialty Guidelines for Forensic Psychologists* hold that psychologists who work in forensic contexts are bound by a "special responsibility for fairness and accuracy" (Committee on Ethical Guidelines for Forensic Psychologists, 1991, Section VII B). Indeed, the *Specialty Guidelines* state:

> In providing forensic psychological services, forensic psychologists take special care to avoid undue influence upon their methods, procedures, and products, such as might emanate from the party to a legal proceeding by financial compensation or other gains. As an expert conducting an evaluation, treatment, consultation, or scholarly/empirical investigation, the forensic psychologist maintains professional integrity by examining the issue at hand from all reasonable perspectives, actively seeking information that will differentially test plausible rival hypotheses. (p. 661)

Draft revisions of the *Specialty Guidelines*, currently under way, also appear to address in straightforward terms the need for evaluator objectivity (Otto, 2006). Grisso (1998, p. 241) summarized the issue quite succinctly:

> One of the substantial threats to a clinician's objectivity when performing forensic evaluations is the subtle pressure to meet clients' objectives lest the flow of referrals begin to wane. It does no good for clinicians to imagine that they are above this sort of economic pressure. It is better to recognize it and to use it to produce better evaluations that have no trouble meeting ethical standards of practice.

One additional benefit of a systematic risk assessment model may be that it offers the structure of a standardized procedure and therefore reduces the opportunity for partisan bias to creep in and influence opinions. Ideally, an evaluator follows the same risk assessment model, and similarly integrates data to form opinions, in a consistent manner regardless of the side retaining services. Nevertheless, every stage in the risk assessment process includes points at which the evaluator may become vulnerable to partisan bias (Murrie & Balusek, in press), and we urge evaluators to assess their own practice for this subtle risk. One reasonable place to start is to review professional guidance on avoiding errors in clinical judgment (for an excellent review, see Borum, Otto, & Golding, 1993). An additional strategy is to monitor one's pattern of psycholegal opinions across cases (Brodsky, 1991, 1999; Murrie & Warren, 2005), particularly examining the degree to which opinions converge with the side retaining one's services.

3

Risk of What?
Defining the Referral Question

For years, authorities on forensic assessment have emphasized the need to carefully define referral questions before commencing any evaluation (Grisso, 2003; Heilbrun et al., 2002). Carefully defining the question can prevent insufficient exploration of critical issues and overzealous analysis of irrelevant issues. A clear referral question limits the scope of an evaluation to the relevant data. Such a focus will also guide the evaluator to instruments designed for the purpose at hand. Finally, it will help protect any resulting legal testimony from exclusion due to lack of relevance—an exclusion allowed by the Federal Rules of Evidence and most state systems.

Ethical guidelines published to date do not specifically address the careful definition of referral issues. However, the Committee on Ethical Guidelines for Forensic Psychologists (1991, p. 658) does indicate that a forensic evaluator must have "a fundamental and reasonable level of knowledge and understanding of the legal and professional standards." The Guidelines go on to direct evaluators to inform the examinee of "the purposes of any evaluation, of the nature of procedures to be employed, of the intended uses of any product of their services" (p. 659). To accomplish this latter task, a thorough knowledge of the purposes and uses would, of course, be essential. Finally, the Guidelines direct forensic psychologists to avoid "offering information from their investigations or evaluations that does not bear directly upon the legal purpose of their professional services and that is not critical as support for their product, evidence or testimony, except where such disclosure is required by law" (p. 662). Thus, if the defined task is in reality quite narrow, including extraneous information could be more prejudicial than probative. It could also waste valuable time and resources.

Questions related to risk assessment are often particularly difficult to define. The pendulum of judicial thought swings at various times between the importance of civil liberties and the need for public protection. Unlike issues such as competence to stand trial and insanity, no specific legal standards define the meaning of risk *across contexts*. Questions of risk arise in contexts as varied as the civil commitment of a person with mental illness to the application of the death penalty. Courts may wish to know the particular type of violence that is likely, across what time periods, and in what situations or settings. The specific cause of the potential violence may also be an issue. Therefore, to clearly define the sometimes ambiguous construct of *risk* in a given evaluation, evaluators must often seek clarification from the court, the attorneys, case law, and/or statutes.

Types of Violence

The first term to be defined in a violence risk assessment is *violence* itself. Does violence mean actual physical violence, or does it include the potential for or threat of violent behavior? For example, some jurisdictions include robbery and any crime involving a weapon under the rubric of violence (Quinsey et al., 2006). Another commonly used term is *dangerousness*. Dangerous behavior may mean behavior that risks physical harm to someone, or it may actually be meant to refer to the broader category of criminal recidivism, which could include crimes such as fraud, trespassing, and drug possession. Some examples will help to illustrate this point.

When civil commitment is at issue, some jurisdictions require actual proof of a recent violent act. Historically, however, courts have often utilized much less precise criteria. For example, in 1983, the U.S. Supreme Court found it not unreasonable for an individual to be committed as a mentally ill and dangerous person simply because he had committed a criminal act while mentally ill. The criminal act in this particular case was attempted theft of a windbreaker from a department store (*Jones v. U.S.*, 1983). However, the justices reasoned "the 'danger' may be to property rights as well as to persons. It also may be noted that crimes of theft frequently may result in violence from the efforts of the criminal to escape or the victim to protect property or the police to apprehend the fleeing criminal" (p. 365). Of course, the base rates of dangerousness are apt to vary considerably depending on whether one is examining the entire spectrum of criminal offenses or whether only those causing physical injury are relevant.

Violence may also be examined in terms of its frequency and severity (Litwack, Zapf, Groscup, & Hart, 2006). Will the consumer of a risk assessment be more concerned about the risk of frequent minor assaults without injury or with the rare homicidal event? This issue is often raised relative to stalkers. A review of literature on stalking suggests that the frequency of physical violence perpetrated by stalkers is quite high; however, the degree of physical injury remains relatively low (Meloy, 1999).

Commitment evaluations under sexually violent predator (SVP) statutes present particular challenges. Some risk assessment texts take the position that any violence is of importance in such assessments (Quinsey et al., 2006). However, evaluators must consult statutes in the relevant jurisdiction to determine if the risk defined is for violent recidivism in general, or (as is more commonly the case) for sex-offense recidivism in particular. Statutes using the term *predatory* often define the term as offending against victims outside the family. If this is the case, potential for incest offenses may not be relevant. It is often unclear to what extent noncontact offenses should be considered, except as a risk factor for offenses that do involve physical contact. Some jurisdictions may go so far as to list the specific sexual crimes for which evaluators should assess risk. (For a complete discussion of SVP evaluations, see Chapter 10.) Sexually violent predator statutes offer an excellent example of the need to clearly understand the referral question in precise terms.

Whereas SVP evaluations may target only extrafamilial abuse, other risk assessments may focus specifically on domestic violence, such as spousal abuse. Not all persons who severely abuse a spouse or intimate companion engage in other violent or criminal behavior. Several studies have identified the "family only" spousal abuser (Hamberger, Lohr, Bonge, & Tolin, 1996; Holtzworth-Munroe & Stuart, 1994). This particular target behavior would require predictors and information sources somewhat different from other types of violence (Kropp & Hart, 1997). For example, discussions with past and potential victims, seldom available in the context of a general violence risk assessment, may provide critical information. Unique predictor criteria such as past violation of no contact orders would need to be explored. On the other hand, a total lack of non-contact or extrafamilial criminal offenses may not constitute a protective factor. If the risk referral question is specific to spousal abuse, specialized instruments, such as the Spousal Assault Risk Assessment Guide (Kropp, Hart, Webster, & Eaves, 1995), should be considered. (See Appendix A.)

In efforts to define violence and risk, there have sometimes been debates as to whether arson should be considered a property crime or a crime of violence. Whether intentional or not, fire setting can cause serious injury and even death. What little is known about arson suggests that perpetrators are more like property offenders than violent criminals (Hill, Langevin, Paitich, Handy, Russon, & Wilkinson, 1982). In one of the rare studies directly addressing arson, Rice and Harris (1996) found that predicting future fire setting shared very little common variance (3%) with the prediction of general violent recidivism. Arsonists were much more likely to reoffend with an unrelated nonviolent crime than with additional fire setting or significant interpersonal violence.

Examples illustrate the need to consider the specific type of violence risk under consideration before beginning any risk assessment. Guidance may be available in statutes (such as those outlining criteria for the commitment of sexually violent offenders) or case law. However, in many instances the evaluator will need to consult the entity raising the issue (e.g., judge, attorney, parole board, release board). The nature of the violence under consideration may well alter significantly the violence base rate data that one consults, the predictors of the violence that one examines, the sources of information that one consults, and the instruments one uses.

Time Periods Covered

Risk assessments vary tremendously in terms of the time span they cover or are expected to cover. Some risk assessments are done in minutes in the face of very immediate risk (e.g., a clinician deciding if a hospitalized patient should be placed in seclusion). However, these emergency judgments often must be made absent collateral information, a review of data, or the application of instruments (indeed, they differ considerably from the forensic evaluations of violence risk, which are the focus of this text). Yet, even some risk periods considered in court hearings are relatively short. Take, for example, the case of *Hinckley v. U.S.* (1998), in which the DC Circuit Court considered at length whether John Hinckley would present a risk to the public if allowed to leave St. Elizabeth's Hospital on a 12-hour pass with his parents. A somewhat longer, but not indefinite, time period is under consideration when courts consider whether an individual would present a significant risk if released pending legal proceedings as addressed in *U.S. v. Salerno* (1987). At the other end of the spectrum are risk assessments expected to project years into the future and those that are expected to cover a lifetime (i.e., risk assessments in death penalty cases, evaluations of sexual reoffense risk in SVP evaluations).

In an evaluation covering a brief period of time, an evaluator can generally be much more confident in the assessment. It is much easier to obtain a clear picture of the circumstances the examinee will face and the context in which the examinee will be living. The examinee's mental status is less likely to undergo marked change. Treatment compliance can more reasonably be assured. Generally, however, the longer the time period covered, the more tentative an evaluator must be. The longer the time period covered, the less precise the information available about future context and circumstances, and the more heavily the evaluator must rely on nomothetic data regarding groups similar to the examinee. The more time passes, the more likely it is that unforeseen change will occur. The longer the period covered by the assessment, the more crucial it is for the evaluator to know whether and how the individual will be monitored and if, and at what intervals, the risk assessment can be reconsidered.

Evaluating juvenile offenders presents an excellent illustration of the importance of time frames. Typically courts request risk assessments of juveniles when considering the need for pretrial detention, confinement during rehabilitation, probation or diversion, and the results of rehabilitation efforts. The pretrial period may be relatively short, allowing the evaluator to gain thorough knowledge of the individual's exact circumstances, to apply an understanding of the specific developmental level involved, and perhaps even to recommend methods of risk reduction. As the period lengthens, however, the task becomes more challenging. Even under the best of circumstances adolescence is a time of monumental change. It is difficult to predict what a 12-year-old will be like in a variety of domains when 15 or 17, even if the criminal justice system were not an intervening variable. If the child is to be in the community, an evaluator must anticipate changes in family structure or living arrangements. However, the greatest challenge comes when the risk is being assessed on a juvenile for potential waiver to adult court. Here the court may wish some assistance in determining level of risk in various environments well into adulthood. However, most delinquents—even those who have engaged in violent crime—desist from criminal activity after entering adulthood (Elliott, 1994; Moffitt, 1993). No clear methodology has been developed to predict with certainty which individuals are in the small group of offenders likely to remain "life-course persistent offenders" (Moffitt, 1993). Given that most young offenders do not become chronic criminals, it would take substantial and specific evidence to estimate a high risk of adult offending. (See Chapter 11 for additional guidance regarding the evaluation of juveniles.)

Finally, there may be risk assessment referral questions in which the evaluator must focus less on recent violent behavior and more on behavior prior to some specific intervention. This issue may be particularly salient in cases regarding the retention of an individual in a mandatory treatment program. For example, in 2002 the New York Court of Appeals considered the case of an insanity acquittee who had been maintained in psychiatric facilities since 1977. In evaluating dangerousness, the justices relied not on recent violent acts but on his inconsistent treatment compliance and evidence that his mental status had not changed appreciably since his original violent offenses. Specifically, the court said:

> A court may consider the nature of the conduct that resulted in the initial commitment, the likelihood of relapse or a cure, history of substance or alcohol abuse, the effects of medication, the likelihood that the patient will discontinue medication without supervision, the length of confinement and treatment, the lapse of time since the underlying criminal acts, and any other relevant factors that form a part of an insanity acquittee's psychological profile. (*In re David B.*, 2002, p. 279)

The Federal Ninth Circuit Court of Appeals used similar logic in affirming the continued commitment of an individual found not competent to stand trial and unlikely to be restored to competence in the foreseeable future. The court denied John Sahhar's contention that a recent violent act was constitutionally essential to justify continued commitment. Instead, the justices considered the plaintiff's ongoing symptoms of paranoid schizophrenia and poor treatment compliance as clear and convincing evidence of his current dangerousness (*U.S. v. Sahhar*, 1990). Although evaluators are responsible for identifying the information necessary to form their opinions about risk, a review of judicial opinions in cases like this may help an evaluator consider the scope of the evaluation and the type of information the court may solicit.

Under What Circumstances

In clarifying the risk assessment referral question, evaluators must also clarify the context (or contexts) for which a risk opinion has been requested. Violence, dangerous behavior, and criminal recidivism are not equally likely under all circumstances. To take an obvious example, one would not opine the same level of risk for a sex offender who was beginning to work at a research facility in Antarctica as for an offender of identical background who was beginning to operate a day care center in Houston. One criticism of the early dangerousness prediction strategies that yielded high false-positive rates (e.g., Kozol et al., 1972; Steadman, 1977; Steadman & Cocozza, 1974; Thornberry & Jacoby, 1979) was the tendency to treat dangerousness as a trait of the individual (Melton et al., 1997). For example, a number of studies based the prediction on evaluations done prior to treatment interventions. Thus, neither the fact that treatment occurred, the established effectiveness of that treatment, nor the individual's response to treatment was considered. In addition, discharge planning would not have been done at the time of initial evaluation, so the circumstances the individual would likely face could not have been considered. One of the principal arguments against heavy reliance on actuarial risk assessment instruments is that these do not address context.

One key aspect of context is the structure of the environment. Will the individual be living in the community or in an institution (i.e., prison or hospital)? For example, in capital murder cases when the options are death or life without parole, the risk question must focus on violence risk within a prison. Violence within an institution may be predictive of violent recidivism (albeit only to a modest degree; see Quinsey et al., 2006). However, the reverse is often not the case. Research suggests that a significant subgroup of offenders are violent in the community yet well behaved in structured environments (Rice, Harris, & Cormier, 1992). In the final analysis, the best predictor of institutional aggression appears to be a history of institutional aggression. Even given this correspondence, however, context may vary from one institution to the next. Quinsey et al. note that some institutional environments tend to be "violence promoting," and staff behavior may be a critical variable.

Access to victims of a preferred type may also be an important contextual variable. For instance, for the exclusive child molester, the degree of anticipated contact with children and the circumstances of that contact should be considered. This takes on added significance when the individual's past violence has tended to be opportunistic rather than premeditated.

An important question in regard to context is whether it can be purposefully altered. For example, if the individual will be institutionalized, is there a choice of institutions or of specific security requirements? In the case of insanity acquittees, courts often consider to what extent they will be allowed access to the community. Are passes into the community generally a component of treatment? For individuals who will be living free, are they under any type of supervision? For how long? Can special conditions be included in that supervision? How will the supervision be monitored? If the person is being discharged from a hospital, can outpatient treatment be mandated? Often a specific question is whether continued psychotropic medication can be a requirement of a patient's release. With this type of knowledge, the evaluator may be in a position to assist the decision maker in determining the least restrictive environment in which the patient's risk can be reasonably managed.

The Cause

Not all risk assessment referral questions specifically require that an evaluator address the causes of anticipated violence. For example, in determining whether an inmate would present a risk to the community if paroled or whether a capital case defendant is apt to commit further violence if not executed, decision makers are not required to demonstrate any particular cause of the potential violence, but only that there is a significant risk of violence (of course, evaluators may still want to consider the causes of violence to better inform a risk management plan, if needed). However, when the issue is civil commitment, evaluators are usually required to establish that perceived risk is related to some mental disorder. Jurisdictions use a variety of terminology (e.g., mental illness, mental disorder, mental disease or defect, severe mental disease or defect) and may not define these terms in the same way—if at all.

In establishing the requisite condition, the issue of *personality disorder* has been particularly thorny. In 1992, the U.S. Supreme Court found that the Louisiana statute allowing the continued detention of an insanity acquittee who was dangerous, but not mentally ill, violated the person's constitutional right to due process (*Foucha v. Louisiana,* 1992). Although Foucha was diagnosed with antisocial personality disorder, he was not considered mentally ill, and his condition was not considered treatable.

Since *Foucha,* courts have continued to struggle with whether to consider a personality disorder a mental illness in terms of meeting statutory requirements. In *Colorado v. Parrish* (1994), the Court of Appeals of Colorado found that it was permissible to retain the individual in confinement based on antisocial personality disorder. Specifically, the court explained that this case differed from *Foucha* because this person had reportedly shown progress over the years in treatment, and there was also evidence of some paraphilias, as well as borderline personality traits. That same year, the Federal Eighth Circuit Court of Appeals ruled that an insanity acquittee could not be retained simply based on antisocial personality disorder and severe alcohol dependence, because he did not have a mental illness (*U.S. v. Bilyk,* 1994). Yet 2 years later, the U.S. Ninth Circuit Court of Appeals found that the diagnosis of *personality disorder not otherwise specified* was a sufficient basis for commitment (*U.S. v. Murdoch,* 1996). Later, the District Court for the Eastern District of North Carolina committed a man who had diagnoses of antisocial personality disorder and borderline personality disorder, explaining that it was the "synergistic effect" of the two disorders that rose to the level of a mental disease or defect (*U.S. v. Henley,* 1998).

In the case of *Kansas v. Hendricks* (1997), the U.S. Supreme Court complicated the issue further. Here, the justices clearly said that some mental disorder was essential to separate persons warranting civil commitment from common criminals. However, they were equally clear that this did not need to be a serious mental illness or even a diagnosis acknowledged in the American Psychiatric Association's *Diagnostic and Statistical Manual of Mental Disorders* (1994). The court used the terms "mental abnormality" and "personality disorder," saying that legislatures were well within their authority to specify and define such concepts for themselves. Because the *Hendricks* case involved an SVP statute, it is uncertain whether this very broad definition of mental disorder was to apply to more general civil commitments. In SVP proceedings it is uncommon for commitments to be grounded on Axis I disorders other than a paraphilia. Personality disorders, however, are frequently identified as ground for commitment. In Texas, for example, antisocial personality disorder is the second most common diagnosis to appear in SVP commitments (Amenta, 2005; Texas Department of Criminal Justice Programs and Services Division, 2002).

These examples are simply to illustrate the myriad ways in which *mental disorder* can be interpreted. We should emphasize that both statutes and case law vary markedly from one jurisdiction to another. What applies in one state may not apply in another; what applies in federal court may not apply in state court; even what applies in one federal circuit may not apply in another. This variety makes it incumbent upon an evaluator to be thoroughly familiar with relevant law in the relevant jurisdiction.

In clarifying the referral question, evaluators must determine whether the cause of the risk matters before commencing a risk assessment. If the answer is yes, the evaluator should try to determine how an acceptable cause is defined. This may mean studying statutes or case law. Absent clarity, one strategy is to avoid ultimate issue opinions, such as "Mr. X suffers from a mental disease or defect that will result in risk of bodily harm to others if he is not committed." Instead, the evaluator may simply report to the court that the individual presents a particular risk and describe the mental condition, or psychological problems, involved. This leaves to the trier of fact the appropriate task of determining whether the disorder meets statutory criteria.

As can be seen from this discussion, defining the risk assessment question is often complicated. Yet it is essential. A good evaluator will investigate the specific type of risk at issue, the time period under consideration, and the circumstances the examinee is most likely to face. In some cases, the cause of the risk may also be an issue. When clarifying the referral question, common sources of information will include statutes, case law, and referring legal professionals. Often, the process of clarifying the referral question becomes a mutually educative exchange between the evaluator and the referring attorney. Only after adequately clarifying the referral question can an evaluator progress to the point of identifying relevant base rate data, examining relevant case considerations, and forming a risk opinion, as described in the remaining chapters.

4

What Do We Know Overall?

Consider Normative Data and Population Base Rates

Once an evaluator has worked with a referral source to articulate a clearly defined risk assessment question, the risk assessment can begin. Yet, the process of forming a risk estimate does not begin with an interview, file review, or other individualized data. Instead, a crucial starting point usually involves pulling back the lens to examine group data, attempting to identify the rate of violence among the population of which the examinee is part. Thus, the evaluator's first task requires examining a base rate, not a person.

What Are Base Rates?

A base rate is simply the prevalence of a particular characteristic or behavior within a particular population (Arkes, 1989). A base rate is a proportion. For example, the base rate of left-handedness in the human population is approximately 10% (Hardyck & Petrinovich, 1977). One can compare base rates across populations: The base rate of pickup truck ownership is greater in Huntsville, Texas, than in Manhattan. Often, base rates become increasingly useful as they reflect more narrowly defined populations. For example, the infant mortality rate for Angola tells us more about the risks that a child in Angola faces than does the infant mortality rate for Africa or the infant mortality rate for the global population. Of course, base rates can be defined so narrowly that they cease to be useful. Meehl (1954) explained that we need base rates from populations that are defined narrowly enough to be useful, but from samples that are large enough that the obtained data are stable and meaningful.

The insurance industry and the field of meteorology have long used base rates to draw inferences about individual policyholders or locations, respectively. Base rates are also a common focus in public health disciplines, where epidemiologists estimate base rates of illness in particular populations to identify untreated cases, identify treatment needs, and plan appropriate responses. Epidemiologists also compare base rates of illnesses across subpopulations to identify risk and protective factors for the illness and gauge the efficacy of public health interventions (Mercy & O'Carroll, 1988). Knowledge of illness base rates also helps physicians who must make diagnostic decisions. For example, physicians know that when administering a diagnostic test in a population that has a very low base rate of a particular disease (e.g., 0.02%), the test is much more likely to yield a false positive than if the base rate is higher. In public health, knowledge of base rates helps us better understand risk factors, interventions, and diagnostic accuracy.

Since at least the mid-1980s, violence has increasingly been understood as a public health problem (Rosenberg & Fenley, 1991; U.S. Department of Health and Human Services, 1986). By studying violence base rates across various populations and subpopulations, scholars have identified violence risk and protective factors and examined the effectiveness of interventions. Base rates also help us properly gauge the predictive power, including the likelihood of false positives and false negatives, of risk assessment instruments.

Why Are Base Rates So Important to Violence Risk Assessments?

For at least half a century, authorities have advised clinicians to consider base rates in diagnostic and predictive decisions (Meehl & Rosen, 1955). For the past quarter-century, the field has recognized that assessments of violence risk, in particular, must consider relevant base rate data. For example, Monahan (1981, p. 60) emphasized that knowledge of the appropriate base rate is the most important piece of information in violence prediction. Conversely, he also emphasized that failing to consider the relevant violence base rates is the most significant error in prediction that clinicians make. Several authorities have observed that the recent advances in the field of risk assessment are attributable in part to recent research documenting violence base rates for particular populations (McNeil et al., 2002; Monahan & Steadman, 1996).

In violence risk assessment, the violence base rate is the proportion of a particular population (e.g., civil psychiatric patients, released sexual offenders, paroled offenders) who commit violence in a particular period of time. Because violence risk assessments are often (though not always) requested for individuals who have already committed a violent offense, we often consider base rates of violent reoffense, or recidivism. Consider this illustration regarding sexual offenders:

> If, for example, 20 out of 100 sexual offenders were reconvicted for a new sexual offense, the recidivism base rate would be 20%. This rate can be used to predict how many offenders will reoffend (e.g., 20 out of 100) as well as to estimate the probability that an individual offender will reoffend (i.e., the "typical" sexual offender has a 20% chance of reoffending). (Hanson, Morton, & Harris, 2003, p. 155)

As we will detail further, violence base rates are essential to violence risk assessment because base rates offer a starting point from which to make use of all subsequent data (Borum et al., 1993; Hanson et al., 2003). Offering guidelines to improve the quality of all types of forensic evaluations (not just risk assessments), Borum and colleagues stressed the importance of considering base rate data. Their instructions about the use of base rates are particularly apt for violence risk assessment:

> The evaluator should use the base rate to set the starting point for subsequent evaluation of probability. That is, higher frequency events will be seen as more likely, and low frequency events will be seen as less likely. With the base rates as a starting point, the

examiner can then consider assessment data and (cautiously) modify these rates accordingly to make a judgment about the individual case. (p. 46)

Why Are Base Rates So Tricky for Violence Risk Assessment?

Given the strong emphasis on base rates in the literature, we might expect references to violence base rates to appear in every forensic evaluation of violence risk. However, neither anecdotal evidence nor the little research available (Heilbrun, Phillipson, et al., 1999) suggests that evaluators routinely reference base rates in violence risk assessments. Apparently, utilizing base rates does not come naturally. For decades, cognitive psychologists who study decision making have demonstrated that most of us tend to neglect normative, base rate, or prior probability information in favor of individuating (case-specific) information that is more available or vivid (e.g., Kahneman, Slovic, & Tversky, 1982; Kahneman & Tversky, 1973; Lyon & Slovic, 1976; Shah, 1978; cf. Koehler, 1996). Indeed, scholars coined terms such as *base rate fallacy* and *base rate neglect* to explain the common human tendency to neglect available empirical data about the probability of an event, and instead rely on anecdotal evidence or individualized data.* Interestingly, one early study of

---

* To be fair, the tendency to ignore base rates when making decisions might not be as pronounced or as pervasive as researchers sometimes suggest. As the terms *base rate fallacy* and *base rate neglect* became increasingly common in the literature, some scholars suggested that these terms are probably overstatements (Bar-Hillel, 1990; Koehler, 1996). On balance, the evidence does not necessarily demonstrate that we ignore base rate information completely; rather, we tend to make use of base rate information only under certain circumstances. For example, individuals tend to use base rate information when a prediction task appears to be strictly statistical or probabilistic (e.g., predicting the likelihood of drawing a king from a deck of playing cards), when there appears to be a causal connection between the base rate and the predicted outcome (e.g., the base rate of car accidents among intoxicated drivers), or when there is no case-specific individuating information available to accompany base rate information. However, most violence risk assessment contexts offer considerable case-specific individuating information. The circumstances in which most violence risk assessments take place appear more similar to the circumstances under which it is typical to neglect base rate information than to the circumstances under which it is typical to utilize base rate information. Thus, a strong caution about our tendency to underutilize base rate information is essential.

base rate neglect was quite specific to risk assessment (Carroll, 1977). Participants were given a variety of base rate information regarding recidivism rates in a population, as well as case-specific information, and asked to predict the likelihood of recidivism. Participants appeared to entirely neglect base rate information when case-specific information was present.

Of course, the field has changed considerably since this 1977 study, and most evaluators have heard at least some admonishments to consider violence base rates. But even among evaluators who recognize the importance of considering base rates, it is often difficult to know which base rates to consider and how best to consider them (Rogers, 2000). Consider the following challenges.

Base Rates Vary by Type of Violence

At the risk of belaboring the obvious, violence is not a unitary construct. Homicide differs from assaults that do not require medical treatment, and both of these differ from verbal threats. Yet, much research has grouped all forms of violence together, resulting in violence base rate estimates that blend a wide range of violent behavior. Indeed, some studies have intentionally grouped together disparate violent acts to increase the base rate of violence to facilitate study analyses (for critiques, see Rogers, 2000; Rosenfeld, 1999). As an aside, varied operational definitions of violence in the research affect not only base rate estimates, but also the observed relationship between risk factors and violent behavior (for details on how the relationship between psychopathy and institutional violence may vary considerably depending on how narrowly one defines violence, see Edens, Petrila, & Buffington-Vollum, 2001; Guy, Edens, Anthony, & Douglas, 2005).

For a comprehensive study that delineates various types of violence, consider Hiday's (1990) study, which followed 727 North Carolina civil commitment candidates over 6 months following their commitment hearings. Although 27% of candidates engaged in some form of "dangerous behavior" during the community follow-up, the rates of particular behaviors varied considerably. For example, only 10% actually engaged in physical assault against others. Examining the severity of assaults revealed that fewer still were severe.

Studying adolescent offenders, Kenny and Press (2006) demon-strated that the varied operational definitions of violence used across research studies result in varied estimates of the frequency of violence and varied relationships with important risk factors. This variety, they argued, hampers the progress of research and the pro-cess of risk assessment.

Many contexts call for evaluators to distinguish between the risk of general violence and the risk of sexual violence. Yet even consid-ering the more narrow category of sexual violence, "there is no such thing as *the* sexual recidivism base rate" (Doren, 2002; see also Chapter 9 of this text). Studies of offense rates vary in terms of whether they include behaviors such as noncontact sexual offenses (e.g., exhibitionism or voyeurism), statutory sexual offenses, or in-cest offenses (see Doren, 1998, for discussion).

Base Rates Vary by Method of Detection
Assuming that violent behaviors are defined with precision, can re-search provide us with meaningful estimates of the base rates of of-fending? Consider some examples.

Douglas and Ogloff (2003) examined records for 193 civil psychi-atric patients who had been released following involuntary hospital-ization. Most had a prior history of psychiatric hospitalization and substance abuse. Following a retrospective follow-up design, re-searchers examined violence outcome measures from three different sources of archival records after patients had spent an average of nearly 2 years (M = 626 days) in the community. They found that detected rates of violence differed depending on the source used to detect them. For example, the proportion of patients engaging in physical violence varied from 6.2% according to psychiatric hospi-tal records, to 7.8% according to criminal records, to 8.3% accord-ing to general hospital records. Combining the sources, it appeared that nearly 19% of the patients engaged in some form of physical vi-olence during follow-up. Thus, we might infer that the true base rate of physical violence was closer to 19% than to any of the lower base rates indicated by individual archival sources.

Of course, the Douglas and Ogloff (2003) study addressed only the difference in base rate estimates generated across three *archival* sources. Base rate estimates may vary even more when we consider other sources of data, such as self-report. The best-known example of this variability comes from the MacArthur study of violence and mental disorder among civil psychiatric patients (see Monahan et al., 2001; Steadman et al., 1998). Researchers followed a large ($N = 1,100$) sample of civil psychiatric patients for over 1 year and reported a 4.5% base rate of violence as documented in agency records. However, adding information from follow-up interviews with the patients themselves brought the prevalence of violence to 23.7%. Interviews with collateral sources revealed acts of violence that had not been reported in agency records or patient self-report; this collateral data brought the known base rate of violent acts to 27.5%. Examining a second category of other aggressive acts (less severe than the main category of physical violence) revealed a similar pattern. Base rates varied from 8.8% (using agency records alone) to 56.1% (total across agency records, self-report, and collateral informant report). Clearly, no single source of information revealed the full scope or prevalence of violent behavior.

Similar results emerged in an earlier study using multiple measures of violence. Mulvey and colleagues (Mulvey, Shaw, & Lidz, 1994) reported data from a large sample of psychiatric patients drawn from a well-known study (Lidz et al., 1993). Depending on the official records examined, the base rates for violence varied from 1% to 9%. However, observed base rates were much higher, as judged by patient self-reports (37% base rate) and reports from collaterals who knew the patients well (31%). It is important to clarify that these rates are probably not representative of psychiatric patients overall (the authors emphasized that participants composed a particularly high risk sample); rather, the salient point here is that reported base rates of violence vary considerably by source. Of course, the tendency for self-reported data to yield higher frequency estimates of crime than official records is nothing new in criminal justice research. Among juvenile offenders, in particular, this pattern has been long recognized (Elliott, Huizinga, & Morse, 1986).

Not surprisingly, a similar pattern holds true among sexual offenders (Falshaw, Bates, Patel, Corbett, & Friendship, 2003; Rice, Harris, Lang, & Cormier, 2006). Indeed, some (Furby, Weinrott, & Blackshaw, 1989) have argued that it becomes difficult to draw any meaningful conclusions about sex offender recidivism due to the varied methods of detecting offenses used across studies (though some aspects of Furby et al.'s critique are less applicable now than when it was first written). To take some examples, Marshall and Barbaree (1988) found that including child protection reports and nonconviction police reports more than doubled the base rate of sexual offense suggested by criminal history records alone. In their well-known studies of men with paraphilias, Abel and colleagues (1987) found that criminal records identified only about 14% of the offenses that participants reported via self-report under a guarantee of confidentiality. Regarding rape in particular, as few as 10% of rapes are reported to law enforcement (Russell, 1982), let alone prosecuted and convicted.

Even when considering only criminal records of sexual offenses, the base rate of reoffense varies considerably depending on whether one examines arrests or convictions for a new sexual offense. In one of the most rigorous, long-term (26-year follow-up) studies of sex offender reoffense, the base rate of *sexual* reoffense among rapists was 19%, 24%, or 39% depending on whether reoffense was measured by imprisonment, conviction, or charges, respectively (Prentky, Lee, Knight, & Cerce, 1997). For child molesters, the base rate of sexual reoffense was 37%, 41%, or 52% depending on whether the researchers examined imprisonment, conviction, or charges as the outcome measure of offense. In his comprehensive review of sex offender recidivism literature, Doren (1998) identified the 52% rate that Prentky and colleagues reported as probably the most accurate estimate available of the base rate of sexual reoffense among child molesters; yet even this, he emphasized, is probably an underestimate because not all incidents of reoffense are detected.*

---

*Of course, one might offer the counterargument that using arrest data reflects an *over*estimate of reoffense, in that some unknown portion of those arrested are likely to be innocent. However, Doren (1998) argued that the number of true offenses that go undetected is probably greater than the number of truly innocent offenders who are erroneously arrested; thus arrest rates, he argued, remain an underestimate. Furthermore, he argued, arrests are a better measure of reoffense than convictions, because convictions may miss many offenses that were truly sexual in nature, but were subsequently plea-bargained to lesser and/or nonsexual categories of offense (for opposing views on a number of issues surrounding the base rates of sexual recidivism by sexual offenders, see Doren, 1998, 2001; Wollert, 2001; see also Chapter 9 of this text).

The studies that reveal varying base rates by data source teach us several lessons. First, and obviously, researchers should attempt to use as many valid violence outcome measures as possible (Douglas & Ogloff, 2003; Monahan et al., 2001; Mulvey et al., 1994). Second, consumers of research—that is, evaluators attempting to conduct research-informed risk assessments—should recognize that published base rate estimates documented from a single source are likely underestimates of violence. Even combining two sources of information is unlikely to yield a perfectly complete picture of violent behavior.

Some Base Rate Information Is Never Detected

At least in theory, there exist true base rates. There exists a specific proportion of a population who commits a particular type of violence, regardless of whether that violence ever comes to the attention of law enforcement or researchers. True base rates, of course, would be the optimal data to inform forensic evaluations of violence risk (after all, we are usually concerned about whether an individual will do harm to others, not whether an individual will do harm that results in legal sanctions). Unfortunately, none of us knows the true base rate for most types of violence. Rather, we know base rates of certain types of violence that are detected by law enforcement or reported by victims. Landmark studies (i.e., Monahan et al., 2001; Steadman et al., 1998) that have incorporated self-report measures of violent or illegal behavior probably offer us more accurate estimates. Yet, it still remains unclear how even the most rigorous research estimates of base rates—detected via multiple measures—are in error with respect to the true (but unknown) base rates. We can probably reasonably infer that our available base rates almost always underestimate the true extent of most forms of violence, in that some violence goes undetected by law enforcement and unreported to researchers, but we know little more than that.

To be clear, we should acknowledge that there are a few select settings in which base rate data can be known with near-perfect precision. For example, researchers or institutions can probably identify homicides of inmates or staff in forensic psychiatric units or prisons; rates of serious assaults on staff, or escape from a secure perimeter.

However, these opportunities for precise base-rate knowledge tend to be the exception rather than the rule.

Base Rates Vary Over Time

Risk for violence is not stable and unchanging over the life span. There tend to be ebbs and flows in the risk for violence—not just within individuals (Douglas & Skeem, 2005), but even within populations. One striking finding from the MacArthur study of violence and mental disorder (Monahan et al., 2001) was that many of the released civil psychiatric patients who engaged in violence did so during the first 20 weeks after discharge. Violence rates declined steadily thereafter (Steadman et al., 1998). Hence a term such as *base rate of violence among psychiatric patients* may be somewhat ambiguous, unless we identify a specific time frame.

In a different sense, though, when we discuss base rates of violent *recidivism*, base rates cannot decrease over time (Doren, 2002). Base rates of reoffense for a given population must remain the same or increase as times passes, because there is no way for an offender to un-recidivate.

Why is this distinction important? Sometimes evaluators are asked to predict whether an individual is likely to *ever* commit a violent offense (consider sexually violent predator evaluations, in which the period of prediction presumably extends over the remainder of the examinee's life; Doren, 1998). At other times, however, risk estimates are for a narrower period in the foreseeable future (consider the phrase "imminently dangerous" in some civil commitment statutes). Evaluators who review the literature for base rate estimates should study carefully the reported follow-up periods and consider implications for the evaluation at hand.

An Illustration of Base Rates

A careful review of violence base rates documented in the literature reveals at least two important themes. First, a review reveals noteworthy variability in base rates, precisely for the reasons just described (varying operational definitions of violence, varied follow-up periods, varied methods of detection). Second, though, a thorough review also reveals some consistency, in that similarly conducted studies tend to converge on similar (though certainly not identical) base rate values. They are often similar enough to infer a *general range* of typical values.

Table 4.1 illustrates research-identified base rate values from a few studies. Our goal is not to identify *the* violence base rate for particular populations (indeed, even a cursory review of the table suggests this is usually not possible, except for rare behaviors such as homicides within prisons). However, a review of the table does suggest a general range of base rate values common across similar studies and reveals how these values tend to differ based on certain study parameters. We should emphasize that a selection bias certainly exists in terms of which few studies are included in the table. We prioritized those that were larger (meta-analyses of smaller studies, as well as large-sample original data), more rigorous, or more recent. Again, this list is illustrative and not exhaustive. It is also dated. Additional studies will emerge in the near future, and evaluators have a duty to stay informed of them, particularly those most relevant to the population(s) with whom the evaluator works.

Making Use of Base Rates

Discussing more general psychodiagnostic issues (rather than risk assessment specifically), Meehl and Rosen (1955, p. 213) emphasized the importance of base rates and lamented, "The chief reason for our ignorance of the base rates is nothing more subtle than our failure to compute them." As evident in the earlier discussion, our current situation with respect to violence base rates is somewhat different. Researchers across scores of studies have computed what could be considered base rate estimates of violence among particular subpopulations. The task for evaluators is to determine whether, and to what extent, any of these available estimates is relevant to the evaluation at hand.

How should evaluators go about considering what base rate estimate is most relevant to a particular evaluation? Essentially, the

Table 4.1 Base Rates of Violence or Reoffense across Studies and Populations

Source	Sample Description	Context	Follow-Up Time	Method of Detection	Violence/Offense Measure	Base Rate
Steadman et al. (1998) Monahan et al. (2001)	1,136 civil psychiatric inpatients, ages 18 to 40	Recruited from acute inpatient facilities in three American cities	Followed 1 year after discharge	Patient interviews + collateral records + collateral interviews	Violence (acts resulting in injury or threat with weapon) Other aggressive acts (violence not resulting in injury)	Total sample: 28% (violence) 32% (other aggression) *Violence among patients with:* Major mental disorder + no substance abuse: 18% Major mental disorder + substance abuse: 31% Other mental disorder + substance abuse: 43% *Other aggression among patients with:* Major mental disorder + no substance abuse: 33% Major mental disorder + substance abuse: 34% Other mental disorder + substance abuse: 32%
Newhill, Mulvey, & Lidz (1995)	812 psychiatric patients	Recruited from emergency service of an urban psychiatric hospital	Followed 6 months after discharge	Official record + patient report + collateral report	"Laid hands on another person or threatened someone with a weapon"	Total sample: 44.3% Males: 42% Females: 48%

Study	Sample	Source	Follow-up	Measure	Definition	Findings
Swanson, Holtzer, Ganju, & Jono (1990)	10,059 randomly sampled community residents	Recruited for the NIMH Epidemeological Catchment Area studies in three American cities	Not followed, but surveyed about past year	Self-report only	Several specific questions about violent behavior (e.g., ever been in more than one fight, ever used weapon in fight, ever fought while drinking, ever hit or threw objects at spouse, ever spanked child enough to bruise)	*Among those with:* No disorder: 2% Schizophrenia only: 8% Substance abuse only: 21% Substance abuse + anxiety: 20% Substance abuse + mood disorder: 29% Substance abuse + schizophrenia: 30%
Bonta, Law, & Hanson (1998) meta-analysis	11,156 mentally ill offenders, with schizophrenia as most common diagnosis (most male)	Drawn from 64 unique samples from various locales throughout United States and Canada	Followed for various periods of time, from 1959 to 1995	Varied across studies, but usually official record of reoffense or rehospitalization	Rearrest, for either violent or nonviolent crime	*For general recidivism:* 46% *For violent recidivism:* 25%
Gagliardi, Lovell, Peterson, & Jemelka (2004)	333 mentally ill inmates	Released from the Washington Department of Corrections	Followed for 27 to 55 months	Arrests or charges	Criminal or violent offense	*For mentally ill offenders:* Felony recidivism: 41% Violent felony recidivism: 10%
	10,809 general population inmates					*For general population offenders:* General recidivism: 38% Violent recidivism: 10%

(*continued*)

Table 4.1 Continued

Source	Sample Description	Context	Follow-Up Time	Method of Detection	Violence/Offense Measure	Base Rate
Sorensen & Cunningham, (2007)	51,527 Florida inmates	Complete cross-section of inmates who served the entire 2003 calendar year in Florida Department of Corrections	Followed for full calendar year (in that researchers reviewed disciplinary records from entire year)	Institutional charges (documented by corrections staff)	Rule violations, including violent and potentially violent charges	Any infraction: 44.8% Potentially violent misconduct: 10.5% Assault: 2.9% Assault with injury: 0.5% Assault with serious injury: 0.2%
Hanson & Morton-Bourgon (2005) meta-analysis	29,450 male sexual offenders	Included in 82 studies, primarily from United States, United Kingdom, Canada	Followed for 12 to 330 months (M = 76, SD = 57)	Primarily rearrest and reconviction	Sexual recidivism Violent (nonsexual) recidivism	13.7% 14.3%
Prentky, Lee et al. (1997)	136 rapists	Evaluated at the Massachusetts Treatment Center	Up to 25 years	Charges convictions imprisonment	Sexual Violent (nonsexual) Nonviolent	For charges: 39% 49% 54%
	115 child molesters			Charges convictions imprisonment	Sexual Violent (nonsexual) Nonviolent	52% 23% 48%

task involves gauging the degree to which a particular examinee is similar to the individuals that compose the base rate sample, and the degree to which the type of violence risk assessed (e.g., sexual, physical) is similar to the violence outcome measure examined in the base rate study (note that "study" can include government documents and other reports that are not formal academic studies). Table 4.2 lists key—though certainly not exhaustive—factors to consider.

When an evaluator has identified a published base rate estimate from a population that is sufficiently similar to the examinee at hand, this base rate information is a reasonable starting point to form an estimate of risk. As Borum and colleagues (1993) discussed, evaluators can consider cautiously the additional relevant data (as detailed in subsequent chapters of this book) to gauge

Table 4.2   *Key Factors to Consider when Making Use of Base Rates*

Sample and examinee characteristics	To what extent does the examinee match the study sample in terms of ethnicity, age, sex, and other demographics?
	To what extent is the population from which the examinee is drawn similar to the population from which the study sample is drawn?
	At the least, consider similarity in terms of: –Geographic region or country –Facility (hospital, prison) –Security level of facility –Prior criminal history of those in the setting
Setting or context characteristics	To what extent is the context of the base rate study similar to the context of the evaluation at hand?
Violence characteristics	To what extent is the violence risk being assessed similar to the violence documented in the base rate study?
Time-frame characteristics	To what extent is the time period for which the risk assessment is made similar to the follow-up period in the base rate study?

whether a given individual presents risk at a greater or lesser level than the population base rate.

An Underutilized Approach: Local Base Rates

As referenced earlier, Meehl and Rosen (1955), in their seminal article, criticized the field for failing to use base rates, such that diagnostic predictions suffer greatly. Although their criticism was specific to clinical diagnosis, it holds true for the task of risk assessment as well. Clearly, the evaluator should begin with some base rate estimate of the behavior or condition (i.e., violence, in the case of risk assessment) to be predicted.

But what if no base rate data are readily available? What if one is evaluating an individual who is substantially different from the populations from whom research-derived base rates are published? What if one conducts evaluations in a context that appears likely to have a substantially higher or lower rate of violence or reoffense? For example, an evaluator who works in a secure, specialized facility for men with multiple violent offenses might wonder whether general or aggregated rates of violent reoffense are applicable to the offenders in this facility. Likewise, an evaluator who works in a specialized program for first-time offenders, most of whom committed a less serious violent offense, might wonder the same.

One of the suggestions that Meehl and Rosen (1955) offered to remedy clinicians' poor use of base rate data is also applicable to risk assessment tasks: *Utilize local base rate data.* By "local" base rate data, we mean data from a specific, narrowly defined population, such as the population from one large facility, statewide system, or other circumscribed population. State correctional facilities and juvenile justice facilities often house, then release, thousands of individuals. Reoffense data (with, of course, their own set of limitations) are usually available through a department of public safety or other law enforcement sources. Many forensic and psychiatric facilities also treat hundreds of patients and can arrange for access to subsequent arrest data. As a general rule, base rate data from a more narrowly defined population will better inform risk assessment for a member of that population (see, generally, Meehl, 1954). However, some local settings may offer such a small sample that base rates would be misleading. Base rate data from a state department of corrections would likely be informative. Base rate data from a small rural county jail would not.

Obviously, we are not suggesting that an evaluator try to hurriedly amass local base rate data where none exist; but, evaluators should make use of such data when they are already available. Administrators of large facilities may wish to begin the process of collecting base rate data to better inform the risk assessments that evaluators conduct in their facilities in the future. Finally, clinicians with a scientist-practitioner orientation may do well to begin looking for opportunities to gather base rate data relevant to their professional niche. Clinicians can join with administrators or academics to analyze and publish this data, eventually using it to inform their practice. Consider Cunningham's (2006) program of research on violence base rates among inmates convicted of capital murder as one exemplar of this approach.

Local Base Rates in Court

Although there is little empirical research to address the issue, a review of case law offers some reason to believe that courts may be more accepting of local base rate data than broader base rate data. Generally, courts tend to be distrustful of nomothetic data (Bersoff & Glass, 1995; Fradella, Fogarty, & O'Neil, 2003; Melton et al., 1997; Redding, 1998; Redding, Floyd, & Hawk, 2001; Redding & Reppucci, 1999; Slobogin, 1998; Tanford, 1990), including base rate data (Koehler, 2002). Instead, courts tend to prefer case-specific, or idiographic, data (see Chapter 7 for a more detailed discussion of this issue). However, one comprehensive legal review that detailed the courts' reluctance to admit base rate data also identified the few circumstances under which courts *do* consider base rate data to be relevant. Koehler observed that courts tend to be more receptive to base rate data from sufficiently narrow or specific groups. That is, "when reference classes are relatively refined, the resultant base rates are more likely to be treated as relevant than when the reference classes are less refined" (p. 395).

Using Actuarial Instruments to Identify a Base Rate Estimate

Actuarial Instruments That Offer Base Rate Data

One approach to identifying relevant base rate data involves using actuarial instruments developed for this purpose. Some of the instruments described as actuarial are based on large-sample recidivism studies and work essentially by guiding the examiner to base rate estimates for particular subgroups of the sample. Typically, the examiner then uses the documented base rate for a subgroup of the instrument development sample as a risk estimate—or at least the starting point for a risk estimate—specific to an examinee who shares certain features in common with the subgroup.

A primary example of this type of instrument is the STATIC-99 (Hanson, 1997; Hanson & Thornton, 1999), a 10-item measure designed to inform estimates of sexual and violent recidivism among men with prior sexual offenses. As detailed in the manual (A. Harris et al., 2003), the STATIC-99 was based on follow-up studies of 1,301 sexual offenders in Canada and the United Kingdom. For the entire sample, the overall average rate of recidivism by *sexual* offense at 5-year follow-up was 18%. For the broader category of *violent* offense recidivism at 5 years, the rate was 25%. The manual also provides recidivism base rates—again, for both sexual and violent recidivism—at 10- and 15-year follow-ups.

A key benefit of the STATIC-99 (and similar actuarial instruments) is that more precise base rates can be identified for specific subgroups of the instrument development sample who manifested specific numbers of the 10 risk factors included on the instrument. For example, the base rate of sexual recidivism at 5-year follow-up for the 204 offenders in the instrument development sample who manifested 2 of the 10 risk factors was 9%. However, for the 100 offenders who manifested 5 risk factors, the base rate was 33%. Recidivism rates for offenders with scores (results of the STATIC-99 are typically discussed in terms of scores rather than risk factors present, although the two are virtually identical) of 6 or more (up to

12) are grouped together, reportedly because there was no increase in recidivism risk as scores exceeded 6. Simply put, the STATIC-99 offers sexual and violent reoffense base rate figures for subgroups who have a specific number (1, 2, 3, 4, 5, or 6 to 12) of selected risk factors. Evaluators may then use these base rate figures to form a risk estimate for a particular examinee with the same number of selected risk factors.

Actuarial Measures That Involve Other Methods of
Combining Data
As detailed earlier, measures such as the STATIC-99 subdivide a research sample to identify base rates for more narrow reference classes (e.g., base rates of 5-year sexual reoffense among offenders with a score of 3). Other actuarial measures are also based on large data sets but configure risk factors somewhat differently to calculate risk estimates. One such measure is the Violence Risk Appraisal Guide (Quinsey, Harris, et al., 1998; Quinsey et al., 2006). Researchers developed the VRAG with a sample of 618 male offenders with mental disorders and convicted offenders assessed in a maximum-security psychiatric hospital in Ontario, Canada. They initially selected approximately 50 variables, coded from files, to predict any new criminal charge (or return to institution) for violent offense within a 7-year follow-up. A series of regression models identified 12 predictors that best corresponded with violent reoffense. Though most predictors were historical (e.g., age at first offense, elementary school maladjustment, alcohol problems, marital status, nonviolent offense history), the most powerful predictor was a psychopathy score based on Hare's (1991) Psychopathy Checklist—Revised. The instrument authors devised a scoring system that involves assigning points, or weights, for each variable based on the degree to which presence of the variable was related to an increase or decrease in violent recidivism as compared to the overall sample base rate. The resulting VRAG scores can range from −26 to +36 and are distributed across nine equal "bins." Researchers have linked a specific probability of reoffense over a specific time period to each bin, with the Bin 1 probability of recidivism being close to zero and Bin 9 probability being close to 100%. The instrument developers emphasize repeatedly that risk estimates derived from the VRAG should stand alone. That is,

they urge clinicians not to alter these estimates based on context or case-specific considerations. It is worth noting that the discourse in the literature surrounding the VRAG and the strict actuarial approach is sometimes heated (for another perspective on the VRAG, and actuarial assessment more generally, see Litwack, 2001, 2002; Litwack et al., 2006).

Limitations to the Use of Actuarial Measures: Generalizability Is Not Universal

Of course, some important caveats are in order when incorporating base rate estimates derived from actuarial instruments. First, actuarial instruments provide relevant data only when the examinee is sufficiently similar to the sample of individuals among whom the actuarial instrument was developed. Of course, what constitutes "sufficiently similar" is a topic of ongoing investigation. Increasingly, studies have applied actuarial measures such as the STATIC-99 (e.g., Looman, 2006) and the VRAG (see www.mhcp-research.com /ragpage.htm for a list, periodically updated, of VRAG research) to new settings and reported results that generally support the generalizabilty of these measures. However, the generalizabilty of these measures cannot be assumed. For example, one recent study (Caperton, 2005) examined STATIC-99 scores for the large population ($N = 1,983$) of sexual offenders in the Texas correctional system. Though presumably this population would be quite similar to the large sample of sexual offenders from Canada and the United Kingdom on which the STATIC-99 was developed, results suggested lower predictive accuracy for the instrument. To take another example, one recent study suggested caution in assuming that the VRAG is applicable across all populations (Edens, Skeem, & Douglas, 2006); results revealed that VRAG scores related to violence but added no predictive value beyond psychopathy. The authors emphasized the need for caution when generalizing about the validity of actuarial instruments, particularly those "that are statistically derived in a particular sample, involve complex scoring and weighting procedures, and include variables that may not be available or relevant across all types of settings" (p. 368). Similarly, one recent meta-analysis (P. R. Blair, 2005) found that actuarial instruments performed better in studies that the instrument authors designed, as opposed to studies in which other researchers employed the measures in other settings. *Simply put, evaluators cannot automatically assume that actuarial instruments are equally applicable across all settings.*

Limitations to the Use of Actuarial Measures: Scope of Inquiry May Not Be Sufficient

Another primary limitation to actuarial measures is that they may not account for all relevant data. In general, authorities tend to characterize actuarial measures as a starting point or an important data source for forming a risk estimate. However, most also emphasize that actuarial measures are rarely sufficient to complete a risk assessment because no existing actuarial measure has adequately identified or operationalized the breadth of data that may be relevant to any given case (for a starkly divergent view, see Quinsey, Harris, et al., 1998; Quinsey et al., 2006).

For example, A. Harris and colleagues (2003, p. 71) emphasize in the STATIC-99 manual and encourage evaluators to convey in written reports that risk estimates from the STATIC-99 "do not directly correspond to the recidivism risk of an individual offender. The offender's risk may be higher or lower than the probabilities estimated in the STATIC-99 depending on other risk factors not measured by this instrument." In a more general discussion of risk assessment with sex offenders, Hanson (1998, p. 53) explained that it would "be imprudent for a clinical judge to automatically defer to an actuarial risk assessment." Hart (1998b) has provided similar guidance. For example, he explained:

> Reliance—at least, complete reliance—on actuarial decision-making by professionals is unacceptable . . . actuarial decisions are made on the basis of a fixed set of factors, determined without reference to the case at hand. This failure to exercise discretion by considering the "totality of the circumstances" means that actuarial assessments may be considered arbitrary. (p. 126)

After a recent review of the literature on violence risk assessment, John Monahan (2003, p. 536) concluded:

I believe that actuarial instruments . . . are best viewed as "tools" for clinical assessment . . . tools that support, rather than replace, the exercise of clinical judgment. This reliance on clinical judgment, aided by an empirical understanding of risk factors for violence and their interactions, reflects, and in my view should reflect, the standard of care at this juncture in the field's development.

In other words, there are often times when an actuarial instrument may yield the most appropriate available base rate data to inform a risk assessment, yet at no time will an actuarial instrument alone complete the entire risk assessment task. Evaluators should follow consideration of base rate data and/or the results of actuarial measures with a consideration of empirically supported risk factors and consideration of idiographic case data, as described in the next two chapters.

What Do We Know about Individuals Like This One?

Empirically Supported Risk and Protective Factors

Although the debate over the efficacy of clinical versus actuarial methods of risk assessment remains unresolved, it is safe to say that no reputable authority on risk assessment recommends totally unstructured clinical judgment as the method of choice. In other words, risk assessments should not be based simply on a clinical interview and the general impression a clinician subsequently forms. However, beyond that, the debate between clinical and actuarial methods often suggests a false dichotomy. Between unstructured clinical judgment and an actuarial formula lies a lengthy continuum of options for structured professional judgment regarding risk. Some have divided the continuum into specific categories, such as clinical assessment, anamnestic assessment, guided or structured clinical assessment, adjusted actuarial assessment, and actuarial assessment (Otto, 2000). Others simply refer to a broad category of structured professional judgment (Litwack et al., 2006). Research continues to demonstrate the importance of including clinical judgment in the risk assessment armamentarium (Andrews, Bonta, & Wormith, 2006; Buchanan, 1999; Dolan & Doyle, 2000; Douglas, Yeomans, & Boer, 2005; Fuller & Cowan, 1999; Hanson & Morton-Bourgon, 2004; Hart, 1998a). However, any risk assessment must first and foremost be grounded in science. Experts generally caution evaluators to adjust actuarial estimates only after careful consideration and with sufficient justification (Webster et al., 1997a).

Risk Factors

Before commencing a risk assessment, the evaluator must possess a thorough knowledge of the research-supported risk factors related to the violence under consideration. This will likely include both static and dynamic variables. Factors considered static are generally historical, unlikely to change, and not amenable to intervention, whereas dynamic factors may change over time. Risk factors may vary depending on the type and context of violence being assessed. Risk factors relevant to particular types of risk assessments (e.g., in capital cases, among juveniles, among sexual offenders) are discussed in this book's later chapters.

Static Factors

A few factors repeatedly emerge in the literature as predictive of violence in a variety of situations. These should be considered in almost any risk assessment. Probably the factor most firmly established as predictive of future violence is *past history of violent behavior* (Andrews et al., 2006; Bonta, Law, et al., 1998; Klassen & O'Connor, 1994; Menzies & Webster, 1995; Monahan, 1981, 2003; Webster et al., 1997a). In a large-scale meta-analysis, Bonta and colleagues found that for predicting violent reoffending, variables from the criminal history domain were the strongest predictors. This appears to hold true for predicting sexual offenses as well (Boer, Wilson, Gauthier, & Hart, 1997). In a study of 346 patients discharged from a psychiatric hospital in the United Kingdom, Phillips and colleagues (2005) found that patients who reoffended had a significantly greater number of previous convictions. In a meta-analysis examining risk factors in juvenile offenders, Cottle et al. (2001) concluded that the overall domain of offense history was the strongest predictor of reoffense. However, even this very robust factor must be considered in context. For example, violence committed in the community may not relate to the probability of violence in a more structured environment.

Psychopathy is a second factor strongly related to violence in the community, as documented throughout a wealth of literature (Hanson, 1998; G. T. Harris, Rice, & Quinsey, 1993; Hemphill, Hare, & Wong, 1998; Quinsey et al., 2006; Salekin, Rogers, & Sewell, 1996). Psychopathy in this context refers specifically to the construct as operationalized by Robert Hare and colleagues and most often measured by the Psychopathy Checklist—Revised (Hare, 1991, 2003). Reporting the results of the first published meta-analysis, Salekin and colleagues concluded, "The PCL-R appears to be unparalleled as a measure for making risk assessments with white male inmates" (p. 212). The authors specified research demonstrating the association of psychopathy to general criminal recidivism, violent recidivism, violence among persons with mental disorders, and sexual offenders. Although subsequent review (Gendreau, Goggin, & Smith, 2002) has raised some concerns about this initial meta-analysis, the basic relationship between psychopathy and violence remains well recognized. Newer meta-analyses with additional studies have consistently identified a relationship between PCL-R scores and violent recidivism (for review, see Douglas, Vincent, & Edens, 2006). For example, Hemphill and colleagues reported a weighted correlation of .27 between PCL-R scores and violent recidivism. Similarly, Walters (2003) observed a modest weighted correlation of .26 with respect to general recidivism across 33 studies. Generally speaking, psychopathy appears to contribute to violence prediction above and beyond the contributions of other relevant risk factors (see Hemphill et al., 1998; Tengström, Hodgins, Grann, Långström, & Kullgren, 2004).

The predictive validity between psychopathy and violence is strong enough that the PCL-R is included in risk assessment instruments designed to predict violent reoffending in general, sexual reoffending, and violence by psychiatric patients. Indeed, the PCL-R tends to be the strongest predictor in risk measures such as the VRAG (G. T. Harris et al., 1993) and the Iterative Classification Tree, developed for use with psychiatric patients (Steadman et al., 2000; see Douglas et al., 2006, for discussion).

In the second edition of the PCL-R manual, Hare (2003) cited a growing body of literature supporting the validity of the PCL-R with ethnic and cultural minorities, as well as women. However, the question of generalizability is certainly not closed, and careful review of current literature is warranted before applying the instrument to diverse populations. Although the PCL-R has been the most widely accepted instrument for measuring psychopathy, others are also available. The Psychopathic Personality Inventory (Lilienfeld & Andrews, 1996), a self-report instrument, has been evaluated in several studies (Edens, Poythress, & Watkins, 2001; Patrick, Edens, & Poythress, 2006). However, at the time of this writing, the PCL-R is the method of choice for clinical and forensic assessment of psychopathy.

Several studies have found the broader diagnosis of antisocial personality disorder (APD) to be highly predictive of risk (Bonta, Law, et al., 1998). However, other research suggests that this category is perhaps too broad to be useful in distinguishing among criminal offenders (Cunningham & Reidy, 1998a; Widiger & Corbitt, 1995). Antisocial personality disorder as a risk factor may have a great deal of sensitivity but is lacking in specificity, given the large percentage of male felons (60% to 80%; Cunningham & Reidy, 1998a) who qualify for the diagnosis. Thus, to use APD as a predictor of violence, let alone a specific type of violence, would likely result in an inordinate number of false positives. In addition, there may be considerable overlap between APD and other predictor variables. For example, Phillips and colleagues (2005) emphasized that the most common basis for a diagnosis of APD is a significant history of criminal offending, which is a more well-established predictor of future offending. The construct of APD, and personality disorder in general, also overlaps with psychopathy. For example, in scoring the VRAG, points can be given for scores on the PCL-R and separately for "any personality disorder." The degree of overlap is unclear.

Age is a third well-documented risk factor; it appears relevant to violence in at least two ways. First, the younger an individual is when committing his or her first offense, the more likely it is that the person will reoffend (G. T. Harris et al., 1993; Lattimore, Visher, & Linster, 1995; Steadman et al., 1994; Swanson, 1994). Second, the likelihood of repetitive violence decreases as offenders age (Cunningham & Reidy, 1998b; Hirschi & Gottfredson, 1983; Swanson et al., 1990). The rate of violent offenses for males appears to peak between the ages of 20 and 30 and then declines precipitously. Among juvenile offenders, age at first commitment and age at first contact with law enforcement are found to be strongly predictive of reoffense (Cottle et al., 2001). This same phenomenon is seen in the community and in prison environments. Regarding sexual offenders, Thornton (2006) concluded that the odds of an additional sexual conviction decreased by approximately 0.02 with every year of increasing age. Hanson (2005a) went so far as to suggest that advancing age be considered as a separate issue in addition to the actuarial score. However, G. T. Harris and Rice (2007) present data suggesting that current age or age at release may not add incrementally to what can be gleaned from age at first offense and criminal history. They argue that what appears to be an effect of aging can be better accounted for by "life-course persistent antisociality" (p. 309). Nonetheless, G. T. Harris and Rice were unable to account for a related variable, namely, time spent without offending while at risk. They agree there is some support for adjustments based on this factor, but insist that any adjustments must be actuarial in nature.

Substance abuse is another factor suggesting general risk for criminal recidivism (Gendreau et al., 1996; G. T. Harris et al., 1993; Klassen & O'Connor, 1988, 1994; Melton et al., 1997; Pihl & Peterson, 1993; Swanson, 1994). The strength of this factor may vary depending on its relationship to previous acts of violence. However, it appears to be robust even when coupled with significant mental illness (Steadman et al., 1998). In a recent meta-analysis, Dowden and Brown (2002) generally confirmed the role of substance abuse in recidivism. However, there were some differences between those who offended violently and those who offended nonviolently. Among violent offenders, drug and alcohol were equally predictive of reoffending. Whereas parental substance abuse was a significant predictor among general offenders, this was not true of the more violent group. One rather surprising finding was that past criminal charges relating to substance abuse were not predictive of recidivism.

Violation of supervision, probation, or any type of conditional release can increase the risk of violent recidivism, whether alone or in combination with other risk factors (Boer, Wilson, et al., 1997; G. T. Harris et al., 1993; Quinsey et al., 2006). In this instance, risk appears to be related simply to the failure to follow prescribed conditions rather than to the specific nature of the conditions. Therefore, the relationship between supervision failure and recidivism should not lead us to assume that a particular condition (e.g., participation in a specific treatment program) necessarily would have effectively eliminated risk. Hanson and Bussiere (1998) found "failure to complete treatment" (irrespective of the type of treatment) to be one of the top four correlates of sexual offense recidivism. Escape from custody is also a form of supervision violation. Bonta, Harman, Hann, and Cormier (1996) found that history of escape correlated significantly with violent recidivism in the community. Given the research on violations of supervision as a risk factor, items related to supervision failure are included on several of the major actuarial instruments and risk assessment guides (e.g., VRAG, Sex Offender Risk Appraisal Guide, HCR-20, Sexual/Violence/Risk Instrument, Minnesota Sex Offender Screening Tool—Revised; for additional information on these instruments, see Appendix A).

Risk and Gender

Most risk assessment research has been conducted on exclusively male populations. Overall, repeated studies have demonstrated that the base rate for violence among females is much lower than that for males in the general community population; in fact, male gender is often noted as a primary risk factor for violence (Nicholls, Ogloff, & Douglas, 2004). However, among psychiatric patients, the rate of violent aggression is similar for males and females (Hiday, Swartz, Swanson, Borum, & Wagner, 1998; Lidz et al., 1993; Newhill et al., 1995; Robbins, Monahan, & Silver, 2003), though the type of aggression and choice of victims tend to differ. For example, females are much more likely to engage in intrafamilial violence. Perhaps unaware of these patterns, mental health professionals tend to significantly underestimate the risk for violence among females (Skeem et al., 2005).

In a review of the literature on misconduct among incarcerated capital murderers, Cunningham (in press) noted that research on violence among incarcerated females is sparse and results are inconsistent. However, as with men, any attempts to draw inferences about prison violence based on community violence may result in error.

In 2002, Cale and Lilienfeld conducted a comprehensive review of the literature in regard to gender differences in APD and psychopathy. They concluded that both psychopathy and APD are seen more frequently among males than females and that much more research is needed to better understand the nature of these gender differences. A preliminary study provides some support for the use of the HCR-20 and Psychopathy Checklist: Screening Version with females who are under psychiatric care (Nicholls et al., 2004).

However, much research is still needed in the area of risk assessment with women, and evaluators are cautioned against applying data collected on male populations to a female subject, as evidence indicates marked differences.

Dynamic Factors

Research on dynamic risk factors is still in its infancy. These factors present special challenges to the researcher, as they range from relatively stable (e.g., antisocial attitudes) to relatively acute (e.g., mood). Some dynamic factors utilized are simply extensions of static factors. For example, a history of substance abuse is a historical factor, but current substance abuse and even current intoxication is dynamic; a history of violation of release conditions can be examined in dynamic terms, such as recently missing a scheduled appointment.

Some evidence has been gathered in support of specific dynamic risk factors. Monahan and colleagues (2001) demonstrated a relationship between current substance abuse and violence. In a prospective study of psychiatric patients who had been violent in the past, substance abuse predicted violence in the very short term; for example, heavy drinking on day 1 led to a higher likelihood of violence on days 2 and 3 (Mulvey et al., 2006). Anger also appears to be a dynamic risk factor (Monahan et al., 2001; Navaco, 1994). A considerable literature has explored impulsivity (Webster & Jackson, 1997), though it may be better considered a trait than a state.

After an extensive review of the literature, Douglas and Skeem (2005) selected seven broad factors that demonstrate promise as dynamic predictors of violence risk: impulsiveness, negative affect, psychosis, antisocial attitudes, substance abuse, problems in interpersonal relationships, and poor treatment compliance. However, the exact contribution of the dynamic variables is still unclear. It remains uncertain how dynamic variables may interact and whether any specific factor actually precedes violent acts. One recent study, conducted in The Netherlands, suggests that dynamic factors do not add incremental validity to a risk assessment when combined with static factors (Philipse, Koeter, van der Staak, & van den Brink, 2006). However, this particular study failed to validate some of the most well-established static factors, such as age at first offense.

Protective Factors

The field of risk assessment has been accused of being "unabashedly one-sided" (Rogers, 2000, p. 597) for placing so much emphasis on risk factors while virtually ignoring factors likely to be protective. Some evaluators appear to define *protective factor* simply as the absence of a particular risk factor. This assumes that there is a risk-protective continuum relative to the various identified factors. For example, if "never having been married" is a risk factor for certain types of violence, would "having had at least one spouse" be a protective factor? If high scores on the PCL-R are predictive of violent recidivism, would a lower score be considered a protective factor? And how low would these scores need to be to be considered protective? We suggest that this approach is appropriate only if specific data demonstrate that the absence of a particular factor is predictive of reduced risk; it is probably not appropriate to assume that a risk-protection continuum exists for all documented risk factors.

Relatively little research has addressed potential protective factors. Unlike research on risk factors that has repeatedly established certain variables as indicative of high risk (e.g., history of violent behavior, psychopathy), no specific protective factors stand out for violence in general. The majority of research conducted to date has targeted protective factors for children and adolescents. Factors found to be protective for this group are generally contextual and interactive.

In 1995, a U.S. Department of Justice paper indicated that female gender, intelligence, positive social orientation, resilient temperament, and social bonding to positive role models were significant protective factors for youth. Hoge, Andrews, and Leschied (1996) identified positive peer relations, good school performance, participation in organized leisure activities, and positive response to authority as important protectors. Rodney, Johnson, and Srivastava (2005) found strong academic performance and bonding to school to be key. Various dimensions of positive parent-child relationships have proven significant (Gorman-Smith, Henry, & Tolan, 2004; Hawkins et al., 1998; K. W. Taylor & Kliewer, 2006). Protective factors unique to specific cultural groups should also be considered. For example, for Latino youth, strong extended family ties and religious and spiritual values may be important (Velasquez, Castellanos, Garrido, Maness, & Anderson, 2006). Several broad factors have been noted in the literature with some frequency and included in actuarial assessment. These include prosocial involvement, strong social support, strong attachment and bonds, positive attitudes toward intervention, positive attitudes toward authority, strong commitment to school, and resilient temperament (Borum, 2006). As with risk factors, one should consider protective factors specific to the type of risk addressed for the particular population involved.

Use of Assessment Instruments to Identify Empirically Supported Risk Factors

Surveys continue to document the wide use of psychological assessment instruments in forensic evaluations (Archer, 2006; Archer, Buffington-Vollum, Stredny, & Handel, 2006; Borum & Grisso, 1995). Well-researched instruments can aid the clinician in weighting and combining variables, going beyond simply addressing each factor. A structured instrument can also help to assure that the evaluation is comprehensive and less biased. However, an instrument must be carefully selected for its validity and reliability, appropriateness to the task at hand, and legal admissibility.

Admission as Evidence

Courts have long struggled with the question of what standard to use in deciding whether evidence proffered as scientific should be admitted as such. In 1923, the DC Circuit Court of Appeals constructed what has become known as the *Frye* rule (*Frye v. United States*). This rule holds that the basis on which scientific testimony is grounded must be generally accepted in the particular field. This so-called general acceptance rule was widely applied throughout the country for many years. It is still the test used by courts in a number of jurisdictions.

However, in 1993, the U.S. Supreme Court outlined somewhat different criteria for courts to utilize (*Daubert v. Merrell Dow Pharmaceuticals, Inc.*). Specifically, the Justices suggested that courts consider (a) whether the theory underlying the testimony had been tested or could be tested, (b) whether the information had been published and peer-reviewed, (c) whether there was an established error rate, and (d) whether the premise on which the testimony was based was generally accepted in the relevant field. This was in keeping with Federal Rule of Evidence 702. Although *Daubert* itself applies only in federal courtrooms, a number of jurisdictions have adopted the standard. Therefore, before deciding to apply a particular instrument as part of a risk assessment, evaluators should first determine what standard is used in their jurisdiction (most commonly *Daubert* or *Frye*) and then carefully consider whether the chosen instrument would meet a challenge under that standard.

Appropriateness to the Task at Hand

To be of value in any forensic context, including risk assessment, an instrument must relate directly to the psycholegal issue being assessed, be appropriate for the individual who is the subject of assessment, and not stray into areas far afield from the intended focus. Section 9.02 of the American Psychological Association's (2002) *Ethical Principles of Psychologists and Code of Conduct* specifies that care must be taken to assure that instruments are used "for purposes that are appropriate in light of the research on or evidence of the usefulness and proper application of the techniques." An increasing number of instruments have been developed and validated specifically for the purpose of assessing risk for various types of violence. A few other instruments (e.g., the PCL-R) were not developed for the purpose of assessing risk but, nonetheless, have yielded a significant database indicating their relevance to this task. Instruments lacking such a database should not be used for risk assessment purposes.

Care must also be taken to assure that any assessment instrument used has validity and reliability "established for use with the members of the population tested" (American Psychological Association, 2002, §9.02[b]). The "Guidelines on Multicultural Education, Training, Research, Practice, and Organizational Change for Psychologists" (American Psychological Association, 2003) further stress the importance of considering the population a test references before deciding to use it, as well as considering specific limitations it may have with other populations. As the research on risk assessment has progressed, instruments have become increasingly specific as to the populations on whom they are normed and whom they are designed to assess.

A forensic evaluation is distinct from a clinical assessment in part due to the forensic evaluation's intense focus. Guidelines for forensic practice suggest avoiding "any information that does not bear directly upon the legal purpose of the evaluation" (Committee on Ethical Guidelines for Forensic Psychologists, 1991, p. 660). A risk assessment is not a fishing expedition aimed at uncovering everything possible about the subject. Rather, it should focus on issues relevant to risk and avoid instruments that cast too broad a net.

Types of Instruments

In recent years, the number of available instruments designed to measure risk has continued to multiply. They differ markedly on the specific items that are included and methods used for scoring and administration. However, the differences do not seem to relate in any systematic way to predictive validity (Philipse et al., 2006).

Therefore, we present a number of approaches and examples and discuss their advantages and disadvantages. (For a catalogue of instruments, see Appendix A.)

Standard Psychological Test Batteries

Recent research suggests that general psychological tests (e.g., Minnesota Multiphasic Personality Inventory-2, Personality Assessment Inventory, Millon Clinical Multiaxial Inventory-III) are still widely used in forensic evaluations, including the assessment of risk (Archer et al., 2006). These instruments may have an appropriate indirect role as part of a risk assessment. For example, if a diagnosis is essential (as in an evaluation for civil commitment), such tests might be very helpful for diagnostic decisions, although not directly related to risk. If malingering is an issue, a well-validated instrument may be useful. If mental retardation is a critical issue, as in death penalty cases, intelligence testing could be very appropriate. In 1992, Heilbrun pointed out that tests may be valuable in the forensic context to measure a construct relating to the issue at hand, even though such a construct is not the ultimate psycholegal concern.

However, results from broad psychological inventories should *not* be interpreted as predictive of risk. Evaluators have been known to attempt broad cognitive leaps based on constructs that appear *potentially* related to acts of violence. For instance, elevations on Scale 4 (*Psychopathic Deviate*) of the Minnesota Multiphasic Personality Inventory-2 may indicate traits such as a lack of remorse, limited empathetic abilities, and an egocentric outlook on life. However, most people with some combination of these traits do not engage in violence, and research has failed to demonstrate meaningful predictive validity for this scale or similar scales with respect to violence.

More generally, administering large test batteries is often ill advised for forensic purposes. Research on types of risk has become increasingly specific, and there is no standard battery suitable for risk assessment in general. In addition, it would be difficult to establish the predictive validity of standardized personality or cognitive instruments for this purpose. Finally, describing numerous test instruments on the witness stand can be difficult, opening the evaluator to many lines of cross-examination and potentially confusing the jury.

The Pure Actuarial Approach

As detailed in the previous chapter on nomothetic and base rate data, actuarial instruments are typically composed of a limited number of variables, combined using a numerical weighting procedure, with results corresponding to a particular rate of recidivism in the instrument development sample. Although true actuarial instruments do include research-supported risk factors, we discussed these instruments in the prior chapter because one of their distinguishing features is their link to nomothetic data provided by the instrument development sample. Another feature is the strictly defined procedure for combining risk factors in a mathematical fashion.

The Structured Guide to Risk Assessment

In contrast to the pure actuarial approach, structured risk assessment guides present a set of variables, backed by ample research, for evaluators to investigate when assessing risk. However, there is no formula by which the factors should be mathematically weighted or combined. Proponents of this approach assert that in the clinical arena,

> It makes little sense to sum the number of risk factors present in a given case, and then use fixed, arbitrary cutoffs to classify the individual as low, moderate, or high risk. . . . It is both possible and reasonable for an assessor to conclude that an assessee is at high risk for violence based on the presence of a single factor. (Webster et al., 1997b, p. 22)

A prominent example of a structured risk assessment guide is the HCR-20. This checklist-style measure includes 10 historical, 5 clinical, and 5 risk management items. It is best used with persons having both a history of violence and evidence of a mental illness or personality disorder. Considerably more clinical judgment is required to employ the instrument than would be the case with an actuarial device. The scores may be summed for purposes of research; however, there is no specific number or cutoff point to assign a final decision for clinical purposes. The authors are adamant that the HCR-20 should be considered one step in conducting a risk assessment and not the entire risk assessment process (Webster et al., 1997b). Although a thorough review of the HCR-20 (and other risk measures based on structured professional judgment) is beyond the scope of this review, there is a wealth of literature regarding the measure's utility in violence risk assessment (for review of this literature, see Douglas, Guy, & Weir, 2005).

Using Risk for Treatment Planning

A final type of instrument attempts to utilize risk assessment as a tool for risk management and treatment planning. After its initial publication, a companion guide was added to the HCR-20 specifically addressing risk management (Douglas, Webster, Hart, Eaves, & Ogloff, 2001). One example of an instrument developed specifically to combine risk with needs assessment is the Level of Service Inventory—Revised (Andrews & Bonta, 1995). The instrument is composed of 54 items covering 10 criminogenic domains. Completion involves a review of records, as well as a semi-structured interview. Items range from the simple and narrowly defined to those requiring considerable clinical judgment. It is designed to aid in the development of treatment targets and treatment plans and in determining the least restrictive environment necessary for risk management. It has also been used in the assessment of treatment outcome (Bonta, Wallace-Capretta, & Rooney, 2000). Both static and dynamic factors are considered. The total score may be used to help in assessing a level of risk, while the subscales are to identify service delivery needs. Andrews and Bonta emphasize that cutoff scores are guidelines only and that the instrument is not a substitute for clinical judgment.

Instrument Selection

Descriptions of a variety of risk assessment instruments are provided in Appendix A. The examples discussed earlier were chosen simply because, along with the PCL-R, they tend to be the risk assessment instruments used by highly trained forensic evaluators to measure general violence risk in the community (Archer et al., 2006) and because they have considerable empirical support. However, they are not the only instruments to consider, and there may be good reasons to choose others for a particular evaluation. New instruments are regularly being developed for the assessment of risk. It may be tempting to select the latest from the increasing options, but evaluators must ensure that there is sufficient validational data to support the use of an instrument in any particular case or given context. Evaluators should be cautious about too quickly adopting new techniques, as these may prove less reliable and valid when subjected to cross-validation and continued study.

The Role of Third-Party Information

In any forensic evaluation, third-party information is generally deemed essential and almost always sought by evaluators (Heilbrun, Warren, & Picarello, 2003; Otto, Slobogin, & Greenberg, 2007). Collateral information is absolutely critical in risk assessment. For a variety of reasons, examinees may be inaccurate or misinformed regarding data critical to the evaluation. In establishing risk or protective factors, misinformation or missing information may significantly alter the landscape. Inaccuracies can be particularly problematic when the evaluator is scoring an instrument. Although it is possible to administer the PCL-R without an interview, Hare (2003, p. 19) is very explicit that "PCL-R ratings should not be made in the absence of adequate collateral information." A single point of history can potentially raise or lower the score on instruments and alter the resulting prediction.

The "Specialty Guidelines for Forensic Psychologists" specifically direct that "forensic psychologists seek to obtain independent and personal verification of data relied upon as part of their professional services to the court or to a party to a legal proceeding" (Committee on Ethical Guidelines for Forensic Psychologists, 1991, p. 662). This would suggest not only verifying information obtained from the examinee, but assuring the accuracy of other records. In our experience, police and criminal justice department records are not

100% accurate in every detail. For example, one of us recently received an official record of an offender's sexual misconduct. One document reported that the offender previously assaulted two 60-year-old females. Further investigation revealed that the victims were actually 6-year-old females. This typographical error made a difference in the evaluation of deviant interests, as well as in risk management strategies.

What We Know from Science

The scientific literature on risk assessment has grown exponentially over the past 2 decades, and this trend appears to be continuing. To provide a competent risk assessment the evaluator must first explore static factors that, over time, have proven predictive for the particular type of risk under analysis. These are apt to vary with the type of risk (e.g., sexual offending, spousal abuse), the type of individual who is the subject of the assessment (e.g., a criminal offender, a person with a mental disorder), and the context (e.g., in the community, in a structured environment). Subsequent chapters discuss specific types of risk most commonly evaluated.

Less research has been conducted on dynamic and protective factors. However, what is available can be of particular value when considering risk management and interventions. The more control that can be exercised over the individual's future circumstances, the more vital these factors become.

Finally, an evaluator must consider whether available risk instruments can enhance the accuracy of the assessment. Critical issues relevant to this decision include whether the instrument will provide information specifically needed to address the issue at hand, whether the instrument would satisfy legal criteria, and whether there is an adequate database to justify its use in the forensic arena generally and with a particular examinee specifically. We are enthused about the increasing availability of risk measures and the empirical support for many of these. However, in the complex task of risk assessment, no single score or set of scores can provide the complete answer. Determining level of risk requires careful integration of numerous pieces of information from a variety of sources.

6

What Do We Know about This Individual?

Idiographic Factors and the Need for Individualized Assessment

Although risk assessment is rooted in research-driven normative data, it also requires a fine-grained individualized assessment of risk. Among the primary principles that Heilbrun (2001, p. 190) identified as relevant across forensic evaluations, he included, "Use case-specific (idiographic) evidence in assessing clinical condition, functional abilities, and causal connection." We agree that the need to consider idiographic data is particularly acute when the issue is risk assessment. The goal is not to sweep aside the empirically derived normative data, but to consider that other factors—particularly dynamic factors—may bear upon risk as well. Does it matter whether delusional beliefs correlate broadly with risk for violence if the examinee killed two people because he harbored the delusional belief that they were agents of Satan? Must a history of sexually molesting children raise the risk of violence for an individual who will spend the rest of his life in prison? Regardless of the number of high-risk factors identified, does the rapist's level of risk change if he is injured severely and becomes quadriplegic?

Janus and Prentky (2003) observed that courts have historically relied too heavily on unsupported clinical judgment in rendering decisions about future risk. However, while arguing in favor of actuarial risk assessment and indicating that relying solely on unstructured clinical judgment may be unethical, the authors still affirmed the highly idiosyncratic nature of human behavior. They concluded, "Best-practice methodology would not, in our opinion, rely exclusively on the results of an actuarial risk assessment and would never knowingly exclude potentially critical, risk-relevant information that is not reflected in the actuarial risk assessment" (p. 1498).

Evaluators need to be aware that actuarial tests and specific risk factors having a strong research base do not exhaust all of the important elements that may be contributing to an individual's propensity to become violent. Rarely will such information allow one to determine the type of violence most likely, the likely triggers for violent events, the potential severity of the incident, the time frames of highest risk, or the most effective intervention (Hart, 1998b; Heilbrun et al., 2002).

In this chapter, we outline the rationale for considering idiographic factors in risk assessment. While we emphasize that the use of nomothetic data is the foundation underlying good risk assessment practice, we also argue that a risk assessment is incomplete without additional consideration of idiographic factors. As Hart (1998b, p. 126) argued, "Reliance—at least complete reliance—on actuarial decision making by professionals is unacceptable." Specifically, a careful consideration of idiographic risk factors is necessary in order to:

- Address the possibility of a truly unique risk or protective factor
- Examine the role of dynamic risk factors
- Acknowledge multicultural variability
- Inform risk management
- Demonstrate the face validity and legal relevance of the risk assessment process

Here, we discuss and illustrate the use of idiographic data in empirically grounded risk assessments.

Addressing the Possibility of Unique Risk or Protective Factors

There are times when a single variable is so powerful that it is likely to override most other considerations. Indeed, the possibility of a rare risk or protective factor is one of the primary reasons that many scholars argue against the exclusive reliance on actuarial instruments (e.g., Hanson, 1998; Hart, 1998b; Monahan, 2003).

What constitutes a unique risk or protective factor? Consider a few illustrations. One of us evaluated an individual who was completing a relatively brief prison sentence for two counts of Indecency with a Child, the only offenses documented in collateral records. The evidence of his culpability was compelling, and he readily admitted his guilt. More important, though, he readily admitted that he had been sexually assaulting children for many years in various parts of the country, and that he had assaulted his first victim over 15 years ago. By his own estimate, he had assaulted or molested over 100 boys, generally between the ages of 12 and 15. He said he was relieved to finally "be stopped" from offending due to incarceration. Given the magnitude of his offense history, it would be difficult to see any actuarial scheme (particularly one that relies heavily on prior *convictions*) that would persuade the evaluator that this person presents a low risk for reoffense if he were simply released without supervision. A strong history of lethal or potentially lethal violence may have a similar effect. Hart (1998b) described an individual who scored in the range of average risk on a well-validated actuarial measure, though he had completed dozens of rapes and three sexual homicides.

Single key variables do not always function to *increase* one's level of risk. For example, an individual may acquire a significant disability that seriously limits his or her capacity to engage in the previous violent behavior. One of us was asked to provide an opinion on risk regarding an individual with a lengthy history of criminality. His offenses included a number of armed robberies, several serious injuries to the victims, injuries to several law enforcement officers, and incidents of assault while in custody. He began his criminal career at age 12, and his history revealed evidence of significant psychopathic traits. However, during his most recent apprehension, he was shot in the head by police. The damage was severe and well documented by neurologists. He could not walk, speak coherently, coordinate his arm movements, or control his bodily functions. Given the nature of the injuries, medical specialists opined that he would never regain his premorbid functioning and that he would require nursing home care indefinitely. Absent the injury, this individual would be at high risk for violent recidivism, but his incapacitation altered that risk considerably. Unique factors with such an obvious impact on risk level may be relatively rare; nevertheless, any risk assessment methodology must allow for consideration of these possibilities. Unless actuarial instruments improve to the point that they can account for *all* possible relevant variables (a scenario that is hard to imagine), it will be necessary for clinicians to remain open to the possibility of unique risk and protective factors.

One category of unique risk factors that scholars often mention is threats (e.g., Hanson, 1998; Hart, 1998a; Litwack et al., 2006; Monahan, 2003). Direct threats of violence would seem to be an obvious target of concern. However, most risk assessment studies do not specify whether the subjects had threatened violence (Litwack et al., 2006). The scant literature addressing threats of violence indicates that these should be taken seriously (Meloy et al., 2004). Correlations between making threats and engaging in violent behavior have emerged in studies of stalking and obsessional harassment (Brewster, 2000; Kienlen, Birmingham, Solberg, O'Regan, & Meloy, 1997).

If threats are an issue, a careful examination of the historical context would be important. Does the individual commonly make threats? Does he or she tend to act on them? Have threats been recent? Are threats made in some contexts and not others? Have the threats been toward a single target? What is the likely availability of that target? Answers to these questions can be important in that the only known target may be deceased or, for other reasons, permanently out of reach. Is the threat plausible? Are the means likely to be available? Answers to these questions can be particularly important when threats are made in correctional environments. Results of the analysis should be incorporated into the risk assessment as appropriate.*

Examining the Role of Dynamic Factors

Mental Illness

Considerable research has documented the relationship between various diagnoses, or specific psychiatric symptoms, and violence (Monahan & Steadman, 1994; Swanson, Borum, Swartz, & Monahan, 1996; Swanson et al., 1990, 2006). However, individuals can experience and respond to mental illness in very idiosyncratic ways.

---

* Although we are discussing threats of violence in the context of forensic assessment of violence risk (in which evaluators typically are assigned a risk assessment to inform some institutional procedure such as release or a decision in a civil or criminal court), it is worth mentioning that scholars have delineated a number of threat assessment protocols for situations brought about specifically due to threats of violence, which tend to differ from standard forensic risk assessment contexts. For example, the U.S. Secret Service has long followed a well-developed protocol for assessing the risk that a threatening individual poses to Secret Service protectees (Borum, Fein, Vossekuil, & Berglund, 1999; Fein, Vossekuil, & Holden, 1995). Addressing a context more familiar to most clinicians, Borum and Reddy (2001) offered a protocol for clinicians to assess threats in "*Tarasoff* situations." Named after the well-known case (*Tarasoff v. The Regents of the University of California*, 1976) that came before the California Supreme Court, *Tarasoff* situations are those in which a mental health professional concludes (or should conclude, based on reasonable professional standards) that a patient presents a serious danger of violence to another person. Depending upon the jurisdiction, the clinician then may incur a duty to make a reasonable effort to protect the potential victim.

More recently, following several highly publicized firearm homicides by youth on school campuses, scholars devoted attention to evaluating threats of violence by students (e.g., Reddy et al., 2001). Targeted violence in schools is an exceedingly low base rate event (Cornell, 2005; 2006; Mulvey & Caufman, 2001), despite public perceptions to the contrary. For assessing this type of risk, authorities from both academia and law enforcement (Cornell, 2004; Cornell & Sheras, 2005; O'Toole, 2000; Reddy et al., 2001; Vossekuil, Reddy, Fein, Borum, & Modzeleski, 2002) are consistent in recommending an idiographic assessment of case facts, including context and nature of the threat, as opposed to "one size fits all" approaches such as profiling or other prediction schemes. Indeed, recent empirical research (Cornell et al., 2004) supports the utility of individualized threat assessment guidelines.

For example, it is helpful to know that in a large national study only 3.6% of patients diagnosed with schizophrenia engaged in serious violent behavior during the follow-up period (Swanson et al., 2006). It is also significant that on one commonly used actuarial tool for assessing violence risk among mentally disordered offenders (the VRAG), schizophrenia is inversely related to violent recidivism. However, these data may not be persuasive of reduced risk when the subject of the assessment, who has a diagnosis of schizophrenia, has a clear-cut history of acting on his or her paranoid delusional beliefs in a manner that involves violence to others. The fact that violent behavior is uncommon in persons with schizophrenia does not negate the very real risk that it may pose in a particular individual.

Response to and compliance with treatment may also be critical to addressing risk in someone with a mental illness. Historically, how has the examinee changed in response to treatment? For example, has antipsychotic medication been effective, and to what degree? Do symptoms other than delusions go into remission, leaving the person more functional but still deluded? If delusions respond positively to treatment, to what degree? Has the individual actively resisted treatment? Does the individual comply with treatment only when it is mandated and monitored? Unfortunately, many of the empirical studies addressing risk and mental illness do not report the treatment conditions under which they were conducted. Nevertheless, an examinee's history of (non)compliance, or idiosyncratic response to treatment, may have some bearing on the violence risk that examinee poses.

Substance Abuse

Research clearly reveals a stronger relationship between substance abuse and violence than between mental illness and violence (Steadman et al., 1998; Swanson, 1994). However, even here, idiographic factors may be important to the complete analysis. Is there an actual direct relationship between the violent acts in a person's history and substance abuse? How consistent is that relationship? That is, does the individual engage in violence only when abusing substances? Does the individual become violent when intoxicated, or report using substances specifically to lower inhibitions to violence? Has any history of mandated sobriety been successful in reducing violence? One paradoxical case involved an individual with a very significant history of alcoholism, including several DWIs and commitments to alcohol rehabilitation programs. However, his only crime of concern was sexually molesting children. A careful review of his history revealed that his only offenses occurred during extended periods of sobriety.

Stressors

Stress has been suggested as a critical moderator in the assessment of violence risk (Klassen & O'Connor, 1994). However, research has been variable as to whether, and to what degree, stress relates to violence. Furthermore, individuals vary in terms of what external factors trigger stress and the degree to which they respond to stress. Isolating individual vulnerabilities will require careful social history analysis.

Acknowledging Multicultural Variability

Increasingly, mental health professionals see culturally pluralistic populations (American Psychological Association, 2003; Sue & Sue, 2003). Nowhere is this more common than in the criminal justice system. Ethical principles dictate that evaluators acknowledge the limitation of any standard instrument as applied to a particular population (American Psychological Association, 2002, 2003; Constantine, 1998; Dana, 2005). Certainly, a number of studies on violence risk assessment and risk assessment instruments have been conducted internationally and with multiethnic samples (e.g., Cooke, Michie, Hart, & Clark, 2005a, 2005b; de Vogel, de Ruiter, Hildebrand, Bos, & van de Ven, 2004; Doyle, Dolan, & McGovern, 2002; Hare, 2003). However, culture involves more than nationality and ethnicity. Individuals are impacted by a wide variety of social influences, and each may be part of an ethnic culture, a religious culture, a regional or national culture, a socioeconomic culture, or a culture based on sexual orientation, to name but a few. To assume that an instrument will provide an accurate assessment of risk for someone simply based on studies that included members of the person's racial or ethnic group grossly oversimplifies cultural context. Unfortunately, professionals engaged in psychological assessment frequently minimize within-group differences, thus making test results appear more definitive (Dana, 2005). This has led researchers in the area of multicultural assessment to advocate for a more holistic, idiographic framework (Ponterotto, Gretchen, & Chauhan, 2001; Ridley, Hill, Thompson, & Omerod, 2001).

We do not contend that every culturally distinct feature of an examinee renders actuarial data irrelevant. (Were this the case, actuarial data could never be used!) But, with multiculturalism in mind, actuarial instruments and assessment schemes should be evaluated with caution and supplemented with more individualized information. This is the case even with the most well-researched and robust techniques. For example, the PCL-R has been researched both internationally and with a variety of ethnic groups across North America. In the most recent edition of the test manual, Hare (2003) described studies of female offenders, African Americans, Hispanic Americans, Aboriginal Natives, and Native Americans. In 2000, Hare, Clark, Grann, and Thornton discussed an array of international studies further validating the instrument. Works compiled by Cooke, Forth, and Hare (1998) seem to reinforce the notion that the PCL-R measures much the same construct across cultures. However, even with data from increasingly diverse samples, Hare (2003, p. 51) cautioned that the issue is not resolved:

> Until more is known about the role played by social and cultural factors in the expression and practical implications of psychopathy, clinicians and researchers should be judicious when interpreting the PCL-R scores of minority and other groups for whom the instrument has not been well validated.

More recently, Cooke et al. (2005a, 2005b; cf. Bolt, Hare, & Neumann, 2007) have conducted additional studies in the United Kingdom. These studies found evidence that scores obtained in the

United Kingdom and in North America may not be wholly comparable, particularly in the area of arrogant and deceptive interpersonal style. They suggested overall evidence of significant cultural bias in PCL-R ratings. As two Westernized industrial areas, the United Kingdom and North America would be expected to have greater cultural similarities than between other, more divergent populations. Yet, even within the same country, there may be variability. Although there is much less research on the relationship between psychopathy traits and violence among youth, relative to adults, the available information suggests variability with respect to ethnicity. In particular, the predictive validity of psychopathy with respect to violence or recidivism appears considerably lower among multiethnic youth samples than among Caucasian youth samples (Edens & Cahill, 2007; Edens, Campbell, & Weir, 2007).

Cultural bias in the PCL-R is particularly important, because the assessment of psychopathy is included (often as the strongest predictor; Edens, Skeem, et al., 2006; G. T. Harris, Rice, & Camilleri, 2004) in a number of the most widely used risk instruments (e.g., the VRAG, the Sex Offender Risk Appraisal Guide, the HCR-20). Cultural competence in risk assessment, as in any other area of psychological evaluation, requires the clinician to consider any and all relevant information about the individual, as well as the individual in context.

One example of an idiographic experience that receives considerable attention in the multicultural literature is oppression (American Psychological Association, 2003; Atkinson, Morten, & Sue, 1998; Fukuyama & Ferguson, 2000; Willie, Rieker, Kramer, & Brown, 1995). Common examples include ethnocentrism, racism, sexism, and homophobia. Individuals may experience individual episodes of oppression, or oppression may be part of the cultural experience of an entire group. Victims of oppression or members of victimized groups may hold unique worldviews that alter their perception of other individuals, other groups, violence, or efforts to prevent violence. Conversely, a few subcultural groups have been formed specifically around *goals* of oppression. For example, we have evaluated inmates involved in prison gangs with explicitly articulated goals regarding violence to other racial or ethnic groups. Obviously, membership in such a gang, particularly when one openly espouses violence to other groups, could be considered a unique risk factor for violence, depending on context.

Recently, the issue of oppression and minority status as it impacts domestic violence has drawn some attention (Kasturirangan, Krishnan, & Riger, 2004). Violence has also been linked to previous oppression and victimization in the context of school bullying (Klein, 2006). Several reviews of school shooting incidents have associated victimization with subsequent violence (Kimmel & Mahler, 2003; Leary, Kowalski, Smith, & Phillips, 2003). Thankfully, such tragedies are rare, and the number of subjects for study is small. However, bullying has also been associated with retaliatory violence of much less severity (Elliott, Hamburg, & Williams, 1998; Hazler & Carney, 2000). Of course, school is not the only time in life that such individuals may be the subject of prejudice and discrimination. Despite the dearth of empirical studies, it would seem that the issue of oppression and victimization could be worthy of analysis as a potential idiographic factor in some cases.

Informing Risk Management

One of the most important reasons to consider idiographic factors is that "the clinical task (of risk assessment) is violence *prevention*, not violence *prediction*" (Hart, 1998b, p. 123). Many risk assessment tasks will require offering some degree of input regarding risk management strategies (Heilbrun, 1997). The evaluator who has examined carefully the past antecedents, nature, frequency, and severity of violence that a particular individual has committed (and also examined incidents in which the individual refrained from violence, or was prevented from violence) is in a much better position to offer detailed, individualized suggestions for risk management. Similarly, a careful examination of how well-established risk factors, such as substance abuse, relate to violence in a particular individual's history tends to improve efforts to identify appropriate conditions or interventions for risk management (see Chapter 8).

Heilbrun and colleagues (2002) described a case to illustrate how nomothetic evidence is critical to risk assessment; however, it also demonstrates very effectively how idiographic information must be integrated in order to analyze the connection between clinical condition and functional abilities. In the case (submitted by Stephen Hart), the PCL-R, the VRAG, the HCR-20, and the Spousal Assault Risk Assessment Guide are first used to establish the nomothetic base. However, the evaluator then proceeded to analyze the role of the examinee's mental disorder (psychotic disorder not otherwise specified)—including delusional components, depressive features, and dissociative features—in the examinee's violent behavior. This analysis became the primary basis for the recommended risk management plan.

Demonstrating the Face Validity and Legal Relevance of the Risk Assessment Process

When data are to be presented in a courtroom, one must not only consider accuracy, but also the perception of accuracy. Scientists rightly say that face validity is the weakest measure of a valid assessment. However, face validity may be the first concern for the trier of fact. As Grisso (2003, p. 52) observed in discussing instruments to assess competence, "It is possible that no amount of empirical validity will be able to overcome a judicial belief in the face invalidity of an instrument's dimensions in relation to the legal construct." Although it may be difficult, particularly for jurors, to grasp the significance of ROC curves as they relate to sensitivity and specificity, they are apt to have little difficulty understanding that, for an offender who intentionally becomes intoxicated to lower inhibitions at the time of each rape, continued substance abuse would be a significant risk factor. Following a survey of state and federal cases, Litwack and colleagues (2006) argued forcefully that courts have generally admitted testimony based on clinical judgments of what precipitates violence, and they may even prefer that actuarial assessments be bolstered by more complete clinical data. As detailed in Chapter 7, courts tend to distrust broad and nomothetic data, while emphasizing unique or case-specific data.

To be clear, we are not arguing that evaluators prioritize idiographic case data simply because courts prefer it. However, a model that allows for consideration of idiographic factors (even if none of these idiographic factors is sufficient to alter the initial risk estimate that is based on nomothetic data) is not only sound practice, but is more likely to enhance our communication with the courts.

Using an Anamnestic Approach to Identify Relevant Idiographic Factors

In risk assessment, an anamnestic approach is "a specific type of clinical assessment whereby the examiner attempts to identify violence risk factors through a detailed examination of the individual's history of violent and threatening behavior" (Otto, 2000, p. 1241). Although an examinee's personal recollections may be a part of the database, the approach goes well beyond the clinical interview, incorporating historical records and information from third parties. In a scientifically grounded assessment, an anamnestic approach is used in addition to, and not as a substitute for, appropriate risk instruments and the established risk factors from the literature.

To conduct an anamnestic assessment, the examiner meticulously studies each incidence of violence in the individual's history, looking for a chain of events that led to each episode and specific triggers of the behavior. Importantly, triggers for serious violence may be different from factors that precipitate minor incidents. The evaluator then attempts to identify patterns of behavior that led to violence with the particular individual, as well as protective factors that might have prevented other violent events. A thorough anamnestic evaluation helps to inform an individualized risk management plan.

The overall result of an anamnestic evaluation should identify how and why a particular individual acted violently. Most commonly, this will produce a combination of personal and situational factors. The approach can perhaps best be illustrated through examples.

Vignette 1

JW had a relatively uneventful childhood. He was the only child of two university professors. He generally did well in school; however, records indicate that he began abusing alcohol and marijuana around age 14. Following high school graduation, he began college. During his freshman year, he was twice convicted of DWI and underwent a 6-week inpatient rehabilitation program. He completed college and went on to graduate school. While working on his master's degree in computer science, he experienced psychological problems. He took a one-semester leave of absence, returning to school stabilized on antipsychotic medication. Following receipt of his degree, he taught at a small community college consistently for 7 years. During this time he married, and the couple had two children.

During JW's 8th year as a college instructor, students complained that he preached religious doctrines in the computer labs. After consultation with administrators, he admitted that he had discontinued mental health treatment and agreed to return to his psychiatrist. His wife noted that she carefully reminded him of his medications and treatment appointments.

The next 2 years of JW's life were uneventful. Then, for the first time, he took off the summer semester to do some writing. He returned to campus for the fall semester several days late, looking somewhat disheveled. He mentioned to colleagues that he and his wife had separated in late May, and she and the children had moved out of state. His colleagues then noted that he was withdrawn and often mumbling about demon possession. Students once again complained that he was preaching religious doctrines, and he was placed on administrative leave pending investigation. The evening after he was placed on leave, he returned to campus and, after seriously assaulting a campus security guard with a large rock, he set fire to the campus bell tower.

JW was found Not Guilty by Reason of Insanity and committed to a hospital. Records indicate that he had not taken any medications for 3 months prior to the incident. He harbored a delusional belief that Satan had infiltrated the campus through the bell tower, and it had become the center of Satanic worship. He received a diagnosis of schizoaffective disorder. A risk assessment was requested as he was pending discharge.

Analysis

JW scored very low on the PCL-R and very low on the VRAG. He had no prior history of violence. He had a stable family history and a stable history of employment. He had maintained a marriage successfully for 9 years. There was no evidence of a personality disorder. He did have a history of abusing substances that began at an early age. However, there was no evidence that substance abuse was involved in the bell tower incident and, in fact, no evidence that he had been drinking alcohol or using drugs at all since his college days. He had not been in trouble with the legal system since he was a freshman in college, had never been on probation, had demonstrated insight into his mental illness, and was generally compliant with mental health treatment over many years. Although some planning was involved in the arson, the assault on the security guard appeared completely impulsive, in that JW became violent when the man tried to foil the arson of the tower. Therefore, one could conclude that JW has few of the well-researched risk factors for violence.

However, an anamnestic analysis would yield important information. Although neither a diagnosis of a schizophrenic condition nor the presence of a delusion is strongly correlated with violence, in this case JW's delusional belief led directly to his assault on the guard to enable his burning the bell tower. The conduct was in no way typical of his behavior, nor did it make sense in any other way. This occurred on one of the few occasions when he had not been compliant with treatment. Untreated, schizoaffective disorder is generally a chronic condition with acute episodes likely to recur. Therefore, his mental illness and treatment rejection were two personal factors that clearly precipitated serious, potentially deadly violence. Beyond the personal factors, two situational variables appear to be directly relevant. He had lost his support system (family)—one that appeared to facilitate his treatment compliance—and he was without the structure usually afforded by his college employment. Taken together, one could conclude that, under certain specific circumstances, JW could pose a substantial risk for additional significant violent behavior. A report integrating the anamnestic approach would delineate the specific factors that led to his violent behavior and outline a risk management plan that would help avoid those factors (e.g., treatment noncompliance) in the future.

Vignette 2

PT was raised by a single mother along with six siblings. His elementary school performance was variable. At age 15, he was charged with Sexual Assault of a female peer. He was given 1-year probation, which he successfully completed. He began working at a convenience store and failed to complete high school. At 17, he was charged with unauthorized use of a motor vehicle and credit card fraud. He spent 6 months in jail, followed by a period of probation that he successfully completed. For the next 3 years he worked at various jobs in the construction industry. He was then charged with raping three adult females and prosecuted and convicted on one of the charges. In each instance he was heavily intoxicated on alcohol.

PT then served 3 years in the state department of corrections and was characterized as an exemplary inmate. He was paroled, but violated after 11 months for failing to report and failing a required urinalysis. He was reincarcerated, served another 3 years with no disciplinary reports, and was again paroled. For the next 3 years, he reported as required, consistently attended sex offender treatment, passed all required drug and alcohol tests, and maintained appropriate employment.

With 1 year of parole time remaining, PT was involved in a serious automobile accident and received a head injury suspected of causing frontal lobe damage. The accident was not his fault, and no substance abuse was involved. Two months later he was arrested for a sudden assault on a neighbor with a tire iron. No precipitant was identified aside from the individual politely asking him to move his car. Results of alcohol and drug testing were negative.

PT's parole was immediately violated, although he was not actually prosecuted on the assault charge. As he was close to his maximum release date, an evaluation was requested as to whether he presented a high risk as a sexually violent predator and should be committed.

Analysis

PT scored relatively high on the PCL-R and had a high score on the most commonly used sex offender actuarial instrument (STATIC-99). He had a history of violence, sexual offending, substance abuse, and violation of conditions of release. He had never been married, and all of his rape victims were unrelated strangers. However, an anamnestic assessment adds important data. The sexual assault as a juvenile was basically consensual sex with an underage partner, according to his report and as documented in records. The one rape for which he was convicted and the additional two for which he was charged all occurred within a 24-hour period of heavy binge drinking. Substance abuse appears to be strongly related to his violent acts, yet, with frequent monitoring, there has been no evidence of substance abuse in the past 3 years. Since his conviction for the sexual offenses, he has lived in the community for a total of 4 years without reoffending. His most recent violent act was nonsexual and apparently extremely impulsive. Prior to this event, when not intoxicated, he appeared to have excellent impulse control (as evidenced by his prison records). The tire iron assault was inconsistent with his previous criminal acts. It would, however, be consistent with uncontrolled impulsivity that can be precipitated by a closed head injury. One might then ask whether the sequelae of the injury itself would put PT at high risk. It would potentially put him at risk for future sudden violence (as in the tire iron incident), but there was no evidence to clearly demonstrate that it necessarily

placed him at high risk for future sexual offending, as required by the
SVP statute.

Both of the vignettes presented here illustrate the often critical
role that idiographic factors can play in a risk assessment. We emphasize that examining idiographic factors is a chance to weigh evidence with a direct, clear bearing on violence risk; it is not an
opportunity to introduce loose subjective impressions or biases. Evidence suggests that clinicians are prone to overpredict violence
based on race (Hoptman, Yates, Patanlinjug, Wack, & Convit,
1999) and sex (Elbogen, Williams, Kim, Tomkins, & Scalora, 2001);
thus evaluators should remain vigilant to ensure that idiographic
considerations remain objective.

Recognizing the heated and sometimes polarized tone (cf. Dvoskin
& Heilbrun, 2001) that often characterizes discussions of strict actuarial prediction versus actuarial-based prediction with additional idiographic considerations, we must reemphasize that *idiographic data
supplement nomothetic data; they do not replace nomothetic data.* Any
risk opinion should be rooted in nomothetic data and consideration
of empirically demonstrated risk and protective factors. However, any
risk assessment *methodology* is incomplete if it does not allow an evaluator to consider truly salient case-specific factors. Furthermore,
consideration of these idiographic factors allows the evaluator to con-
textualize risk and develop a case-specific risk management plan, as
discussed in later chapters.

7

What Can We Say about the Results of a Risk Assessment?

Risk Communication

In the third chapter, we emphasized the importance of working with the referring party to identify a precise referral question. A precise referral question establishes clear parameters for the risk assessment process and guides inquiry through the central stages of the risk assessment (i.e., identifying base rate data, considering empirically demonstrated risk factors, considering idiographic factors). Near the end of the risk assessment process, the referral question also defines how evaluators provide meaningful feedback that is appropriate in content and scope. Indeed, even a well-conducted and empirically sound risk assessment is useless if evaluators cannot convey findings in a precise yet easy-to-understand manner. As Heilbrun, Dvoskin, and colleagues (1999, p. 94) emphasized,

> Assessments of risk are valuable to the extent that they can improve legal or clinical decisions. . . . The only way risk assessors can influence decisions is by effectively communicating their findings to the legal and clinical actors whose decisions they wish to influence.

In this chapter, we detail the research on risk communication and then offer practical guidance for communicating the findings from a risk assessment, whether in written report or in expert testimony.

Research on Risk Communication

Research on risk communication is fairly recent. This is not surprising when we consider that the conceptual shift in our field, from violence prediction to risk assessment, was also fairly recent (see Chapter 1). To complete a task conceptualized as *violence prediction*—in which likelihood of violence is understood as a dichotomous (present or absent) individual characteristic that is unchanging over time and stable across contexts—an evaluator may communicate evaluation results with little more than a yes-or-no, dangerous-or-not-dangerous response to the referral question. On the other hand, when risk is understood to be dimensional rather than dichotomous, dynamic rather than static, and contextual rather than fixed, the task of communicating risk assessment results becomes much more complex. For example, evaluators must now communicate in terms of probabilities rather than dichotomies and emphasize the importance of context. Not surprisingly, then, the literature offered virtually no research on risk communication prior to 1990. Yet, beginning in the mid-1990s, several articles addressed the process of risk communication (e.g., Grisso & Tomkins, 1996; Heilbrun, Dvoskin, et al., 1999; Schopp, 1996), and several studies compare strategies for communicating violence risk estimates.

Options in Risk Communication

Most research that has addressed risk communication has addressed the following options in communication. Not coincidentally, many of these options correspond to decisions that an evaluator must consider before presenting the findings from a risk assessment to a decision maker. These decisions include the following.

Description versus Prediction versus Management

Is the evaluator's role only to identify risk factors that a particular individual demonstrates? If so, should the evaluator also offer suggestions to manage or minimize these risk factors? Perhaps the evaluator should instead offer a precise prediction as to the likelihood of violent behavior? In other words, evaluators choose from three general options for risk communication. These options were presented in the clinician surveys by Heilbrun and colleagues (2000, 2004), discussed later in the chapter. More recently, Borum and Verhaagen (2006) summarized the three primary risk communication styles in their text on violence risk assessment among youth:

1. *Descriptive risk communication,* as the label implies, involves identifying and describing the risk factors that are present in a given case. These may be nomothetic (broad, empirically identified) or idiographic (individualized, case-specific) risk factors, and the evaluator may be more or less explicit in describing how these contribute to greater risk. However, descriptive risk communication does not end with any particular conclusion or prediction about the likelihood of violence.

2. *Prediction-oriented risk communication* moves beyond simply identifying the relevant risk factors and concludes with a formal prediction as to the likelihood of violence. As described later, evaluators who convey a risk prediction may choose from several options—each with unique strengths, limitations, and risks of their own. However, prediction-oriented risk communication involves expressing only the perceived likelihood for violence; prediction models do not include communication regarding actions or strategies that may reduce the likelihood of violence.

3. *Management-oriented risk communication* involves the most active, or expansive, evaluator role. Here, evaluators move beyond simply identifying risk factors and take the next step of offering intervention strategies designed to reduce each observed risk factor. For a management-oriented risk communication message, authorities (e.g., Heilbrun et al., 2000) recommend a format such as "The examinee's risk for violence depends on a number of factors, including . . . (*evaluator describes salient risk factors or high risk circumstances*). To reduce this risk . . . (*evaluator prescribes specific interventions for each risk factor*)." Management-oriented risk communication is often the most comprehensive and practical final product of a formal risk assessment. However, there are also circumstances in which offering management-oriented communication extends beyond the evaluator's legally defined role.

The decision about whether to communicate risk in terms that are descriptive, predictive, or management-oriented is not an arbitrary one. The context of the evaluation most often dictates which style of communication an evaluator should adopt. Certain legal questions (e.g., the initial stage of civil commitment) call for *only* a prediction to help inform a particular judicial decision. However, there are also a number of situations in which the decision maker retains control over the examinee (e.g., probation, parole, conditional release from a hospital), and a risk management model of communication is much more helpful to inform the course of action (Heilbrun, 1997). For evaluators who have reached an *a priori* agreement with the party requesting a risk assessment, in which a precise referral question is articulated, there is rarely any ambiguity in deciding whether to present risk assessment findings in a prediction versus management model. In other words, a clear referral question (see Chapter 3) should lead to clear risk communication.

Categorical versus Probability Estimates

For clinicians who do choose to follow a prediction model (either alone or in combination with a risk management model) and offer an estimate of risk, how might they do so? The literature has recently featured several articles addressing the format via which evaluators communicate risk: categorical or numerical (numerical messages can be expressed in terms of probability or frequency).

- *Categorical estimates of risk* are perhaps the most commonly used format for risk communication, with the most common form being a simple ordinal scale of *low, moderate,* or *high* risk (Heilbrun, Phillipson, Berman, & Warren, 1999). Structured clinical judgment guides for risk assessment (e.g., the HCR-20 or the Structured Assessment of Violence Risk in Youth) often lead to risk estimates that are expressed as low, moderate, or high. A categorical risk communication message might read as follows, "Considering the risk factors previously described, Mr. Johnson presents a *high* [or *medium* or *low*] risk of violence."

Monahan and Steadman (1996) offered an innovative discussion of categorical risk estimates, suggesting that the field of violence risk assessment has much to learn from the more established field of meteorology. Like forensic evaluators, meteorologists also use base rate information and prediction models to form an estimate of risk, which they communicate to decision makers. The field of meteorology, the authors observed, no longer offers dichotomous predictions ("It *will* rain today") but instead now communicates in probabilistic language that may be either numerical (80% chance of rain) or categorical (no message, hurricane watch, hurricane warning).

Monahan and Steadman (1996) proposed a hypothetical illustration of categorical violence risk communication that is roughly analogous to storm warnings offered by the National Weather Service. Illustrative categories included:

> *Low violence risk:* Few risk factors are present. No further inquiry into violence risk or special preventive actions are indicated. . . .
>
> *Moderate violence risk:* Several risk factors are present. Gather additional information and monitor the individual more closely than usual. . . .
>
> *High violence risk:* A number of key risk factors are present. Give priority to gathering additional information and close patient monitoring. Make preparations for preventive action should the situation deteriorate. . . .
>
> *Very high violence risk:* Many key risk factors are present. Enough information is available to make a decision. Take preventive action now. (pp. 935–936)

Their illustration demonstrates the possibility of categorical risk estimates that are specific to the forensic assessment of violence and appear more precise and practical than the common low-medium-high trichotomy. Their illustration also follows a concept and communication format (i.e., meteorological forecasts) with which most decision makers would already feel familiar and comfortable. Indeed, some decision makers may be particularly grateful for categorical risk communication that outlines clear steps for actions (e.g., "Take preventive action now").

However, the aspect of this model that many decision makers would find appealing—that is, the combination of a risk estimate with recommended action—is sometimes controversial. Schopp (1996) cautioned that combining a description or estimate with a formal prescription for action blurs important professional boundaries between the clinician and the decision maker (usually a court). He warned:

> To the extent that institutions of mental health law adopt a comparable categorical system of risk communications, such as that tentatively proposed by Monahan and Steadman (1996), they extend the risk assessment roles of the psychologist from those of description and explanation to those of evaluation and prescription. Thus, this form of communication system entails an extension of the scope of psychologists' responsibilities from describing and explaining risk to interpreting and applying social values and priorities. (p. 941)

In some respects, a detailed study of Schopp's (1996) critique of the Monahan and Steadman (1996) meteorology analogy might seem like an academic exercise. Certainly all three scholars agreed that Monahan and Steadman offered the analogy only to stimulate discussion and investigation. No clinicians (at least to our knowledge) have adopted into practice the risk forecasts illustrated in the article. However, Schopp's critique offered an important caution: The most practical or well-received risk communication messages may not be legally or ethically appropriate *if* they involve evaluators overstepping their assigned role.

For example, some forensic evaluations of violence risk involve a clear (in theory, at least) delineation between the evaluator as an objective informant who describes risk level and the court as the decision maker with responsibility for deciding (a) what degree of risk is sufficient to justify intervening and (b) what intervention is warranted. Thus, in these situations, categorical risk communication must be descriptive without being directive.

On the other hand, many—probably a majority—of risk assessments conducted in routine practice require that a clinician fulfill all roles ranging from evaluation, to prescription, to preventive action. Consider, for example, the staff psychologist in a small secure unit of a psychiatric facility who determines that a patient is approaching violent behavior and must make administrative or clinical decisions to prevent violence. Likewise, routine risk assessments conducted in psychiatric hospitals often consider the release of a voluntary, but potentially dangerous, patient. If the clinician (or group of clinicians) decides to petition for civil commitment, the clinician is clearly recommending to the court that specific action be taken now. In other situations, the clinician (or group of clinicians) may decide that the risk is not sufficient to petition for civil commitment. In such instances, the clinician has actually made the ultimate decision (i.e., no preventive action needed) and is commonly required to go on record justifying that decision.

Along these lines, any consideration of categorical risk communication should also consider the long-standing debate over offering *ultimate issue* opinions in forensic mental health evaluations. Simply put, ultimate issue opinions are those that explicitly address the decision a trier of fact (i.e., judge, jury, parole board) must make. For example, in an evaluation of competence to stand trial, an evaluator who explicitly states the opinion that a criminal defendant is not competent to stand trial would be expressing an ultimate issue opinion. An evaluator would not be offering an ultimate opinion, however, if that evaluator explained only that the defendant has little rational understanding of the charges against him and appears unable to communicate meaningfully with his attorney. In the context of risk assessment, offering an ultimate opinion might involve an unequivocal statement that an individual "is dangerous" as defined by civil commitment statutes that specify "dangerousness to self or others" as the criterion for commitment. Another example might involve offering the opinion that a particular examinee is a sexually violent predator, as defined by statutory criteria.

The field has long debated the appropriateness of offering ultimate opinion testimony. Whereas some professional guidance advises clinicians to avoid ultimate issue testimony (e.g., Grisso, 1998; Heilbrun, 2001; Melton et al., 1997; Tillbrook, Mumley, & Grisso, 2003), other authorities (e.g., Rogers & Ewing, 2003) have argued, on both theoretical and practical grounds, against prohibiting ultimate issue testimony. In some states, the statutes that govern risk assessment (or other types of forensic evaluation) essentially require clinicians to offer an ultimate issue opinion. Even in situations in which statutes do not require an ultimate issue opinion, some judges explicitly ask for ultimate issue testimony, even when evaluators avoid it. Finally, in cases such as civil commitment (or release from civil commitment), the clinician is often the petitioner, and the case would not come before the court absent a specific opinion and recommendation for action. Reviews of written reports from forensic evaluations (Heilbrun & Collins, 1995; Skeem, Golding, Cohn, & Berge, 1998), including some related to risk assessment (Amenta, 2005), reveal that evaluators frequently offer ultimate opinion conclusions. Without offering an opinion on the "ultimate issue issue," we do caution that certain forms of categorical risk estimates are essentially ultimate issue opinions (e.g., a patient is/is not dangerous). Evaluators who offer these should be aware of the conflicting professional guidance on ultimate issue opinions, including the pros and cons of these opinions.

Whereas categorical risk estimates tend to be expressed with descriptive labels (e.g., "low to moderate"), numerical estimates of risk may be communicated in terms of *probability* or *frequency*.

- *Probability estimates of risk* involve offering a particular percentage of likelihood of risk for violence (theoretically, risk communication expressed in probabilistic terms could instead feature other mathematical expressions of probability, such as odds ratios, but this is apparently rare in practice). A risk communication message expressed in probability terms might read as follows: "Considering findings from the assessment procedures previously discussed, Mr. Johnson presents a 33% chance of violence." The use of actuarial measures tends to facilitate the use of probability estimates, in that many actuarial measures (e.g., the VRAG, the Sex Offender Risk Appraisal Guide) essentially calculate probability estimates based on a particular research sample. Some scholars have speculated that probabilistic risk communication statements will become increasingly commonplace as the field becomes more sophisticated and further grounded in actuarial data and as predictions become more accurate (e.g., Monahan & Steadman, 1996).
- *Frequency estimates of risk* involve expressing risk level in terms of a frequency. For example, a risk communication message might read "Research suggests that of 100 men with risk factors similar to Mr. Johnson's, 33 engage in violence."

Intuitively, it would seem that the numerical risk communication messages (whether expressed as probabilities or frequencies) would offer several advantages over categorical communication. After all, most of us understand that 40% represents the same numerical value as 40 out of 100, and all of us should interpret 40% as representing the same numerical value, even though we may vary considerably in terms of what we consider low risk or high risk (see Kwartner et al., 2006, for an example of individual variability in terms of what is considered low, moderate, or high risk). However, research reveals—exactly as cognitive psychologists (e.g., Gigerenzer, 1996; Hoffrage & Gigerenzer, 1998; Wallsten, Budescu, Zwick, & Kemp, 1993; Yamigishi, 1997) would have warned us to expect—that our use and understanding of numbers is neither reliable, logical, nor consistent when it comes to estimates of risk.

First, clinicians' numerical estimates of risk appear to be influenced by the response scale that is used to express those estimates. Slovic and Monahan (1995) presented 191 college students, then 137 forensic mental health professionals, with case vignettes describing psychiatric patients. They asked participants about the probability that a patient would harm someone, and whether coercion should be used to ensure treatment. However, they varied the response scale by which participants could offer risk estimates. Some received a "large probability" response scale format with options of 0% (no chance) through 100% (certain to harm) in increments of 10 (i.e., . . . 20%, 30%, 40%). Others received a "small probability" response scale that included smaller options: less than one chance in 1,000, 1 in 1,000, 1%, 2%, 5%, 10%, 15% . . . 40%, and greater than 40%. Results revealed that participants who received the large probability format (i.e., 0%, 10%, 20%) judged the hypothetical patient's level of violence risk as much higher than did participants who received the small probability format. For example, in the large probability format, in which two response options were ≤10%, only a small minority of participants judged violence risk to be ≤10%. Yet, in the small probability format, when six response options were ≤10%, the *majority* of participants rated the patient's risk of violence as ≤10%. In other words:

> Respondents appear[ed] to have used the probability response scales as if they were rating scales . . . with no meaning to the numbers

other than their rank. This behavior is more than just a methodological artifact. It strongly implies that the concept "probability of harm" was not represented in . . . respondents' minds in a consistent, quantitative way. The numbers circled on the probability scale appear to have been meaningless in an absolute sense, though they were consistent and meaningful in a relative sense. (pp. 61–62)

Concerned about these findings, the researchers (Slovic et al., 2000) conducted another series of studies with several hundred forensic psychologists and psychiatrists, adding modifications to the study design. They used discharge summaries from actual patients, provided tutorials on the response scale bias, and included options for frequency estimates (e.g., "1 out of 100") in addition to probability estimates (e.g., "1%"). Regardless of modifications, results were strikingly similar. Clinicians estimated that violence was more likely when researchers gave them a scale with large probability values (e.g., 1%, 10%, 20%, 30%) to express their estimates, as compared to when researchers gave them a scale with options for smaller probability estimates (e.g., 1%, 2%, 5%, 10%, 15%).

Admittedly, these results (Slovic & Monahan, 1995; Slovic et al., 2000) seem fairly removed from clinical practice. We probably need not worry that some judges will offer evaluators a small probability format scale by which to offer a risk estimate and other judges will offer a large probability format scale, thereby leading to discrepant risk estimates. Typically, evaluators are free to offer risk estimates in the format they choose, and there are no direct concerns about bias due to the gradations of a response scale. On the other hand, the bottom line implication of these studies is sobering: *Even clinicians may not conceptualize risk in terms of consistent, absolute numerical values.* Schwarz (1990, as cited in Slovic et al., 2000) explained that response scale format biases occur because raters assume that the response options provided on a response scale reflect the true distribution of behavior or events in the real world. However, we would expect clinicians who conduct risk assessments to have a working knowledge of violence base rates, typical reoffense rates, and other nomothetic data that should anchor a risk estimate (or at least a risk estimate range) more so than any response scale offered.

The second compelling finding to emerge in the recent risk communication research involves the differing influences of frequency versus probability risk estimates. In one of the experiments by Slovic and colleagues (2000), 479 forensic-clinical psychologists read a vignette that reported the conclusions of a "state-of-the-art" assessment of a psychiatric patient. Survey questions then asked clinicians to provide opinions regarding the patient's risk level (in categorical terms) and appropriateness for discharge and monitoring. Vignettes varied in the ways they expressed the conclusions from the risk assessment; some featured a probability format (e.g., "Patients similar to Mr. Jones are estimated to have a 20% probability of committing an act of violence to others during the first several months after discharge"); others featured a frequency format (e.g., "Of every 100 patients similar to Mr. Jones, 20 are estimated to commit an act of violence to others during the first several months after discharge"). Results were striking in that clinicians who reviewed a frequency estimate (e.g., 20 out of 100 patients) were much more likely to perceive higher risk and recommend against hospital discharge than clinicians who reviewed a probability estimate (e.g., 20%) *even when the mathematical value of these estimates was exactly the same.* Apparently, use of the frequency format evoked images of *individuals* (even if only a small minority of a much larger group) committing acts of violence, whereas probability estimates evoked consideration of the less than likely chance of one person committing an act of violence. In other words, it is easier to visualize frequencies than to visualize probabilities. In a follow-up study, researchers found a similar frequency effect, though only among clinicians who worked in forensic facilities as opposed to clinicians who worked in other settings (Monahan et al., 2002). Overall, these findings related to a frequency effect raise a number of questions, discussed in more detail later in the chapter, about how evaluators should best present risk estimates.

Clinician Practices and Preferences

Given the several options available to communicate findings from a risk assessment, how do clinicians typically go about communicating risk estimates? In what was apparently the first study of clinician practices, Heilbrun, Phillipson, and colleagues (1999) asked 59 psychiatrists and psychologists in Virginia how they communicated findings and opinions related to risk. Nearly all reported that they avoided numerical probability figures in communicating risk, with most explaining that the state of the research does not support such precise estimates, that they could not offer such precise estimates, or that such precise estimates are easily misinterpreted. Instead, clinicians reported that they tended to identify risk factors that raise or lower risk, describe risk level in categorical terms, or simply describe history and present behavior with no attempt at prediction. In the second survey of an additional 59 participants, similar results emerged. Very few clinicians supported the practice of communicating risk by way of probability estimates.

Researchers (Heilbrun et al., 2000) next used an experimentally manipulated case vignette to survey 71 recognized experts in the field of violence risk assessment. Overall, participants most highly valued a management-oriented approach to communicating risk. For example, an evaluator might conclude, "'Mr. J's risk of committing a violent act toward others is dependant on (identified risk factors); to reduce risk (specify interventions to address each factor)'" (p. 143). Although this approach was favored overall, participants were particularly likely to value this approach in a vignette describing a patient who was clearly at high risk for violence. Overall, participants rated as least valuable the approach in which the evaluator identified the examinee's "percentage of likelihood" to commit another violent act.

Finally, Heilbrun and colleagues (2004) conducted a similar study with a broader sample of 256 practicing psychologists. Again, the participants demonstrated an overall preference for the risk communication style that identified applicable risk factors and specified interventions to reduce risk. Also replicating prior findings, participants overall were least supportive of an approach that offered a definitive conclusion that an individual was "x% likely to commit a violent act toward others" (p. 192). Examining interaction effects, the authors reported that participants were particularly supportive of a management style of risk communication when the examinee was high risk and the observed risk factors were dynamic. On the other hand, participants were more supportive of a prediction model when risk was high and risk factors tended to be static (historical, unchangeable). Not surprisingly, the authors observed that this pattern may have emerged "because clinicians prefer a model that 'makes sense' in light of the kind of risk factors that are present—dynamic risk factors are particularly well-suited for management-oriented communication—and when the case seems particularly problematic because risk is high" (p. 193).

Distilling the programmatic research by Heilbrun and colleagues (Heilbrun, Phillipson, et al., 1999; Heilbrun et al., 2000, 2004), what can we observe? Clinicians clearly support a practical approach that identifies risk factors and offers guidance to reduce the risk factors; this finding was particularly strong when the hypothetical examinee appeared particularly high risk. One reason that clinicians prefer a management-oriented approach in high-risk cases may be that they consider it less prejudicial to identify and suggest remediation for risk factors than to simply declare the person to be high risk (Heilbrun et al., 2004). Another possibility may be that, particularly in high-risk cases, clinicians support a practical approach that suggests methods for intervention, as opposed to a statement that an individual is at high risk without corresponding guidance to reduce this risk.

Another clear trend across Heilbrun and colleagues' (Heilbrun, Phillipson, et al., 1999; Heilbrun et al., 2000, 2004) studies was that clinicians tended *not* to support highly specific numerical estimates of risk, such as "This individual poses a 33% likelihood of recidivism." Interestingly, this clear and pronounced pattern stands in stark contrast to results from risk communication in other fields. For example, adults report a preference to receive risk estimates from a physician (e.g., an estimate that a given test result may be indicative of cancer) in terms of specific numerical values, such as a fraction or percentage, rather than in categorical or descriptive terms; indeed, such precise risk communication increases their trust in the physician (Gurmankin, Baron, & Armstrong, 2004). Why, then, might clinicians report such a *dissimilar* reaction to precise numerical estimates of another serious risk, that is, that of physical violence? Participants in the first study by Heilbrun, Phillipson, and colleagues (1999) explained that they simply did not consider the existing research literature or assessment instruments sufficient to provide such precise estimates. Likewise, several years before the Heilbrun studies were published, Monahan and Steadman (1996, p. 935) suggested that "clinicians may find it both pretentious and potentially misleading to produce risk assessments along a 100-point probability scale." Another, perhaps related, interpretation is that clinicians may not be sufficiently familiar with the relevant base rate data, or the methodology that employs base rate data (such as some actuarial measures), that would allow them to offer a numerical estimate.

What Risk Communication Strategies Do the Courts Prefer?

Judges

The Heilbrun studies (Heilbrun, Phillipson, et al., 1999; Heilbrun et al., 2000, 2004) offer considerable data about clinician preferences, and these data are helpful in describing common practice in terms of risk communication. However, it is important to note that whereas clinicians often deliver risk communication, they are not always the ones to receive risk communication. Often, the primary consumers of risk communication are judges. First, judges tend to make decisions about civil commitment. Even when considering risk estimates from clinicians, judges must (implicitly or explicitly) identify *decision thresholds* at which they impose interventions to manage risk (Monahan & Silver, 2003). In criminal cases, even when judges are not the finders of fact, they usually impose sentences and make decisions about whether to admit mental health evidence and testimony (Redding & Murrie, 2007). In short, judges play a crucial role, if not the only role, in many of the decisions that risk assessments inform. However, relatively little research has investigated judges' preferences or responses regarding risk communication.

The limited data available hint that presenting the results of a science-based risk assessment to judges may feel like an uphill battle. For example, Redding and colleagues (2001) surveyed 59 trial court judges and 72 trial attorneys in Virginia using a vignette design based on a hypothetical insanity defense case. The authors concluded:

> Judges and lawyers were relatively disinterested in statistical or ac-
> tuarial data as compared to other types of testimony, contrary to
> the scholarly consensus among social scientists that such informa-
> tion provides important contextual or "social framework" evidence
> (see Monahan & Walker, 1998) in which to interpret the reliabil-
> ity and relevance of the clinical evidence brought to bear. These
> findings suggest that judges may not fully understand the rele-
> vance of such evidence. As Redding and Reppucci (1999) found
> in a national survey of trial judges, judges and lawyers frequently
> "did not appreciate the value of research evidence, believing in-
> stead that nomothetic research had no bearing upon individual
> cases." (p. 592)

Results from the studies by Redding and colleagues (2001; see also Redding & Reppucci, 1999) would not surprise other legal scholars, who have long observed the courts' apparent distrust of so-cial science data and statistical evidence (see generally Bersoff & Glass, 1995; Fradella et al., 2003; Melton et al., 1997; Redding, 1998; Tanford, 1990). Slobogin (1998) reported that judges were more likely to exclude mental health testimony based on research evidence than mental health testimony based on case-specific clin-ical evidence. Similarly, one review of federal judicial opinions con-cluded that the courts became increasingly resistant to social science evidence over the course of the 1990s (Fradella et al., 2003).

Unfortunately, none of the literature that has examined judges' preference for clinical over actuarial data has directly investigated their preferences regarding risk assessments. However, considering the literature on judges' preferences about mental health evidence in general, we can attempt some reasonable inferences regarding judges' preferences for specific types of risk communication in particular. Specifically, we would expect judges to be more recep-tive to risk communication that is rooted in clinical description and less receptive to risk communication based on nomothetic statistical data. Of course, such a preference would stand in stark contrast to most professional guidance (including our own) that suggests risk assessment be rooted in nomothetic data, more so than unstructured clinical observation. So the challenge for the clinician becomes one of explaining the relevance of the nomothetic data to the individual case and, in the case of court testimony, presenting nomothetic data in a fashion that will engage the jury.

At the time of this writing, there appears to be only one published study in which judges conveyed specific preferences regarding risk communication.* Kwartner and colleagues (2006) used a vignette design (modeled after the Heilbrun et al., 2000, study) to survey 116 judges regarding preferences for various risk communication formats. Overall, judges gave higher probative value ratings to risk messages communicated in a categorical format versus probability or frequency formats. When asked to choose a preferred risk format, most (54%) judges chose a categorical format, and the rest were similarly divided between preferring probabilistic (26%) and frequency (20%) formats. Among judges who preferred that risk messages be communicated in more than one format (66% of the total sample), most preferred a combination of categorical + probabilistic (46%) or categorical + frequency (35%), with relatively few reporting a preference for a probabilistic + frequency combination (19%) without categorical terms. On a practical level, results suggest that, when appropriate, evaluators may opt to communicate risk estimates to judges using some combination of categorical and numerical terms, as discussed in more detail later in the chapter.

Laypersons and Mock Jurors
Some recent risk assessment research using undergraduate mock jurors provides results that converge with research and commentary regarding judges. Although one must consider the results of under-

---

* In fact, one other study (Monahan & Silver, 2003) related to forensic assessment of violence risk also surveyed judges. However, the study was not specific to risk communication. Rather, the authors surveyed 26 judges as to what they considered an appropriate threshold for civilly committing an individual as "dangerous to others," offering response options that corresponded to the risk classes developed in the MacArthur study of violence risk. Judges offered a wide range of responses, but as a group, responses converged on the MacArthur Risk Class 3 (a 0.26 likelihood of violence) as the decision threshold for civil commitment based on dangerousness to others.

graduate mock juror research with a number of caveats in mind (Diamond, 1997; cf. Bornstein, 1999), it is clear that mock jury research can offer at least an initial impression of how nonclinicians make sense of risk communication. Krauss's (Krauss & Lee, 2003; Krauss, Lieberman, & Olson, 2004; Krauss & Sales, 2001) programmatic research on mock jury deliberations in death penalty cases suggests that, like judges, jurors are more responsive to clinically descriptive testimony than to testimony based solely on actuarial data. Indeed, findings from his studies challenge the Supreme Court's conclusion that jurors are consistently savvy consumers of expert testimony regarding future dangerousness.

As detailed in Chapter 1, Justice White conveyed that the Supreme Court was "not persuaded that [mental health testimony on future dangerousness] is almost entirely unreliable and that the fact finder and adversary system will not be competent to uncover, recognize, and take due account of its shortcomings" (*Barefoot v. Estelle*, 1983, p. 3398). In other words, the Court expressed faith that consumers of risk communication could consider a message about risk, and even the underlying risk assessment methodology, in order to "seperat[e] the wheat from the chaff" (p. 3398).

Krauss and Sales (2001), however, engaged 208 undergraduates in mock sentencing proceedings for a death penalty case and found that they were more persuaded by testimony based on unstructured clinical judgment (an expert summarized his interview and clinical opinion that the defendant was sociopathic and dangerous) than by actuarially based testimony using the Violence Risk Appraisal Guide (G. T. Harris et al., 1993). Furthermore, a vigorous cross-examination did more to alter the impressions of those exposed to actuarial-based testimony than those exposed to purely clinical testimony; in other words, adversarial procedures were not sufficient to reverse the conclusions drawn from pure clinical testimony (Krauss & Sales, 2001).

In a follow-up study (Krauss & Lee, 2003), researchers again found that undergraduate mock jurors were more influenced by pure clinical opinion testimony than by actuarially based testimony. Even after simulated jury deliberation (and simulated cross-examination, as in the prior study), jurors who heard purely clinical testimony maintained perceptions and were more persuaded of a defendant's dangerousness than jurors who heard actuarially based testimony. The fact that mock jurors appear more responsive to purely clinical testimony than to actuarially based testimony is not surprising when we consider social psychological research on persuasion (e.g., O'Keefe, 1990), but it does suggest that the evaluator who plans to convey results based on actuarial data may face some challenges.

Interestingly, a recent study suggests that there may be ways to help laypersons better understand and respond to more actuarially based risk communication. Krauss and colleagues (2004) repeated their death penalty deliberation paradigm, asking undergraduates to participate in a mock death penalty sentencing phase, in which they responded to expert testimony (purely clinical, actuarially based, or based on the HCR-20) regarding future dangerousness. The authors developed this study based on cognitive-experiential self theory (Epstein, 1994), which posits that individuals tend to process information via two systems: experiential and rational. The default processing approach is experiential—a crude, rapid, emotionally based approach that efficiently (albeit intuitively) handles new information. But, individuals can also be induced to use a rational approach, which involves careful, conscious deliberation based on logic and evidence.

Krauss and colleagues (2004) hypothesized that jurors typically operate on an experiential basis, considering case information at an intuitive level, which explains their receptivity to clinical over actuarial risk communication (Krauss & Lee, 2003; Krauss & Sales, 2001). However, in this study (Krauss et al., 2004), researchers attempted to induce some participants into an experiential mode of information processing (by asking them to draw a "picture that describes your gut-level feelings about your emotional state right now"), and induce others into a rationale mode of information processing (by asking them to solve math problems). As the researchers expected, experientially induced participants were most influenced by clinical testimony, whereas rationally induced participants were most influenced by actuarial testimony.

Of course, in the narrowest sense, this study (Krauss et al., 2004) has few practical applications; certainly, neither attorneys nor evaluators would assign math problems in court proceedings to induce laypersons to be more receptive to actuarially based testimony. In the more general sense, however, the results offer implications for risk communication. Even though layperson consumers of risk communication may, by default, respond more to (less scientifically valid) pure clinical testimony and respond less to (more scientifically valid) actuarially based testimony, it may be possible to encourage laypersons toward a more rationale, analytical style of information processing that leaves them more responsive to empirical data. Generally, it may be possible to educate a risk communication audience in a manner that helps them better understand risk communication, as we describe next.

Practical Guidance for Risk Communication in Written Reports and Expert Testimony

So how does an evaluator best communicate findings related to violence risk? Whether communicating risk via written evaluation report or courtroom testimony, certain general principles apply. These principles are drawn not only from the recent research on risk communication, but also from more general guidelines and best practices related to psychological assessment, forensic evaluation, and expert testimony. The overall goal of these principles is to make the evaluation and opinion-formation process *transparent*. In other words, evaluators convey clearly how they gathered and considered data to arrive at a well-reasoned opinion. As with any forensic evaluation, risk assessment reports document the purpose of the evaluation and limits of confidentiality as explained to the examinee. The report should also include a list of sources of information used in the assessment. More specific to risk assessment, the following guidelines are suggested:

1. *Clearly reiterate the specific risk assessment referral question and the boundaries of the evaluation.* Most general guidance on psychological evaluations (e.g., Groth-Marnat, 2003) encourages evaluators to begin reports or communication by reminding the audience of the evaluation's purpose and scope. This becomes particularly important in forensic evaluations of violence risk, however, because audiences may attach a variety of meanings or expectations to the process we label "risk assessment."

Begin risk communication with a clear message that includes:

- Reason for the evaluation (e.g., statutory requirement, agency requirement, court petition to be filed, attorney or court request): What decision is the assessment expected to inform?
- The nature of the risk assessment requested: Is the referral source requesting risk prediction, risk management strategies, or both?
- What, if any, legal statute(s) or institutional policy defines this assessment or the legal decision for which this assessment was requested.
- The nature of the violence for which risk is being assessed.

In most instances, one can communicate this important information succinctly. For example:

In preparing for the parole board's review of Mr. Henderson's case, his attorney requested that I conduct the following risk assessment. Specifically, the attorney requested that I offer an opinion regarding Mr. Henderson's likelihood of physical or sexual violence upon release, explain the reason for that opinion, and identify any management strategies that may reduce that risk.

An example that requires a specific legal statute might read:

Mr. Jones is due to complete his prison term on July 1, 2007. This assessment was completed pursuant to Title 18, USCS §4246 to determine whether in the opinion of the evaluators he is presently suffering from a mental disease or defect as a result of which his release would create a substantial risk of bodily injury to another person or serious damage to property of another.

Because risk communication should correspond to the process of risk assessment (Dvoskin & Heilbrun, 2001), reiterating the specific referral question is a form of introduction, which orients the audience so that the evaluator can tell the story of the risk assessment process. In effect, the evaluator is able to say, "Because I was given this specific question, I went about answering it in these particular ways . . . (detail the risk assessment process, as described later)."

2. *Assume the role of educator.* Typically, decision makers solicit risk assessments from evaluators because evaluators possess knowledge, training, or experience specific to risk assessment that the decision makers do not possess. In other words, the intended audience rarely knows the risk assessment process. Some teaching is required.

Without condescending, good evaluators communicate to the audience the rationale and science behind risk assessment procedures. This will involve providing some understandable definitions of key concepts (e.g., base rates) and taking the time to explain procedures that are sometimes hastily communicated in professional jargon. For example, an evaluator should probably initially phrase "I reviewed the empirically identified risk factors that Mr. Smith manifests" as something more like "Scientific research has shown us several risk factors, or features that tend to be related to criminal reoffending, across large groups of offenders. One step of the risk assessment process involves reviewing which of these research-identified risk factors were present in Mr. Smith's case."

Assuming the role of educator also increases the chances that the audience better understands the complex aspects of an evaluation. For example, considering the research reviewed earlier in this chapter, communicating results of a science-based risk assessment may be challenging. If many among the risk communication recipients, such as judges (Kwartner et al., 2006; Redding et al., 2001) and mock jurors (Krauss & Lee, 2003; Krauss et al., 2004; Krauss & Sales, 2001), tend to prefer risk messages that are more purely clinical than purely actuarial, then evaluators who plan to express opinions rooted in nomothetic data must adopt the role of educator. An actuarial measure should not be introduced out of the blue or as a technical testing procedure that appears unrelated to the individual examinee. Rather, a more educative approach is to guide the audience through the risk assessment procedure (clarifying the question → considering base rates → considering research-identified risk factors → considering idiosyncratic risk factors), specifying when and how an actuarial measure provides key information. In this process-driven approach to communication, the audience may better understand that actuarial measures and base rate data help us consider the case at hand in the context of accumulated scientific data from similar cases. The audience should also understand that evaluators consider carefully case-specific data that may not be accounted for in the broader first steps that are explicitly linked to research.* In other words, the audience may come to view actuarial data less as a technical procedure detached from the case at hand and more as a crucial starting point for understanding the case.

3. *Clearly delineate the procedure used to arrive at a risk opinion.* Generally, authorities on psychological assessment (Groth-Marnat, 2003; Kamphaus & Frick, 1996), and forensic assessment in particular (Borum & Verhaagen, 2006; Grisso, 1998; Melton et al., 1997), recommend that evaluators convey clearly their evaluation procedures and the basis for their opinions. Describing the evaluation procedure facilitates transparent practice. A transparent evaluation allows the risk communication audience to review how an evaluator obtained and considered data and arrived at an opinion. Ideally, it allows one reviewing the evaluation to see that the evaluator's "work is based upon established scientific and professional knowledge of the discipline," as detailed in the *Ethical Principles of Psychologists and Code of Conduct* (American Psychological Association, 2002, p. 5).

4. *Present clearly the relevant data.* Offering general guidance about communicating the results of forensic evaluations, Grisso (1998, p. 249) encouraged evaluators to "include all data that are necessary in order to support or question your opinion." This general guidance on forensic evaluations and expert testimony (see also Shuman & Greenberg, 2003) holds true for the specific task of risk communication. As part of transparent practice, evaluators make clear the data that inform their opinions.

---

* In a recent review of research on expert witness testimony across disciplines, Kwartner and Boccaccini (in press) identified "case-specific testimony" as one of the four primary factors contributing to effective courtroom communication. The authors also reviewed literature that supported the effectiveness of combining case-specific clinical *and* research-derived data in testimony.

5. *Avoid "red herring" data.* Presenting clearly the *relevant* data implies, of course, that evaluators should not include *irrelevant* data. However, a review of risk assessment reports in the field suggests that an additional reminder might be in order. In particular, we urge evaluators to avoid what we label "red herring" data, or data that have no demonstrable bearing on risk level and that distract from a risk opinion rooted in nomothetic data and relevant idiographic data.

In most evaluation contexts, it is necessary and even important to provide some general case history of the examinee and, of course, a detailed description of clinical and historical factors that have a bearing on violence potential. However, evaluators who have gone to great lengths to collect voluminous data or who have engaged in lengthy detailed interviews may feel pulled to include some data, even when not directly relevant. This seems particularly likely to occur when the data are unusual or sensational. Certainly the population of individuals who tend to be referred for evaluations of violence risk tend to be a population with a history of colorful life events and behaviors—some tragic, some disturbing, and some poignant. However, only a portion of these events or behaviors have any bearing on potential for violence. Of course, we are not arguing that evaluators serve as public relations experts who attempt to protect examinees by omitting unflattering information that is salient to violence risk (e.g., past violence, active substance abuse). But we do encourage evaluators to consider carefully the degree to which each data point in their report or testimony is relevant to an objective evaluation of violence risk.

Consider risk assessments of sexual offenders, for example. Campbell (2004) detailed numerous factors that evaluators often identify in sex offender risk assessments (e.g., sexual abuse as a child, denial of offense). Yet meta-analysis (Hanson & Bussiere, 1998) has demonstrated no significant relationship between these factors and recidivism. Even when evaluators do not explicitly suggest that a particular event or behavior contributes to the evaluator's risk estimate, the data may influence the conclusions that the audience draws. It may be necessary to address these factors directly, however, to explain why they are not considered relevant.

We have reviewed risk assessment reports in which evaluators provide detailed and sensational information about the behavior of an examinee's spouse or family members or explicit information about the examinee's past legal sexual behavior (even in cases where sexual behavior was not at issue)—all when there was no discernable link between these accounts and the examinee's clinical status or violence potential. At best, this irrelevant information takes up valuable report space and inconveniences the reader who is seeking relevant data. At worst, the irrelevant information encourages erroneous and ill-founded conclusions about the examinee.*

Apparently attuned to the risk for evaluators to stray from the topic at hand, the "Specialty Guidelines for Forensic Psychologists" (Committee on Ethical Guidelines for Forensic Psychologists, 1991, p. 662) state:

> With respect to evidence of any type, forensic psychologists avoid offering information from their investigations or evaluations that does not bear directly upon the legal purpose of their professional services and that is not critical as support for their product, evidence or testimony, except where such disclosure is required by law.

---

* At the risk of complicating matters, one caveat is probably in order. There may be times when an evaluator is aware that an opposing evaluator (or another party) has erroneously identified a particular data point as relevant to violence risk. In this instance, it may be important for the evaluator to demonstrate awareness of this data point, while also offering a reasoned conclusion that the data point does not have a predictable relationship with violence risk. Consider the following illustration, which has occurred repeatedly in the context of sex offender risk assessments. It is not uncommon for some evaluators to emphasize the examinee's past history of experiencing sexual abuse and suggest that this history places the examinee at greater risk of future sexual offending, even though there is no reliable relationship between past victimization and sexual reoffending (Hanson & Bussiere, 1998). In this situation, we have tended to acknowledge the examinee's history of sexual victimization, lest others assume we failed to consider the data and came to an erroneous decision based on insufficient data. However, we have also made it clear that the past history of sexual abuse is not a factor that predicts sexual reoffense.

6. *Discuss tests and test results carefully.* Few in the risk communi-cation audience have completed graduate coursework in testing and measurement. Thus, any discussion of testing will require a brief and understandable description of the test, its design, and its rele-vance. For example, evaluators who report the results from the Psy-chopathy Checklist—Revised (Hare, 1991, 2003) might include a statement such as the following:

> Clinicians conducting evaluations in criminal justice contexts often employ an assessment of psychopathy using the Psychopathy Checklist—Revised (PCL-R) because research demonstrates that PCL-R scores relate to criminal violence and recidivism. The PCL-R is completed and scored by the clinician (not the individual being evaluated), based on a clinical interview and a review of clinical and criminal records. Clinicians can then compare the examinee's score to results from large samples of others who have been scored on the PCL-R.

The goal is not to provide a professional or psychometric review of the test, but simply to provide a general description of the test, the manner in which it is completed (e.g., self-report, clinician-scored), and the way it may inform the evaluation at hand.

7. *Clearly articulate the reasoning behind conclusions.* The Supreme Court emphasized that an evaluator's opinion "rises no higher than the reasons on which it is based" (*U.S. v. Horowitz*, 1973, p. 777). Thus, it becomes important for evaluators to make clear how the data they considered led to the risk estimate they offer. As Grisso (1998, p. 249) urged forensic evaluators working in the juvenile justice system, "Provide clear explanations for each of your opinions (i.e., spell out the reasoning that links your data to your conclusions)."

A clear articulation of one's reasoning should be evenhanded. That is, evaluators should acknowledge conflicting data or unavail-able data that would have better informed the conclusions. Fortu-nately, this evenhanded approach usually increases the evaluator's credibility and underscores the weight of the data sources that are congruent (Melton et al., 1997).

The following brief excerpt from an SVP risk assessment may be illustrative:

> Previous sexual offending is one of the strongest predictors of future sexual offending, and Mr. H. has one prior conviction for a sexual offense. Specifically, he offended against his 3-year-old stepdaughter, indicating the presence of deviant interests. On the other hand, there is no evidence of a lifetime pattern of criminal sexual behavior.
>
> Mr. H demonstrated an early and lengthy history of nonsexual offenses, increasing his risk for general recidivism. He also has a history of substance abuse and was under the influence of alcohol during at least one of his (nonsexual) offenses. Mr. H. also violated his parole conditions with one of his nonsexual offenses.
>
> There are a number of important risk factors for sexual reoffending that Mr. H. does not exhibit. Research indicates that offenders who offend against females and know their victims are at somewhat less risk of sexual recidivism (as compared to men who offend against boys or strangers). Mr. H has been involved in two stable romantic relationships, demonstrating an ability to maintain a relationship with an appropriate adult partner. He is well past the age of highest risk for recidivism, sexual or nonsexual. His score of 23 on the PCL-R is within the average range compared to other offenders.
>
> In my opinion, based on the available information (listed earlier in this report) and the risk factors just described, Mr. H. would most appropriately be described as being at low to moderate risk for sexual reoffending relative to other sexual offenders facing release from this state correctional system. However, given his lengthy record, his risk for nonsexual reoffending may be somewhat higher.

8. *Consider communicating risk in multiple formats.* In the risk communication research described earlier, Slovic and colleagues (2000) observed that clinicians perceived greater risk and offered more cautious decisions when they reviewed risk estimates communicated in frequency terms (e.g., 10 out of 100 patients) as compared to mathematically identical risk estimates communicated in probability terms (e.g., 10%). Based on this finding, Doren (2002, p. 186) suggested that evaluators should present estimates *only* in

percentage format, "based on the ethical stance that evaluators should bias their conclusions and communications toward lower versus higher risk in the face of ambiguity." However, several authors (Borum & Verhaegen, 2006; Kwartner et al., 2006; Slovic et al., 2000) suggested that evaluators handle the possibility of a frequency bias by communicating risk messages in multiple formats to reduce the bias due to any single reporting format. Stepping outside the forensic mental health field, cognitive psychologists (e.g., Wallsten et al., 1993) have argued that a combination of numerical *and* descriptive terms is necessary to convey information as complex as a risk estimate.

Although the suggestion to use multiple risk communication formats is offered often in the literature, we would argue that this is not a rule to be followed in all instances. Rather, different cases call for different risk messages. For example, in a risk assessment in which it was appropriate to use an actuarial measure, and no subsequent considerations substantially altered the risk estimate derived from the actuarial measure, it may be quite feasible to report a percentage estimate from the measure, accompanied by a descriptive label. For example:

> Of individuals like Mr. Smith, with scores of 1 on the STATIC-99, on average, 7% committed a new sexual offense within 15 years. Given that there were no additional considerations that would substantially alter Mr. Smith's risk level beyond the estimate derived from the STATIC-99, he can be best described as presenting a low risk of sexual reoffense.

However, there are cases in which an evaluator cannot apply an appropriate actuarial measure, and no relevant base rate data is available. In these instances, an evaluator would be hard-pressed (or even irresponsible) to offer a formal percentage estimate of risk. A categorical label (e.g., low, moderate, high) is all that one could offer with any confidence.

Under certain circumstances, it may also be appropriate to modify a numerical estimate using categorical terms. As detailed in previous chapters, a rare idiographic factor may prompt the evaluator to estimate lower or higher risk than the score from an actuarial measure suggests. In this circumstance, the evaluator might convey a message such as:

> Mr. Smith's score of 5 on the STATIC-99 provides an appropriate starting point for considering risk of sexual reoffense. Of offenders who scored a 5 on the STATIC-99 in the instrument's development sample, 33% reoffended sexually within 5 years. However, because Mr. Smith (describe compelling idiosyncratic factor that raises or lowers risk), his actual risk for sexual recidivism appears somewhat (higher/lower) than 33%.

To summarize, assessment methodology and relevant findings will be the primary factors determining the risk communication format.

9. *Communicate risk with a point of reference.* Although judges (Kwartner et al., 2006) and clinicians (Heilbrun, Phillipson, et al., 1999) appear to prefer risk messages that are framed in categorical terms, categorical terms are amorphous without a clear point of reference. Should a judge infer that "low risk" means that an individual poses virtually no risk of violence? Or does it mean that the individual poses significantly less risk of violence than other individuals charged with similar offenses? Should a parole board infer that "high risk" means an individual is more likely to be violent than nonviolent? Or does it imply only that the individual's likelihood of committing violence is greater than the documented base rate of 4% for the population of similar offenders? To complicate matters, the limited research available suggests that judges may assign values to the concepts of low, medium, and high risk that differ from clinicians' assigned values (Kwartner et al., 2006). Indeed, some might argue that labels such as "high risk" or "low risk" are essentially social value judgments that may differ among individuals.

The best way to reduce ambiguity is to communicate risk estimates relative to a reference point. Usually, base rates—reviewed early in the evaluation and discussed early in the risk communication process—serve as the logical point of reference. Note that sometimes a risk communication message may include little more than base rate data for a particular population and a conclusion that the risk assessment evaluation revealed no data that would raise or lower the risk estimate relative to the population base rate. At other times, a risk communication message will describe how various salient factors lead to a risk estimate that is somewhat higher or lower than the population base rate for violence.

Here are some examples of risk communication messages that use base rates as reference points:

- A 2005 report from the State Department of Corrections (SDOC) indicates that of the 1,250 offenders who had previous violent offenses and were released from SDOC in 1999, 24% were rearrested for another violent offense within 3 years. Obviously, these figures do not account for reoffenses that were not detected by law enforcement or offenses that occurred after the 3-year follow-up period. However, the 24% base rate provides an initial point of reference for estimating risk of violent reoffense. As discussed earlier in this report, Mr. Jones demonstrates a number of factors that research has shown to relate to violent reoffense (i.e., repeated parole violations, an unusually high score on the Psychopathy Checklist—Revised, and substance abuse even under conditions of mandated monitoring or treatment). Therefore, it is my opinion to a reasonable degree of professional certainty that Mr. Jones's risk of reoffense should be considered relatively high compared to other violent offenders released from SDOC and higher than the 24% base rate for violent reoffense.

- Institutional research from the Bigcity Juvenile Probation Department (BJPD) revealed that of the 19,850 boys age 12 to 15 referred for preadjudication evaluations from 1998 to 2003, 13% returned to the BJPD within 1 year, having been arrested for a violent offense. Based on the risk and protective factors described earlier in this report (i.e., no offenses prior to the instant offense, absence of substance abuse, home stability including relatively frequent supervision), Calvin's risk of violent reoffense appears to be somewhat lower than the 13% base rate of violent reoffense within this population.

Of course, these examples involve ideal scenarios in which the evaluator has access to local base rate data. As detailed in Chapter 4, such data are often unavailable, and evaluators may instead rely on statistics from national law enforcement or criminal justice agencies, large research studies, or meta-analyses of smaller research studies. There are also situations in which absolutely no base rate data are available. In these circumstances, the evaluator has the option of identifying a reference group more generally. For example, Borum and Verhaagen (2006, p. 128) offered the following example: "In my opinion, relative to other 14-year-old juvenile offenders on probation, Johnny is at an average/moderate risk for committing a violent offense within the next six months." A similar example might read, "Compared to other inmates appearing before this parole board, Mr. Smith . . ." (see Grisso, 1998, for similar examples). Again, a more precise estimate linked to base rate data is ideal, yet this is feasible only when the relevant base rate data are available. A second approach might be to use the examinee as his or her own reference group when there is sufficient historical information to do so. Heilbrun, Dvoskin, and colleagues (1999, p. 102) introduced the possibility of a "conditional risk statement" and gave the following illustration: "Mr. A currently appears at higher risk to commit a violent act than he has at any other time in his life, with the exception of his hospitalization in 1992. To lower his risk . . . [specified interventions]." Again, such an approach is particularly appropriate when there are no applicable actuarial data but when rich historical information is available.

10. *Emphasize context.* In law and in psychology, the accurate answer to most questions is "It depends." To what extent does an examinee pose a risk of violence? It depends on context. As detailed earlier in this text, risk levels may vary dramatically based on an examinee's circumstances and surroundings. To take an obvious example, evaluators tasked with conducting risk assessments as part of death penalty proceedings in Texas are expected to address whether the defendant "would constitute a continuing threat to society" (Texas Code of Criminal Procedures, 37.071.2, 1996). Yet, "threat to society" may differ greatly depending on whether society is defined as living in the community with no supervision or as in-

carcerated in a maximum-security prison with substantial security, supervision, and structure. The latter would be the only alternative for someone convicted in a capital case (see Cunningham, 2006a; Cunningham & Reidy, 1998b, 1999, 2001, 2002; Chapter 12 of this text).

Of course, context matters in less extreme examples as well. To what extent will the examinee have access to illicit substances? If the examinee has sexually offended against children, to what extent would he or she have access to a similar victim pool?

If the risk assessment referral question (see Chapter 3) requires a risk management approach, then the evaluator has the flexibility to describe numerous contextual conditions under which risk level would be reduced. However, even when the risk assessment question relates strictly to prediction, an honest answer almost always requires answering with respect to a particular set of anticipated circumstances. Good risk communication makes those anticipated circumstances *explicit*. Evaluators may handle this with a preface as brief as the following:

> Assuming Mr. Nelson returns to the community under the conditions that the parole board typically assigns . . . (i.e., list conditions).

or

> If Ms. Wilson is returned to the community under circumstances identical to those before her evaluation (i.e., she does not consume her prescribed medication, and follow-up psychiatric visits remain optional).

Sometimes, communicating risk estimates with respect to context requires if-then statements that detail how risk level would vary depending on context. These are most common when an examinee has a violence history that is fairly specific and circumscribed (see Chapter 6 for discussion of idiographic factors in risk assessment). Consider the following examples:

- Each of Mr. Smith's seven known encounters with law enforcement have followed a similar pattern, wherein he discontinued his psychotropic medication and became increasingly suspicious and irritable toward his elderly mother, with whom he has lived for most of the past several years. He has responded to her innocuous comments with verbal threats, sometimes escalating to the point of striking her, at which point she has called the police. This pattern appears to have become more frequent in recent history, with four of the seven incidents occurring within the past year. Notably, Mr. Smith has *not* engaged in similar behaviors during the months when he lived in supervised group housing. If he is released to his mother's care and returns to her home, it appears more likely than not that Mr. Smith will engage in a similar assault within the next few months. However, if released to a group home in which his weekly visits with his mother are supervised, or if released to the care of his uncle, and his medication compliance is monitored, Mr. Smith appears to manifest no greater risk of violence than other patients receiving outpatient psychiatric treatment.

- In each of Mr. Olstein's three documented sexual offenses, he has sexually assaulted women who were under the influence of crack cocaine while in a home or building that served as a "crack house." Although Mr. Olstein maintained that sexual contact was consensual, each instance resulted in reports to police and documented victim injuries. Records, including drug testing, indicate that Mr. Olstein committed the assaults both when using crack cocaine and when free from illicit substances, as per his earlier probation conditions. If Mr. Olstein is paroled under conditions in which he can socialize and visit with drug-abusing acquaintances (even if Mr. Olstein himself receives regular drug screening), his risk of committing similar offenses should be considered high relative to other sexual offenders released from the State Department of Corrections. However, if paroled to a halfway house and work release program that provides intensive monitoring during both day and evening hours, his likelihood of sexual reoffending would be considerably lower.

Note that a working knowledge of community resources, typical supervision arrangements, and typical agency practices often enhances the degree to which an evaluator can be context-specific in risk communication. Of course, there may be many situations in which the context that an examinee will encounter is completely unknown.

11. *Acknowledge limits.* By definition, risk assessment involves developing an opinion in the context of some uncertainty. Indeed, uncertainty about an examinee's future behavior is precisely what prompted someone to request a risk assessment. Even in a well-conducted risk assessment, some questions may remain unanswered, or an evaluator cannot offer a risk estimate that is as precise as the decision maker would like. Research data and instruments are not applicable to every case and may be less precise than desirable even when they do apply. Evaluators are ethically bound to be open in acknowledging these limits.

For example, psychologists interpreting assessment results "indicate any significant limitations of their interpretations" (American Psychological Association, 2002 p. 14). Similarly, "the forensic psychologist maintains professional integrity by examining the issue at hand from all reasonable perspectives, actively seeking information that will differentially test plausible rival hypotheses" (Committee on Ethical Guidelines for Forensic Psychologists, 1991 p. 661). Likewise, authorities on forensic evaluation consistently emphasize the need to discuss in a straightforward manner the limits to one's data and opinions (Brodsky, 1991, 1999; Heilbrun, 2001; Heilbrun et al., 2003; Melton et al., 1997; Shuman & Greenberg, 2003). Common examples of limitations include sparse collateral information, conflicting information from records, and individuals who refuse to be interviewed or refuse to discuss certain relevant issues.

The evaluator who has clearly detailed the risk assessment process has already addressed any conflicting data, discussed alternative theories and rival hypotheses, and presented an opinion based on the weight of available evidence. Nevertheless, some final clear statements about the limits to a risk estimate may be in order. Evaluators acknowledge limits first and foremost because this represents honest and ethical practice. As an added benefit, however, acknowledging the limits to one's opinion during expert testimony (and probably in written reports) often does much to enhance an evaluator's credibility (Brodsky, 1991, 1999; Melton et al., 1997; Shuman & Greenberg, 2003).

12. *Throughout the communication, use language that is clear and simple, yet precise.* Once again, guidance on psychological assessment in general (Groth-Marnat, 2003) and forensic mental health assessment in particular (Grisso, 1998; Heilbrun, 2001; Heilbrun et al., 2002; Heilbrun, Dvoskin, et al., 1999; Melton et al., 1997) bears repeating in any discussion of risk communication. The most astute or well-founded opinion, if phrased in a manner that the audience cannot understand, is useless. In their review of 62 studies of expert witness testimony across disciplines, Kwartner and Boccaccini (in press) identified clarity of communication as the first empirically supported variable essential to effective expert testimony. Clarity is certainly just as important in written work.

Clear language involves clear diction, using words the audience understands. Clear language also requires speaking in a logical, linear manner, usually avoiding the digressions common to academic discourse. Bear in mind that even popular publications, such as *Newsweek*, are written at a sixth-grade level (Harvey, 1997), yet reviews tend to find that mental health professionals write much more complex reports (Brenner, 2003). The goal of risk communication is not to demonstrate an evaluator's sophistication, but to convey concepts—sometimes complex concepts—in a language the recipients can understand.

Doren (2002), discussing evaluations for civil commitment of sexual offenders, suggested that risk communication in expert testimony can be improved by the use of metaphors to explain concepts that may be new to the audience. Obviously, metaphors should be chosen carefully. Few are perfect in all respects, and the audience may draw inferences or analogies the evaluator has not anticipated. However, a well-crafted metaphor can be a valuable tool in clear communication. As an illustration, here are two of the metaphors Doren offered:

"Risk factors": When one goes for a physical checkup, the doctor checks out your [sic] heart, among other things. This is done by assessing the person's heartbeat, cholesterol level, blood pressure, family history of heart problems, if the person is a smoker, and so on. These characteristics are looked at because research has shown these considerations to be related to heart problems. Each is a risk factor.

"Multiple pathways/dimensions to recidivism": During that same physical, the doctor checks out more than just one's heart, but also one's lungs, nervous system, and so on. Each of these can affect one's overall health. If the doctor tells me that my heart is in great shape, I will still feel very worried if the doctor also says that I have a malignant brain tumor. That is because my overall health depends on many different parts all working well. (p. 187)

Similarly, Cunningham (personal communication, 2007) when testifying about actuarial approaches or group-based data, discusses car insurance rates (a topic with which most adults are familiar) as an example. He uses another automotive example when discussing the importance of context in violence risk assessment. He describes an adolescent male whose driving behavior on a Saturday night with peers differs greatly from his behavior when driving his parents to church the following morning; though the teenager and the car remain the same, the context—and thus the behavior—differs.

13. *Throughout the communication, know your audience.* To communicate clearly to an audience, an evaluator must be reasonably familiar with the audience. Some consumers of risk communication (e.g., a parole board) may be quite familiar with the criminal justice system, but less familiar with the behavioral sciences or mental health. For other audiences, the reverse may be true. For still other recipients of risk communication (e.g., laypersons on a jury), the evaluator should assume no advanced knowledge of the topics at hand.

Additional Resources

A few clinicians who conduct risk assessments spend much of their time in court and offer testimony regarding most of the evaluations they conduct. But for most clinicians, and in most cases, a written evaluation report is the only form of communication we offer to a decision maker (indeed, a well-prepared and clear report may preclude the need for testimony; Melton et al., 1997). Therefore, reports must be clear, complete, and credible. They must be written in such a manner that they can stand alone, without additional verbal explanation. For additional suggestions regarding report writing generally, see Brenner (2003), Harvey (1997), and Groth-Marmat (2003). For additional suggestions regarding forensic report writing in particular, see Melton et al. (1997) or Weiner (2006).

For the minority of cases that do result in expert testimony to the court or other decision makers (e.g., a parole board), the general principles described in this chapter certainly still apply. However, we encourage a review of several guides developed specifically to prepare mental health professionals to testify in court (i.e., Blau, 1998; Brodsky, 1991, 1999; Hess, 2006; Kwartner & Boccaccini, in press).

To summarize, risk communication, whether in writing or in testimony, is the link between assessment and decision making (Heilbrun, Dvoskin, et al., 1999). Often, the decision making involves high stakes for society and the examinee. Cautious, balanced, clear, and specific risk communication is a necessity.

8

From Risk Assessment to Risk Management

Thus far, we have concentrated on how an evaluator can best assess the level of risk an individual presents and under what circumstances. Substantial research is now available to assist the forensic clinician in such an assessment. However helpful it may be to have a well-founded risk estimate, this simply leaves the system with a choice of accepting the risk or somehow incapacitating the individual. Only a decade ago, Heilbrun (1997) proposed going one step further, moving from a paradigm of risk assessment to one of risk management. Risk assessment involves evaluating the level of risk presented; risk management involves reducing that risk. Risk assessment tends to be a one-time evaluation; risk management must be ongoing and fluid. Research to date on risk assessment puts primary emphasis on static variables; risk management stresses factors that are dynamic in nature and amenable to intervention. Risk assessment delineates the factors and combination of factors that tend to raise the individual's risk for violent behavior; risk management then moves to addressing these issues (Glancy & Chaimowitz, 2005). Both models assume that some level of risk is probably unavoidable; however, the risk management model gives more flexibility to the community or decision maker to determine what level of risk is tolerable.

Therapeutic Jurisprudence

Risk management moves beyond the usual forensic evaluation into a realm that Wexler (1992) labeled "therapeutic jurisprudence." Therapeutic jurisprudence has been defined as "studying the role of law as a therapeutic agent" (Daicoff & Wexler, 2003, p. 561). Numerous statutes authorizing the evaluation and potential containment of violent individuals allow judges great leeway in defining what constitutes violence, how much risk is tolerable, and what specific measures may be taken to reduce the risk. This presents opportunities to implement risk management plans, based on the best clinical science available, to protect the public *and* prioritize constructive interventions for the individual involved. Stated differently, risk management opens the door to using the law in ways both protective and therapeutic. Well-formulated risk management plans can potentially strike an agreed-upon balance between society's need to feel safe from threat and an individual's civil liberty.

Such an approach is not without controversy and may not be appropriate in every circumstance in which risk is assessed. Some courts have openly rejected the idea of managing risk, asserting that risk should instead be eliminated. For example, the Supreme Court of Wisconsin recently considered whether conditions of release should be taken into account when determining whether one meets the definition of sexually violent predator (SVP). The justices opined that a mental disorder *within* the person, and not external factors, was what statute intended courts to consider. They therefore concluded that any discussion of release conditions was irrelevant (*In re Mark*, 2006).

Some risk assessments specifically lend themselves to a single, static evaluation. For example, in the case of assessments for the penalty phase of capital cases, the evaluator will present evidence to a jury at only one point in time, and future circumstances are usually not open to negotiation. In other cases, the issue is long-term commitment to a designated facility, with the facility having control over future interventions. Even when some type of outpatient commitment is considered, the commitment is completed separately from the imposition of conditions in some jurisdictions. In Texas, for example, in SVP outpatient commitment proceedings, a risk assessment is a critical element the court considers; however, once a decision is made that an individual meets the state's criteria for commitment, the responsibility for supervision conditions, treatment planning, and monitoring passes to a separate agency (the Texas Council for Sex Offender Treatment). Finally, there are circumstances in which there is no authority to provide interventions, alter circumstances, or monitor outcome.

However, if the opening does exist for the exercise of therapeutic jurisprudence in the form of risk management planning, it can have significant value. This may, however, be a new concept to the layperson and require some education. One of us recently presented this concept to a group of judges in a large metropolitan county. Initially the judges were skeptical, offering reactions much like that of the Supreme Court in Wisconsin: Anyone who presents a risk should be incapacitated! However, three arguments raised interest in risk management applications: (1) practicality, (2) cost effectiveness, and (3) constitutional concerns about civil liberties.

The current reality is that most offenders under the control of some correctional agency are supervised in the community (Bureau of Justice Statistics [BJS], 2006; Hart, Webster, & Douglas, 2001; Stalans, 2004). Prison, jail, and hospital space is finite and often inadequate to accommodate current populations. Jurisdictions must increasingly accommodate new referrals. As of 2005, federal prisons were operating at 34% above capacity, and state prisons were operating at up to 14% above capacity (BJS, 2006). Given these circumstances, no one would seriously argue that everyone presenting any risk of violence can simply be incarcerated indefinitely. For the safety of the public, the most prudent response involves carefully selecting the population for which institutional space is best allocated.

The financial cost of maintaining someone in an institution far exceeds that of supervising the same individual in a community setting. Despite the majority of offenders being supervised in the community, prison operations accounted for 77% of state correctional costs in fiscal year 2001 (BJS, 2006). Legislators are loath to increase taxes for any reason, and budget managers are anxious to stretch available dollars to the limit. Therefore, the least expensive method to achieve the greatest public protection is understandably attractive.

Whereas sentences for criminal conduct serve the purposes of justice and retribution, civil commitment procedures do not. Approximately two-thirds of states have laws following the doctrine of *least restrictive alternative* (Melton et al., 1997). In general, this doctrine suggests that individual liberty cannot be curtailed to a greater degree than is necessary to prevent the potential harm. For example, it would be inappropriate to confine someone to a secure hospital if his or her risk for violence could be ameliorated by a regimen of outpatient treatment. Beyond court or statutory mandates, long-term improvements are more likely and more sustainable if community environments have more effective treatment options than do institutions. Finally, it is worth considering the potentially negative effects of long-term institutionalization.

Formulating a Risk Management Plan

Scientifically sound risk management plans can have great utility; however, a poorly formulated plan can be hazardous. Before describing the mechanics of risk management planning, we describe some of the most common errors to avoid.

Common Errors

Perhaps the most common error in risk management involves building an intervention around conventional wisdom or illusory correlations with no scientific support. A prime example is common to sex offender risk management strategies. Sex offender treatment programs throughout the country concentrate most treatment efforts on "breaking down denial" and developing victim empathy (Conroy, 2006). However, most research on sex offender recidivism reveals no relationship between recidivism and denial and/or victim empathy (Hanson & Bussiere, 1998; Hanson & Morton-Bourgon,

2004), and no studies indicate that changes in denial cause changes in risk level. Therefore, including these elements as the foundation of a risk management plan appears to be a misdirected effort.

The frequency of recommendations for counseling or psychotherapy made by mental health professionals might lead one to believe that every offender requires counseling. It is a somewhat attractive intervention because it is readily available in most areas and easily monitored for compliance. Before requiring psychotherapy, however, the risk management planner should assess whether there is strong research evidence or idiographic data to demonstrate that it has proven effective in reducing violent behavior for the individual in question. It is possible that counseling may at best be an expensive inconvenience and at worst a detriment. For example, the effectiveness of conventional psychotherapy for persons scoring high in psychopathy—a group often among the highest risk offenders—is the subject of great debate. Whereas some reviews are more optimistic (D'Silva, Duggan, & McCarthy, 2004; Salekin, 2002), other studies offer little support for the effectiveness of treating high-psychopathy offenders with traditional counseling approaches (Looman, Abracen, Serin, & Marquis, 2005; Rice, 1997; cf. Skeem, Monahan, & Mulvey, 2002). In 2003, Hare suggested that therapy programs "may help psychopaths to develop better ways of manipulating, deceiving, and using people, but do little to help them understand themselves" (p. 159). In proposing some new approaches that remain as yet untried, Wong and Hare (2005, p. 2) conclude that the literature to date has provided "more direction on what *not to do* than on what *should be done* in order to provide effective treatment for psychopaths."

Setting aside the ongoing debate regarding psychopathy and traditional psychotherapy approaches, a more general concern may be that traditional psychotherapy is rarely crafted specifically to address criminogenic needs in a manner that reduces recidivism. For example, a review of the literature on risk management with juveniles (see Borum, 2003, for an excellent narrative review) reveals that delinquency-specific interventions addressing specific criminogenic factors are far more effective than vague therapies to improve psychological well-being or self-esteem, which appear to have little effect on reducing recidivism risk (for meta-analyses, see Dowden & Andrews, 1999; Lipsey, 1992, 1995). Of course, detailed assessments may indeed reveal specific psychiatric symptoms (e.g., attention-deficit/hyperactivity disorder, chronic anger) that increase risk among many youth, and targeted treatment for these tends to prove effective, as does targeted treatment for cognitive and emotional skills related to risk (e.g., self-control; see Dowden & Andrews, 1999). In sum, psychological or psychiatric interventions may be important components of risk management strategies *if* careful assessment suggests they are necessary, but there is no reason to reflexively recommend psychotherapy services be employed with all offenders.

Another common risk management error is the tendency to focus on a single target, generally the one most commonly addressed by one's profession. For example, psychologists and psychiatrists may be especially prone to targeting a mental illness or personality disorder. Probation officers may emphasize containment and monitoring techniques. To be effective, a risk management approach requires interdisciplinary cooperation (Douglas et al., 2001). No single discipline can address, or even identify, all of the significant risk factors and potential interventions.

Finally, there is a tendency for the courts and administrative bodies to seek a one-size-fits-all solution to vexing problems. This has been particularly evident in sex offender risk management, where there is often a set of conditions applied to all offenders in the group regardless of needs or circumstances (Conroy, 2006). Unfortunately, such models fail to recognize the heterogeneity of such groups and the fact that intragroup variance may well exceed variance between groups. Such plans may waste valuable resources applying interventions not needed—and perhaps contraindicated—for a given individual. They may also overlook a unique need that is central to ameliorating individual risk.

The Planning Process

Heilbrun (1997) suggested a generic template for a risk management plan that could be adapted to a variety of individuals and circumstances. Specifically, the planner generates a list of risk factors identified through a thorough risk assessment, using both nomothetic and idiographic analysis. The next steps are to determine which factors are amenable to intervention, specify the interventions, and establish a review schedule. This scheme can form the basis for solid risk management planning.

Once it is clear that a risk management plan is appropriate for a particular individual, the first step is an analysis of risk factors. Evaluators should consider these factors in light of the "need principle" articulated by Andrews and Bonta (2003). This principle was developed specifically for those engaged in correctional treatment. It states that emphasis should be placed on criminogenic rather than noncriminogenic needs. However, this can be broadened beyond the criminal realm by concentrating on those factors that may in some way precipitate violent behavior rather than those that simply cause the individual discomfort. Although helping the individual feel better may be a noble goal, feeling better may not necessarily reduce the risk for violence.

Factors examined can be roughly categorized from major to minor, depending on their salience to risk. Both the static and the dynamic factors should be examined. It is important to take note of static factors that cannot be changed (i.e., risk that cannot be reduced); however, some static factors may worsen over time (e.g., more violent acts). Time may also mitigate some static factors. For example, the individual may have a history of serious substance abuse, but may have been clean and sober while living in the community for several years. In management, primary emphasis should be on dynamic risk factors—those that have the potential for change through intervention.

Once the risk factors have been enumerated, each should be examined to determine which interventions might best ameliorate each of them. Interventions should be considered in light of the "responsivity principle" (Andrews & Bonta, 2003). That is, interventions need to be adapted to the particular abilities and personal style of the target individual. Factors to consider would include, but are not necessarily limited to, cognitive abilities, cultural background, social attitudes, learning style, and personal circumstances. Some will directly address the risk factors; others may be more indirect. For example, regular urinalysis may directly address substance abuse. However, the degree to which one's occupation exposes one to opportunities for substance abuse may also be important, but less direct and perhaps less obvious. Interventions for a comprehensive plan must be multisystemic. That is, mental health professionals must think beyond the tools of their profession (e.g., psychotherapy, medications) to consider training and mentoring, family services, financial counseling, monitoring and containment strategies, social supports, victim access, and a list of other possibilities. Interventions must be pragmatic and reasonably available. For example, if a great deal of structured treatment is required, it may prove very difficult for the individual to simultaneously maintain steady employment. Certain interventions are more readily available in some areas than others. One of us was recently involved in the case of a sex offender released on condition that he attend a biweekly sex offender group therapy program. Unfortunately, he lived in a rather remote rural area where the only therapist qualified as a sex offender treatment provider did not have enough clients to compose a group. After some negotiation with the supervisory agency, a substitution of individual therapy was approved.

A Sample Risk Management Plan

Risk management can be best explained using an example. Consider the case of a 42-year-old male (HP) who is eligible for conditional release from a federal prison hospital, where he was committed following a finding of Not Guilty By Reason of Insanity for Threatening the President of the United States. He had previously served a federal prison sentence for a similar offense. In the most recent incident, he was apprehended while attempting to scale the White House fence armed with a hunting knife and saying he "must destroy the antichrist." HP was diagnosed with schizophrenia in his early 20s. He has been intermittently compliant with treatment but has a consistent delusion about a secret sect replacing the president of the United States with the antichrist, who is trying to destroy Christianity. By age 30 he had begun writing threatening letters. He previously served 4 years in federal prison for Threatening the President through the U.S. Mail. He has no other criminal record, with the exception of a charge for Public Intoxication. However, given his approach with a weapon, the Secret Service was very concerned about his risk to their protectee.

Risk Management Proposal

Table 8.1 shows a proposed risk management plan.

Justification

Risk Factor 1 indicates a history of threatening or pursuing violent behavior that has escalated over time from writing strange letters, to writing specific threats, to approaching the target with a weapon and verbalized intent. Although a significant concern that needs to be seriously considered, this factor is static and not amenable to intervention.

Factor 2 is a symptom of HP's psychotic disorder. Although the research literature on the role of delusional thinking in violence is not clear-cut, in this case, each threat and/or provocative action HP

Table 8.1   HP Risk Management Plan

Risk Factor	Intervention	Review
1. History of threats and attempted violence	None possible	
2. Delusion: The president has been replaced by the antichrist	Antipsychotic medication	Monthly
3. Treatment noncompliance	Medications in form of long-acting injectable medication	Monthly
4. Alcohol abuse	Random testing AA attendance Family support Job selection	Monthly
5. Isolation	Social support (AA & family) Employment training	Monthly
6. Specific target: U.S. president	Secret Service monitoring Geographic restriction	Annually

undertook was specifically motivated by the delusions that the president had been replaced by the antichrist and that HP needed to eliminate the antichrist to save Christianity. Careful review of the man's past treatment history reveals that he has directed no threatening communications or actions toward anyone during periods when he was being treated with antipsychotic medications. When stabilized, HP still says that he believes there is a secret sect trying to undermine the presidency; however, there is nothing he can do about it, and protecting the president is the responsibility of others. He also agrees that he needs to continue his medications. During these periods of stability, HP has held a job and avoided conflict with the law.

Problems arise when HP discontinues his treatment. To assure ongoing medication compliance, the plan calls for a long-acting, injectable form of medication. This has proven effective in the past.

HP has had a problem with the abuse of alcohol that once led to his arrest for Public Intoxication. Abuse of alcohol is also associated with increased risk for violent behavior. HP had not been drinking at the time of his most recent offense, nor was there evidence of alcohol abuse involved in his threatening letters. However, a review of records led to the conclusion that alcohol abuse had frequently precipitated discontinuation of antipsychotic medications. It was, therefore, a less direct, but important risk factor in the chain. HP's immediate family do not use alcohol at all; therefore, this appeared to be a positive living situation for him. HP himself suggested participation in AA as a strategy that has kept him sober in the past. Job selection became an important issue because his most frequent occupation was that of bartender, placing him in close proximity to alcohol.

Risk Factor 4 was added because a careful review of HP's history indicated a pattern of losing friends, becoming socially isolated, beginning to drink, discontinuing medication, and becoming actively delusional. Assuring a variety of social support seemed advisable.

The final risk factor is important in that all of this man's violent focus has been on a single target. Especially because the target was a prominent public figure, victim access in this case could be controlled. The U.S. Secret Service would be monitoring the case and placing geographic restrictions on HP regardless of his status as an insanity acquittee. This could save the resources of other agencies, and the decision maker should be made aware of this additional intervention.

The risk management plan called for reviewing each of the proposed interventions on a monthly basis, with the exception of factor 6. This would allow for revisions in elements of the plan that were ineffective and reconsideration of any that appeared unduly onerous. Overall, risk management planners made an effort to determine the most significant risk factors and whether intervention was feasible. Interventions were selected that were reasonably available and fit with HP's abilities and lifestyle. In this example, it would then be up to the designated decision maker (in this case, a federal judge) to determine whether the potential for risk is sufficiently reduced to allow HP to once again live in the community.

Principles of Effective Risk Management

Based on a review of the extant literature and personal experience, we offer 10 principles we believe appropriate for effective risk management. We attempted to make these guidelines sufficiently general so that they could be applied to a wide variety of individuals, circumstances, and types of violence. In each instance the degree to which the principles can be applied will depend on what ongoing authority is available.

1. *Maximum energy and resources should be devoted to the individuals at highest risk for violent behavior.* This is in keeping with the risk principle articulated by Andrews and Bonta (2003). The idea here is to select the very highest risk offenders for the most intense concentration of interventions. In fact, concentrating intensive treatment efforts on very low risk individuals may actually increase their likelihood of repeated violence (Andrews, Bonta, & Hoge, 1990). Since the early 1990s this idea has been the subject of meta-analytic review. Repeatedly, studies have demonstrated that, in both adults and youth, delivering intensive services to the highest risk offenders will result in the greatest decreases in violent recidivism

(Andrews et al., 2006). This concept may be met with some understandable resistance among those delivering interventions. It may seem much more attractive to concentrate on low-risk offenders whose success may be gratifying on the surface. It may also seem simple to apply a one-size-fits-all model in which everyone receives the same services. However, if the goal is to achieve the greatest reduction in overall violence (or even to maximize financial efficiency), science suggests that risk managers should concentrate on those at highest risk (Hart et al., 2001; Monahan et al., 2001).

2. *Identified risk factors must be directly linked to management strategies.* This is perhaps one of the most important—and most commonly ignored—principles of risk management. For example, there is a tendency among large community correctional systems to try to apply a set of tools to a wide variety of offenders. One such practice has been labeled "the containment approach." It has become an increasingly common approach to the management of sexual offenders. In an effort to assure public safety, programs typically apply every conceivable intervention strategy. These include various types of counseling, testing for substance abuse, polygraphs, geographic restrictions, frequent reporting requirements, and even electronic monitoring. Applying such intensive measures to low-risk offenders would likely be an intrusive ordeal and a waste of scarce resources. Even if the individual is at high risk for recidivism, this may be due only to one or two significant risk factors. Perhaps most disturbing is the potential for missing those one or two most salient risk factors due to the excessive emphasis on a broad set of interventions.

3. *A clearly identified centralized entity should monitor the risk management plan.* A common error in administering a risk management plan is to have a wide variety of disciplines involved and reporting separately to the court. For example, courts have been known to set up outpatient commitment plans that involve psychiatric treatment, housing, substance abuse programming, employment, and other potential areas of intervention and then require each provider to monitor the individual and report accordingly. This is a recipe for failure for several reasons: (a) The various elements may need to interact

(e.g., individuals indicate to their residential supervisors that they are working the night shift when they may actually be unemployed); (b) one of many reporters failing to do so may be easily overlooked; (c) agencies may change personnel and lose track of their obligations; (d) mental health providers are not generally trained to police their clients; and (e) such an arrangement may create ethical conflicts. For management plans to work, infrastructure must be available. Ideally, if interventions are court-ordered, a single entity will have responsibility for monitoring the entire plan and will have the training and authority to do so. A single monitoring authority also eliminates conflicts for treatment providers trying to fulfill the dual roles of therapist and overseer.

4. *Planners must think beyond conventional treatments.* We noted earlier that not every offender needs traditional counseling. Reducing risk factors may require a broad interdisciplinary approach, as exemplified in the multisystemic therapy approach advocated for some violent juveniles (Henggeler, Schoenwald, Bourdin, Rowland, & Cunningham, 1998; Howell, 1999). Interventions may require mentoring, tutoring, use of an educational ombudsman, family financial planning, respite care, sex education, medical treatment, vocational training, or conflict resolution training, to name but a few. Risk management strategies must be matched to needs and not to what any single practitioner can provide.

5. *Plans must be tailored to situational realities.* Experts have often debated whether a risk management plan should put forth the best possible known risk reduction strategies or whether the plan should recommend only options known to be readily available. It is often the case that many more programs and opportunities exist in large metropolitan areas than in small rural communities. Financial resources may also determine which approaches are reasonable. Transportation can be a very real barrier. For almost any intervention, there is the issue of qualified providers. One compromise would be to draft a plan that would use available resources, followed by an explanation of additional interventions that would reduce risk further if they could be arranged or if some reasonable substitute could be crafted. However, courts may quickly lose interest in

the concept of risk management if they receive a comprehensive, elegant scheme that they see no way of implementing.

Plans that are overly complex and onerous may result in almost immediate failure for even the most motivated individual. Plans that are beyond the capability of the person involved (e.g., a person who is illiterate or who has limited English-language capabilities assigned to a group program requiring the use of workbooks and completion of written homework) are also a recipe for failure.

6. *Clear channels of communication must be identified.* One of us has been involved in a number of cases in which risk management plans have failed because communication went awry. In one instance, an individual had been released on condition that he continue compliance with his regimen of psychotropic medication. Any deviation from this requirement would result in his immediate return to a secure hospital environment. However, when he missed his scheduled appointment, the first response of his treatment providers was to give him time to call and reschedule. When some time had passed, they contacted the officer in charge of monitoring the release. However, this individual made numerous attempts to contact the patient without notifying authorities. The situation ended tragically as the patient decompensated into a psychotic state and murdered two other individuals before killing himself.

It is essential to clarify who is responsible for ongoing communication with the court (or other appropriate decision maker) and at what intervals. It is further important to identify how those responsible for each facet of the plan will communicate among one another and with the central monitoring entity. Recognizing that the management of individuals who are prone to violence does not always go smoothly or predictably, it is essential to specify how sudden, urgent communication should be routed. For instance, in the example of risk management planning presented earlier, if HP were found to have obtained part-time employment tending bar, it would be foolish to wait until the official monthly reporting date to initiate action.

7. *The plan must be specific yet flexible, involving the subject as much as possible.* It is only fair that anyone released from confinement on conditions understands exactly what is required to remain

free. This could be construed as an essential element of due process. Assuring that mandatory conditions are clear to all involved can avoid counterproductive debates and hostility. It can also assure that, should an individual need to be returned to custody, this can be done quickly and efficiently.

However, some flexibility should be allowed to avoid draconian measures when simple, reasonable substitutions could be made. In one case, one stipulation of an individual insanity acquittee's conditional release was that he live with his parents. He successfully fulfilled all conditions of release for 2 years. Then, however, his father died, his mother was transferred to a nursing home, and the acquittee went to live with his sister. Soon thereafter the hospital from which he had originally been released (located in a distant state) received a letter from the court saying that, although he appeared to be functioning in a very satisfactory manner, it would be necessary to rehospitalize him as he had violated a key component of his release plan. The hospital administrator quickly rewrote and resubmitted the plan, and revocation was avoided. However, the consternation could have been avoided had the plan used language such as "maintain a living environment approved by his local probation officer" rather than the unnecessary specificity of living with his parents at a particular address.

The more one can involve the subject of the risk management in the plan the more likely it is to succeed (Hart et al., 2001; Heilbrun, 1997). The individual can provide input on the types of interventions he or she will readily accept and respond to in satisfactory fashion. The subject may also be able to point out problems before they are irrevocably set in place. The more ownership the individual takes of the conditions, the more likely it is the individual will work to comply.

8. *Mechanisms should be in place for immediate intervention and graduated response.* Protection of society is a critical value of risk management. Mechanisms should be designed to anticipate and prevent violence rather than simply incapacitating and/or punishing the perpetrator after it happens. Well-planned risk management as described here will have carefully examined those factors that elevate risk and have led to past violence. Methods of immediate intervention should be in place so that situations are not allowed to

escalate. For example, if substance abuse has been established as a risk factor, intervention should occur as soon as it is evident that the individual has taken a substance. However, interventions need not be all or nothing. In other words, every violation does not need to result in immediate confinement if more graduated sanctions are in place. These could include (but are not limited to) more frequent reporting, more frequent random drug testing, random visits by the monitoring agent, overnight confinement, movement to a supervised residence, or a change in employment.

Risk management plans can also be conceived in stages. For example, one of us worked for a number of years in secure forensic hospitals that were charged with designing conditional release plans. After some years of experience, these plans came to include stages: release to a less secure local facility, release to a halfway house, and finally release to the community. At each level, a violation of any condition could result in a return to the previous level of restriction and not necessarily to the secure hospital. The individual could then again be released to a less restrictive environment at any time that treatment providers were satisfied that all conditions would be met. Treatment providers explained that knowing consequences for an individual's noncompliance would be modest, rather than catastrophic, prompted them to intervene more quickly.

9. *Issues of confidentiality and legal reporting should be clarified.* Confidentiality is an ethical issue dear to the heart of any mental health professional. However, in the area of risk management, some reporting to legal authorities will likely be necessary. It must be clear at the onset to all involved what is confidential and what is not. It is commonly accepted that in the area of forensic assessment, the actual client is the legal system and the evaluator owes no duty of confidentiality to the person being assessed (Ogloff, 2001). However, mental health providers involved in carrying out risk management plans are often primarily providing treatment and not forensic evaluation services. Trust within the therapeutic relationship is generally considered essential to success. Although some correctional systems may push to have completely open communication among those involved in risk management, to date there is no actual evidence that this is essential to reducing risk (Conroy, 2006). We

would encourage agreements that report to legal authorities only the information necessary to affirm that conditions of release are being met. For example, it is reasonable to report whether the individual is keeping appointments, taking prescribed medications, and generally cooperating with the treatment provider. It may also be appropriate to report precursors of violence (e.g., direct threats); however, much of the content of psychotherapy sessions can be kept in confidence without presenting a risk to society.

One argument for protecting confidentiality as much as possible is simply that confidentiality makes it more likely that the individual will offer more important issues to address therapeutically. Whatever the agreement made, it must be clear from the start to all involved who will report what to whom.

The issue of dual roles is also relevant here. To some extent, any treatment provider involved in risk management with the legal system is functioning both as a therapist and as law enforcement; this may be unavoidable. However, legal authorities may go beyond this and suggest that treatment providers also become forensic evaluators who perform the formal risk assessment periodically required. Although a risk assessor should have access to treatment records, it is very difficult for the treating clinician to remain objective in performing a risk assessment, and it is very difficult for the examinee to establish a truly therapeutic relationship with the individual who will report his future level of risk (Ogloff, 2001). Such dual roles should be strongly discouraged (Committee on Ethical Guidelines for Forensic Psychologists, 1991).

10. *There should be a mechanism in place for regular reassessment and modification of the plan.* Risk management is based on the idea that risk factors are dynamic and level of risk is fluid, necessitating reevaluation and reformulation of interventions (Douglas et al., 2001; Heilbrun, 1997). Mechanisms should be incorporated to assure that all elements of a plan are reevaluated on a regular basis. Those that are not accomplishing the expected results should be modified or dropped. New risk factors may also emerge and require attention. This is essential to reduce risk, but also to conserve scarce resources, assuring that they are not invested in useless or inappropriate interventions.

Passage of time should also be considered. If the individual has not reoffended over a lengthy period of time, should he or she be required to remain in a counseling program forever? Submit to regular drug testing forever? Be subject to certain restrictions regardless of changes in his or her physical or mental condition? If there is no time limit on conditions, should one be set? There are no concise answers to these questions, but mechanisms need to be in place to consider them periodically.

To summarize, risk management can be a valuable tool for violence prevention when used appropriately. It is appropriate when there exists ongoing authority to monitor and intervene with a potentially violent individual and his or her future context. Risk management also acknowledges an important reality: that risk is not wholly stored within the individual, but rather is to some extent a function of circumstances. Advantages include protection of society, allowing individuals to function in the least restrictive environment, and appropriate utilization of scarce resources. In addition, it allows society (or its representatives) to determine what level of risk is tolerable. Risk management is less commonly understood and applied than risk assessment and may require education of authorities involved.

Risk Assessment of Patients with Serious Mental Illness

Psychopathology is one factor to be considered in a variety of the violence risk assessments outlined in this book. This chapter, however, addresses risk assessments in which mental illness is the central and essential factor. Typically, this type of risk assessment occurs in the context of commitment to or discharge from a psychiatric hospital, particularly for individuals subject to civil commitment or those found Not Guilty by Reason of Insanity (NGRI). Though risk assessments of this sort are not unheard of among youth (see Chapter 11 for a discussion of juveniles with mental disorders), this chapter focuses on adults, among whom this type of risk assessment is much more common. Civil commitment of those alleged to be sexually violent predators is also addressed separately in Chapter 10.

The public perception that persons with mental illness are inherently dangerous has persisted for decades (Monahan, 1992, 1993a; Norko & Baranoski, 2005), resulting in many laws designed to confine or otherwise incapacitate the mentally ill. Given that severe mental illness is relatively rare when compared to the broader population of those prone to violence (Swanson, 1994), implementing some of these resource-intensive laws—which often involve curtailing civil liberties—may not be the most efficient use of resources or the most direct means of reducing violence.

Up until the mid-1980s, the general consensus of the mental health profession was that there was no scientifically demonstrated relationship between mental illness and violence risk (Monahan, 1981). Most argued that when demographic and historical factors were taken into account, the apparent relationship between violence and mental disorder disappeared. However, large-scale studies conducted over the next decade suggested otherwise (Klassen & O'Connor, 1988, 1990; Steadman, Fabisiak, Dvoskin, & Holohean, 1987; Steadman & Felson, 1984; Swanson, 1994; Swanson et al., 1990). In 1992, following a detailed review of the literature, Monahan concluded:

> The data that have recently become available, fairly read, suggest the one conclusion I did not want to reach: Whether the measure is the prevalence of violence among the disordered or the prevalence of disorder among the violent, whether the sample is people who are selected for treatment as inmates or patients in institutions or people randomly chosen from the open community, and no matter how many social and demographic factors are statistically taken into account, there appears to be a relationship between mental disorder and violent behavior. Mental disorder may be a robust and significant risk factor for the occurrence of violence. (p. 519)

Although severe mental illness is relatively rare and the relationship between mental disorder and violence is moderate, decisions to hospitalize or to discharge persons with severe mental illness are fairly common for mental health professionals. Concern for the rights and best interests of the patient must often be balanced against the concern for the welfare of society and the potential liability in the case of a bad outcome. It is therefore essential that decisions be based on the best science and practice in the field.

Defining the Question

Risk assessments among the severely mentally ill are fairly common practice, but these assessments may vary depending on the specific referral question. Certainly, as described elsewhere in this text, it may be necessary to discuss specifics about a particular referral question with the particular referring party. However, an essential first step in understanding any of these referral questions is to understand the legal contexts in which these questions are raised. Specifically, evaluators must be familiar with the primary ways by which courts commit persons with mental illness to psychiatric treatment (i.e., civil commitment and commitment through the criminal justice system) and must be familiar with the broader doctrines that influence these procedures (e.g., the doctrine of least restrictive alternatives). In other words, evaluators must understand the legal context to understand referral questions within that context.

The Legal Context

The issue of when and how society should restrict the civil liberties of persons with mental disorder has a long and tortured history in the courts. Over time, the pendulum has swung between intense concerns over civil liberty and a strong emphasis on protecting the public. Any evaluator working in this area should maintain current knowledge of relevant case law, because the pendulum is apt to continue its shifting motion. In the following, we briefly summarize case law in relation to civil commitment and commitment from the criminal justice system. In the interest of setting the stage for risk management, we discuss the doctrine of *least restrictive alternative*, outpatient commitment options, the legal concept of mental disorder, and special issues surrounding treatment with psychotropic medications.

Civil Commitment

Until the late 1960s, patients suffering from mental disorder often could be confined to a hospital based only on the signature of a physician. Such commitments were often indefinite and potentially lifelong. This was accomplished under the auspices of the state's *parens patriae* powers. That is, the state had a duty to provide for "the protection of those who are incapable of acting for their own welfare or those who are incompetent to make decisions in their own interest" (Mrad & Nabors, 2007, p, 232). During the decade that followed, however, the courts began to emphasize civil liberties of the mentally ill. In 1972, the U.S. District Court for the Middle District of Alabama issued a precedent-setting ruling, often referred to as the "Patient's Bill of Rights." Among these is the right to an assessment resulting in an individualized treatment plan that must be reviewed; if no further treatment is deemed necessary, the patient must be discharged (*Wyatt v. Stickney*, 1972). That same year, the U.S. District Court for the Eastern District of Wisconsin issued a ruling that outlined what became a model for civil commitment statutes. Specifically, the court declared that because civil commitment involved such a substantial curtailment of an individual's liberty, there must be evidence that the individual presented a danger to self or others and that danger should be narrowly defined (*Lessard v. Schmidt*, 1972). In 1975, the U.S. Supreme Court affirmed this finding: "The state cannot constitutionally confine, without more, a nondangerous individual who is capable of surviving safely in freedom by himself or with the help of willing and responsible family members or friends" (*O'Connor v. Donaldson*, 1975, p. 576). In 1979, the Supreme Court went further. The justices declared that the standard for civil commitment must be proven by clear and convincing evidence and not simply a preponderance of evidence (*Addington v. Texas*, 1979). By the close of this decade the primary justification for civil commitment had swung from the state's *parens patriae* authority to its *police power*. That is, involuntary hospitalization would be based on an established danger to self or others and not simply a patient's need for treatment.

Evaluators should be aware that "danger to others" has been defined differently across jurisdictions. Some states include the concept of emotional harm in addition to bodily harm; some use the term *serious bodily harm*; some require a recent overt act of violence; some distinguish between likelihood and substantial likelihood; and some include danger to property (Melton et al., 1997). "Danger to self" may refer to the probability of suicidal behavior or self-mutilation; however, many jurisdictions include the construct *gravely disabled*. That is, the person is not actively attempting to harm himself or herself but lacks the ability to meet basic needs such as food, shelter, and hygiene. Suffice it to say that evaluators must be aware of the exact requirements for risk in the jurisdiction in which they practice.

Commitment through the Criminal Justice System

Contrary to popular opinion (Hans, 1986), the defense of insanity is rarely used and rarely successful (Silver et al., 1994). However, when an individual is found NGRI, the verdict almost always results in the individual's being committed for further evaluation and treatment. In 1983, the U.S. Supreme Court ruled that an individual found to be NGRI can be presumed to be mentally ill and dangerous given that the individual was found to have committed a criminal act and has admitted to a severe mental illness by virtue of having entered an insanity plea. Specifically, the justices said, "It comports with common sense to conclude that someone whose mental illness was sufficient to lead him to commit a criminal act is likely to remain ill and in need of treatment" (*Jones v. U.S.*, 1983, p. 366). Therefore, there may be no requirement for a formal investigation of risk at the time of initial commitment. However, protection of the public becomes a principal issue when NGRI patients are being considered for discharge. In the Insanity Defense Reform Act of 1984, the federal government placed the burden on the defendant to prove by clear and convincing evidence that "his release would not create a substantial risk of bodily injury to another person or serious damage of property of another due to a present mental disease or defect" (18 USCS §4243). Numerous states followed with similar legislation. Given the heavy burden to be met, the majority of NGRI acquittees are released conditionally (Callahan & Silver, 1998). Conditional release is unlike probation or parole, in which the time frame for supervision is finite. Although a few jurisdictions limit the duration of conditional release to the maximum sentence one could have received if found guilty, conditional release can be a life sentence in many jurisdictions. By definition, this involves ongoing risk assessment and risk management.

A few jurisdictions provide mechanisms for persons other than insanity acquittees to be committed through the criminal justice system. For example, The Insanity Defense Reform Act of 1984 also allows for committed (including conditional release) of persons who are about to complete their prison sentences but are mentally ill or who have had charges dismissed for reasons of mental disorder (e.g., those found incompetent and unlikely to be restored to competence; 18 USCS §4246). The standard for release is the same as that for the insanity defense, except that the burden of proof rests on the government. Once again, implementation of this law requires ongoing risk assessment and risk management.

The Doctrine of Least Restrictive Alternative

In *Lessard v. Schmidt* (1972), the Supreme Court conveyed that, when attempting to protect the rest of society, the states should consider the alternative that least restricts an individual's liberty. Although initially applied to civil commitments, the concept quickly expanded to include the overall conditions of confinement and the person's right to refuse treatment (Perlin, 2003). The basic idea was that a person could not be confined in a secure hospital if both the individual and society could be adequately protected with the person in the community. Less restrictive options might include residential facilities, day treatment, family supervision, or other available alternatives.

More recently, the U.S. Supreme Court interpreted the doctrine of least restrictive alternative in light of Title II of the Americans with Disabilities Act (1990). Specifically, the court ruled that persons with mental disabilities must be afforded community-based treatment rather than confined to an institution if the following conditions are met: (a) The treating professionals affirm such a setting to be appropriate, (b) the individual agrees, and (c) resources are reasonably available (*Olmstead v. Zimring*, 1999). On the last condition, courts have varied in their interpretation. To what degree the state is required to create least restrictive alternatives remains unclear.

Outpatient Commitment

Outpatient commitment statutes come in three types: (1) conditional release requirements when an individual is discharged from hospitalization, (2) the option of mandatory outpatient treatment as a less restrictive alternative to inpatient commitment, and (3) preventive outpatient commitment, in which the individual does not have to meet the requirements needed for inpatient commitment but appears likely to reach that point in the absence of intervention. Almost all jurisdictions now have at least one of these three options (Petrila, 2007). Kendra's Law (N.Y. Mental Hygiene

Law), passed in New York in 1999, is probably the most widely known and critiqued of these statutes. It allows for preventive outpatient commitment—the most controversial type. Although it retains the dangerousness requirement, an individual can be subject to commitment if experiencing deterioration likely to result in harm to self or others. In 2002, the Supreme Court of Wisconsin affirmed this lesser standard (*In re commitment of Dennis H.*). (For a complete discussion of the controversy surrounding these approaches see Perlin, 2003; Petrila, 2007.)

Mental Disorder Defined

One consistent message from the courts regarding the definition of mental disorder has been that, when considered by the judicial system, it is a legal, moral, and policy judgment—not a medical one (*U.S. v. Lyons*, 1984; *U.S. v. Weed*, 2004). The U.S. Supreme Court in *Kansas v. Hendricks* (1997) went so far as to say that states could define the mental disorder any way they wished, and it need not relate to any category in the current *Diagnostic and Statistical Manual of Mental Disorders* (DSM). In this same ruling, the justices declared that, for persons to be committed, their "mental abnormality or personality disorder" need not be amenable to treatment. Thus it is critical for evaluators to be familiar with both statutory and case law in the jurisdiction in which they practice. Some states exclude mental retardation, and some exclude diagnoses relating to substance abuse; others have separate statutes addressing these issues. Some states exclude antisocial personality disorder (e.g., Florida); some exclude all personality disorders (e.g., Arizona). Ultimately, it will be up to the court to determine whether the condition, disorder, or abnormality described by the clinician fulfills the appropriate legal requirement.

A second series of court decisions addressed which conditions may be considered a *current* mental disorder. In *Foucha v. Louisiana* (1992) the Supreme Court ruled that an insanity acquittee could be retained in the hospital only so long as the acquittee is both mentally ill and dangerous. Dangerousness, absent mental illness, was not sufficient. However, more recently, the U.S. Tenth Circuit Court of Appeals considered the issue of possible "latent" mental disorders (*U.S. v. Weed*, 2004). In this case, an insanity acquittee was found to have suffered from a psychotic episode at the time of the crime. Seventeen months passed with no apparent recurrence of psychosis. However, the court ruled that, even though the individual was showing no current symptoms of psychosis and currently met no *DSM-IV* criteria for mental illness, the statutory requirements for continued commitment were nonetheless fulfilled. The justices reasoned that because experts agreed that there may be a latent condition that simply had not been prompted recently, the person could once again present a substantial risk of violence if prompted.

Medication

For psychiatric patients with a history of violence, psychotropic medication is often the most critical issue to be addressed in managing risk. Courts have generally considered involuntary medication among the most intrusive forms of treatment. Historically, case law has deemed involuntary medication acceptable only for persons who lacked the capacity to provide consent (*Rivers v. Katz*, 1986) or in emergency situations where the person presented an imminent risk to self or others and medication was the least restrictive (but effective) remedy (*Rennie v. Klein*, 1981; *Rogers v. Okin*, 1980; *Sell v. U.S.*, 2003). These cases, however, dealt with the involuntary treatment of an institutionalized person.

In recent years, hospital stays have become increasingly brief (Mulvey & Lidz, 1995; Silver, 2006). Thus, the need for mandated outpatient conditions has become much more salient. Courts have generally been very hesitant to order a noninstitutionalized individual to comply with a regimen of psychotropic medication. However, Kendra's Law, the outpatient commitment law in New York, allows courts to order ongoing medication in addition to numerous other services. This aspect of court-ordered treatment was tested in the New York courts in the case of *In re K. L.* (2004). The court acknowledged that the order for continued medication was a critical element of the statute. The justices found an order for medication to be constitutional and consistent with previous rulings because the court could order the individual to comply with a medication regimen but could not forcibly administer the medicine. Therefore, what teeth the law has remains quite unclear. The outpatient commitment law in North Carolina is of similar construction:

When an outpatient committed person stops taking medication or fails to keep scheduled appointments, the treating clinician may request that law enforcement officers bring the individual to a mental health center to be examined and, it is hoped, persuaded to comply with treatment. Medication cannot be forcibly administered in that setting; however, the clinician may remind the patient that failure to take medication could result in the need for hospital admission. (Swanson et al., 2001, p. 161)

Conditional release under federal statute (18 USCS §4243, 4246) often mandates that the individual continue a regimen of psychotropic medication. Failure to comply with this provision of the plan can, and often does, result in a warrant for the U.S. marshals to return the released person to custody.

The Shifting Legal Landscape

We present this very brief summary of key legal issues to provide background, and to raise consciousness about the need to keep abreast of current law in the applicable jurisdiction. This landscape is ever shifting, and, by the time this book is in print, new laws and cases will have already emerged.

Base Rates and Nomothetic Data

Reasonably accurate base rates for violence among those with mental disorder are very difficult to obtain, in part because disorder is defined differently across research reports. Likewise, researchers have used a variety of indexes of violence.

One of the most extensive studies of this topic was the National Institute of Mental Health's Epidemiologic Catchment Area (ECA) project, completed in the 1980s (see Swanson, 1994, for a discussion of methodology and limitations). This large study of community residents examined self-reported symptoms, and posed a few questions related to violence. Based on diagnoses given at the time of the study, approximately 7% to 14% of persons with *no* mental disorder committed a violent act at some time in their lives, with 1% to 2%

committing violence in a given year. Among those with a major mental illness these percentages increased 16% to 33% in a lifetime and 4% to 7% in a given year. However, for participants with a co-morbid diagnosis of substance abuse, the violence rate over a lifetime rose to over 63%. Substance abuse, absent any mental disorder, yielded a lifetime rate of approximately 55% (Swanson, 1994). These data appear to suggest that individuals with a major mental illness are more than twice as likely to engage in violence than those with no diagnosis. However, these data also indicate that a large majority of those with major mental illness never hurt anyone. One significant limitation to the study was that the questions about violence were quite brief; thus no data were available regarding the frequency or severity of violent acts. In addition, there was no attempt to establish a proximal relationship between the acute phase of an illness and acts of violence, so no causation can be inferred.

In a later study that specifically defined major mental disorder as psychosis or major mood disorder, 13% of those with mental disorder reported an episode of violence over a 1-year period (Swanson et al., 2002). In 2006, Hiday summarized a broad review of the extant literature, both North American and European, and concluded that males with a serious mental disorder were 3 to 7 times more likely to engage in violence than those in the general population. However, consistent with the ECA data, those who abused substances were at much greater risk. Hodgins (2001) reviewed literature dating back to the early days of the deinstitutionalization movement and reached a similar conclusion. The National Comorbidity Survey (Corrigan & Watson, 2005), as well as the MacArthur Violence Risk Assessment Study (Monahan et al., 2001), also revealed that those with mental disorder and substance abuse were at greatest risk for violence.

Moving from community populations to mentally disordered offenders, however, the picture changes. Quinsey and colleagues (Quinsey, Harris, et al., 1998; Quinsey et al., 2006) found that the presence of psychosis, particularly schizophrenia, was negatively related to violence risk among offenders. Consistent with community samples, however, alcohol abuse seriously elevated violence risk. The group concluded:

We believe these discrepancies can be explained by the fact that our sample was (because of past history of violence) at high risk for

future violence compared with a sample from the general population and that among high-risk samples, many nonschizophrenic
offenders are likely to be personality disordered. (Quinsey et al.,
2006, p. 113)

So what conclusions can be drawn from what is known about the
base rates of violence among persons with mental disorders? Persons
diagnosed with a major mental illness who are not involved in the
criminal justice system are at somewhat higher risk for some violent
acts than persons with no diagnosis. However, contrary to popular
belief, the vast majority of persons with mental illness do not engage
in violence of any kind. Substance abuse is a greater risk factor for
violence than any mental illness. And finally, those with a history
of antisocial behavior are probably at higher risk for violence than
those with a diagnosis of a major mental disorder.

Empirically Supported Risk Factors

Broadly speaking, mental disorder and substance abuse both relate
to risk of violence. However, when conducting risk assessments
with patients with mental disorders, the task is less a matter of simply determining whether mental disorder is present and more a
matter of closely examining how the present disorder relates to
risk. Thus, we first discuss risk factors related in some way to the
mental disorder.

Risk Factors Specific to Mental Disorder

It has become clear to mental health professionals that a diagnosis
alone provides very little information relative to risk. Diagnoses are
much too broad, and within-group heterogeneity is much too great,
for a diagnosis alone to provide substantial information relevant to
risk. Therefore, researchers have increasingly investigated specific
symptoms. One conclusion with general acceptance is that positive
symptoms (the presence of disordered responses or behaviors, e.g.,
hallucinations) may be related to violence, but negative symptoms
(i.e., the absence of expected responses or behaviors such as speech
or emotional expression) usually are not (Shah, 1993; Swanson

et al., 2006). For example, flat affect, by itself, appears to have no relationship to violence.

Probably the two most common positive psychotic symptoms are delusions and hallucinations. When someone is found NGRI due to a psychotic disorder, delusional thinking is among the most common reasons. Experts generally agree that most violence perpetrated by psychotic individuals is not directly precipitated by delusions; however, a minority of this behavior may be (Appelbaum, Robbins, & Monahan, 2000; P. J. Taylor, 1985). Although delusions among patients certainly vary, two broad types have evoked considerable concern. One type involves perceiving a specific threat that in reality does not exist; another type involves perceiving that an outside entity is attempting to take control of one's mind. These have become known as threat/control override delusions, or TCOs. A number of studies were conducted on the relationship between TCOs and violent behavior. Results appeared to demonstrate that TCOs are related to violence (Link & Stueve, 1994), and subsequent research indicated that patients with TCO symptoms were twice as likely to report violence than those with other symptoms of psychosis (Swanson et al., 1996). Chronic schizophrenic patients who behaved violently were significantly more likely to report persecutory delusions than their nonviolent counterparts (Cheung, Schweitzer, Crowley, & Tuckwell, 1997). Link, Monahan, Stueve, and Cullen (1999) reported a study conducted in Israel demonstrating that the prevalence of violence rose steadily along with scores on a scale designed to measure TCOs. Their analysis suggested that other psychotic symptoms were associated with violence simply because they covaried with TCOs.

Just as it appeared that data consistently supported the link between TCOs and violent behavior, evidence to the contrary emerged in the large-scale MacArthur Violence Risk Assessment Study. In 1998, Steadman and colleagues reported that the prevalence of violence among discharged psychiatric patients was not significantly different from the prevalence in a group of community controls unless substance abuse was involved. Further study by the MacArthur group failed to support the link between TCOs and violence (Appelbaum et al., 2000).

Several ideas have emerged regarding how to reconcile these apparently incompatible results. In a study examining schizophrenic patients who had been found NGRI, researchers (Stompe, Ortwein-Swoboda, & Schanda, 2004) found TCO delusions to be associated with severe violence. More recently, Teasdale, Silver, and Monahan (2006) found that in a mixed-sex sample, males were distinctly more apt than females to be violent in response to TCOs. Several of the previous studies had sampled males only, and there seemed to be a distinct possibility that in a mixed-sex sample, results from each sex canceled each other out. The researchers went on to suggest other potential moderating variables, such as race, culture, ethnicity, and socioeconomic status that needed further research. They concluded, "The results of this study suggest that a 'one-size-fits-all' main effects approach to risk assessment may be unwarranted" (p. 656).

There are a few other considerations that make it difficult to draw firm conclusions about the role of TCOs in the MacArthur findings. First, a significant portion (almost one third) of potential subjects declined to participate in the follow-up research. There is a possible interaction between consent to research participation, lower violence potential, and treatment compliance; however, the authors took several steps to examine the impact of selection effects as a possible confound in their results (see Monahan et al., 2001). Second, it is unclear exactly to what extent patients were medication-compliant when discharged from the hospital and throughout the follow-up. Third, it is unclear to what degree the TCO symptoms were in remission when patients were discharged from the hospital. Even with very successful psychiatric treatment, delusions frequently remain present to some degree. When asked, the individual may still affirm the delusional belief, though describe it as more of a concern in the past or a less pressing preoccupation at present. Presumably, these patients would be less likely to act on such delusions. Therefore, before dismissing TCOs as a significant risk factor, it will be important (for researchers studying TCOs in general and for clinicians considering TCOs in specific cases) to understand whether TCOs that remain untreated (or treatment-resistant) are predictive of violent behavior. Even some of the researchers who found no support for TCOs as a risk factor in the MacArthur data argued that delusional beliefs can most certainly lead to violence in individual cases and should not be ignored (Appelbaum et al., 2000; Monahan, 2003).

The second most common psychotic symptom addressed in the literature is hallucinations, particularly those that involve commands. Data on the relationship between command hallucinations and violence are rather sparse and appear mixed. Earlier writers concluded that, even in the case of violent command hallucinations, people rarely followed the commands (Cheung et al., 1997; Goodwin, Alderson, & Rosenthal, 1971; McNeil, 1994; Zisook, Byrd, Kuck, & Jeste, 1995). Later, McNeil, Eisner, and Binder (2000) found that command hallucinations were related to violent behavior, but only in conjunction with other psychotic symptoms. This would be consistent with other studies suggesting that people were more apt to comply when the hallucination was in the context of a delusional belief (Junginger, 1995). In a review of the literature, Bjorkly (2002) found confounded results, as well as inconclusive evidence for an interaction between delusions and hallucinations. Before drawing any conclusions about hallucinatory commands, it would be important to investigate the specific content and tone of these commands, as well as the individual's beliefs about the source of the commands (Barrowcliff & Haddock, 2006).

The one risk factor on which there is almost universal agreement in the literature is comorbid substance abuse (Corrigan & Watson, 2005; Hiday, 2006; Monahan, 2003; Monahan et al., 2001; Norko & Baranowski, 2005; Pihl & Peterson, 1993; Silver, 2006; Silver, Mulvey, & Monahan, 1999; Swanson, 1994; Swanson et al., 1990, 2002). This appears to raise the risk of violent behavior regardless of other diagnoses or evident symptoms.

Results from the MacArthur studies suggest that a diagnosis of personality disorder, particularly one with antisocial features, is associated with a higher risk of violence than is a major mental illness (Monahan, 2003; Monahan et al., 2001). Of particular concern is the construct of psychopathy, generally found to be strongly correlated with violent behavior. Estimates suggest that among patients with a major mental illness, substantial psychopathic features (high PCL-R scores) are present in anywhere from 1% to 25% of cases (Crocker et al., 2005). Research supports the conclusion that psychopathy (as measured by the PCL-R) is predictive of future violent behavior among psychiatric patients, as well as among the general offender population (Abushualeh & Abu-Akel, 2006; Appelbaum et al., 2000; Silver et al., 1999; Skeem & Mulvey, 2001 Tengström, Grann, Långström, & Kullgren, 2000). Research appears to favor Factor 2, the aspects of psychopathy related to an impulsive and antisocial lifestyle, as more strongly related to violence (Monahan, 2003). One study that did not reveal a relationship between psychopathy and violence among those with psychiatric illness (Crocker et al., 2005) measured psychopathic traits via self-report, as opposed to the PCL-R.

Risk Factors beyond Mental Disorder

Mental illness and its direct symptoms are not the sole risk factors to consider when conducting risk assessments among patients with mental disorders.

Neighborhood Context

Social and environmental issues are not to be ignored. Research clearly reveals that patients who are released into disadvantaged neighborhoods tend to have a higher probability of becoming involved in violence than patients released to less disadvantaged neighborhoods (Silver, 2000a, 2000b; Swanson et al., 2002). In fact, Silver et al. (1999) found that 23.3% of patients discharged to neighborhoods characterized by concentrated poverty committed acts of violence, compared to 9.9% of those discharged elsewhere. This problem is compounded by the fact that persons with serious mental illness are much more likely to live in disadvantaged neighborhoods (Silver, 2006). In analyzing the ECA data, Swanson (1994) also concluded that lower socioeconomic status was related to violence. Violence-related effects of release to a disadvantaged neighborhood may be confounded by such factors as easy access to illicit drugs, active sales efforts by drug dealers to exploit disability checks, victimization, chaotic interactions, and a general lack of social support.

Problematic Relationships

Impaired social support is another complex variable that appears related to violence risk (Estroff & Zimmer, 1994; Silver & Teasdale, 2005; Swanson et al., 1998). However, this becomes a very difficult variable to disentangle, and one about which it becomes difficult to make definitive statements, because this general variable includes several interacting factors, such as one's level of functioning, the quality of social relationships, frequency of contact, and context, to name but a few.

Institutional History

A history of violent behavior is very significant in any risk assessment. However, among those with major mental illness, a history of any arrest or psychiatric hospitalization is also important. In the ECA data analysis, researchers compared those with no mental illness to those with a major mental illness (schizophrenia or major affective disorder) and to those who had a major mental disorder and a problem with substance abuse. Those with a major mental illness were significantly more likely to be violent than those with no mental illness, and those with mental illness and substance abuse had a higher probability of violence than either of the other groups. However, within each of the groups, there were significant differences based on institutional history. Within each group, persons with no history of arrest or hospitalization had the lowest probability of violence, followed by those with a history of hospitalization only, followed by those with a history of arrest only. In each group, *the highest probability for violence was among those who had both a history of hospitalization and a history of arrest.* Within the group having major mental illness but who did not abuse substances, those with no history of arrest or hospitalization had a 13% 1-year probability of violence, whereas those with a record of both arrest and hospitalization had a 42% 1-year probability of violence (Swanson, 1994).

Current Mental Status

Any and all of the risk factors for violence among those with mental disorder—most especially those diagnosed with a major mental illness—must be considered in light of the patient's current mental status. In 1992, Link, Andrews, and Cullen found that for persons with active psychosis, many of the established risk factors applied; however, those not currently suffering from a psychotic disorder may be at no greater risk for violence than the average person in the community. Depending on the exact nature of the legal proceedings, the trier of fact may be most concerned about *imminent* risk rather than general risk over a lifetime.

Using Specialty Instruments to Examine Risk Factors

In determining whether someone presents a significant risk for violence based on a mental disorder, the first step in the process may be to determine diagnosis. For purposes of diagnosis only, a number of standard psychological tests or structured diagnostic interviews, familiar to most clinicians, may be helpful. Although these may assist in clarifying the presence of psychopathology, they have little *direct* bearing on violence risk.

In considering the use of a specialty instrument, the evaluator needs to carefully assess the focus: Is it on violence risk assessment in general (where mental disorder may be one factor), or is it on violence specifically stemming from the mental illness? In considering correctional decisions such as parole, risk in general (regardless of etiology) would probably be the primary focus. However, risk questions related to civil commitment—that is, commitment for psychiatric treatment—will almost always require a focus on risk that stems directly from mental disorder. Statutes often contain language similar to that used in the Insanity Defense Reform Act of 1984, directing courts to establish that "the person is presently suffering from a mental disease or defect *as a result of which* his release would create a substantial risk of bodily injury to another person or serious damage to property of another" (18 USCS §4246; italics added). This would seem to clearly imply a nexus between the mental disease or defect and the perceived risk.

Some currently available guides for structured professional judgment (e.g., the HCR-20) are geared more toward the clinically impaired population than others. However, the MacArthur group developed one instrument specifically for psychiatric patients. Their Iterative Classification Tree (ICT) resulted from a study of 900 psychiatric patients who were released to the community (see Monahan et al., 2001). It was predicated on "an interactive and contingent model of violence, one that allows many different combinations of risk factors to classify a person as high or low risk"

(Monahan, 2003, p. 534). By using a classification tree approach, the developers were able to go beyond a simple list of questions asked of participants or an algorithm that combines variables to yield a single numerical answer. The ICT has combined five different predictive models, allowing for different pathways through which people may become violent (Monahan, Steadman, Appelbaum, et al., 2005, 2006; Monahan, Steadman, Robbins, et al., 2005). Such calculations are beyond the capability of most practicing clinicians, but the necessary software is now commercially available (see Monahan et al., 2007; Monahan, Steadman, Appelbaum, et al., 2005).

However, as we've emphasized elsewhere in the text, evaluators should be cautioned against blind reliance on any actuarial instrument, even one as well developed as the ICT, to assess risk. Monahan (2003 p. 536) described the ICT procedure as one of the empirically derived "tools that support, rather than replace, the exercise of clinical judgment."

Idiographic Risk and Individualized Assessment

Among all types of violence risk assessment in forensic contexts, none necessitates thorough anamnestic analysis more than those addressing risk due to mental disorder. Despite the arguments for the superiority of pure actuarial risk assessments (Hilton, Harris, & Rice, 2006; Quinsey, Harris, et al., 1998; Quinsey et al., 2006), these rarely suffice to evaluate the risk of a psychotic person committing a violent behavior for a psychotic reason over a particular span of time and under specific circumstances. To illustrate the role of idiographic assessment in risk assessment with psychiatric patients, we present the following case.

Vignette

CH was a 42-year-old male found NGRI for detonating an explosive device that resulted in a death. He had a diagnosis of schizophrenia, and, in response to his delusional beliefs that he had been sent by Jesus Christ to stop a Jewish conspiracy against Christianity, he attempted to bomb a large synagogue. Although his explosive device only partially detonated and relatively little damage was done to the building, a female bystander was killed.

CH was raised in a close family, did very well in school, and was married for 4 years during his early 20s. Although he had been hospitalized on three previous occasions, this was his first encounter with the criminal justice system. His score on the PCL-R was low, he had never been diagnosed with a personality disorder, and he had no history of substance abuse. Although his bomb malfunctioned on this occasion, he had been a munitions expert in the military and was highly skilled in the use of weapons and explosives. He continued to say that it was his mission to stop the "Jewish conspiracy" by any means possible. He refused psychotropic medication, and, given that he presented no immediate threat within the secure forensic hospital, there was no justification for involuntary treatment.

Applying actuarial methods using the most well-researched risk factors, CH would appear to be in the low-risk category. His VRAG score would, at most, fall in Bin 2, indicating only a 10% probability of recidivism over the next 10 years. Would a recommendation for immediate release back to the community be appropriate? Could an evaluator reasonably opine that he was at low risk for violence if released to live in the same circumstances he lived in just prior to the offense? He had only one substantial risk factor: his delusional belief. Yet, he still strongly endorsed this belief on which he had previously acted, and stated clearly his perceived need to continue acting on the belief until he completed what he emphasized was his God-ordained mission. Based on recent history, his risk appeared very high and the consequences potentially lethal.

One might argue that the case of CH is unique, and we would agree in most respects. However, only with an idiographic assessment can one identify this type of unique factor that may have considerable bearing upon violence risk. Although scientifically derived risk factors and instruments are crucial to risk assessment, it would be folly to ignore risk and protective factors unique to an individual. It would also be important to consider the potential frequency and severity of violence that might occur.

Factors Specific to Mental Disorder

Any anamnestic assessment will involve a careful review of the individual's history, with specific attention to all issues surrounding violent or potentially violent behavior. By their vary nature, many of the factors identified will be unique. However, there are five issues of particular importance.

1. *In what way is the disorder related to the violent behavior?* The relationship may be very direct, as in the case of CH. However, it is also possible that there is little, if any, relationship. For example, consider the case of a man who has an erotomanic delusion about a famous female athlete. He has traveled widely to watch her compete, written her passionate letters, and told a number of associates that they are secretly married. However, he has never approached or threatened her in any way. Yet he has a history of significant violent behavior; he supports himself by selling cocaine and has been involved in a number of violent encounters with others in the drug trade. For legal purposes, one could probably conclude that the man has a history of "violence and mental disorder," but not that he is "violent as a result of mental disease or defect."

   Finally, there are some occasional cases in which violence and mental disorder appear to be inversely related. One of us evaluated an individual who had a substantial history of violence in the context of organized criminal activity, some of which involved contract killings. However, he began to experience psychotic episodes, and, when psychotic, he would become quite withdrawn and seemed incapable of engaging in routine social contact, let alone his usual criminal activities.

2. *What is the pattern of mental illness in this person?* Does it tend to cycle in any predictable way? For example, if the person suffers from bipolar disorder with psychotic features, it is probable that delusional thinking occurs only during times of manic or depressive episodes. Is substance abuse a factor? If so, does it precipitate a violent episode? Is it the trigger that precipitates noncompliance with treatment? Does the individual engage in violence whether or not he or she has been abusing substances?

3. *In what context does problem behavior occur?* What stressors tend to trigger mental decompensation, treatment noncompliance, or violence in this individual? What social connections

are available? Are these helpful or harmful? Do degrees of structure in the environment make a difference? Is the individual focused on a particular victim or type of victim? For example, someone may have a delusion focused on a specific public figure. In the federal criminal justice system, the president of the United States is a common focus. In such instances, an evaluator may find that the individual is not at risk for violence to anyone else. Or the individual's past violence may have been directed toward a single target who is no longer available.

4. *What has the response to treatment been?* What types of treatment, if any, has the patient tried, and with what effect? Is the response rapid or slow? Is treatment effective with all critical symptoms? For example, it is not unusual for a patient's thought disorder and hallucinations to respond quickly, yet delusional thinking may be more treatment-resistant and less obvious absent the other symptoms. What has the person's pattern of treatment compliance been in the past? History of treatment compliance may be a better predictor of future compliance than insight or plans expressed in the moment.

5. *What is the person's pattern of violent or potentially violent behavior?* Is it opportunistic, and, if so, what provides the ideal opportunity? Is it apparently sudden and unprovoked, or can early triggers be identified? Is it related to treatment compliance? A very important concern, often overlooked, is whether potentially violent behavior is escalating. Take the case of an individual who harbors some delusional thoughts about the nefarious conduct of federal judges. He is now in jail charged with attempting to bring an unauthorized deadly weapon into a federal building. In examining his history, it appears that a year or so earlier he began talking to anyone who would listen about corruption in the federal court. He then wrote letters to the newspaper and eventually began writing angry, but not threatening, letters to certain judges. This was followed by a period in which he spent many of his days sitting in federal courtrooms "monitoring" the proceedings and following up with letters demanding certain changes. He was arrested trying to evade officers at a federal

courthouse metal detector, where officers found he had two concealed and loaded pistols. His only comment was, "Talking has failed, it is time for action." Although at this point the individual has harmed no one and made no direct threats, his pattern is of obvious concern.

Risk Communication regarding Patients with Mental Disorders

In risk assessment with patients who suffer from mental disorders, there are generally two elements required: mental disorder and risk. To what extent the risk must arise from the mental disorder is often an issue for the trier of fact to determine. However, an evaluator should address that relationship.

This is one type of risk assessment in which addressing the ultimate issue may be mandatory, not optional. Many hospitals that house potentially dangerous patients (whether civil or forensic) have established some specific procedure to determine if a patient should be discharged or if petition for involuntary commitment may be in order. Sometimes there are formal panels of mental health professionals; sometimes only the treating clinician makes a decision. A formal system has the advantage of ensuring that records are carefully reviewed and risk factors are addressed. It also assures that consultation takes place, and it serves to separate the roles of forensic evaluator and treatment provider. However the decision is made, if the decision is simply to discharge the patient, the mental health professional has *made* the ultimate issue decision. This is a very reasonable procedure, as it would be totally impractical to submit every patient who is to be discharged to a court for final determination. It is nonetheless important for clinicians to realize that they have made the decision that a patient's risk for violence is sufficiently low that the patient may be returned to the community.

In cases where civil commitment is sought or under review, or if discharge of a committed patient is at issue, clinicians may have no choice but to address the ultimate issue. For example, federal statutes mandate that such an opinion be filed with the court in order to initiate commitment procedures:

If the director of a facility in which a person is hospitalized certifies that a person . . . is presently suffering from a mental disease or defect as a result of which his release would create a substantial risk of bodily injury to another person or serious damage to property of another. . . he shall transmit the certificate to the clerk of the court for the district in which the person is confined. (18 USCS §4246)

If the director is not a clinician, that individual generally requires this opinion from an appropriate clinician. Discharge statutes contain similar language:

Discharge: When the director of the facility in which a person is hospitalized pursuant to subsection (d) determines that the person has recovered from his mental disease or defect to such an extent that his release would no longer create a substantial risk of bodily injury to another person or serious damage to property of another, he shall promptly file a certificate to that effect with the clerk of the court that ordered the commitment. (18 USCS §4246)

In the case of persons found NGRI, the criteria for discharge are parallel:

Discharge: When the director of the facility in which an acquitted person is hospitalized pursuant to subsection (e) determines that the person has recovered from his mental disease or defect to such an extent that his release, or his conditional release under a prescribed regimen of medical, psychiatric, or psychological care or treatment, would no longer create a substantial risk of bodily injury to another person or serious damage to property of another, he shall promptly file a certificate to that effect with the clerk of the court that ordered the commitment. (18 USCS §4243)

Many jurisdictions have similar requirements.

Of course, when evaluators *are* communicating with courts or other decision makers, it will be helpful to follow the general guidance included in Chapter 7. Note that, in the risk communication role of educator, it may be helpful to dispel many of the public misconceptions we mentioned earlier in this chapter (e.g., the impression that those with mental illness are inevitably at high risk for violence). Judges who regularly preside over civil commitments are quite unlikely to need education of this type. However, when presenting risk information in a context in which mental illness is less often a central issue (e.g., some parole or probation settings), more education might be in order.

Risk Management

Outpatient commitment, by definition, involves some type of risk management plan. A variety of studies have come to the conclusion that such plans, applied over time, can reduce violent behavior (Hiday, 2006; Hodgins, 2001; Swanson et al., 2000; Swartz et al., 2001). However, often a major difficulty is the dearth of adequate services to make the plan a success (Hiday, 2006; Hodgins, 2001; Petrila, Ridgely, & Borum, 2003). A further difficulty in interpreting and applying the promising data on outpatient commitment is the variety of complex outpatient commitment schemes available across jurisdictions (for a complete discussion of the many options and the advantages and disadvantages of the various alternatives, see Winick & Kress, 2003). Finally, there is the issue of coercion and the way coercion can impact treatment. This has ethical and legal implications as well as concerns regarding outcome. Petrila (2004, p. 14) has aptly characterized the research on this issue as in the "embryonic stage."

In formulating a risk management plan for those suffering from a mental disorder, the issue of psychotropic medication is likely to be paramount. Sometimes medication is a somewhat indirect factor, in that a specific symptom places the individual at risk for violent behavior, as in the case of CH, who engaged in violent conduct due in large part to a psychotic delusion. If medication eliminates or reduces the intensity of the delusion, it may be an important intervention. Additionally, some research is now emerging comparing the effectiveness of various psychotropics in the direct reduction of violence (Krakowski, Czobor, Citrome, Bank, & Cooper, 2006; Swanson, Swartz, & Elbogen, 2004; Swanson, Swartz, Elbogen, & Van Dorn, 2004). However, before relying heavily on medication as an element of a community risk management plan, the evaluator needs to carefully investigate the degree to which such treatment can be required in a particular jurisdiction. For some individuals, history may indicate that simply having a requirement in place and the knowledge that someone is monitoring it may be sufficient to assure compliance. For others, this will not be the case.

A special challenge for risk management planners is the person who has a major mental illness, but who also scores high on psychopathy. Scholars debate the extent to which psychopathy may be responsive to treatment (for contrasting perspectives, see D'Silva et al., 2004; Gacono, Nieberding, Owen, Rubel, & Bodholdt, 2001; Salekin, 2002; Skeem et al., 2002; Wong & Hare, 2005). Salekin suggested some optimism after a review of diverse treatment studies with antisocial and psychopathic patients. However, Wong and Hare criticized the selection and methodologies of the various studies reviewed. Also in 2002, Skeem et al. presented data suggesting that sufficient dosages of some types of treatment (i.e., some combination of verbal therapies and medication) could reduce violence potential among psychiatric patients who were high in psychopathy. However, it is unclear whether any positive results among the dually diagnosed patients stemmed from changes to psychopathic traits or to other important risk factors relating to other psychopathology. Given the current state of the literature, one cannot identify a demonstrated, effective treatment for psychopathy per se (Wong & Hare, 2005). However, a high score on the PCL-R does not preclude the possibility that an individual has other important risk factors for which effective interventions are clearly available. For example, a patient who scores high on psychopathy may also suffer from a psychotic disorder, and an anamnestic evaluation may demonstrate that the patient's violent behavior has stemmed primarily from some delusional belief. In such a case there would be a key risk factor potentially amenable to treatment, whether or not the psychopathic traits remained.

Despite the divergent perspectives, it is certainly safe to say that there is no basis on which to withhold treatment from individuals scoring high in psychopathy, as some bleak conventional wisdom might sometimes suggest. And, even without a psychopathy specific treatment, a high score on the PCL-R does not preclude the possibility that an individual has other important (or even *more* important) risk factors for which effective interventions are clearly available.

To summarize, risk management planning for patients with mental disorder will depend on carefully reviewing all nomothetic and idiographic risk factors, formulating a strategy to address each in a feasible fashion, considering protective factors that may assist in this endeavor, and recognizing factors that may not be amenable to available interventions. The plan needs to be formulated with the particular legal constraints of the jurisdiction in mind.

CHAPTER

10

Risk Assessment with Sexual Offenders

Of all the areas of risk assessment, the largest single body of research is directed toward sexual offenders. Additional studies appear in print almost daily. Therefore, please understand that this chapter in no way purports to provide a comprehensive review of the literature. Rather, the goal is to sample critical data and provide a framework for evaluators.

Defining the Risk Assessment Question

Individuals who commit sexual offenses have long been viewed with special fear and loathing by the larger society. Since 1990, the number of sexual offenders has risen faster than any other criminal population except drug offenders (LaFond, 2005). On an average day, there are over 200,000 sexual offenders overseen by some correctional agency in this country; of those, 60% are treated in a community setting (Stalans, 2004).

In a variety of contexts, and through a variety of mechanisms, evaluators may receive requests to evaluate the risk of reoffense that a sexual offender poses. Like other violent offenders, those with a history of sexual crimes may be considered for probation or parole, and evaluators can approach these cases following the violence risk assessment model described throughout this book (e.g., defining the exact referral question, considering empirical and idiographic risk factors, communicating risk, and considering appropriate risk management). There will be one important addition: Evaluators must also consider the research-supported risk factors for sexual reoffense, summarized later in this chapter. Certain sex offenders may also present as part of other populations—for example, some forensic psychiatric patients may have histories of sexual offenses—and evaluators should bear in mind the data and guidance specific to both sexual offenders and other relevant populations (e.g., patients with mental illnesses; see Chapter 9).

However, an increasingly common venue for assessing risk among sexual offenders has emerged, given the widespread implementation of legislation related to civil commitment of sexual offenders, also called sexually violent predator legislation (for overviews, see Campbell, 2004; Doren, 2002; H. A. Miller, Amenta, & Conroy, 2005). Because this legislation has prompted so many sex offender risk assessments, and because these risk assessments involve unique considerations not found in other sex offender risk assessments, we devote particular attention throughout this chapter to SVP evaluations.

The Legal Context for Sexually Violent Predator Risk Assessments

From the 1930s through the 1970s, a number of states relied on sexual psychopath statutes in an effort to control or rehabilitate sexual offenders. These laws generally allowed for commitment to a treatment facility in lieu of criminal prosecution. However, by the late 1970s, these were rarely applied. The laws had fallen into disfavor due to increasing skepticism toward the effectiveness of treatment for sexual offenders, as well as opposition from prominent legal and professional associations (Brakel & Cavanaugh, 2000). Simultaneously, however, public concern about sexual offenders remained strong, becoming particularly acute following a number of high-profile sexual crimes.

In 1990, Washington passed the first of the SVP statutes (Rev. Code Wash. [ARCW] §71.09.010). In contrast to the earlier sexual psychopath laws that were applied in lieu of criminal penalty, SVP statutes generally applied *after* a term of imprisonment was completed. Although presented in terms of civil commitment, most SVP statutes did not specifically require the presence of a mental illness, nor was providing treatment a central component. By the year 2000, sixteen states had enacted such legislation; two additional jurisdictions have since done so. These laws are primarily applied to adult males who commit rape or molest children.

Civil libertarians were quick to challenge SVP statutes in the courts. They contended that the statutes were unconstitutional due to the absence of a requirement for mental illness, the alleged punitive nature of this civil commitment, the issue of double jeopardy, and the imposition of an ex post facto law. In *Kansas v. Hendricks* (1997), the U.S. Supreme Court ruled that the Kansas SVP statute did meet constitutional rigor. Specifically, the Court declared that the act was civil and therefore not punitive, and that, as such, it did not constitute double jeopardy, nor did it violate ex post facto provisions. Most important to mental health professionals were positions the court articulated regarding mental disorder and treatment requirements. The Kansas statute had used the term "mental abnormality or personality disorder," and the justices said:

> Contrary to Hendricks' assertion, the term "mental illness" is devoid of any talismanic significance. Not only do "psychiatrists disagree widely and frequently on what constitutes mental illness," *Ake v. Oklahoma*, 470 U.S. 68 (1985), but the court itself has used a variety of expressions to describe the mental condition of those properly subject to civil confinement. (*Kansas v. Hendricks*, 1997, p. 2080)

Nonetheless, the Court left no doubt that some disorder was an essential basis for the civil commitment:

> The Kansas Act is plainly of a kind with other civil commitment statutes: It requires a finding of future dangerousness, and then links that finding to the existence of a "mental abnormality" or "personality disorder" that makes it difficult, if not impossible, for the person to control his dangerous behavior. The precommitment

requirement of a "mental abnormality" or "personality disorder" is consistent with the requirements of these other statutes that we up-held in that it narrows the class of person eligible for confinement to those who are unable to control their dangerousness. (p. 2080)

In regard to essential treatment, the Court went on to say:

While we have upheld civil commitment statutes that aim both to incapacitate and to treat . . . we have never held that the Constitu-tion prevents the State from civilly detaining those for whom no treatment is available, but who nevertheless pose a danger to others. (p. 2084)

State statutes have approached the commitment of SVPs in a va-riety of ways, but appear to have three requirements in common: (1) The person must have some mental, personality, or behavioral ab-normality; (2) the abnormality must somehow interfere with the in-dividual's capacity for behavioral control; and (3) as a result, the person must present a significant risk to society (H. A. Miller et al., 2005). This risk must be specific to *sexual* offenses and not simply a risk for general reoffending. In all but one jurisdiction, commitment results in confinement, usually long term, to a secure inpatient set-ting (the exception is Texas, where only outpatient commitment is permitted). From 1990 until 2003, only 5% of those committed had been released (LaFond, 2003).

On other issues state statutes and/or case law may differ, and it is important for evaluators to maintain current knowledge about their jurisdiction. For instance, most states use the term *predator* or *preda-tory act*. In Texas, for example, predatory act is defined as one that victimizes a stranger, casual acquaintance, or someone with whom the relationship was established specifically for the purpose of vic-timization (Texas Health & Safety Code, 2000). Thus, this defini-tion eliminates the majority of incest offenses from consideration.

Although the Supreme Court was very clear that SVP proceed-ings were to be considered civil and not criminal, states differ on how closely specific procedures conform to those utilized in regular civil commitments. The issue of whether a defendant must be legally competent for SVP proceedings has arisen in several jurisdictions. The Supreme Court of Texas overruled lower courts in saying that, given the civil nature of SVP proceedings, a defendant was not entitled to a determination of competence, as would be the case in a criminal trial (*In re Fisher*, 2005). On the other hand, Florida courts have ruled that, under the Ryce Act, a defendant is entitled to be competent to testify for commitment proceedings, and if found not competent, competence must be restored before the matter can go forward (*In re Branch*, 2004).

It would also be important to know in a specific jurisdiction what, if any, Fifth Amendment rights a defendant retains and when a defendant is entitled to counsel prior to an evaluation. Professional guidelines indicate that a psychologist should not conduct a forensic evaluation until the individual has access to counsel (Committee on Ethical Guidelines for Forensic Psychologists, 1991). Most states assure a right to counsel once official judicial action has been initiated. However, risk assessments are often conducted as part of the process to determine whether a petition for commitment will be initiated; under such circumstances, the right to counsel may not exist (*Beasley v. Molett*, 2002).

A first step, then, for professionals planning to conduct an SVP risk assessment is to make certain they have *current* knowledge of the statutes, case law, and rules of the jurisdiction in which the evaluation will be done. The legal landscape is ever shifting; new laws are passed and new case law is decided.

Base Rates and Nomothetic Data

Once an evaluator is clear as to the precise risk assessment referral question and the rules of the jurisdiction in which it is raised, the next step is to examine available scientific data, beginning with base rates for the type of risk involved. Ideally, the base rate would provide a figure against which to compare a specific offender's likelihood of reoffending. However, the already challenging process of identifying relevant base rates (see Chapter 4) becomes even more challenging when the issue is risk of sexual reoffending. Reputable, peer-reviewed studies of sex offense base rates have reached very different conclusions. In 1989, Furby et al. reviewed research-documented rates of sexual reoffending that ranged from 0% to 50%. Hanson and Bussiere (1998) examined reconviction rates for sex offenders over 5 years and found the average to be 13.4%. Although the common perception is that sex offenders reoffend at phenomenally high rates, Heilbrun, Nezu, Keeney, Chung, and Wasserman (1998) examined Bureau of Justice statistics from the mid-1990s and concluded that sex offenders violated parole no more often than other offenders. However, when type of offender and follow-up period are examined, results may differ. Prentky, Lee, et al. (1997) studied 136 rapists after their release and observed a 9% reoffense rate in the first year; however, the authors estimated that the reoffense rate reached 39% by the 25th year. In a comparable study of child molesters, these researchers found a recidivism rate of 6% in the first year, but estimated a 52% reoffense rate by the 25th year. In a recent longitudinal study in Canada that spanned 25 years, Langevin and colleagues (2004) found that 3 in 5 sex offenders (60%) had reoffended, as measured by charges or convictions for a sexual reoffense. However, this figure increased to 4 out of 5 (80%) if all offenses and undetected sexual offenses were examined.

Problems in establishing recidivism base rates for sex offenders are complex. Such data are often presented as though sex offenders are a homogeneous group. This assumes that the drunken felon who commits a rape of opportunity in the process of a home burglary would have the same sexual reoffense rate as the otherwise upstanding athletic coach who molests dozens of children on his sports teams. Yet in reality, base rates often represent averages of diverse samples. Recent literature has attempted to improve precision by subtyping sexual offenders by type of victim, motive, psychopathology, etiology, and the other variables that are relatively accessible for research purposes (Campbell, 2004; Lalumiere, Harris, Quinsey, & Rice, 2005). Research has indicated some significant differences among subgroups of sexual offenders grouped by these approaches, including in rates of recidivism (e.g., Doren & Epperson, 2001; Furby et al., 1989; Hanson & Bussiere, 1998; Rice & Harris, 1997).

As illustrated by the Langevin et al. (2004) study, the time period over which recidivism is studied can be an important consideration in the results. Sex offenders tend to reoffend over a broader range of time than most other groups of offenders (Hanson, Steffey, & Gauthier, 1993; G. T. Harris, Rice, & Quinsey, 1998). Given that the majority of research on reoffense rates covers 5 years or less, the resulting base rates may be gross underestimates (Doren, 1998).

Perhaps the most significant variable affecting calculation of base rates is the criterion utilized. Are researchers measuring recidivism using convictions only, convictions and charges, self-report, or other, less official data? Although one might argue that convictions are the most rigorous criterion, there is general agreement that using convictions alone results in serious underestimates (Barbaree & Marshall, 1988). Past research has demonstrated that a significant portion of the offenses committed by chronic sexual offenders goes unreported (Abel et al., 1987; Doren, 1998). Other offenses are dismissed for insufficient evidence or plea-bargained down to a charge that appears nonsexual. Finally, the very small subset of the most serious of sexual offenses (those resulting in murder) are often classified as homicide (Quinsey et al., 2006).

Given the grave difficulty of calculating a reliable base rate estimate for sexual reoffending, such figures should be used only with great caution. Prentky and Burgess (2000, p. 113) aptly summarized the dilemma:

> Perhaps the simplest summary is that consideration of base rate data is indeed critical to accurate decision-making, but that (1) the unreliability of such data on sex offenders compromises their usefulness and (2) the overarching goal of community safety may place a higher premium on inaccuracy.

Empirically Supported Risk Factors

Though accurate base rates of sexual reoffending remain somewhat elusive, substantial research documents factors that relate to recidivism among sexual offenders. Several variables have demonstrated robust relationships with reoffense over time and across studies. If a risk assessment is to be grounded in science, it is essential to examine key factors empirically associated with reoffense.

Prior Sexual Offenses

Not surprisingly, a past history of sexual offending is consistently one of the strongest correlates with recidivism (Hanson & Bussiere, 1998; Prentky, Knight, & Lee, 1997; Quinsey, 1986; Rice, Harris, & Quinsey, 1990). Some would argue that the predictive history should be limited strictly to sexual offenses. However, following a broad review of the literature, Quinsey and colleagues (2006) argued that general violent offenses are just as accurate as predictors of sexual recidivism. While reviewing offense history, it is important to examine the pattern of offending, since chronic sexual offenders tend to repeat the same type of offense (Quinsey et al., 2006).

Deviant Sexual Interests

A second factor with substantial empirical support is deviant sexual interests (Hanson & Bussiere, 1998; G. T. Harris et al., 2003; Proulx et al., 1997; Rice et al., 1990). Deviant interests are generally considered to be a sexual interest in children or a special interest in hurting or humiliating one's victim. However, one criticism of examining deviant sexual interests is that the construct is too loosely defined (Campbell, 2004). Though such methods may not be available to most evaluators, researchers often assess deviant interests using phallometric methods (i.e., the penile plethysmograph), which creates further controversy. Use of the plethysmograph has been criticized due to the lack of standardized stimuli and procedures, the lack of uniform training requirements for plethysmographers, the variability of data interpretation, and the lack of norms for subgroups of sexual offenders (Marshall & Fernandez, 2000; Prentky & Burgess, 2000). Phallometric testing appears much more useful for identifying child molesters than identifying rapists (Hanson & Bussiere, 1998; Marshall & Fernandez, 2000), although it is also possible for individuals to fake results of phallometric testing, particularly if tested repeatedly (G. T. Harris et al., 1998; H. A. Miller et al., 2005). Posttreatment application of phallometric testing has generally failed to predict recidivism (Quinsey et al., 2006).

Other mechanical methods used to assess deviant interests include measures based on response time when viewing sexual stimuli (Abel, Huffman, Warberg, & Holland, 1998) and the polygraph (Ahmeyer, Heil, McKee, & English, 2000). However, research on these latter two methods has been directed more toward distinguishing subgroups of offenders based on past behavior rather than predicting future offenses (Beech, Fisher, & Thornton, 2003). Use of either the plethysmograph or the polygraph requires both special equipment and specially trained operators. One simple alternative to these methods is to draw inferences about deviant interests based on verified past behavior (e.g., repeated sexual offenses against children).

Psychopathy

A third risk factor often associated with sexual reoffending is psychopathy (Barbaree, Seto, Langton, & Peacock, 2001; Hanson & Bussiere, 1998; Hanson & Morton-Bourgon, 2004; Langton, Barbaree, Harkins, & Peacock, 2006; Serin, Mailloux, & Malcolm, 2001). As discussed in prior chapters, psychopathy is distinct from antisocial personality disorder (a much broader concept), and is most commonly measured by Hare's (1991, 2003) Psychopathy Checklist-Revised. While PCL-R scores correspond strongly with violent reoffense, research also demonstrates that they correlate significantly (though somewhat less so) with sexual recidivism. For example, in a sample of 178 released sex offenders, Quinsey, Rice, and Harris (1995) found PCL correlations of .33 with violent reoffending and .23 with sexual reoffending. An elevated PCL-R score is more likely to be associated with recidivism in rapists than in child molesters, as a much smaller proportion of child molesters are psychopathic (Hare, 2003; Porter et al., 2000; Rice & Harris, 1997). Again, a low score on the PCL-R does not demonstrate low risk; rather, a low score simply indicates that psychopathy is one risk factor the individual does not have. For example, very low PCL-R scores are not at all uncommon among child molesters who are otherwise law-abiding citizens with steady employment and no nonsexual criminal history (Porter et al., 2000). This is most likely the case because PCL-R scores are influenced by characteristics evidenced across a variety of life contexts. On the other hand, the rare individual who has a high score on the PCL-R and a pattern of deviant interests in young children is among those at highest risk for reoffending (Hildebrand, de Ruiter, & Vogel, 2004; Rice & Harris, 1997; Serin et al., 2001).

Antisocial Lifestyle

Beyond psychopathy, antisocial personality disorder, or a general antisocial lifestyle (e.g., impulsivity, rule violation, and reckless behavior) tends to correspond with sexual reoffense (Hanson & Morton-Bourgon, 2005). Numerous antisocial traits have been associated with sexual offending, particularly among rapists (Firestone, Bradford, Greenberg, & Serran, 2000). However, relying heavily on antisocial traits to assess the risk of sexual reoffending tends to cast too wide a net and overpredict reoffense. One difficulty is that sex offenders generally are more likely to recidivate with a nonsexual crime (Hanson & Morton-Bourgon, 2005). Although there may be good reason to assess risk for (and prevent) *any* violence, most SVP statutes specifically target sexual recidivism. As previously discussed, antisocial personality disorder is the most common diagnosis among incarcerated adult male offenders, with anywhere from 49% to 80% of inmates meeting the criteria (Cunningham & Reidy, 1998a). However, most of these individuals are never arrested for a sexual offense.

Age

Young age also relates to risk for sexual reoffending. Using a large, combined sample of released sex offenders, Hanson (2002) found that the highest risk for sexual reoffending was in young adulthood (18 to 30). However, this was more true for rapists than for child molesters; the rate of recidivism among child molesters declined much more slowly over time. Recidivism for any offender released after the age of 60 was less than 5%; however, very few in this sample were that old. Age at the onset of an individual's sexual offending is also related to risk. Much like the relationship between age and general violence, the younger the individual was at the time of the first offense, the more likely it is the person will reoffend (Hanson & Bussiere, 1998; Quinsey et al., 2006).

Sex and Relationship of Victim

Both the sex of the victim and the relationship of the victim to the perpetrator have been correlated with recidivism. Offenders who choose male victims and those who offend against strangers are more likely to reoffend (Hanson & Bussiere, 1998; Proulx et al., 1997). Offenders who have never been married or otherwise maintained a stable sexual relationship with an appropriate adult partner are also at higher risk (Hanson & Bussiere, 1998).

Past Failures

Finally, failure to cooperate with treatment providers (as evidenced by treatment rejection) or law enforcement officials (as evidenced by conditional release violation) appears to be related to future recidivism (Epperson et al., 1998; Hanson, 1998; Hanson & Bussiere, 1998; Hanson & Harris, 1998). However, this pattern should not be interpreted as affirming the effectiveness of any particular treatment nor as suggesting that a lack of treatment guarantees recidivism. Rather, the salient factor appears to be the offender's choice to refuse (or fail to meet) the requirements that past risk managers have imposed.

Dynamic Factors

The risk factors just described have been heavily researched over the past decade, yielding fairly consistent results. However, all of these factors are static in nature; that is, they are historical and unlikely to change over time. This makes them particularly valuable for a one-time assessment such as an initial commitment evaluation. However, they are not generally applicable for an additional evaluation focusing on change, nor are they helpful to an evaluator attempting to assess an individual's changing needs. Currently, research on dynamic risk factors for sexual reoffending is in its infancy. Preliminary results suggest that poor social supports, an emotional preoccupation with children, attitudes tolerant of sexual assault, antisocial lifestyles, hostility, poor self-management strategies, substance abuse, poor cooperation with supervision, employment instability, and sexual preoccupations are among the factors that likely relate to dynamic risk (Hanson & Harris, 2000; Hanson & Morton-Bourgon, 2004, 2005).

Dynamic risk factors can be further subdivided into stable dynamic and more acute dynamic. Stable dynamic factors are those that are subject to change but generally change slowly over time (e.g., intimacy deficits, impulsivity), whereas acute dynamic factors may change from day to day or even moment to moment (e.g., anger, severe emotional distress, intoxication). To measure some of the more dynamic variables, researchers Hanson and Harris (2001) are developing The Sex Offender Need Assessment Rating.

Misleading Risk Factors

A discussion of important sex offender risk factors would not be complete without a review of factors that *do not* relate to risk of recidivism. Over the years, evaluators conducting sex offender risk assessments have too often guided their evaluations by intuition, conventional wisdom, or the factors generally included in treatment protocols. Unfortunately, much of the conventional wisdom has received minimal, if any, research support. Among the most commonly used, but unsupported, risk factors are: verbally accepting responsibility for the offense, expressing empathy for the victim, expressing motivation for treatment, and completing sex offender treatment. Research has repeatedly found that the correlation between each of these factors and recidivism is close to zero (Hanson & Bussiere, 1998; Hanson & Morton-Bourgon, 2004, 2005; Marques, Wiederanders, Day, Nelson, & van Ommeren, 2005). Research has also repeatedly failed to establish a positive relationship between treatment goal completion and recidivism (Barbaree & Marshall, 1998; Quinsey, Khanna, & Malcolm, 1998; Rice, Harris, & Quinsey, 1991; Seto & Barbaree, 1999). Another factor commonly thought to predict recidivism is an abusive childhood, particularly if the abuse was sexual. However, though many sexual offenders report a history of childhood sexual abuse, the research has failed to support any relationship between childhood sexual abuse and sexual reoffense (Hanson & Bussiere, 1998; Hanson & Morton-Bourgon, 2004, 2005).

Instruments for Assessing Sex Offender Recidivism Risk

We have a wealth of data regarding risk factors for sexual reoffending, but lively debate continues regarding the most effective way of combining these data into an overall assessment of an individual's risk. As discussed in earlier chapters, the debate often compares clinical versus actuarial prediction, and the variety of actuarial instruments designed to measure sexual reoffense risk has made the debate particularly intense. Despite some arguments for a strict actuarial approach (Quinsey et al., 2006), others emphasize that research on actuarial devices for the assessment of risk in sexual offenders is in its infancy and would not meet either ethical or evidentiary standards currently held by the courts (Campbell, 2004; Otto & Heilbrun, 2002). Others have pointed out that actuarial instruments are not comprehensive and could not possibly address all the potential risk factors for a given individual in a given situation (Hanson, 1998).

A variety of instruments designed to assess the risk of sexual reoffending are described in Appendix A. At the time of this writing, the oldest of these instruments had been in use for less than 10 years, so we caution evaluators to review emerging research before using an instrument. Some devices initially looked very promising, but subsequent research reveals poor reliability or validity. For example, early research on the Minnesota Sex Offender Screening Tool-Revised (Epperson et al., 1998) suggested that the instrument was quite promising; however, later study called its predictive validity into question (Barbaree et al., 2001; Seto & Barbaree, 1999).

Some instruments (e.g., the STATIC-99) apply a strict algorithm to a set of static variables; others (e.g., the SVR-20) call for the clinician to make structured professional judgments based on a set of more general variables to be assessed. Although a few studies have compared the predictive validity of the various instruments, results have been inconsistent, and there are as yet insufficient data from which to draw definitive conclusions (Barbaree et al., 2001; Bartosh, Garby, Lewis, & Gray, 2003; de Vogel, de Ruiter, van Beek, & Mead, 2004; Rice & Harris, 1997; Stadtland, Hollweg, Kleindienst, Dietl, Reich, & Nedopil, 2005).

Because the results of actuarial instruments are presented in statistical or numeric terms, they may give the layperson the impression of excellent precision or scientific rigor. However, Campbell (2004) presented a detailed critique of the research and statistical basis of these instruments. Wollert (2006) applied Bayes's theorem to sexual recidivism rates by age and concluded that most actuarial instruments are reasonably accurate only for the youngest group of offenders. This is particularly concerning given that many SVP risk assessments are conducted with individuals who have already spent a number of years in prison.

Finally, the role that an instrument should play may depend on the exact nature of the evaluation. Regarding SVP statutes, most states commit only a very small percentage of sexual offenders released from confinement (Meyer, Molett, Richards, Arnold, & Latham, 2003). Is the objective of assessment identifying a relatively large group of fairly high-risk offenders (i.e., screening) or isolating a very small group that is at highest risk for reoffense (i.e., selecting)? If the object is the latter, an actuarial device such as the STATIC-99 may function best as a screening instrument prior to conducting more in-depth evaluation.

To date, numerous research efforts have been devoted to creating a number of actuarial instruments to assist in assessing sex offender risk. However, caution is recommended, as the instruments are still relatively new, additional research is constantly emerging, and most instruments are based on static variables. None allows for a comprehensive assessment of the risk presented by an individual sexual offender. In fact, despite the utility of data from group studies, it is impossible to say how accurately any actuarial instrument would predict the future behavior of a single individual (Berlin, Galbreath, Geary, & McGlone, 2003), in part because actuarial instruments do not take account of context or future circumstances. As of this writing, it is uncertain whether actuarial procedures are equally predictive across ethnicities (Langstrom, 2004).

Idiographic Risk Factors and Individualized Assessment

It is essential to rely on data drawn from group studies; it is also essential to go beyond data drawn from group studies and consider the individual sexual offender and context. Again, to endorse idiographic assessment is not to endorse assessment by way of feelings, intuition, or vague clinical impressions. Rather, idiographic assessment involves carefully reviewing the offender's history, particularly as related to sexual offenses, and considering the future circumstances into which the person is likely to be placed. One reasonable starting point involves considering *how* the empirically supported risk factors impact the specific person. For example, never having been married is one of the correlates of elevated risk for sexual reoffending (Hanson & Bussiere, 1998; Quinsey et al., 2006). Conversely, demonstrating the ability to maintain a long-term relationship with an appropriate adult partner is sometimes viewed as a protective factor. However, this group pattern must be examined in light of the individual's experiences. There may be instances in which a typically protective factor such as adult romantic relationships relates to risk in idiosyncratic ways. We have each evaluated several pedophilic offenders who engage in serial relationships with adult women, offending against the woman's children in every one of the relationships. In this instance, it seems misleading to consider the history of adult relationships a protective factor. Similarly, consider the unusual (though not unheard of) adult relationship in which the partners collaborate in committing sexual crimes. One of us evaluated an individual who had been married for 16 years, whose spouse professed her love for him and her intention to resume the relationship once he was released from prison. She described their sexual activity as both frequent and satisfying. Although the relationship initially appeared to be a protective factor, this appearance changed when it became clear that the wife also enticed child victims to their apartment and served as operator for the video camera recording the molestation. In another evaluation, a woman who appeared to be an accomplice in her boyfriend's sexual offenses against her children eventually acknowledged a long-standing pattern of abusing her children alone or with prior partners. In short, idiographic assessment acknowledges the possibility of instances in which well-established risk factors operate atypically and the possibility of unusual risk factors.

As noted earlier, past history of sexual offending is unquestionably a key element in predicting future risk. However, in individual cases evaluators may find it difficult to determine what to consider as past sexual offending. For example, should one include only charges of which the offender has been convicted? What about other sexual offenses, detailed in records, that were dismissed or not prosecuted for unknown reasons? What about new admissions? There is often some ambiguity when deciding which past-offending data to consider as relevant. The decision is generally based solely on professional judgment as to whether the evidence supporting past offenses is credible. When relying on offenses that did not result in convictions, it would, of course, be important to be clear in any report or testimony so that the trier of fact can determine if the evidence should be excluded. However, evaluators should keep in mind that in cases of general civil commitment, the individual may never have been convicted of any violent offense; yet other evidence of past behavior will surely be considered.

The age at which the offender first committed a sexual offense and his or her current age have a demonstrated relationship with potential recidivism. However, the individual's specific pattern of offending must be considered. For example, one of us recently evaluated an individual who admitted to numerous offenses against children, whose first known offense was at age 45, whose last offenses were at age 59, and who had been incarcerated since the last offense. Nomothetic data suggest that his age would leave him at relatively low risk. However, the fact that he began offending late in life and continued frequent offending regularly into his late 50s suggests that he probably still posed more risk than one might initially expect.

Substance abuse is common among sexual offenders. It tends to be a significant predictor of criminal recidivism generally (Gendreau et al., 1996). Although it is included in a number of instruments specifically designed to predict sexual recidivism (Boer, Wilson, et al., 1997; Epperson et al., 1998; Quinsey et al., 2006), it demonstrates only a modest relationship to sexual recidivism (Hanson & Bussiere, 1998). To seek additional data about the substance abuse-risk relationship for a particular sex offender, the evaluator will need to examine the history to see if alcohol or drugs have contributed in any way to past offenses—particularly sexual offenses. If so, the next question is whether there is reason to believe the offender will abuse substances in the future. Has the offender been in the community for a significant period of time voluntarily abstaining? Has substance abuse treatment been demonstrated to be effective with this individual? What, if any, monitoring of the person's substance abuse will be done, and for what length of time?

An individual's pattern of offending may be very important to analyze. For example, various studies have suggested that nonsexual offending, as well as sexual offending, correlates with sexual offense recidivism, and it has been included in several instruments (Hanson, 1997; Hanson & Bussiere, 1998; Quinsey et al., 2006). Although this is true, using it is apt to be problematic in jurisdictions that require an assessment specifically of the risk for *sexual* reoffending. Given the presence of considerable criminal versatility (as is often the case with rapists, in particular), it may be possible to say that the individual's risk for recidivism in general is high, but it may not be possible to say, with any degree of clinical certainty, whether his or her next offense is apt to be sexual in nature.

Patterns of offending can also be characterized as opportunistic or carefully planned. Some offenders commit sexual offenses on the spur of the moment simply because the opportunity presents itself: the burglar who unexpectedly finds the house occupied and rapes the occupant, the perpetrator who unexpectedly finds himself home alone with a small child. Others plan offenses carefully over time: the rapist who stalks his victim and orchestrates the event down to the smallest detail to avoid detection, the pedophile who grooms his victims for months before molesting them. In the case of the opportunistic offender, restricting access to victims may have a greater effect at risk reduction than with the goal-directed planner.

Individualized assessment is especially important when the evaluator is confronted with an offender who is, for some reason, atypical. For example, a sex offender with severe Axis I psychopathology (aside from substance abuse) is relatively rare. However, it is possible that someone commits sexual offenses in a psychotic state due to some delusional belief (e.g., the offender who believed he was commanded by God to impregnate a virgin). It is also possible that a severe mood disorder contributes to the offending (e.g., he offends when he cycles into depression, or he offends when mania removes his inhibitions). In these unusual cases, the principal risk factor may be mental illness, and the most important circumstance to analyze would be whether the offender will receive, or be mandated to receive, psychiatric care. Finally, a subpopulation of sexual offenders has significant intellectual or developmental disabilities (Boer, Tough, & Haaven, 2004). Factors that may contribute to sexual offending in this group include a tendency to prefer the company of children due to shared interests and abilities, significant difficulty in establishing a sexual relationship with an appropriate adult partner, a misperception of social cues, and a basic misunderstanding as to why certain behaviors are not appropriate. Here again the primary risk factor may be the disability, not the well-established risk factors that are more germane to most subjects in the sex offender literature.

Any risk assessment in regard to a sexual offender should include what some have called a "detailed functional analysis" of past offenses (Beech et al., 2003, p. 340). This involves examining the motives, precursors, specific behaviors, and consequences of the events. Such an analysis could reveal any personal triggers and/or inhibitors for the individual's behavior. This analysis would also form the basis for examining the likely future circumstances an individual faces, and how these relate to risk. Finally, it is important to examine the degree to which future circumstances are open to modification.

Risk Communication regarding Sexual Offenders

Most of the principles regarding risk communication in sex offender cases are no different from those outlined in Chapter 7. However, communicating results of a risk assessment in the context of an SVP evaluation is more complex than simply communicating an opinion regarding risk alone. Most jurisdictions require findings similar to those considered in the case of *Kansas v. Hendricks* (1997). Specifically, the Kansas statute's criteria for commitment specified that the individual have

> a congenital or acquired condition affecting the emotional or volitional capacity which predisposes the person to commit sexually violent offenses in a degree constituting such person a menace to the health and safety of others. (Commitment of Sexual Violent Predators Act, Kansas, 2002)

States that subsequently enacted an SVP statute often patterned it after this one. Regardless of the exact wording, statutes generally require proof of three elements: (1) The person has some disorder, (2) the disorder makes it more difficult for the person to control certain behaviors, and (3) as a result he or she presents a significant risk of sexual reoffending.

The first element requires a basic diagnostic evaluation with which most mental health professionals are familiar. Many state statutes allow for diagnoses not included in the *DSM* (e.g., a diagnosis related to repeated rape). The court in *Kansas v. Hendricks* (1997) also made clear that the required "abnormality" did not need to be diagnosed from established psychiatric or psychological texts. However, if mental health professionals were to begin developing individual syndromes, there would be no way to assess any type of diagnostic reliability. Therefore, this practice should be avoided.

Once a diagnosis is established, it may be difficult to connect that diagnosis with the second element (H. A. Miller et al., 2005). The second element basically requires an expert opinion on whether the individual's volitional capacity is somehow impaired by his or her disorder. For years, the legal community has been vocal in challenging the mental health professional's ability to render such an expert opinion (Mercado, Bornstein, & Schopp, 2006; Mercado, Schopp, & Bornstein, 2003; Morse, 1998; Schopp, Scalora, & Pearce, 1999;

Winick, 1998). To date, no scientific method has been developed to differentiate the irresistible impulse from the impulse that simply was not resisted. To carry the argument a step further, there is no instrument or recognized assessment procedure that can establish whether a particular individual has more or less difficulty controlling his or her impulses than the average person or the average sex offender (whoever that may be). Yet, in 2002, the U.S. Supreme Court was very clear in stating the necessity that this connection be made:

> With respect to the civil commitment of dangerous sexual offenders under the statute, the Federal Constitution required the state to prove that such offenders had serious difficulty in controlling their behavior. Such required proof—when viewed in light of such features of the case as the nature of the psychiatric diagnosis and the severity of the mental abnormality itself—had to be sufficient to distinguish the dangerous sexual offender whose serious mental illness, abnormality, or disorder subjected the offender to civil commitment from the dangerous but typical recidivist convicted in an ordinary criminal case. (*Kansas v. Crane*, 2002, p. 607)

It is difficult to connect a specific diagnosis to volitional impairment when the *DSM-IV-TR* emphasizes that no particular diagnosis implies any particular degree of control over specific behaviors (American Psychiatric Association, 2000). To date, the few disorders scientifically demonstrated to inhibit impulse control involve neuropsychological impairments generally in the form of orbitofrontal abnormalities (Bechara, Damasio, & Damasio, 2000; R. J. R. Blair & Ciplotti, 2000; Burns & Swerdlow, 2003). However, the target sexual offenses frequently involve complex planning (e.g., grooming children for sexual assault), in contrast to the impulsive acts precipitated by brain abnormalities. Furthermore, these are almost never the disorders at issue in an SVP evaluation. The most commonly identified diagnoses in SVP cases are personality disorders and paraphilias (H. A. Miller et al., 2005).

Prosecutors frequently argue that, given the likely consequences, the very fact that an offender continues to reoffend demonstrates a particular difficulty controlling his or her behavior. This conclusion, they argue, is common sense. However, the expert is not credentialed to testify to common sense. Rather, the expert witness is expected to assist the court in understanding scientific evidence that is beyond the ken of the layperson.

The wisdom and/or ethical implications of mental health professionals testifying to the ultimate legal issue in a courtroom has long been a matter of great debate in the field (Fulero & Finkel, 1991; Slobogin, 1989). Even if ultimate issue testimony is scientifically appropriate, it certainly needs to be clinically or scientifically based. However, in the case of SVP proceedings, the central element that must link the disorder to the risk presented—impaired volition—does not meet this criterion. Evaluators must give careful thought, therefore, to whether they believe they are qualified to present an ultimate issue opinion.

An alternative strategy is to present one's findings as a pure assessment of sex offender risk. Sex offender risk assessment has a rich database from which much relevant information can be provided. As with any risk assessment, dichotomous predictions are to be avoided in favor of an opinion as to level of risk given specific circumstances.

Risk Management

Whether an evaluator should include a formal risk management plan depends on the demands of the circumstances and jurisdiction. Certainly, risk management recommendations are common, and tend to be valuable, in evaluations for probation and parole. However, with respect to SVP evaluations, many jurisdictions seek evaluations only to help answer the question "Should a petition be filed to have this individual committed as an SVP?" In such circumstances, the individual is usually still incarcerated at the time of the evaluation but continued incarceration is not an option. If the court commits the person, he or she will be transferred to a secure residential facility indefinitely. Under such circumstances, risk management planning is probably not possible. Even in circumstances where outpatient commitment is likely (i.e., in Texas), set conditions may already be in place, and input on risk management would not be welcome.

When some type of release is finally considered, however, risk management may be very appropriate. Effective risk management in this situation involves acknowledging that sex offenders are a heterogeneous group who may be functioning in a wide variety of contexts (Conroy, 2006). Evaluators should avoid the one-size-fits-all models, however common these may be. Three such models are commonly assumed to be effective, yet have significant flaws. The first is a sex offender treatment program. A number of studies produced data indicating moderate reduction in recidivism from programs based on a cognitive-behavioral approach (Hall, 1995; Hanson et al., 2002). However, research methodologies were often found to be less than ideal (Marshall & Anderson, 1996; McConaghy, 1999), and other studies found little to no positive effects (Hanson, Broom, & Stephenson, 2004; Marques et al., 2005). Variations in research results may be due to the variation in programs and treatment providers, problems with research methodology, or a failure to take into consideration the diversity of individuals who may be treated as sex offenders. Despite inconsistent outcomes, one cannot conclude that sex offender treatment programs are *not* effective, only that it is unclear for whom they are effective. Specific programs may well be warranted in some cases.

A second approach commonly applied to large groups of offenders is medication. Specifically, progestronal hormone compounds are used to reduce sexual drive. These medicines appear effective in reducing recidivism among some child molesters (G. T. Harris et al., 1998). However, there is little evidence to indicate that many sex offenders have exaggerated sexual drives (Rosler & Witztum, 2000), and the treatment does not change the object of one's attraction. In addition, these medications have been known to have very negative side effects (Kravitz et al., 1995; R. D. Miller, 1998) and may be counteracted by ingesting testosterone or anabolic steroids.

A third intervention model is often called the "containment approach." Under this model, every conceivable restriction and treatment intervention may be imposed upon the offenders. All involved are generally made to waive confidentiality entirely. Probation officers across the country who have used this approach generally endorse it (English, Pullen, & Jones, 1996). However, the pure complexity of the approach makes it almost impossible to conduct solid outcome research (Conroy, 2006). If positive results are obtained, which of the many elements were effective? Given the large number of sexual offenders in the community, this costly and intrusive method potentially pulls resources from other criminal justice programs.

Effective risk management of an individual sexual offender will still require an analysis of risk factors, both nomothetic and idiographic, that put that particular individual at risk. Certain sex offender treatment programs may be one intervention, as may medications to reduce sexual drive or unwanted fantasies—particularly for those obsessed with aberrant thoughts and fantasies. Specific containment efforts (e.g., geographic restrictions, work restrictions) may also have utility in some cases. However, we would emphasize that to obtain the most risk reduction at the most reasonable cost, plans must be individualized, as detailed in Chapter 8.

CHAPTER

11

Risk Assessment with Juvenile Offenders

Efforts to assess risk are ubiquitous in the juvenile justice system (Weibush, Baird, Krisberg, & Onek, 1995). Mulvey (2005) detailed at least three general ways in which the juvenile justice system makes some effort to delineate youth at higher and lower risk of violent offending. First, broad statutes reflect some attempt to identify youth at greater or lesser risk, so that these youth may be differently processed through the system or punished. Second, Mulvey explained, administrators use guidelines and sometimes even actuarial measures (based on instant offense or past offense history) to make decisions about placing youth in varied settings, depending on their level of perceived risk. Finally, clinicians or other court professionals (e.g., juvenile probation officers) form opinions about a youth's level of risk based on an individualized assessment of the youth's characteristics and history.

In this chapter, our focus is on Mulvey's (2005) third category, assessing risk on an individual basis to help the court make a decision about a given youth. Of course, courts and juvenile justice agencies are not the only entities that seek individualized violence risk assessments for youth. Juvenile psychiatric facilities, like their adult counterparts, often rely on risk assessments to inform decisions about hospitalization and release. Increasingly, school administrators seek risk assessments to inform decisions about a youth's placement. Even other clinicians and social service agencies may request a risk assessment for a youth about whom they have become concerned. Violence by juveniles is a prominent concern, both among the general public and among policy makers. Thus, requests for risk assessments of juveniles are likely to remain commonplace, or become even more so.

A Cautionary Note about Evaluator Competence to Assess Risk among Juveniles

Although calls for risk assessments of juveniles are commonplace, not all clinicians should respond to these calls. As Borum (2000, 2003, 2006)* has articulated, assessing risk among juveniles differs from assessing risk among adults. As we detail in this chapter, the base rates of violence differ markedly, some risk factors differ or at least operate differently, and a developmental perspective is essential. More generally, forensic assessment of youth differs from forensic assessment of adults, and evaluators must bring additional, youth-specific knowledge and skills to the task (Grisso, 1998). Cornell (2002, p. 187) explained:

> The ideal forensic examiner for a juvenile should be a mental health professional who is experienced in clinical work with adolescents and who has knowledge of the forensic issues germane to juvenile proceedings. . . .
>
> Capable forensic examiners who work with adults should be cautious about evaluating a juvenile without adequate training or supervision. It is possible to conduct a seemingly competent evalu-

---

* Shortly before this text went to press, Borum and Verhaagen (2006) released a text specific to assessing and managing violence risk in *juveniles.* Although our chapter illustrates juvenile risk assessments as one application of the risk assessment model we present throughout our text, we also recommend the Borum and Verhaagen text as essential reading for evaluators who anticipate performing risk assessments among juveniles. More generally, we recommend Grisso's (1998) text on forensic evaluation of juveniles. For the evaluator new to forensic work with juveniles, both of these texts are necessary, but probably not sufficient. Ideally, evaluators would also engage in supervised training in juvenile forensic assessment, combined with broader continuing education in developmental psychopathology and clinical skills applied to children.

ation but fail to obtain the data necessary to construct a complete picture of the developmental and familial context for the youth's clinical presentation and delinquent behavior. Interview styles and techniques that work well with adults may elicit limited or even misleading information from youths, resulting in an incomplete or inaccurate case formulation. . . . Examiners must broaden the scope of evaluation to include information from parents and schools and must use psychological tests and measures appropriate to this age group.

Essentially, evaluators must not only be able to address the necessary forensic issue (in this case, risk for violence), but must do so with child-appropriate clinical skills and an understanding of the multiple contexts (e.g., schools, families, and peer relationships) and developmental transitions that shape juvenile behavior. Grisso (1998) has often characterized juveniles as "moving targets," because their cognitive and emotional capacities develop (and even stall or regress) in sometimes unpredictable patterns. Thus, evaluators should approach juvenile forensic evaluations with an appreciation for the ways development influences a juvenile's ability to, for example, appraise risk, control impulses, resist peer influences, and take the perspective of others (Borum & Grisso, 2007). Evaluators should consider carefully these requisite knowledge and skills, as well as the ethical guidance to accept referrals only within one's area of expertise (Committee on Ethical Guidelines for Forensic Psychologists, 1991; Heilbrun et al., 2002) before conducting risk assessments among juveniles.

A Changing Juvenile Court

Evaluators who do conduct risk assessments of juveniles should, of course, be knowledgeable about the juvenile justice system. As detailed in other discussions of justice-involved youth (e.g., Grisso, 1996; Grisso & Schwartz, 2000; Krisberg, 2005), the juvenile justice system has changed dramatically over the past 2 decades. Originally designed as a nonadversarial arrangement to act in the best interests of troubled youth, the early *parens patriae* model of juvenile justice placed little emphasis on due process protections, and instead operated more informally, with the assumption that rehabilitation was a primary goal. However, as the U.S. Supreme Court extended certain constitutional due process rights to juveniles (*In re Gault*, 1967; *In re Winship*, 1970; *Kent v. United States*, 1966), as youth accused of serious crimes were more often waived to adult court (Redding, 2003), and as goals of public safety tended to receive more emphasis than goals of rehabilitation, the juvenile justice system has grown increasingly similar to the adult criminal justice system (Grisso, 1996; Grisso & Schwartz, 2000; Krisberg, 2005; Scott, 2000). Overall, the adultification of the juvenile court has led to a system with sometimes mixed goals and procedures. On the one hand, there are efforts to acknowledge developmental differences and emphasize rehabilitation, but on the other hand, certain procedures and outcomes (including the potential for long-term sanctions) are more similar to those in the adult court (Redding, Sevin Goldstein, & Heilbrun, 2005).

What does the altered juvenile justice landscape mean for evaluators who conduct risk assessments? The first implications are evident in the type of risk questions that evaluators face.

Defining the Question

Balancing goals of public safety and rehabilitation, the modern juvenile court seeks risk assessments for a number of clearly defined questions. Grisso (1998, p. 127) listed the following:

- To assess the need for secure pretrial detention
- To assess the risk of harm to other youths during pretrial secure detention
- To address the public safety standard in juvenile court hearings on waiver of a juvenile to criminal court for trial as an adult
- For youths adjudicated delinquent in juvenile court, to assist the court in determining the degree of security needed during rehabilitation (for the juvenile court sentencing or disposition hearing)
- After a period of commitment to a secure rehabilitation program, to assess whether rehabilitative efforts have resulted in

reduced risk of future harm to others that would allow for placement in a less secure program
- To assess the need to extend juvenile court custody in states that allow extension of juvenile jurisdiction beyond the usual maximum age based on an assessment identifying continued risk of violence if released to the community

A review of Grisso's list reveals that the courts may ask evaluators to conduct risk assessments for certain precise, statutorily defined questions, such as the issue of waiver to adult court (see *Kent v. United States*, 1966). In these circumstances, the evaluator can easily clarify the referral question with the referring party, usually with reference to the relevant legal code or statute.

However, there are instances in which the juvenile justice system still operates less formally, or perhaps with somewhat blurred boundaries, due to the long-standing goal of rehabilitating troubled youth. It is not uncommon for some decision makers (probation officers, judges) to request that general psychological evaluations also include some opinion regarding a juvenile's risk for violence. Sometimes, the referring party may not articulate questions of risk explicitly or may not understand the distinctions between a general clinical evaluation and a forensic assessment of violence risk. Yet even in a system in which some decisions are made less formally, *any* opinions about risk that an evaluator offers to the juvenile justice system could *potentially* result in the same types of grave decisions made in adult court (e.g., substantial restrictions on liberties and long-term sanctions). Thus, we encourage evaluators—whether working on an independent basis or as part of a juvenile court clinic—to settle on a clearly defined referral question, which allows the evaluator to conduct an assessment that is appropriate in content and scope and is communicated with appropriate caveats. A comprehensive risk assessment should be presented as such, and it is rarely feasible to include a risk assessment as a minor component of a general assessment. That said, there are situations in which it is quite appropriate to conduct multiple, distinct evaluations for distinct purposes as a youth progresses through the justice system. In short, the dual goals (rehabilitation and public safety) that characterize the modern juvenile court (Redding et al., 2005) make it increasingly important to clarify the boundaries of one's role and tasks in any given evaluation of a juvenile.

Distinguishing Risk Assessment from Threat Assessment

There is a second trend to which evaluators should be attuned when clarifying a referral question related to juvenile risk. Courts, psychiatric facilities, and other agencies have long requested risk assessments for *general* violence, that is, the possibility that a youth will commit any violence to any victim over a specified period of time. This referral question is most congruent with the forensic assessment of violence risk as we discuss it throughout this text. However, schools, parents, and other sources increasingly approach clinicians to request risk assessments for *targeted* violence (Borum, 2000, 2006; Cornell, 2004; Halikias, 2004). Risk assessments of this type are probably better termed "threat assessments" (Borum, 2000; Reddy et al., 2001) in that the referral question was prompted by a perceived threat, whether explicit (e.g., a student formally threatens a peer or school staff, a student writes a list of likely targets) or implicit (e.g., a student makes vague remarks or writings that worry authorities). Borum (2006, p. 193) explained that the distinction between risk assessment and threat assessment

> becomes important because the factors considered and the assessment approach may differ (Borum & Reddy, 2001; Reddy et al., 2001). . . . These (threat) assessments should arguably rely on a fact-based assessment approach and may—for a variety of reasons—not rely primarily on base rates or a tally of empirically based risk factors for general violence.

Essentially, the threat assessment approach as articulated by Borum and colleagues affiliated with the U.S. Secret Service (e.g., Borum et al., 1999; Borum & Reddy, 2001; Fein et al., 1995; Reddy et al., 2001; Vossekuil et al., 2002) involves a detailed and case-specific analysis of the examinee's patterns of behaviors. Similarly, Cornell and colleagues (2004; Cornell & Sheras, 2005; O'Toole, 2000) developed threat assessment guidelines specific to responding to threats by students; they offered empirical research to support the use of threat assessment procedures in schools (Cornell et al., 2004).

Detailed guidance on threat assessment is beyond the scope of this chapter, in which we focus on assessment of general violence risk. But we emphasize the need for evaluators to remain attuned to the distinction between risk assessment and threat assessment as they work to clarify the referral questions. Referral questions prompted by threats or related to concerns about targeted violence will likely require an assessment approach detailed in the resources described earlier. Referral questions related to risk of general violence can be answered with the approach we describe in this chapter. Although most discussions of threat assessment with youth center around schools, it is important to emphasize that it is the *question,* not the *setting,* which determines whether a risk assessment or threat assessment approach is warranted. Schools may request a risk assessment for a youth who has a long-standing pattern of generally aggressive behavior; conversely, juvenile justice agencies could request a threat assessment for a youth who has made specific threats of violence against a particular individual.

Base Rates and Nomothetic Data

Although it is always essential to consider base rates in violence risk assessment, the need to do so is even more pronounced in violence risk assessments of juveniles. Why? First, delinquent behavior, including some violent behaviors, are so commonplace among youth that they are statistically normative, or typical. Second, the vast majority of youth who engage in delinquent or violent behavior cease doing so by the time they become adults. These two axioms reflect decades of the most rigorous research that the social sciences have to offer (as summarized later), and these two axioms should guide any assessment of risk among juveniles. Simply put, some degree of delinquent or even violent behavior is not uncommon among youth, and such behavior does not necessarily indicate long-term, substantial violence risk. Thus, a base rate-informed default assumption in any juvenile risk assessment is that the youth will not engage in violence on a *long-term* basis; one would require substantial case-specific facts to alter this assumption (Grisso, 1998).

Understanding these broad patterns, an empirically informed risk assessment still starts with base rate estimates. As detailed in Chapter 4, local base rates may be helpful, particularly when performing risk assessments in a large institutional setting (e.g., a metropolitan juvenile probation department). However, local base rates will not be available in many instances, and it will be necessary to consider broader research-derived base rates. Fortunately, several large-scale studies offer useful base rate data regarding violent behaviors, and we summarize a few of these for illustrative purposes. Again, these rates (or any other rates drawn from research) will be more or less appropriate depending on the examinee and the examinee's context in the case at hand.

Table 11.1 offers some important overviews of violence base rates among juveniles, but it is important to note that these base rates tend to vary by age. For example, in the Centers for Disease Control and Prevention (CDC; 2006) Youth Risk Behavior Survey, half (49.6%) of boys in ninth grade reported having engaged in a fight during the past year, whereas the proportion declined to 38% among 12th-grade boys.

However, the strongest age trends in youth violence relate to onset and desistance from violence. Generally speaking, most youth initiate violence in the teen years and desist before entering adulthood (Moffitt, 1993, 2002, 2006; U.S. Department of Health and Human Services [USDHHS], 2001). For example, in the National Youth Survey, 16 was the most common age to initiate serious violence. However, a small proportion of youth begin engaging in violence before puberty (Moffitt, 1993, 2002, 2006; Tolan & Gorman-Smith, 1998; USDHHS, 2001). As detailed later in this chapter, these youth who demonstrate early-onset violence are at substantially higher risk of continued violence. Indeed, they appear to be responsible for the majority of crime committed by juveniles (and later, adults), even though they compose only 5% to 6% of juvenile offenders (Moffitt, 1993).

Table 11.1 *Base Rates of Violent Behavior among Juveniles*

Source	Sample	Data Type	Behavior	Rate
CDC Youth Risk Behavior Surveillance Summary (Centers for Disease Control and Prevention, 2006)	13,917 students in grades 9 to 12, in U.S. schools, surveyed during 2005	Self-report survey responses	Engaged in physical fight during past year	36% overall Males: 43% Females: 28%
			Engaged in physical fight on school property during past year	14%
			Carried a weapon onto school property during past month	7%
Monitoring the Future survey as reported in the Surgeon General's Report on Youth Violence (USDHHS, 2001)	50,000 8th-, 10th-, and 12th-grade students in U.S. schools surveyed 1980 to 1998 (data at right reflect 12th-grade students only)	Self-report survey responses	Committed violent crime during past year	30%
			Committed an assault causing injury	10% to 15%
			Committed robbery with a weapon	2% to 5%
The National Longitudinal Survey of Youth 1997, as reported in the Office of Juvenile Justice and Delinquency Prevention's Juvenile Offenders and Victims: 1999 National Report (Snyder & Sickmund, 1999)	8,984 youth ages 12 to 16 (as of 1996)	Self-report telephone survey responses	Committed an assault during the past year	12%
			Committed an assault ever	18%

210

Data source	Sample	Data type	Measure	Rate
The National Longitudinal Survey of Youth 2001 as reported in the Office of Juvenile Justice and Delinquency Prevention's Juvenile Offenders and Victims: 2006 National Report (Snyder & Sickmund, 2006)	Subsample of above; youth age 17 or older by 2001		Committed an assault ever (as of age 17)	27%
National Youth Survey, as reported in the Surgeon General's Report on Youth Violence (USDHHS, 2001)	1,725 youth from across the United States who were 11 to 17 in 1976, followed longitudinally	Self-report interview responses	Serious violence (i.e., aggravated assault, robbery, gang fights, rape); incidents by age	Males (ages 12–18): 10% to 13%
Denver Youth Survey, Pittsburgh Youth Study, and Rochester Youth Development Study, as reported in the Surgeon General's Report on Youth Violence (USDHHS, 2001)	4,500 youth at high risk for delinquency, ages 7 to 15 in 1988, and followed longitudinally	Self-report interview responses	Serious violence (i.e., aggravated assault, robbery, gang fights, rape); incidents by age Serious Violence; cumulative prevalence by age 17	Males (12–20): 8% to 20% Females (12–20): 1% to 18% Males: 30% to 40% Females: 16% to 32%
The Office of Juvenile Justice and Delinquency Prevention's Juvenile Court Statistics 2001–2002 (Stahl et al., 2005)	National Juvenile Court Data Archive (covering areas with jurisdiction over 75% of U.S. youth)	Arrests as reported by courts	Arrested for crimes against person	0.012% (12 per 1,000 juveniles)

Data sources reflect most recent available data/resources as of January 2007. In all of the data sources, violence base rates differed by age, sex, and ethnicity. Please see original sources for more specific details.

211

Are Actuarial Measures Available to Guide Juvenile Risk Assessment?

Evaluators familiar with adult risk assessment procedures often ask a question such as "Is there something like a VRAG for kids?" In other words, can a widely-used, widely-researched instrument offer a base rate estimate or initial risk estimate for juveniles? The short answer is no. Actuarial measures have a long history in criminal justice administration (Burgess, 1928, 1936) and a moderately long history in juvenile justice administration (e.g., Baird, 1984). Indeed, most juvenile justice authorities emphasize the value of actuarial approaches to standardize the many classification decisions made in the system (Howell, 1995, 2003), and many, if not most, juvenile justice agencies use some form of screening measure for classification. However, many of these are not actuarial measures, strictly defined (Schwalbe, in press). Although they may feature a brief list of (presumed) risk factors, these factors are often determined by expert consensus rather than the strict actuarial approach (Schwalbe, in press).

A few juvenile justice instruments have been developed with a stricter actuarial approach that involves successive validations in differing samples (e.g., Krysik & LeCroy, 2002). However, research often demonstrates that actuarial measures developed in one jurisdiction fail to generalize to other jurisdictions (Howell, 1995; Wright, Clear, & Dickson, 1984) and that the predictive validity of actuarial-like instruments is often hampered by gender or ethnic bias (Schwalbe, Fraser, Day, & Arnold, 2004; Schwalbe, Fraser, Day, & Cooley, 2006). Thus, at present, there appears to be no actuarial juvenile risk measure validated across enough settings to be considered widely generalizable. This is not to say there are no useful or research-supported risk instruments, though, as we discuss later in this chapter.

Empirically Supported Risk Factors

Few topics in the social sciences have generated as much attention and careful study as have efforts to identify risk factors for youth crime and violence. Consequently, the literature offers a wealth of data on the many factors that correspond with (though may not necessarily cause) an increased risk for violence (for reviews, see, e.g., Cottle et al., 2001; Lipsey & Derzon, 1998; USDHHS, 2001). These factors remain fairly consistent even as new research emerges (Mulvey, 2005). Though it is not possible to thoroughly describe each of these factors in a few pages, we summarize some key factors that warrant attention in practical risk assessment. For ease of discussion, these are grouped into categories (individual, family, school, peers, neighborhood), though discrete grouping is somewhat misleading, as these factors are interactive and synergistic in reality (see, generally, Dishion & Patterson, 2006; Mash & Dozois, 2003).

Individual and Historical Risk Factors

Prior Violence

Not surprisingly, as among adults, previous violent offending is a well-established predictor of subsequent violent offending among youth (Brame, Mulvey, & Piquero, 2001). A history of aggression across multiple settings in the preadolescent years is a particularly strong predictor of later violence (Loeber, Farrington, Stouthamer-Loeber, Moffitt, & Caspi, 2001). Quite reasonably, Borum and Verhaagen (2006, p. 31) concluded that "prior violent behavior is perhaps the best single predictor of future violence."

Despite the predictive validity of past violence with respect to future violence, there is no one-to-one correspondence between past violence and future crime in terms of offense type or offense severity. For example, minor delinquency such as stealing, smoking, and destruction of property at an early age is associated with increased risk of adolescent violence (Hawkins et al., 1998). Conversely, detailed studies of juvenile homicide offenders reveal a substantial proportion who demonstrated no serious violence prior to committing homicide (Benedek & Cornell, 1989; cf. Meyers, Scott, Burgess, & Burgess, 1995). Because the severity of past offenses is not necessarily a strong predictor of future offenses, it is important to examine past violence and past offending in terms of the chronicity and recency of the prior offenses (Grisso, 1998) instead of simply examining types of offense.

Early-Onset Violence

In a recent meta-analysis that analyzed 30 possible predictors of re-offending among delinquent youth (Cottle et al., 2001), the two strongest predictors were younger age at first institutionalization (effect size = .35) and younger age at first contact with law enforcement (effect size = .34). Though this study examined reoffending generally, the same pattern held true in a comprehensive review that addressed youth violence specifically (Hawkins et al., 1998, 2000) and holds true in the most rigorous long-term studies of youth violence. In the large-scale prospective Pittsburgh Youth Study of over 1,500 urban boys, an onset of delinquency before age 10 was one of the strongest predictors of violence in adolescence and adulthood (Loeber et al., 2005). Likewise, in the National Youth Survey (Elliott, 1994), half of the youth who first committed violence before age 10 continued violence into adulthood; only 10% of youth who first committed violence in adolescence did so. Farrington (1995, as cited in Hawkins et al., 2000) found that 50% of the boys who were adjudicated for a violent offense between ages 10 and 16 were subsequently convicted of violence as adults; in contrast, only 8% of those not charged with violent offenses in their early years were subsequently convicted of violence as adults. Simply put, early onset of violence suggests increased risk for subsequent violence (Loeber, Farrington, & Waschbusch, 1998; Piquero, Farrington, & Blumstein, 2003; Thornberry, Huizinga, & Loeber, 1995; Tolan & Gorman-Smith, 1998).

Substance Abuse

Substance abuse is often considered the strongest predictor of juvenile delinquency in general, and there is ample evidence that many, if not most, incarcerated youth were under the influence of substances at the time of offending (DeMatteo & Marczyk, 2005). But the influence of substance abuse on violence risk is less straightforward than we might assume. In a comprehensive meta-analysis, substance abuse was one of the strongest predictors of future violence for children ages 6 to 11; however, it was one of the weakest predictors for children 12 to 14 (Hawkins et al., 2000). In the aggregate, substance abuse does not appear to be a strong predictor of reoffending (Cottle et al., 2001), perhaps because substance abuse is so common among youth with prior offenses as to be of little predictive value.

Impulsivity

Impulsivity has been cited as the most powerful personality factor increasing the risk of violent behavior (Lipsey & Derzon, 1998). Measures of impulsivity predict delinquency even during preadolescence (White et al., 1994), and longitudinal studies reveal that early impulsivity predicts violent offending during adulthood (Brennan, Mednick, & Mednick, 1993). Related to impulsivity, *sensation seeking* during middle adolescence tripled the risk of violence (Hawkins et al., 2000). Also related to impulsivity, failure to inhibit an angry reaction can certainly lead to violence, but evidence also suggests that state anger is a risk factor for violence (Cornell, Peterson, & Richards, 1999).

Violence-Conducive Social Information Processing

Violence-conducive social-information processing may be somewhat related to impulsive thinking but probably deserves separate attention as a risk factor for violence. Programmatic research by Dodge and colleagues (for reviews, see Coie & Dodge, 1998; Crick & Dodge, 1994) reveals a variety of errors in social information processing that leave youth more likely to engage in violence. Generally speaking, social information processing requires a youth to (a) encode and interpret social cues, (b) consider and decide on a response, and (c) act out the selected response and evaluate its success. Considerable research reveals that

> aggressive youngsters display deficits and distortions at various levels of this information-processing model. At an overview level, such children and adolescents (in comparison with nonaggressive youths) underutilize pertinent social cues, misattribute hostile intent to ambiguous peer provocations, generate fewer assertive solutions to social problems, and expect that aggressive responses will lead to reward [references omitted]. Importantly, such effects are found in both community and clinical samples of aggressive youths, including severely violent offenders (Lochman & Dodge, 1994). (Hinshaw & Lee, 2003, p. 178)

Although violence-conducive social information processing is an empirically supported risk factor by even the most rigorous standards, we emphasize that practically speaking, evaluators can infer information about social processing only through an in-depth clinical interview that reviews past episodes of violence with the young examinee (collateral records may also help).

Psychiatric Illness
Psychiatric illness is commonplace among youth who are involved with the juvenile justice system (Grisso, 2004; Teplin, Abram, McClelland, Dulcan, & Mericle, 2002). However, the relationships between violence and psychiatric illness depends on the type of disorder and specific symptoms (in addition to individual and contextual factors). Ample research documents that conduct disorder and oppositional defiant disorder are strongly associated with aggression, although this relationship is tautological and not particularly informative, in that aggressive behaviors can meet diagnostic criteria for these disorders. More informative, the combination of conduct disorder and attention-deficit/hyperactivity disorder appears to correspond with increased risk for aggressive behaviors throughout adolescence and into adulthood (Lynam, 1996, 1997). Although there does not appear to be substantial research that directly links depression to violence risk, Vincent and Grisso (2005) noted the tendency for depression to manifest as anger or irritability among youth and the tendency for anger and irritability to contribute to violence. Likewise, they noted that although anxiety symptoms usually leave youth less aggressive, chronic anxiety may relate to conduct problems (Frick, Lilienfeld, Ellis, Loney, & Silverthorn, 1999). Posttraumatic stress disorder, in particular, when combined with conduct disorder appears to relate to aggression (Vincent & Grisso, 2005). Schizophrenia and other disorders that result in psychosis are quite rare in children and appear to play little role in youth violence overall. A relatively large study of juvenile homicide offenders documented that fewer than 10% manifested psychotic symptoms (Benedek & Cornell, 1989).

Psychopathic Personality Features
Psychopathic personality features deserve special attention in this discussion of youth risk factors, not because psychopathy features

are a stronger risk factor than others discussed in this section (indeed, the research base on youth psychopathy is smaller and more recent than most of the other risk factors we discuss), but because there appears to be greater ambiguity and potential for misunderstanding regarding how psychopathy features should be considered in juvenile risk assessment. We suspect that many clinicians are likely to embrace psychopathy assessment approaches with juveniles, given how often psychopathy assessment is employed in forensic evaluations of adults (e.g., Lally, 2003; Otto & Heilbrun, 2002). Indeed, given the well-documented relationship between psychopathy scores and measures of violence and recidivism (Hemphill et al., 1998; Salekin et al., 1996; Walters, 2003), researchers have devoted considerable attention to identifying psychopathic features among youth (for reviews, see Forth & Mailloux, 2000; Frick, Bodin, & Barry, 2000). This research has attempted to identify precursors of adult psychopathy to find meaningful distinctions among youth with conduct problems, thereby improving early intervention and treatment (Frick & Ellis, 1999; Frick, O'Brien, Wootton, & McBurnett, 1994; Lynam, 1996). Research has also generated a series of juvenile psychopathy assessment measures, two of which are commercially available for clinical use: the Psychopathy Checklist: Youth Version (PCL:YV; Forth et al., 2003) and the Antisocial Process Screening Device (Frick & Hare, 2001). A substantial body of literature has examined the validity of these juvenile psychopathy measures and generally supported their validity (Salekin, 2006). For example, youth scoring high on psychopathy measures tend to be more thrill seeking (Frick, Lilienfeld, Ellis, Loney, & Silverthorn, 1999) and fearless (Barry et al., 2000) but less empathic and less prone to emotional distress (Pardini, Lochman, & Frick, 2003). Just as adult psychopathy is considered a more homogeneous and pernicious condition than the broader diagnosis of antisocial personality disorder, a subgroup of youth high in psychopathy-like features appear to be distinguishable from the more heterogeneous group of youth who qualify for diagnoses of conduct disorder (Frick & Marsee, 2006).

Much like adult psychopathy predicts criminal violence and recidivism (Salekin et al., 1996), psychopathy scores among youth correspond with similar outcomes. For example, youth psychopathy features are associated with general and violent recidivism (Brandt,

Kennedy, Patrick, & Curtain, 1997; Gretton, Hare, & Catchpole, 2004; Gretton, McBride, Hare, O'Shaughnessy, & Kumka, 2001; cf. Edens & Cahill, 2007), institutional violence (Stafford & Cornell, 2003), instrumental violence (Murrie, Cornell, Kaplan, McConville, & Levy-Elkon, 2004), and self-reported aggression (Frick, Stickle, Dandreaux, Farrell, & Kimonis, 2005). In short, mounting evidence suggests that a small subgroup of youth manifest personality and behavioral features that are at least phenotypically similar to psychopathy, as conceptualized among adults.

However, several authorities have raised important concerns about applying the psychopathy construct to adolescents (Edens, Skeem, Cruise, & Caufman, 2001; Seagrave & Grisso, 2002). First, some scholars warn that some transient developmental characteristics that are relatively common to adolescents (e.g., irresponsibility or impulsivity) could be mistaken for long-standing adult psychopathy traits (Edens, Skeem, et al., 2001; Seagrave & Grisso, 2002). For example, clinicians might misconstrue typical adolescent egocentrism as a psychopathic lack of empathy. Indeed, adolescence is a time of rapid transition, with day-to-day variability in terms of emotional expression and emotional maturity; clinicians attempting to reliably assess any condition among adolescents must make many difficult distinctions (e.g., distinguishing clinical depression from irritability, discouragement, or loneliness). Borum and Verhaagen (2006, p. 58) responded to this concern as follows:

> While some of the criteria for psychopathy are clearly not typical of adolescents, there is enough overlap to cause some professionals to question how reliably this construct can be assessed among a teenage population (Edens, Skeem, et al., 2001; Seagrave & Grisso, 2002). This is a valid concern, but in our view, not an insurmountable one. It does, however, call for different norms so that young people can be compared on relevant dimensions to others who are at a similar age and developmental level (Frick, 2002). Impulsivity, for example—a trait associated with psychopathy—may be normal and common in adolescence, but it still should be possible to distinguish among more and less impulsive teens.

A second, more compelling concern regarding the assessment of psychopathy among youth is that we have few data to indicate whether those who exhibit psychopathic features as juveniles will continue to manifest such traits as adults (Edens, Skeem, et al., 2001; Hart, Watt, & Vincent, 2002; Steinberg, 2002). On the one hand, a few recent studies described samples in which youth psychopathy scores corresponded with a higher incidence of conduct problems during follow-up several years later (Frick, Kimonis, Dandreaux, & Farell, 2003; Frick et al., 2005) or violent criminality in early adulthood (Gretton et al., 2001, 2004; cf. Edens & Cahill, 2007). A recent meta-analysis found a moderate relationship between psychopathy scores and recidivism, although this relationship varied considerably across studies (Edens, Campbell, & Weir, 2007). However, available data regarding the long-term stability of psychopathic personality traits are far too sparse to make long-term predictions with any degree of confidence, particularly considering that many individuals who commit crimes in adolescence desist from crime by adulthood (see, e.g., Moffitt, 1993).

Considering the rapidly developing juvenile psychopathy literature as a whole, then, what are the implications for risk assessment among juveniles? First, there is a sufficient body of literature linking youth psychopathy features to violence that evaluators may reasonably investigate psychopathy features as *one* possible risk factor for violence (Vitacco & Vincent, 2006). Second, the bulk of data linking psychopathy features to violent outcomes involve only brief follow-up periods, and even these studies reveal more variability than is sometimes assumed (Edens et al., 2007). This means that any inferences an evaluator draws from psychopathy scores should be *short term* in nature. The need to focus on short-term inferences certainly reflects our limited knowledge about the long-term implications of youth psychopathy features. More generally, an emphasis on short-term predictions reflects our modern understanding of youth risk and development: Nearly all risk indicators are more valid in the short term than in the long term (Mulvey, 2005). It is much safer and more responsible to offer inferences about the next *stage* of development, as opposed to the next *stages*.

The emerging literature also suggests that additional caveats are in order, even when one uses psychopathy scores only in a circumscribed fashion to help inform shorter term assessments of risk. First, there are few data to support the utility of psychopathy assessment among girls (Edens et al., 2007; Odgers, Moretti, & Reppucci, 2005;

Odgers, Reppucci, & Moretti, 2005; cf. Penney & Moretti, 2007). Second, PCL:YV assessments should be conducted with minority youth cautiously, if at all. Emerging research appears to suggest that, roughly stated, the predictive validity of PCL:YV assessment decreases as the proportion of non-Caucasian youth in the study sample increases (Edens & Cahill, 2007; Edens et al., 2007).

Overall, there appears to be some role for the assessment of psychopathy as *one* component of a comprehensive assessment of *short-term* violence risk (Vitacco & Vincent, 2006), though probably only with male juveniles. Several scholars have speculated about the likely hazards of using the label "psychopath" (e.g., Steinberg, 2002), and we discuss issues of labeling and language in more detail later in this chapter (see Risk Communication). However, it is worth emphasizing that designating any youth as "a psychopath" is simply misleading (regardless of the label's putative effects) given that psychopathy features appear to lie on a continuum rather than reflecting a distinct class or category of youth (Murrie, Marcus, et al., 2007; see Edens, Marcus, Lilienfeld, & Poythress, 2006, for a similar discussion related to adult psychopathy).

Contextual Risk Factors

Family Variables
Family variables contribute to violence risk in a number of ways. First, experiencing violence or other maltreatment as a child increases one's risk of later becoming violent to others (e.g., Hawkins et al., 2000; Malinosky-Rummell & Hansen, 1993; Maxfield & Widom, 1996; Smith & Thornberry, 1995; Widom, 1989, 1994). So does witnessing family conflict and violence (DeMatteo & Marczyk, 2005; Elliott, 1994; Kashini & Allan, 1998). Landmark longitudinal studies revealed that aggressive discipline and poor supervision by parents predicted violent offenses in youth many years later (McCord, 1979), and more recent studies have yielded similar results. Generally, antisocial personality in parents also corresponds with conduct problems, including violence and aggression, in children (Lipsey & Derzon, 1998).

To summarize, data that link adversity in early home life to subsequent aggression is voluminous (for reviews, see Farrington, 2005;

Hawkins et al., 2000; Lipsey & Derzon, 1998), and this relationship holds true for reoffending as it does for the initiation of offending. Family problems, broadly defined, was one of the strongest predictors of reoffense in the Cottle et al. (2001) meta-analysis, with an effect size in the medium range. However, it is important to note that the influence of family-based risk factors may vary considerably on a case-by-case basis. For example, in the context of a risk assessment, we would consider a high-conflict family environment to be a much more salient risk factor for a youth returning from a facility to his or her conflictual home than we would for a youth who will soon be placed in a group home or independent living facility.

Peer Influences

Peer influences are strongly associated with delinquency in general and violence in particular (Hawkins et al., 2000; Lipsey & Derzon, 1998). First, *rejection* by peers relates to aggression. Not only does peer rejection serve as a marker of aggressive, intrusive, or impulsive behavior among young children; rejection actually appears to be a causal factor in terms of continuing and escalating aggressive behavior as an adolescent (Hinshaw & Lee, 2003).

Even more research has addressed *delinquent peer affiliation* as predicting delinquency, aggression, and violence. These findings do not simply reflect the fact that birds of a feather flock together. Rather, long-term studies with sophisticated analytic procedures reveal a direct causal relationship between delinquent peers and subsequent delinquency and aggression (Elliott & Menard, 1996; Patterson, Capaldi, & Bank, 1991) and violence in particular (Farrington, 1989). Related to delinquent peer affiliation, *gang affiliation,* in particular, is associated with increased risk for violence (Hawkins et al., 1998, 2000) *even beyond* the risk attributable to delinquent peers alone (Battin, Hill, Abbott, Catalano, & Hawkins, 1998).

Finally, a lack of peer relationships is also problematic; youth who are isolated or withdrawn tend to be at greater risk for violence (USDHHS, 2001).

Neighborhood Context

Neighborhood context appears to play a considerable role in violence, generally speaking (Sampson, Raudenbush, & Earls, 1997), as well as juvenile violence in particular (Farrington, 1989; Ludwig, Duncan, & Hirschfield, 2001, as cited in Mulvey, 2005; Thornberry et al., 1995). Borum and Verhaagen (2006) echoed other researchers who suggested that one reason disorganized, criminogenic neighborhoods relate to violence is because these neighborhoods are likely to expose youth to crimes at earlier ages, thereby predisposing them to early-onset violence. Ingoldsby and Shaw (2002) explained that although researchers typically speculate about the indirect effects of neighborhoods on early child development, it is youth in middle childhood who are particularly vulnerable to the influence of a criminogenic neighborhood.

Caveats Important to Considering Risk Factors among Juveniles

The list of risk factors just reviewed is necessarily brief and incomplete. Clinicians who anticipate conducting risk assessments with juveniles should spend time in the rich literature at the intersection of criminology and developmental psychopathology (see, e.g., Dishion & Patterson, 2006; Hinshaw & Lee, 2003; Howell, 2003; Howell Krisberg, Hawkins, & Wilson, 1995; Loeber & Farrington, 1998; Moffitt, 2006; see also the *Surgeon General's Report on Youth Violence,* USDHHS, 2001), considering not only lengthy lists of identified risk factors for violence, but the ways these interact. Four other caveats are also in order.

First, with only a few exceptions, the empirically supported risk factors for youth violence are much more helpful in predicting the near future than the distant future (Mulvey, 2005). Although we mentioned this as a limitation to the use of psychopathy assessment, it holds true for the vast majority of risk factors. Youth who begin with very similar risk factors may eventually arrive at very different outcomes (multifinality), and youth who begin with very different risk factors may eventually arrive at the same adverse outcome (equifinality), such as violence (Cicchetti & Rogosch, 1996). Thus, developmental psychopathologists emphasize a humble approach to long-term prediction. Of course, this corresponds well with general guidance on risk assessment, which holds that evaluator opinions about short-term risk are more likely to be valid than opinions about longer term risk.

Second, these empirically identified risk factors tend to be more important in the cumulative sense than in the individual sense. For example, in the prospective Pittsburgh Youth Study of over 1,500 urban boys, those with four or more risk factors for homicide were 14 times more likely to later commit homicide than boys with fewer than four risk factors, *regardless of which risk factors were considered* (Loeber et al., 2005). Developmental scholars have long emphasized that it is much more likely to be the cumulative effect of risk factors, rather than any specific risk factor, that contributes to negative outcomes (see generally Sameroff, 2000; see Mulvey, 2005, with respect to juvenile risk assessment). Of course, this does not preclude the possibility that one particular risk factor could, alone, create a very high risk for violence in a particular case (e.g., consider the youth with an escalating pattern of domestic assaults in an already high-conflict home). But, empirically speaking, the accumulation of risk factors is almost always more influential than any specific risk factor.

Third, as mentioned in the case of substance abuse, many of the risk factors may vary by age. For example, meta-analysis revealed that delinquent peers was one of the strongest ($r = .37$) predictors of late-adolescent violence among youth in the 12 to 14 age range; yet, delinquent peers was the weakest predictor ($r = .04$) of late-adolescent violence among youth in the 6 to 11 age range (USDHHS, 2001, adapting data from Hawkins et al., 1998, and Lipsey & Derzon, 1998).

Fourth, we discuss empirically supported risk factors because considering such factors is a crucial part of any risk assessment strategy. However, risk factors are just that: factors that increase *risk*. No single factor or set of factors can accurately predict violence for all youth, and many youth—even with many accumulated risk factors—do not become violent (USDHHS, 2001). These are basic truths of risk assessment, of course. But they bear repeating in any discussion of youth violence because youth violence, in particular, has been plagued with numerous and widely publicized, simplistic efforts to construct profiles or checklists that identify violent youth.

Instruments to Guide
Consideration of Risk Factors

Although there are currently no widely applicable actuarial measures to provide risk estimates, there are a few recently developed measures that guide evaluators through consideration of relevant risk factors.

The Structured Assessment of Violence Risk in Youth (SAVRY; Borum, Bartel, & Forth, 2000, 2006) is composed of risk factors drawn from youth violence research. The SAVRY exemplifies the structured professional judgment approach to risk assessment. Under ideal circumstances, a well-trained evaluator scores the measure based on an interview with the examinee and a detailed review of collateral records. The measure includes 24 broad risk factors distributed across three categories (historical, individual, and contextual); it also includes six broad protective factors. As in the HCR-20, evaluators code each item on a 3-point scale (low, moderate, or high) based on the degree to which the risk factor is present in the case at hand; protective items are scored as present or absent. Although at the time of this writing no peer-reviewed, published studies of the SAVRY are available, Borum and colleagues (Borum, 2006; Borum, Bartel, & Forth, 2005; Borum & Verhaagen, 2006; www.fmhi.usf.edu/mhlp/savry/statement.htm) provided strong preliminary evidence for the measure's reliability and validity.

The Youth Level of Service/Case Management Inventory (YLS/CMI; Hoge & Andrews, 2002) is somewhat broader than a typical risk measure, in that it also includes factors related to service needs. Like its predecessor, the Level of Service Inventory—Revised (Andrews & Bonta, 1995) for adults, the YLS/CMI was based on the well-known risk/needs perspective (Andrews et al., 1990). This perspective holds that (a) services should be proportional to the offender's level of risk, with more intensive intervention for those at higher risk; (b) services should be specific to the offender's individual intervention needs; and (c) intervention decisions should take into account individual offender characteristics that may influence one's response to the intervention. Juvenile justice professionals—they need not be clinicians—complete the YLS/CMI on the basis of file review and interview.

The measure includes 42 risk and needs items (across eight sub-scales), which the evaluator can designate as present or absent; one can also designate the particular subscale as an area of strength for the youth. The measure then includes a mechanism for summarizing the risk/needs factors, identifying other factors that may be relevant to case planning. The measure allows for a professional override that allows the evaluator to consider all available information to form a risk estimate. Notably, "the User's Manual stresses that the YLS/CMI is not to be used in a rigid fashion to dictate decisions based on a scoring algorithm" (Hoge, 2005, p. 285). Generally, research supports the YLS/CMI in terms of concurrent validity with similar measures; perhaps more important, research tends to provide moderate support for the measure's predictive validity with respect to reoffending (for review, see Hoge, 2005).

The Early Assessment Risk Lists, one for boys and one for girls (Augimeri, Koegl, Webster, & Levene, 2001) were developed specifically for young (<12) children who are demonstrating aggressive behaviors and appear at risk for escalating conduct problems (Augimeri, Koegl, Levene, & Webster, 2005). The measure includes items related to the child and the child's context (family, neighborhood, poverty, peers) that research has shown to correspond with future antisocial behavior. Like the HCR-20, the measure includes a number of empirically supported items across a number of domains, allowing the evaluator to code each item on a 3-point scale, based on the degree to which it is salient to the child examinee. Like other youth risk measures, research appears to be in the early stages, with little in the way of peer-reviewed, published validity data. However, the authors reported promising preliminary results (Augimeri et al., 2005; see also www.childdevelop.ca/public_html /research/research_risk.html).

Idiographic Risk Factors and Individualized Assessment

As should be clear, clinicians can access a wealth of research-derived data to examine empirically supported risk factors for a particular juvenile. However, a review of idiographic factors remains essential. As among adults, there may be unique manifestations of well-known risk factors. For example, substance abuse is a risk factor in general, but may become even more salient for juveniles who ingest substances specifically to reduce their inhibitions or increase their aggression. Grisso (1998) described violent youth who *only* engaged in violence when using substances, youth who *never* engaged in violence when using substances, and youth who engaged in violence *regardless* of whether they were using substances. Thus, data regarding a youth's past pattern of substance abuse vis-à-vis violence are essential. Likewise, a youth may manifest a history of responding to psychiatric symptoms with aggression and violence or, conversely, becoming more passive when psychiatric symptoms are active.

Although we have stressed the importance of context for risk assessments in general, an idiographic assessment of context becomes especially important with juveniles. One reason is that social relationships compose a large part of a juvenile's context. As most adults remember, the role of peer relationships during the adolescent years is profound. Indeed, there is a large subgroup of youth who commit violence only as part of a peer group. Consider, for example, youth who fight only in the context of their gang affiliation or who commit robbery only with peers. One of us recently evaluated a young man with a history of school success and no juvenile record of any sort, until his affluent family moved to another state and he found new friends, with whom he began a lengthy series of violent crimes (carjackings, bank robberies, and a rape) that spanned age 17 through 19.

Consideration of peer rejection may also reveal important information about the types of situations in which violence may be more likely. Some youth have a history of engaging in violence only in response to teasing or ostracism. One colleague tells the story of conducting an evaluation with a shy adolescent who had no history of violence until he murdered a peer who had teased him about his facial acne.

Idiographic consideration of relationships might decrease, rather than increase, perceived risk. Research suggests that a stable relationship with a caring adult is one of the strongest factors that protect high-risk youth against negative outcomes (Luthar, 2006; Werner, 2000). Many youth are less likely to engage in violence when in close proximity to a parent, grandparent, or other adult with whom they maintain a long-term supportive relationship. Conversely, knowing that a youth has recently separated from a significant adult (through death, relocation, etc.) might prompt an evaluator to query how this loss influences the risk for violence.

Another reason context is so important to consider in juvenile risk assessment involves the role of family. Youth, more so than adults, may have difficulty extracting themselves from a high-conflict home environment simply because they may have fewer options for independent living outside the home. Consider, for example, the common situation in which conflict erupts between an adolescent son and his mother's new live-in boyfriend. Family may have little bearing on an adult's risk for violence, but family should almost always be a consideration in juvenile risk (the only exception being if a juvenile will clearly be confined far from his or her family for the foreseeable future).

Evaluators should consider carefully the contexts to which a juvenile is likely to return after the risk assessment and examine the extent to which he or she has engaged in (or refrained from) violence in similar contexts in the past. Is the context one in which it would be difficult to refrain from violence even if highly motivated to do so (e.g., a house with a lengthy history of police visits, in which family members handle most conflicts with physical aggression)? Conversely, is the context one in which it would be difficult to engage in violence even if highly motivated to do so (i.e., a highly secure juvenile correctional facility)? What types of individuals is the youth likely to encounter, and how has the youth fared with similar individuals in the past?

Risk Communication

In the Chapter 7 discussion of risk communication, we emphasized the need to communicate risk with respect to particular contexts. For reasons just discussed, this becomes especially important in juvenile risk assessment. Grisso (1998, pp. 129–130) emphasized the importance of context in risk communication:

> A clinical opinion about the likelihood of future harm must always be provided with reference to some social context. It makes no sense, and is of little assistance to a court, to say that a youth "is likely to be violent in the future." For a given youth, clinicians should strive to describe the likelihood of harmful behavior in the specific setting or social circumstance that the youth will face. . . . Clinicians often should form several opinions about a youth's prospects for future violence, corresponding to various future social contexts. For example, the clinician might have one opinion about the likelihood of violence if the youth is returned home, another if the youth is placed in a group home, and a third about aggression if the youth is placed in a secure youth facility.

We echo Grisso's advice, and emphasize that forming and communicating opinions with respect to context may require additional work from the evaluator. First, this requires that the evaluator has carefully studied past violent incidents across their contexts, as already discussed. Second, it requires that the evaluator know the likely contexts in which a youth might reside. This may involve becoming familiar with the likely community placements and conditions of confinement, probation, or living arrangements. Nevertheless, this extra research leads to better informed and more useful risk communication.

A second essential component in any risk communication message about a juvenile is a clear time frame (Mulvey, 2005). Again, this holds true for risk assessments overall, but becomes more important because adolescence is a state of flux. Also, as reviewed earlier, the vast majority of delinquent youth do not engage in violence as adults. Specifying the time-limited nature of any risk estimate helps prevent the risk communication audience from misperceiving risk as an enduring, static trait of a juvenile, who may change considerably as he or she ages. Other aspects of the risk communication that we covered in Chapter 7 hold true for juveniles as well. For example, risk should still be communicated with a reference group (e.g., other youth in the same psychiatric facility or probation department; other youth who have passed through the state juvenile justice system and for whom recidivism data are available).

A Note about Language and Labels

Clinicians who conduct forensic evaluations are participating in—and usually influencing—the weighty, life-changing decisions that courts make about the individuals under their jurisdiction. Thus, forensic clinicians should always offer opinions carefully and precisely. However, the need for cautious and thoughtful communication is heightened further in forensic evaluations of juveniles. Scholars have long emphasized—indeed, the juvenile court was founded on—the premise that adolescence is a time of malleability and rapid change preceding an adulthood in which personality and behavior become more fixed and less flexible. Decisions or experiences during adolescence may shift profoundly one's course of development, in ways that may be difficult to alter once one reaches adulthood. In this sense, the stakes are higher when evaluators contribute to court decisions about juveniles as compared to decisions about adults; decisions about juveniles may have more pronounced or far-reaching consequences. Thus, evaluators should be even more careful to strive for clarity and avoid misunderstandings.

Recently, scholars have devoted considerable attention to the potential impact of diagnostic labels and language in juvenile court with respect to the construct of youth psychopathy. Results of a psychopathy assessment are most likely to emerge in juvenile court in the context of a risk assessment. However, even those who recommend youth psychopathy assessment as one aspect of evaluating short-term violence risk understandably admonish clinicians to "avoid diagnostic labeling" (Vitacco & Vincent, 2006, p. 34). Likewise, many concerned scholars have understandably emphasized the "negative label" (Vincent & Hart, 2002, p. 154) or even the "damning label" (Edens, Skeem, et al., 2001, p. 76) of psychopathy and expressed concern that describing juveniles as psychopathic may increase the likelihood of transfer to adult courts, longer or harsher sentences, or other adverse consequences (Petrila & Skeem, 2003; Seagrave & Grisso, 2002; Steinberg, 2002).

However, systematic studies of juvenile court personnel, including judges (Murrie, Boccaccini, McCoy, & Cornell, 2007) and juvenile probation officers (Murrie, Cornell, & McCoy, 2005), suggest that decision makers are influenced little by *labels* per se.* Generally, juvenile justice participants in these studies were much more influenced by a juvenile's history of antisocial behavior and, to a somewhat lesser extent, a description of psychopathic personality traits (e.g., charming but manipulative, poor empathy and remorse, denied responsibility) than they were influenced by the diagnostic labels psychopathy or conduct disorder.

Do these findings suggest that evaluators can loosely apply provocative labels, comfortable that they yield little influence? Not at all. Study results like these should expand—not narrow—the range of communication about which an evaluator is cautious. In other words, the need for evaluators to use caution in communication extends far beyond simple diagnostic labels, to include even the descriptive narrative about a juvenile or that juvenile's past behaviors. Clinicians should consider carefully whether there is sufficient evidence to support grave claims such as whether a youth has a substantial history of antisocial behavior, lacks empathy for others, or has little remorse for his or her actions. Reports should include information that is directly relevant to violence risk but, if there is no discernable link to violence potential or risk management, avoid background data that might come across as provocative, sensational, or disturbing.

Risk Management

Because most juveniles desist from delinquency by the time they enter adulthood, and because adolescence is a time of malleability, an optimistic approach might conceptualize most (though not all) risk management of juveniles as a short term task that is likely to become unnecessary within a few years. This perspective seems even more plausible when we consider that most youth who enter the ju-

---

*One notable exception was juvenile justice clinicians (Rockett, Murrie, & Boccaccini, 2007), who, perhaps not surprisingly, did appear to be somewhat influenced by diagnostic labels, in contrast to the nonclinical juvenile justice personnel.

venile justice system never return for a new referral and most young offenders are managed in the community (Snyder & Sickmund, 1999). How then, is risk management best carried out?

First, back to risk assessment. Any risk management plan will involve repeated risk assessments (Vitacco & Vincent, 2006), probably at briefer intervals than would be typical among adults. This is necessary because adolescents change rapidly in many respects, and we assume risk state is likely one more domain in which change is frequent.

The remaining components of risk management for juveniles are much like the general risk management principles we detailed in Chapter 8 and reflect the risk/needs and responsivity principles discussed by Andrews and colleagues (e.g., Andrews & Bonta, 2003; Andrews et al., 1990; Hoge & Andrews, 1996). In other words, maximum energy and resources should be devoted to the highest risk offenders, identified risk factors must be linked to management strategies, and a centralized entity must monitor the plan.

Borum (2003) detailed a similar risk management approach specific to juvenile offenders that involved the following: (a) Apply intensive resources selectively in high-risk cases; (b) choose criminogenic targets for intervention; (c) do what works; and (d) implement, follow up, and modify. Key in Borum's model was an emphasis on *addressing those factors that are clearly related to recidivism risk*, a principle that sometimes gets overlooked in the enthusiasm over broader goals such as improving psychological functioning or improving self-esteem.

It is important to note that there may be more risk management options for juveniles than are available in the adult criminal justice system. Well-designed, empirically supported interventions for youth with conduct problems are increasingly disseminated beyond universities and teaching hospitals and are being adopted by community and justice agencies. For example, multisystemic therapy (Henggeler et al., 1998) is increasingly popular and has demonstrated some success even with serious, violent young offenders. Likewise, multidimensional family therapy (Henderson, Marvel, & Liddle, in press) and parent management training (Kazdin, 2005) have proven effective with delinquent, including violent, youth. A key component to these successful interventions is the emphasis on addressing a range of risk factors simultaneously. When feasible and appropriate, these approaches can serve as the backbone of a sensible risk management plan.

Three Common Risk Assessments in Juvenile Court

Three distinct types of juvenile proceedings are so common as to merit separate discussion, albeit as a brief overview. The first type involves aiding the juvenile justice system in determining pretrial decisions; the second, dispositions; and the third, assisting the court in deciding whether the case should be transferred to adult court.

Pretrial Proceedings

One issue to be determined is whether the youth should be placed back in the community while awaiting further proceedings. A second is determining whether the case should proceed to formal adjudication at all. It is fairly common for juvenile courts to consider some form of deferred adjudication for young offenders. In both of these instances, the required risk assessment may be relatively short term, and the court has considerable control over conditions of release. The evaluator may also have the opportunity to evaluate the exact circumstances the youth will confront. Idiographic factors for analysis would include (but are not limited to): options regarding living arrangements, restrictions on movement and associations, access to victims, degrees of supervision, availability of services, and efficacy of services recommended. Again, many referral questions related to pretrial proceedings are particularly conducive to a risk management model and allow the evaluator considerable flexibility in offering recommendations to reduce risk.

Disposition

In juvenile court, the stated function of disposition is for the purpose of rehabilitation and prevention of further criminal conduct rather than for punishment or retribution. At the disposition phase, options are broader and often include confinement to a structured environment. Time frames to be considered are generally longer than during the pretrial phase. Courts are usually concerned about both risk of violence and risk of reoffending. Risk management plans are often a primary focus in this type of evaluation. Special factors to be considered in determining this type of risk include: types of structured environments available, length of time for which the court will have jurisdiction, and all potential community resources.

Transfer to Adult Court

This type of evaluation is much less common than evaluations for pretrial conditions or disposition. However, the consequences are profound. In the extreme, it could mean the difference between a few years under the jurisdiction of the state youth authority and a lifetime in an adult prison facility. In *Kent v. United States* (1966), the U. S. Supreme Court suggested a set of factors that courts could consider when determining whether a youth should be transferred (also referred to as waived or certified) to adult court. Among them was protection of the public. In a 1997 national survey, Heilbrun, Leheny, Thomas, and Huneycutt found that risk of future criminality was one of five factors typically included in state statutes.

Salekin, Yff, Neumann, Leistico, and Zalot (2002) noted that dangerousness is now explicitly included in these statutes in all 50 states; however, the meaning is almost never specifically defined. Some courts interpret the issue as dangerousness extending into adulthood. Given what we know about the potential for violent juveniles becoming nonviolent adults, this is probably an impossible question to answer with any reasonable degree of clinical certainty. Other more immediate questions, however, include: Is the court concerned about risk to other juveniles if the individual is placed in a juvenile facility? Is the court concerned because there is insufficient time for interventions from the juvenile justice system (a particular concern with older juveniles)? Is the court concerned about risk due to early release? To do a thorough assessment when transfer is being considered, evaluators need to assess a variety of risk management options and attempt to project future risk under each condition. A final dilemma for evaluators revolves around the issue of the alleged offense. The individual is presumed innocent until proven guilty. Should the evaluator consider the offense behavior at all? Should the evaluator talk with the juvenile about the offense? Important, in many jurisdictions, reports drafted for transfer decision purposes become part of the defendant's file in adult court. (For a more complete discussion of issues in transfer evaluations, see Grisso, 1998.) As with all juvenile risk assessments, this type requires a thorough knowledge of development, including the tendency for most delinquent youth to desist from offending.

12

Risk Assessment of Death Penalty Defendants

A t the time of this writing, 38 states, in addition to the military and the federal government, allow for capital punishment. The number of actual executions varies widely, from the five states that have not carried out an execution since 1976 to Texas, where 379 persons were executed between 1976 and 2006. The number of death sentences pronounced nationwide has declined steadily since an all-time high of 277 in 1999 to 128 in 2005. Actual executions declined during that same period from 98 in 1999 to 53 in 2006 (Death Penalty Information Center, 2007; for additional statistics regarding capital punishment, see www.deathpenaltyinfo.org).

The U.S. Supreme Court has traditionally singled out capital punishment as qualitatively different from any other sanctions imposed by the state (*Woodson v. North Carolina*, 1976). The justices have further expressed the strong belief that, because the penalty, when completed, is final and irrevocable, great care must be exercised to assure that a sentence of death is imposed in a reliable manner (*Lockett v. Ohio*, 1978).

Data indicate that testimony with regard to risk in the punishment phase of capital trials has become almost routine in some jurisdictions (Edens, Buffington-Vollum, Keilen, Roskamp, & Anthony, 2005). Although many perceive that juries in these cases are very concerned with future risk (Sorensen & Pilgrim, 2000), it is not clear to what degree expert testimony influences perceptions about future risk. Nonetheless, mental health professionals must be cognizant of the gravity of the decision with which they are assisting the trier of fact and the irrevocable nature of its potential result. In this endeavor it is essential that the best available methodology be used and the best available evidence be presented.

Defining the Question

Given the gravity of capital cases, it becomes even more important to reach a clear understanding with attorneys about the nature and scope of the evaluation and the ways evaluation findings will be presented. However, the actual risk assessment question is essentially similar across capital cases. Evaluators are tasked with a risk assessment that will be used to inform jury considerations about risk, or future dangerousness, in the penalty phase of a death penalty trial. To understand this general risk assessment question, evaluators must also understand the broader legal context of the death penalty in the United States and the series of landmark cases that defined this context.

The Legal Context

In 1972, the U.S. Supreme Court ruled that the death penalty as then applied was unconstitutional because it amounted to cruel and unusual punishment, violating the 8th Amendment to the U.S. Constitution (*Furman v. Georgia*). In a somewhat unusual step, each of the justices wrote separately. Two justices held that the death penalty was simply morally untenable; however, the remainder of the Court objected, not to the penalty itself, but to the dearth of guidelines for its imposition and the resulting arbitrariness. Most death penalty states quickly set to work redrafting more specific statutes that would govern capital punishment. Texas was the first state to specifically charge the jury with addressing future risk as a special issue. Specifically, Texas law requires the jury to determine, if the individual is not executed, "whether there is a probability that the defendant would commit criminal acts of violence that would constitute a continuing threat to society" (Texas Code of Criminal Procedure Annotated, art. 37.071 §2(b)(1) 2002). The statue went on to say, "The state must prove each issue submitted under Subsection b of this article beyond a reasonable doubt" (Texas Code of Criminal Procedure Annotated, art. 37.071 §2(c) 2002). Oregon quickly followed suit.

As expected, the new statute was challenged in court, and in 1976, the U.S. Supreme Court declared the recrafted Texas law to be constitutional (*Jurek v. Texas*). Although the justices acknowledged that the concept of dangerousness was vague, they reasoned that it was the key element of many types of legal decisions and, therefore, should not present unique problems in the context of capital sentencing. In 1983, the Supreme Court revisited the issue of assessing risk in capital cases. On this occasion, the Court ruled that psychiatrists should continue to testify regarding dangerousness in death penalty cases, even though data indicated they were wrong more often than not (*Barefoot v. Estelle*, 1983).

At the time of this writing, 21 states either allow or require juries to consider risk in death penalty cases (Buffington-Vollum, Edens, & Keilen, 2006). If not expressed in law as a special issue, it can be addressed as a statutory or nonstatutory aggravating factor. In practice, future dangerousness is commonly alleged against a varied group of capital defendants. For example, in federal capital cases, it was alleged in 21 of 37 (57%) instances prior to 1995 and in 75 of 84 (89%) cases between 1995 and 1999 (Cunningham & Goldstein, 2003; Cunningham & Reidy, 1999).

Death penalty trials are bifurcated proceedings; that is, guilt or innocence is decided in the first phase. If the defendant is found guilty, a second phase commences in which the same jury then proceeds to hear evidence and determine punishment. Rules of evidence are often much less strict during the penalty phase, and evidence not allowed during the guilt-innocence phase (e.g., the defendant's history of criminal or violent conduct) can be presented. In addition to evidence of future risk, courts have allowed presentation of evidence that suggests positive future adjustment (*Skipper v. South Carolina*, 1986). Almost all death penalty states now offer the option of life without parole (LWOP), though it remains to be seen what effect this additional option will have on juries.

Base Rates and Normative Data

In assessing risk among capital defendants, the most critical issue is base rates (Cunningham & Goldstein, 2003; Cunningham & Reidy, 1999). In the penalty phase of a capital case, the jury has the choice of sentencing the individual to life in prison or to death. Release to the community is not an option for any time in the foreseeable future. Therefore, when one is considering base rates of violent behavior, base rates of community violence are basically irrelevant. Rather, the evaluator needs to examine base rates of violence among capital offenders *while incarcerated.*

Base rates of prison violence are widely misunderstood by laypersons, who are apt to be selected for a jury. Over many years, prisons have been portrayed in the popular media as gladiator schools, where serious violence is a daily occurrence and inmates generally live in fear. After all, these are institutions populated by persons with a serious history of criminal violence. In actuality, however, incidents of serious violence in U.S. prisons are relatively rare (Cunningham & Sorensen, 2006a). In a broad review of criminal justice statistics, Cunningham and Reidy (1999) found rates of homicide in state correctional institutions to be lower than rates of homicide in the general community. More recent statistics indicate that the rate of homicide in the Texas Department of Criminal Justice was one-eighth the rate of homicide in the open U.S. population (Cunningham, 2006a). Serious assaults were also less frequent than in the community and generally limited to a very small group of offenders (Buffington-Vollum et al., 2006). In addition, as the seriousness of the assaultive behavior increases, the likelihood of occurrence decreases (Sorensen & Pilgrim, 2000). Finally, Cunningham (2006a) reported evidence of significant improvement in prison management in recent years, further reducing violence. Specifically, there was a 93% reduction in inmate-on-inmate homicide in the nation's prisons from 1980 to 2002.

Turning to specific base rates for violence among capital offenders, a rich literature has developed since the post-*Furman* return of capital punishment and the redrafting of statutes regarding future risk. Early studies compared inmates with commuted death sentences to control groups of noncapital inmates. Violent behavior by those with commuted death sentences was generally low compared to controls (Marquart, Ekland-Olson, & Sorensen, 1989, 1994; Marquart & Sorensen, 1988). More recent studies have yielded similar results. Edens, Buffington-Vollum et al. (2005) studied the prison disciplinary records of those inmates who had been sentenced to death based (at least in part) on testimony that they posed a risk of future dangerousness. These inmates had been on Texas's death row for an average of 9.5 years, including some time during which the unit was run as an open population and some time in which the unit was locked down. The researchers reported that no prison homicides were perpetrated by these offenders, and only 5.2% of this population committed any serious assaults. A study of Indiana data found that, over an average of 16 years, 15.4% of capital offenders committed assaults resulting in injury (Reidy, Cunningham, & Sorensen, 2001). Sorensen and Pilgrim (2000) reviewed prison records of over 6,000 inmates who had been convicted of murder. Based on their analysis, they projected that 83.6% of this sample would engage in no serious violence if incarcerated for 40 years. (For recent reviews of this growing body of literature, see Cunningham, 2006b; Cunningham, Reidy, & Sorensen, 2005; Edens, Buffington-Vollum, et al., 2005.)

Researchers have used several types of institutional data to quantify the behavior of capital inmates. One measure is confinement to disciplinary segregation; studies have suggested that disciplinary segregation is rare for former death row inmates (Marquart et al., 1989; Reidy et al., 2001). Some states have offered the eventual possibility of parole for this population. Rates of return to prison following parole violations summarized in a variety of studies ranged from 20% to 33% (Cunningham & Reidy, 1999). Rates were generally below return rates for the general population, and parole violations did not necessarily result from additional violent offenses.

Now that almost all jurisdictions offer the alternative of LWOP, observers have questioned whether those confined to LWOP would be more likely to commit violent acts within the prison system. Commentators have speculated, and prosecutors have argued, that, unlike those with the possibility of parole in the distant future, LWOP inmates would have nothing to lose. However, available research does not indicate any greater risk of violence among the

LWOP population (Sorensen & Wrinkle, 1996). Of particular interest are data generated at the Potosi Correctional Center in Missouri. At this high-security facility, death-sentenced, LWOP, and parole-eligible inmates are intermingled and have equal opportunity to engage in violence. However, in an 11-year review of inmate records, LWOP inmates were half as likely to engage in violence as their parole-eligible counterparts (Cunningham, Sorensen, & Reidy, 2005). In a large-sample study in the Florida Department of Corrections, Cunningham and Sorensen (2006b) found that LWOP inmates were not at a disproportionate risk of institutional violence compared to other long-term inmates.

Review of base rate data relevant to prison violence is complicated by varied operational definitions of this misconduct. Evaluators reading any empirical research on this topic should carefully note how the investigators define violent misconduct. Some studies review "prison misconduct" or "disciplinary infractions," and these terms may seriously inflate the measure of violence (Cunningham & Reidy, 1998a; Cunningham, Reidy, & Sorensen, 2005; Edens, Buffington-Vollum, et al., 2005). For example, we doubt that legislatures concerned about risk for future criminal violence were referring to an inmate interfering with the taking of count, misusing his or her commissary privileges, hoarding extra snacks, or shouting obscenities; nevertheless, all of these are commonly documented as institutional infractions. Even the term *assault* can be misleading. For example, pushing someone or throwing a relatively harmless object at him or her will generally be classified as assault for disciplinary purposes. It is helpful when researchers are specific in their definitions. Sorensen and Pilgrim (2000, p. 1260) specify violent acts as "assaultive or dangerous acts that either cause, or have the imminent potential to cause, serious bodily injury." Minor assaults are much more common than assaults that result in serious bodily injury. For instance, Buffington-Vollum and colleagues (2006) found a yearly rate of minor assaults to be 9.46 per 100 inmates, but only 0.32 per 100 inmates for serious assaults. A recent series of studies have disaggregated rates of assaultive misconduct in prison by potentially violent misconduct, assaults, assaults with injuries, and assaults with serious injuries (Cunningham & Sorensen, 2006a, 2006b).

When we present seminars or workshops on this topic, it is not uncommon to hear questions such as "Isn't this a totally biased review?" or "Where are the data for the prosecution's expert?" We would caution against the idea that there are "prosecution data" and "defense data"; there are simply scientific data. As of the time of this writing, we have found no data reported in the literature to suggest that the rate of violent behavior among incarcerated murderers, whether on death row or not, is appreciably higher than that of other inmates or that capital-convicted inmates, as a group, present a greater risk in the prison system than any other inmates. However, evaluators should be aware that this flies in the face of opinions held by the typical juror. In interviews with former capital jurors, Sorensen and Pilgrim (2000) found that among jurors who issued death sentences, the median estimate was an 85% probability that the individual would commit another violent crime if not sentenced to death. They estimated a 50% probability that this crime would be a homicide. This research team found that, in reality, among 6,000 incarcerated murders, only seven homicides had been committed during their collective 29,074.5 years of confinement.

Empirically Supported Risk Factors

The low base rate of prison violence among those convicted of capital murder suggests that extremely small subsets of capital inmates are likely to commit violence. Though this alone makes it difficult to distinguish the small subset of inmates who will commit prison violence from those who will not, we turn now to specific risk factors. In examining the potential variables, we should perhaps begin by dispelling certain myths about what is predictive of violent misconduct during incarceration. Probably the most commonly held misunderstanding is that a history of violence in the community reliably predicts violence while incarcerated. This would seem to be consistent with the age-old truism that past behavior is the best predictor of future behavior. However, research to date suggests that this is not the case. If it were, maximum security prisons, by definition populated by those who have committed the most violent crimes, should be exceedingly violent. They are not, as is evidenced by the low base rates of violence cited earlier. In studies in which clinicians have used violence in the community as a criterion, predictive validity tended to be very low (R. Cooper & Werner, 1990). The environment of a prison and the environment of the open community are fundamentally different, and behavior in one is not predictive of behavior in the other (Cunningham & Reidy, 1999; Flanagan, 1980). To illustrate, Cunningham (2006a) summarized data from the Texas Department of Criminal Justice for 2005. Despite the many persistently violent individuals housed in the department, the rate of inmate-on-inmate homicide was only 1.28 per 100,000. No staff members were victims of homicide during 2005; the national average in U.S. correctional facilities is one staff homicide per million inmates per year. The seriousness of offenses an inmate committed in the community is also unrelated to prison conduct (Alexander & Austin, 1992; Stephan, 1989). Prior convictions and even history of escape are also very weak predictors of future prison violence (Cunningham & Reidy, 1999).

Another misunderstanding meriting attention is that a diagnosis of antisocial personality disorder (APD) is a good predictor of violent misconduct while incarcerated. The problem with the assumption is that APD is too pervasive in prisons. Well-conducted studies place the prevalence of APD at anywhere from 49% to 80% in the male prison population (Cunningham & Reidy, 1998a). A feature common to 80% of a population gives us little help in identifying the small percentage of that population likely to commit acts of violence. Along these lines, Cunningham (2006a, p. 835) proposed the following maxim: "Any characteristic that is present in the majority of subjects in a targeted population will fail to predict a low base-rate (i.e., highly infrequent) behavior."

One variable that seems to be associated with increased risk for violent behavior in almost every domain is substance abuse (Gendreau et al., 1996; G. T. Harris et al., 1993; Klassen & O'Connor, 1988, 1994; Lindqvist, 1991; Melton et al., 1997; Pihl & Peterson, 1993; Swanson, 1994; Swanson et al., 1990). Many violent offenders were abusing substances at the time of, or in the days preceding, their offenses (Cunningham & Reidy, 1999). However, substance abuse has limited utility when addressing violence in a correctional environment. The first reason for this limitation is much the same as that expressed in regard to APD: A history of substance abuse is so pervasive among prison inmates (in this case, women as well as men) that it would not differentiate the small group at high risk for violence (Cunningham & Reidy, 2002). Second, although alcohol and illegal drugs are available in prisons, they are not available to nearly the degree they are in the community, and their use is apt to be detected and punished.

What factors, then, *do* bear any empirical relationship to violence in prison? At the top of the list is age at the time of incarceration (Cunningham & Sorensen, 2006a; Sorensen & Pilgrim, 2000). Age appears to be inversely related to propensity for assault.

Beyond the age of initial incarceration, rates of rule infractions decline dramatically as inmates age within the system (Cunningham & Reidy, 1998b; Flanagan, 1980; Sorensen & Pilgrim, 2000; Sorensen & Wrinkle, 1996). Hirschi and Gottfredson (1983) presented dramatic data from the New York prison system in 1975 indicating that inmates in their 20s were 10 times more likely to commit rule infractions than were inmates in their 60s, with steady decline in between. In addition, disciplinary infractions were more likely during the first few years of confinement (Cunningham & Sorensen, 2006b). Steadily increasing age and time in confinement are particularly important in death penalty evaluations, as it is highly likely the individual who is sentenced to death will spend a number of years on death row prior to execution. Therefore, an inmate's years of highest risk may be past before an execution will occur.

Not surprisingly, another factor associated with future violent behavior while incarcerated is prior prison violence (Sorensen & Pilgrim, 2000). There is some evidence that simply having served a prior prison term may elevate risk (Cunningham & Sorensen, 2006a; Sorensen & Pilgrim, 2000). However, having completed a probated sentence does not.

Another issue to be considered is length of sentence. Counterintuitively, evidence suggests that persons with shorter sentences are more likely to engage in violence (Cunningham & Reidy, 1999; Cunningham & Sorensen, 2006a; Flanagan, 1980). Perhaps inmates with longer sentences perceive greater need to adapt to prison rules. One other factor to be considered is gang membership (Sorensen & Pilgrim, 2000).

A potential protective factor is education, which correlates inversely with prison disciplinary infractions (Cunningham & Sorensen, 2006a; Toch & Adams, 1986). In other words, more educated inmates appear somewhat less likely to engage in violence or other misbehavior.

Overall, in terms of important risk factors, we would echo the conclusion Cunningham and Reidy (1999) offered:

> Past community violence is not strongly or consistently associated with prison violence.
> Current offense, prior convictions, and escape history are only very weakly associated with prison misconduct.
> Severity of offense is not a good predictor of prison adjustment.

The literature on this issue is complex and rapidly growing. While we hope the risk factors reviewed here provide an accurate overview, any mental health professional who steps into the weighty task of evaluating capital defendants must be prepared to carefully review the most current research available.

Using Instruments to Assess Risk Factors

Given the unique context of the prison environment, it seems unlikely that instruments developed on other populations or for different purposes would be applicable. A recent survey of case law found that Hare's (1991, 2003) PCL-R, the leading measure of psychopathy in applied settings, had been addressed as part of a capital sentencing evaluation in only four published cases (DeMatteo & Edens, 2006); however, there is no way of knowing how often it has been used in cases that have not been published. Still, there are significant reasons to question the use of the PCL-R in capital evaluations, given that it does little to predict the very low base rate occurrence of prison violence (Cunningham & Reidy, 2002; Edens, Buffington-Vollum, et al., 2005; Edens, Petrila, et al.,

2001). Recognizing the PCL-R's poor applicability to capital case evaluations, in at least two cases the court specifically excluded the use of PCL-R evidence in capital sentencing (*U.S. v. Lee*, 2000; *U.S. v. Taylor*, 2004).

Initial research suggested that PCL-R scores might have a positive relationship with institutional misconduct (Hare & McPherson, 1984). However, later review of this material noted that the misconduct included suicidal behavior, verbal threats, and belligerent attitudes (Cunningham & Sorensen, 2006a). The relationship of scores to violence could not be determined. Over the past 20 years, a rather large body of literature has developed examining the relationship between PCL-R scores and violent behavior in correctional institutions. In 2001, Edens, Petrila, et al. reviewed what evidence was then available, organized the data into tabular form (pp. 448–450), and concluded that there was little solid evidence that psychopathy was associated with the types of violence generally considered in capital cases. In 2005, Edens, Buffington-Vollum, and colleagues reviewed work published since 2001 and reached a similar conclusion: "In most recent studies using samples of U.S. male prison inmates, the PCL-R has demonstrated minimal ability to predict future aggressive institutional behavior, however broadly or narrowly one chooses to define it" (p. 68). Other reviewers have also failed to find data supporting the use of the PCL-R for risk assessment in capital cases (Cunningham, Sorensen, et al., 2005). A recent and rigorous meta-analysis of the PCL-R and institutional infractions (Guy et al., 2005) found the weakest effect sizes when physically violent misconduct was addressed. Effect sizes were especially small for U.S. prison samples.

Given the very weak relationship thus far established between PCL-R scores and institutional violence, it appears indefensible to use this instrument in a violence risk assessment conducted in a capital case. In addition, recent findings suggest that presentation of PCL-R data or labeling the defendant psychopathic can have a prejudicial effect, resulting in jurors taking a more negative view of the defendant (Edens, Colwell, Desforges, & Fernandez, 2005; Edens, Desforges, Fernandez, & Palac, 2004). These factors would raise serious ethical concerns about any application of the PCL-R in these proceedings.

Very little research has been done to date specifically addressing the relationship between other established risk assessment instruments (e.g., VRAG, Level of Service Inventory-Revised, HCR-20) and future violent conduct while incarcerated. Given the VRAG's heavy dependence on the PCL-R score, its use would be questionable for reasons already discussed. Considering the instruments overall, there are too few data to justify their use at the present time (Cunningham, Sorensen, et al., 2005; Edens, Colwell, et al., 2005).

Scholars have recognized a need to develop an instrument uniquely suited to risk assessment in capital cases, that is, one designed to assess the risk of serious violent conduct in secure prison environments. However, this effort is constrained by the low base rate of such conduct, making it much like finding the proverbial needle in a haystack. In prediction, low base rates of the relevant behavior lead to significant numbers of false positives and low positive predictive power. These factors would be of particular concern when the issue of life and death is being decided.

Nonetheless, Sorensen and Pilgrim (2000) began the development of an actuarial instrument specific to capital cases. To do this, they reviewed records of over 6,000 men incarcerated for murder in the Texas Department of Criminal Justice. Violent acts were defined as "assaultive or dangerous acts that either cause, or have the imminent potential to cause, bodily injury" (p. 1260). From a broad inventory of possible predictors, six were found to be significant: (1) age, (2) prison gang membership, (3) contemporaneous offenses of robbery or burglary, (4) multiple murder victims, (5) additional attempted murder or assault related to the offense, and (6) having served a prior prison term. Initially results suggested that the scale could prove useful. Edens, Buffington-Vollum, and colleagues (2005) agreed that the scale had promise but needed more research. Later research indicated that it performed somewhat better for nonviolent infractions than for violent ones (Buffington-Vollum et al., 2006).

Cunningham, Sorensen, et al. (2005) continued work on the development of an actuarial measure at the Potosi Correctional Center in Missouri. For comparison, they broadened the base of offenders beyond just those incarcerated for murder. Again results were promising, yielding an effect size (AUC) of .72. Next, the researchers went to the Florida Department of Corrections with the instrument, now titled the Risk Assessment Scale for Prison. At this point, predictors were restricted to those that would be available at the time of sentencing, such as variables reflecting age, education, offense type, prior prison terms, and sentence. The study once again confirmed that a violent offense conviction did not predict future prison violence. Age and education remained key predictive variables. Nevertheless, this instrument is still in its infancy, and it is not ready for clinical or forensic applications. Overall, there is no specific instrument currently available to assist in death penalty risk assessment efforts. However, it remains essential that evaluators maintain awareness of new developments in the field.

Idiographic Risk Factors and
Individualized Assessment

As with any risk assessment endeavor, collateral information is critical. In capital case risk assessments, past prison or jail records are especially important. As noted earlier, violent behavior in the community may be predicated on factors very different from behavior in an institution. Although a record of violence in the community is not predictive of prison violence, past behavior in a context similar to the one in which the inmate will reside is (Cunningham & Goldstein, 2003; Sorensen & Pilgrim, 2000). Individuals may respond very differently to a structured environment; for some it provides a remedy for inadequate behavioral controls. In some cases, an individual with a long record of assaultive behavior in the community becomes a model inmate; in other rare cases, nearly the opposite occurs.

If violent behavior occurred during a previous confinement, it should be carefully explored. What was the frequency of the behavior? Did it occur early in the incarceration? How long ago was it (remembering that the propensity for violence is typically reduced with age)? Was it in an open dormitory setting or in an administrative segregation unit? Did it involve staff or inmates or both? Was it focused on a specific victim (e.g., gang member, prior enemy, authority figure)? Was it instrumental or reactive? Did it involve a weapon? Were there injuries? What appears to have triggered the violence? Was it in response to some perceived threat? What was the response to immediate intervention? Were any strategies successful in alleviating the problem? Whether the individual has been incarcerated before with no record of violent behavior or a lengthy violence record, it is important to ascertain the nature of the correctional setting and determine if it is similar to his or her future context.

Gang membership has been addressed as one of the general risk factors for violence in a correctional institution. However, if present, it needs to be explored in terms of the particular individual. If the person is a known gang member, the evaluator should be very familiar with the particular gang. For example, membership in the Aryan Brotherhood, a gang known to carry out lethal acts of violence in prisons, is quite different from membership in a local street gang. As a starting point, most correctional systems can provide information about prison gangs known to function in their institutions. Other questions include whether the individual has been currently active in the gang. Does he hold a leadership position? Has he attempted to, or succeeded in, disaffiliating himself from the organization? Has he been the target of gang violence?

Particularly in the case of anyone with a mental disorder, past response to treatment and treatment compliance when institutionalized should be explored. Anyone who has worked in a forensic hospital can describe individuals who function very well in a hospital setting simply because treatment (most often medication) is available, monitored, and encouraged. It would be important to note what type of medical treatment or monitoring will be available.

Risk Communication

Initial Negotiation

Communication of a risk assessment in a capital sentencing case must begin long before any report is written or testimony is planned.

It is beyond the scope of this chapter to explore all of the concerns and standards for working with attorneys and the courts on death penalty cases. Other authors have discussed these topics well, and any evaluator entering this arena should thoroughly digest their work (Cunningham, 2006b; Cunningham & Reidy, 2001). However, a few clarifying comments are important.

It is rare for a death penalty risk assessment to be court-appointed. Rather, the mental health professional will more likely be retained by either the prosecutor or the defense attorney, who will then become the client. Whoever is the retaining party, it is important to clarify one's exact role in the risk assessment. Is it to be consultant, teaching witness, or expert evaluator? If it is the last, will it involve direct contact with the defendant? The mental health professional will want to adopt a consulting or testifying role in any given case, but not both.

The Consultant

The consultant's primary role is to assist the attorney(s) in developing the case. The consultant generally becomes part of the attorney's team, working behind the scenes, but not providing court testimony. Tasks may include explaining the complex data and methodology of risk assessment to the attorney, searching the literature for additional data, and recommending questions that might be posed to opposing experts. Although bias may certainly enter the picture when one is working closely with staunch advocates, the consultant's role involves providing all of the available information—the good, the bad, and the ugly—to the retaining party for consideration.

The Teaching Witness

In this role, the expert will be expected to explain to the jury the science of risk assessment. The pure teaching witness should know nothing specific about the defendant and will not be expected to relate any of the general scientific data to the specific case at trial.

The Evaluator

If this type of testimony is expected, the mental health professional should initially explore with the attorney whether there will be direct contact and clinical evaluation of the defendant. There may be circumstances in which the defense attorney will decide not to have the defendant interviewed. In such cases, the evaluator must glean information relevant to risk from other sources. This is really not as daunting as it may sound, as any risk assessment relies heavily on collateral information. If there is to be a full clinical evaluation, the clinician should then discuss whether psychological testing may be included and whether there can be any discussion with the defendant of the offense charged or past unadjudicated offenses. There may be sound strategic and legal reasons (e.g., protection of 5th Amendment rights) not to engage in any of the foregoing.

Regardless of the role, the evaluator will want to come to agreement with the client initially as to whether a written report is expected, whether electronic recording will be done, and what collateral information can be sought. If this is done at the beginning of the relationship, the mental health professional can decline to participate if arrangements are not satisfactory. For example, in such a risk assessment, if the defense attorney wanted to withhold prior prison records, this would probably present an undue impediment to the evaluation.

Communicating the Risk Assessment to the Trier of Fact

We hope the discussion earlier in the chapter makes it clear that base rates must anchor the assessment and are, in death penalty cases, "the single most important piece of information necessary to make an accurate risk assessment of a particular individual" (Cunningham & Goldstein, 2003, p. 426). However, base rates may be among the most difficult items to communicate effectively. Courts often need to be educated as to the relevance of base rates to a particular case. The concept of group data may be new to the layperson, who frequently does not understand that all of science is based on group methodology. Cunningham and Reidy (2002, p. 514) have pointed out that such statistics are routinely used in many courts:

> Mental health experts testifying at federal capital sentencing since 1994 have routinely employed group statistical methods to assess

the likelihood of serious violence within a prison context over a capital life term if a defendant was sentenced to life without parole. According to the Federal Death Penalty Resource Counsel Project (Defender Services Division of the Administrative Office of the United States Courts), since 1994, 50 federal death penalty trials, involving 68 defendants, have resulted in guilty verdicts at trial and proceeded to the penalty phase (K. McNally, personal communication, December 3, 2001). In 18 of these penalty phases, mental health experts have provided violence risk assessments. Group statistical methodology and data from psychologists or sociologists were heard in all 18 of the federal death penalty trials in which mental health experts testified regarding violence risk assessment.

A second difficulty comes in conveying base rates and other critical statistical information to juries in a manner that is engaging and understandable. Research suggests that mock jurors are more impressed with pure clinical opinion than with the presentation of actuarial data (Krauss & Sales, 2001). It seems that the more complex the scientific data becomes, the more jurors rely on the expert's credentials rather than the content of his or her testimony (J. Cooper, Bennett, & Sukel, 1996). Social psychologists might say that, when the science becomes complex, jurors are more likely to take the peripheral route to persuasion than the central one. This is not meant to suggest that mental health professionals should avoid statistical and actuarial data. Rather, it indicates that the expert must plan carefully how best to present such information in an engaging fashion that leaves no doubt as to the relevance to the specific defendant.

Two principal dangers to be avoided in capital case risk assessments are overpredicting and underpredicting risk. Of these errors, the former seems to be much more common. Examples are rampant in testimony provided in capital cases over the years by the late James Grigson, MD (who was given the moniker "Dr. Death"). A prime example comes from the now famous case of *Barefoot v. Estelle* (1983):

Doctor Grigson then testified that, on the basis of the hypothetical question, he could diagnose Barefoot "within reasonable psychiatric certainty" as an individual with "a fairly classical, typical, socio-pathic personality disorder." He placed Barefoot in the "most severe category" of sociopaths (on a scale of one to ten, Barefoot was "above ten"), and stated that there was no known cure for the condition. Finally, Dr. Grigson testified that whether Barefoot was in society at large or in a prison society there was a "*one hundred percent and absolute*" chance that Barefoot would commit future acts of criminal violence that would constitute a continuing threat to society. (emphasis supplied; cited in Reisner & Slobogin, 1990, p. 422)

Obviously, there are no known data to support an opinion that any-one is 100% likely to reoffend. Nonetheless, over the years, Dr. Grig-son remained a sought-after witness in the state of Texas. In fact, some defense attorneys were known to contract with him—having no intention of using his testimony—to assure that prosecutors could not call him as a witness. Such absolute—although baseless—testimony can be persuasive to juries; Mr. Barefoot was sentenced to death by the jury. The mental health community must do better.

Less common, however potentially misleading, is the underpre-diction of risk. Examples of such testimony are statements such as "This man presents no threat to society" and "He is no more apt to be violent than you or I." In addition to having no basis in our sci-entific discipline, universal statements such as these come per-ilously close to the ultimate issue. In this case, that issue is that the defendant should or should not be executed. However open one may be to ultimate issue testimony regarding clinical conclusions, life-and-death decisions do not appear to fall into that category. Yet, by characterizing a defendant as categorically "a psychopath," "beyond cure," or "dangerous in all contexts," the expert clearly implies that the only solution is death—a conclusion much beyond a clinician's competence.

Risk Management

The concept of risk management is somewhat unique in cases of death penalty risk assessment. No mental health professional would be expected to present a specific plan to reduce the various risk factors present. If the jury decides that the defendant should not be executed, the person will be sent to a correctional institution that will then become responsible for managing risk. However, it is helpful for the expert to be well informed of risk management techniques that are actually in place to make a sound decision in regard to context. Research has demonstrated that situational factors within institutions can affect inmate behavior (Gendreau et al., 1997; Steinke, 1991).

It would be important to know about levels of custody available in the particular system. Assuming someone convicted of murder would begin in maximum custody, what does that actually mean? Both physical security measures and staffing patterns may be very different in high-security institutions. In what ways can conditions of confinement be modified if level of risk rises? For example, most systems have various levels of administrative segregation and/or supermax facilities. If the defendant has a history of gang association, how is that managed by the system? For example, most prisons have systems in place to allow for separate housing of known enemies or individuals that would be at risk for violence if contact were allowed. Other strategies include limiting telephone usage and specific visitation privileges. Finally, if the risk assessment has identified a treatment that has been effective with the particular defendant, will it be available?

To summarize, risk assessment in death penalty cases is unique, and the consequences potentially dire. Experts who enter this arena must be cognizant of the most recent data regarding base rates and risk factors. Any new instruments developed should be carefully studied. The collateral database must be as detailed as possible to assess any unique individual risk factors; likewise, the evaluator must be diligent in researching the conditions of future confinement. Only with special diligence on the part of knowledgeable mental health professionals can the field improve its role in capital sentencing evaluations.

Epilogue

There is a substantial demand for risk assessments within the fields of mental health and criminal justice, and there is reason to believe that the demand for risk assessments will only increase (Heilbrun, Dvoskin, Hart, & McNeil, 1999). Risk assessments influence decisions that have very significant consequences for society and for the individual assessed. Release of an individual who subsequently commits serious acts of violence may result in injury and/or death to innocent people in the community. Conversely, offering the opinion that an individual is at high risk for violence may result in major curtailment of his or her liberty or even in application of the death penalty.

As detailed throughout the text, the nature and parameters of risk questions clearly vary by context and by legal statute, and new legislation may create a need for entirely new categories of risk assessment with their own unique features (consider the emergence of sexually violent predator [SVP] statutes, for example). However, a common core runs through nearly all of these diverse risk assessments: all require consideration of group data on violence base rates and violence risk factors. All also require a systematic (not vague or impressionistic) consideration of the individual, history, and context. In many cases, once a risk assessment has been completed, the next step is to develop strategies for reducing or managing that risk in a way that maximizes protection for society and minimizes undue curtailment of civil liberties. Although much empirical data on risk

management has yet to be collected, we present a broad set of practice principles into which emerging data can be integrated.

In this book, we have attempted to articulate a model to help
clinicians work through the core tasks common to nearly all risk
assessments. We have also described ways this model, or guide,
could apply to a few of the more common risk assessment referral
questions, though there are certainly other types of risk assessments that evaluators could approach using this guide. We have
not attempted to introduce a new technique, instrument, or school
of thought for risk assessment. Rather, we have attempted to describe what good risk assessment does: clarifies the question of risk
and the legal context, considers broad population data, considers
specific well-established risk factors, considers the individual in
context, and forms a reasonable opinion to communicate clearly.
We hope clinicians striving to conduct risk assessment will consider this a helpful guide.

However, it is also worth reiterating that a guide is, simply, just a
guide. We do not argue that this approach is appropriate for all
conceivable questions of risk, and aspects of the guide may warrant
greater or lesser emphasis depending on the case. We also reiterate
that a guide to risk assessment—like any guide to a science-
informed task—works only when used with appropriate data. We
have presented data that was current at the time of this writing.
Certain well-documented trends might change little; for example,
we expect that past violence will always have some predictive
value for future violence within similar contexts. However, if the
history of risk assessment has taught us anything (see Chapter 1),
it is that our knowledge base can change rapidly and that even
commonly accepted ideas require ongoing investigation. Risk research will certainly reveal greater detail about the ways in which
risk and protective factors operate. Assessment researchers may develop new measures that better guide the collection of risk-relevant
data or the aggregation of this data. Thus, we repeat, evaluators
must maintain a current knowledge of the relevant scientific literature. Case law and statutes governing risk assessment change; to
practice ethically, evaluators must maintain current knowledge of
these, too.

We expect that a sound model, combined with vigilant attention to emerging knowledge and practice guidelines, will help clinicians in the challenging process of violence risk assessment. Ultimately, we hope that these clinicians will provide increasingly sound, science-based, and practical information to the courts, hospitals, and other decision makers who are tasked with making difficult decisions that influence individual lives.

Risk Assessment Instruments

This appendix provides short descriptions of a variety of risk assessment instruments currently available to clinicians, many of which were referenced elsewhere in this text. We have also included guidance for obtaining additional information about each measure. Our coverage of each instrument is intentionally brief and descriptive and should *not* be considered a psychometric review or critique. Indeed, we intentionally resisted the temptation to summarize validity data because such data emerge fairly rapidly, and it is essential for evaluators to stay abreast of this data and conduct an updated search before using an instrument. Furthermore, evaluators need more than a simplistic summary of whether an instrument *is valid*. Evaluators must seek data to gauge the validity of an instrument as applied to particular persons, from particular populations, for particular risk assessment tasks.

The Classification of Violence Risk

This approach emerged from the MacArthur study of violence and mental disorder. Unlike most currently available risk assessment instruments that are based on main effects linear regression models, this approach utilizes an *iterative classification tree* decision model. The developers argue that the typical linear regression model is a one-size-fits-all approach, assuming that the same risk factors are applicable to everyone and to the same degree. Using a decision tree allows the evaluator to include a wide range of variables (the project used a total of 134). Software is commercially available to make the approach more practical for practicing clinicians. The measure was developed specifically with and for psychiatric patients and is not appropriate for correctional settings or other nonpsychiatric populations.

References

Monahan, J., Steadman, H., Appelbaum, P., Grisso, T., Mulvey, E., Roth, L., et al. (2005). *The classification of violence risk.* Lutz, FL: Psychological Assessment Resources.

Monahan, J., Steadman, H., Appelbaum, P., Grisso, T., Mulvey, E., Roth, L., et al. (2006). The classification of violence risk. *Behavioral Sciences and the Law, 24,* 721–730.

Web Site

www.ParInc.com

Level of Service Inventory-Revised

The LSI-R was researched and developed for use in risk and needs assessment for general offenders. It is for use with persons 16 and older for treatment planning and placement. It consists of a structured interview and expert rating form and generally takes 30 to 45 minutes to complete. A screening version (LSI-R-SV) has been constructed, as well as a computer application.

Reference

Andrews, D. A., Bonta, J., & Wormith, J. S. (in press). *Manual for the Level of Service/Case Management Inventory (LS/CMI).* Toronto: Multi-Health Systems.

Web Site

www.MHS.com

Hare Psychopathy Checklist-Revised

The PCL-R was developed by Robert Hare and his colleagues to assess psychopathic personality as characterized by Hervey Cleckley (this is *not* identical to the antisocial personality disorder in the *DSM-IV-TR*). Scoring requires review of collateral information and direct interview. It generally takes several hours to complete. The evaluator should engage in substantial training before using the instrument.

Reference

Hare, R. D. (2003). *Hare Psychopathy Checklist-Revised (PCL-R): Technical manual* (2nd ed.). Toronto: Multi-Health Systems.

Web Sites

www.MHS.com
www.Hare.org

Historical, Clinical, Risk-20

The HCR-20 is a structured guide for the assessment of violence developed for use with civil psychiatric, forensic, and criminal justice populations. It consists of 20 items (including a PCL-R score). There are 10 historical variables, 5 clinical variables, and 5 risk management variables, each scored 0, 1, or 2. The HCR-20 is not an actuarial measure, but rather an empirically based guide to aid evaluators in considering known risk factors for violence.

Reference

Webster, C. D., Douglas, K. S., Eaves, D., & Hart, S. D. (1997). *HCR-20: Assessing risk for violence, version 2*. Burnaby, British Columbia, Canada: Simon Fraser University, Mental Health, Law, and Policy Institute.

Web Sites

www.PAR.inc
www.sfu.ca/~mhlpi/publications.htm

Minnesota Sex Offender Screening Tool-Revised

The MnSOST-R is a 16-item inventory developed for use by the Minnesota Department of Corrections. As developed in 1996, it is based on actuarial data and very different from the original Mn-SOST protocol developed in 1991, which was primarily based on clinical observations. The instrument includes 12 static and four dynamic variables and was designed to be completed by persons such as case managers. Suggested cutoff scores are provided and matched with expected rates of recidivism. Given that this is a very new instrument, research has been limited and has been primarily done by those who developed it.

Reference

Epperson, D. L., Kaul, J. D., & Hesselton, D. (1998b). *Minnesota Sex Offender Screening Tool-Revised (MnSOST-R): Development, performance, and recommended risk cut scores.* Iowa State University and Minnesota Department of Corrections.

Web Site

www.psych-server.iastate.edu/faculty/Epperson

Rapid Risk Assessment for Sexual Offense Recidivism

The RRASOR is a brief actuarial scale created from four variables found through meta-analysis to independently predict recidivism among sex offenders. These include prior sexual arrests (most heavily weighted), age, targeting of male victims, and whether any victims were unrelated to the offender. Taken together, these variables correlate moderately with sex offender recidivism.

Reference

Hanson, R. K. (1997). *The development of a brief actuarial scale for sexual offense recidivism* (User Report No. 1997-04). Ottawa, Ontario, Canada: Department of the Solicitor General.

Screening Scale for Pedophilic Interests

The SSPI has four dichotomously scored items and was initially designed to be used when phallometric assessment was not possible. Preliminary research found the results to be positively correlated with actual phallometric measurements, as well as with both sexual and violent recidivism.

Reference

Seto, M. C., Harris, G. T., Rice, M. E., & Barbaree, H. E. (2004). The Screening Scale for Pedophilic Interests predicts recidivism among adult sex offenders with child victims. *Archives of Sexual Behavior, 33,* 455–466.

Source

Michael C. Seto, PhD, Law and Mental Health Program Centre for Addiction and Mental Health, Unit 3, 101 Queen Street West, Toronto, Ontario, Canada M6J 1H4, michael_seto@camh.net

Sex Offender Risk Appraisal Guide

The SORAG is a 14-factor risk assessment instrument developed by the Canadian research group who also developed the VRAG. In its current form, it includes administration of the Hare Psychopathy Checklist-Revised. It necessitates collection of accurate historical data but can be completed without substantial cooperation by the offender. It is designed to assess the probability that a sex offender will recidivate.

Reference

Quinsey, V. L., Harris, G. T., Rice., M. E., & Cormier, C. (1998). *Violent offenders: Appraising and managing risk.* Washington, DC: American Psychological Association.

Web Site

www.mhcp-research.com/ragpage.htm

Spousal Assault Risk Assessment Guide

The SARA was developed by the risk assessment research group at Simon Fraser University in British Columbia. It recognizes that persons who principally assault their spouse are a heterogeneous population, but also may be quite different from those who engage in other types of assault. It is brief, comprising 20 items and two summary ratings. It has four sections and a five-level scoring system. It is not a test per se, but rather a checklist or guide to assure that pertinent information is considered.

Reference

Kropp, P. R., Hart, S. D., Webster, C. D., & Eaves, D. (1995). *Manual for the Spousal Assault Risk Assessment Guide* (2nd. ed.). Vancouver, British Columbia, Canada: British Columbia Institute on Family Violence.

Web Site

www.sfu.ca/mhlpi/publications.htm

Structured Anchored Clinical Judgment

Also known as "the Thornton," the SACJ-Min was designed to assess the risk of sex offender recidivism on the basis of a stage approach. Stage 1 considers official convictions, Stage 2 potentially aggravating factors, and Stage 3 treatment variables (usually available only for those who have been in a sex offender treatment program). Available research is limited and conducted primarily by the developer.

Reference

Grubin, D. (1998). *Sex offending against children: Understanding the risk* (Police Research Series Paper 99). London: Home Office.

Source

David Thornton, Sand Ridge Secure Treatment Center, Department of Health and Family Services of Wisconsin, 1111 North Road, Mauston, Wisconsin 53948, thorndm@dhfs.state.wi.us

STATIC-99

This instrument combines items from the RRASOR and the SACJ-Min. Studies thus far indicate that its predictive accuracy exceeds that of either of the previous instruments used alone. It is based completely on static variables, including prior sex offenses, unrelated victims, stranger victims, male victims, age, never married, noncontact sex offenses, prior sentences, current nonsexual violence, and prior nonsexual violence. It is designed to measure long-term risk potential. A revision, the STATIC-2002 is currently in the final research stages.

Reference

Hanson, R. K., & Thornton, D. (1999). *Static-99: Improving actuarial risk assessments for sex offenders* (User Report 99-02). Ottawa, Ontario, Canada: Department of the Solicitor General.

Web Site

www.sgc.gc.ca

Sexual/Violence/Risk Instrument

The SVR-20 was developed by the risk assessment researchers at Simon Fraser University in British Columbia. It is a checklist designed to assess the risk of future sexual violence by examining psychosocial adjustment, past sexual offenses, and future risk management options.

Source

Boer, D., Hart, S., Kropp, R., & Webster, C. (1997). *Manual for the Sexual Violence Risk—20*. Burnaby, British Columbia, Canada: Simon Fraser University, Mental Health, Law, and Policy Institute.

Web Site

www.sfu.ca/mhlpi/publications.htm

Violence Risk Appraisal Guide

This approach was developed by Christopher Webster, Grant Harris, Marnie Rice, Catherine Cormier, and Vernon Quinsey in Canada. It was originally published as the Violence Prediction Scheme. In its current form, the VRAG includes administration of the Hare Psychopathy Checklist-Revised. It has been validated primarily on populations of violent offenders.

Reference

Quinsey, V. L., Harris, G. T., Rice, M. E., & Cormier, C. (2006). *Violent offenders: Appraising and managing risk* (2nd ed.). Washington, DC: American Psychological Association.

Web Site

www.mhcp-research.com/ragpage.htm

Instruments for Use with Juveniles

Early Assessment Risk Lists for Boys and Girls

The EARL-20B and EARL-21G were developed specifically for young (<12) children who are demonstrating aggressive behaviors. Evaluators use a 3-point scale to code items related to the child and the child's context (family, neighborhood, poverty, peers) that research has shown to correspond with future antisocial behavior.

Reference

Augimeri, L. K., Koegl, C. J., Webster, C. D., & Levene, K. S. (2001). *Early Assessment Risk List for Boys: EARL-20B, version 2.* Toronto: Earlscourt Child and Family Centre.

Web Site

www.earlscourt.on.ca

Estimate of Risk of Adolescent Sexual Offense Recidivism

The ERASOR is an empirically guided checklist to assist evaluators in estimating short-term risk for juveniles ages 12 to 18. It considers a total of 25 risk factors (16 dynamic, 9 static).

Reference

Worling, J. R. (2004). The Estimate of Risk of Sexual Offense Recidivism (ERASOR): Preliminary psychometric data. *Sexual Abuse: A Journal of Research and Treatment, 16,* 235–284.

Source

Dr. James Worling, Consultant Psychologist/Coordinator of Research SAFE-T Program, Thistletown Regional Centre, 51 Panorama Court, Toronto, Ontario, Canada M9V 4L8

Juvenile Sex Offender Assessment Protocol II

The JSOAP is an actuarial instrument consisting of four rationally derived factors, two historical and two dynamic. It was initially designed to assess risk and change among juveniles who have committed sexual offenses. Though still in the early research stage, some initial findings regarding reliability and validity have been positive.

Reference

Prentky, R. A., Harris, B., Frizzell, K., & Righthand, S. (2000). An actuarial procedure for assessing risk with juvenile sex offenders. *Sexual Abuse: A Journal of Research and Treatment, 12,* 71–93.

Web Site

www.csom.org/pubs/JSOAP.pdf

Structured Assessment of Violence Risk in Youth

The design of the SAVRY is modeled after existing assessment protocols for adult violence risk (e.g., the HCR-20), but the item content is focused specifically on risk in adolescents. It is composed of 24 items (historical, individual, and contextual) drawn from existing research and professional literature in adolescent development and on violence and aggression in youth. An additional five protective factors are also provided. The individual and social/contextual sections emphasize dynamic risk/needs factors.

Source

Borum, R., Bartel, P., & Forth, A. (2006). *Manual for the Structured Assessment for Violence Risk in Youth (SAVRY)*. Odessa, FL: Psychological Assessment Resources.

Web Sites

www.ParInc.com
www.fmhi.usf.edu/mhlp/savry/statement.htm

Youth Level of Service/Case Management Inventory

This guide was developed at Carleton University to assist those tasked with the management of potentially violent juveniles. It is divided into nine sections: prior offenses, family circumstances, education, employment, peer relationships, substance abuse, personality variables, interests, and attitudes. It is designed as an aid and not a psychometric instrument.

References

Hoge, R., & Andrews, D. (1996). *Assessing the youthful offender*. New York: Plenum Press.

Hoge, R. D., & Andrews, D. A. (2002). *The Youth Level of Service/Case Management Inventory manual and scoring key*. Toronto: Multi-Health Systems.

Web Site

www.mhs.com

B

Sample Risk
Assessment Reports

A variety of clinicians have contributed reports to be included as samples. They illustrate a variety of ways in which practitioners analyze and communicate risk assessment data. Although all utilize sold empirical data, consider the individual in context, and combine a varied database to reach their conclusions, each has a unique style of doing so. Brief editorial comments preceding each report explain its context. Each report has been thoroughly de-identified but represents a real case. In addition, it was necessary to shorten several of the reports in the interest of conserving space. However, we believe that, although many details are omitted, the samples are true to the essential context of the originals.

FORENSIC EVALUATION

The following report was provided by Linda Berberoglu, PhD, ABPP. A pre-sentence evaluation is required in this jurisdiction in regard to virtually all persons convicted of sexual offenses. This report includes a formal risk assessment as well as recommendations for risk management planning.

Name: Doe, John
File No.: XXXXXX
Date of Birth: 00/00/1952
Date of Report: 00/00/2006

Identification and Reason for Referral

John Doe is a 54-year-old, divorced, African-American male. He was referred by the Honorable xxx for a psychological evaluation to assist the Court with its pre-sentence proceedings. Records indicated the defendant recently pled guilty to Criminal Sexual Conduct in the Third Degree. The victim was his 12-year-old stepdaughter. He was in custody at the time of this assessment.

Evaluation Procedures

Prior to participating in the clinical interview, the defendant was informed about my role as well as the nature and purpose of the assessment. He was told that the usual doctor/patient relationship would not exist, that the information obtained from him was not confidential, and that it would be summarized in a written report to the Court, both attorneys, and the probation officer in this case. He was also told that in the event he was referred for sex offender treatment, his treatment provider was also likely to receive a copy of this report. He indicated that he understood this information and agreed to proceed.

As part of the assessment, I reviewed the available records, which included the undated court order; the criminal complaint dated xxx, 2006; and the accompanying xxxx Police Department reports. The defendant participated in a clinical interview at the xxx County Adult Detention Center on xxxx, 2006. He was administered psychological testing on xxx, 2006 by our staff psychometrist. Specifically, he was administered the

Wechsler Abbreviated Scale of Intelligence (WASI) and the Minnesota Multiphasic Personality Inventory—Second Edition (MMPI-2).

Background Information/Interview Data

John Doe was born in Omaha, Nebraska, on xx xxx, 1952, the seventh of nine sons to an intact family. He said his father was absent throughout most of the defendant's life. He said his mother supported the family through employment as a housekeeper and a laundry worker. He said they were a closely knit family, with church activities comprising core family values until his maternal grandmother died when he was 11 or 12 years old. At that point, he described increased fragmentation in the family. He said, "Everyone started drinking, and the whole thing blew up." He denied that his mother had a substance abuse problem, but he indicated that other family members did. He reported a history of sexual abuse as a child, but verbalized shame about this experience.

The defendant reported that he had a tenth grade education. He dropped out in the eleventh grade, stating, "I started hanging out with the boys at the candy store all day long." He denied ever repeating any grades but believed he might have been a slow learner. He reported cheating on exams in order to conceal his academic problems. He reported some behavior problems in sixth or seventh grades for minor stealing and fighting with his peers. He reported that the police intervened when he was picked up for stealing from stores on several occasions.

The defendant reported that after he dropped out of school he got a job in order to help his mother with the bills. He said he worked at a restaurant as a dishwasher and busboy. He said he continued living at home with his mother until he was around 21 years old, at which point he got married because his girlfriend at the time was pregnant. The marriage lasted less than a year. He said he joined the Army Reserves in 1974. He said he completed two 3-year tours of duty and said he received Honorable discharges each time. He denied any disciplinary problems.

The defendant described a somewhat unstable and irresponsible relationship history. He reported that he has five biological children with four different women, but typically has not maintained contact with his children. The first was a son born in 1974 or 1975, who was the product of his first marriage, which lasted less than a year. The second significant relationship lasted approximately 5 years. He said he had a daughter with this woman, who is now approximately 21 years old. Mr. Doe said he moved to Minnesota in 1993. He got involved with a woman with whom he had another daughter, who is now 17. He described the relationship as lasting about 2 years. He reported that he and the mother smoked crack cocaine. The fourth relationship lasted approximately 4 years. They had a daughter together who is now 12 or 13 years old. The fifth relationship was with his second wife. He said they were divorced in approximately 2002 or 2003. They had one son together, born in 1997, and his wife had a daughter from a previous relationship, whom the defendant said he raised from the time she was around 2 years old. She was the victim of the instant offense. When asked why his second marriage failed, he said, "They say my drinking. I guess that's what it was."

The defendant described an employment history that has been characterized by a number of relatively short-term positions at fast food restaurants. At the time of his arrest for the instant offense, he was working in the laundry of a casino. When asked if he was ever fired from any jobs, he said, "Yeah, I guess." Reasons included not showing up for work and tardiness. Since he separated from his second wife, he reported that he has been homeless and has stayed in hotels and shelters.

The defendant denied a serious criminal history prior to his arrest for the instant offense. He was charged with Fifth Degree Assault at least twice and pled guilty to disorderly conduct each time, first in July 1999 and again in March 2006. There was no evidence or prior felony convictions. He told me that when he was arrested for domestic assault in the past, he was always intoxicated.

Psychiatric History

The defendant denied any history of psychiatric hospitalizations or outpatient mental health treatment, including treatment with psychotropic medications. He denied any history of suicide attempts or suicidal thinking. He denied any periods of prolonged depression. He said he has never participated in outpatient counseling.

The defendant described a history of significant substance abuse that has included alcohol, marijuana, and crack/cocaine. He tended to minimize the seriousness of these problems. He said he began drinking when he was in the military, and he reported years of daily alcohol use. He said he also began using marijuana and smoking crack cocaine. He said he voluntarily sought inpatient chemical dependency treatment, which he said he completed in the 1990s, although he was unsure when. He said he has abstained from cannabis and cocaine use for approximately 12 years.

Instant Offense

The defendant was accused of having sexual intercourse with his step-daughter, who was 12 years old at the time the offense occurred. He told police that he was intoxicated at the time. Records indicated that he also told the police that the victim did not want to have sex with him and that he forced himself on her when he was intoxicated.

Psychological Testing

The defendant was administered the Wechsler Abbreviated Scale of Intelligence (WASI), which is an individually administered screening test that provides a quick estimate of cognitive functioning. It yields the three traditional Verbal, Performance, and Full Scale IQ scores and is linked to the widely used Wechsler intelligence tests for adults and children. His Full Scale IQ score estimate of 75 was within the Borderline range. His Verbal and Performance IQ score estimates of 75 and 79, respectively, were also within the Borderline range.

The defendant was also administered the Minnesota Multiphasic Personality Inventory—Second Edition (MMPI-2), which is a 567-item, true-false, self-report inventory designed to assess psychopathology in adults. Because of the inconsistencies in his response pattern, the resulting clinical profile was viewed as not valid or interpretable.

Additional Measures

STATIC-99. The STATIC-99 is one of the most widely used actuarial instruments designed to assist in the prediction of sexual and violent recidivism for sexual offenders. The recidivism estimates provided by the STATIC-99 are group estimates based on reconvictions and were derived from groups of people with these characteristics. As such, these estimates do not directly correspond to the recidivism risk of an individual offender. That is, the offender's risk may be higher or lower than the probabilities estimated in the STATIC-99. Scores on the instrument range from zero (0) to twelve (12), with scores of 0 indicating low risk and scores of 6 and above indicating high risk.

Mr. Doe's score of 1 placed him in the Low risk category for sexual and violent re-offense, relative to other adult male sex offenders who have committed contact sex offenses. Additional dynamic risk factors not reflected in the STATIC-99, but which likely elevate his level of risk for violent and sexual recidivism, include his history of chronic alcohol dependence and his persistent lifestyle instability, as evidenced by employment, housing, and intimate relationship problems.

Diagnostic Impressions

Axis I: Alcohol Dependence Cocaine Dependence, in Sustained Full
          Remission

          Cannabis Dependence, in Sustained Full Remission

Axis II: Antisocial Personality traits Borderline Intellectual Functioning
          (Provisional)

Summary and Recommendations

John Doe appears to be a man of below average intelligence who did not demonstrate evidence of a major mental illness. The most significant clinical problem appears to be his self-reported history of severe, chronic alcohol dependence, for which he received treatment a number of years ago, but quickly relapsed. Although he was viewed as an appropriate candidate for long-term residential substance abuse treatment and aftercare, his ability to benefit from such treatment would be largely dependent upon his level of motivation, which was uncertain. His risk for relapse in the absence of a structured and supervised treatment environment and aftercare setting was viewed as high.

Regarding sexual re-offense risk, although no single risk factor can reliably predict recidivism, the research literature suggests that sexual offense recidivism is best predicted by characteristics associated with deviant sexual preferences (such as a history of sexual preferences for children). The relationship between victim and offender has also been identified as a significant risk predictor, with incest offenders such as Mr. Doe generally showing a lower risk for sexual re-offense than offenders who select unrelated victims. However, his chronic alcohol dependency problem and reports that he was intoxicated at the time of the offense raise his level of risk. In terms of his age, although the recent literature on sex offenders and re-offense risk has suggested that older offenders (i.e., those over the age of 50) may present a lower level of recidivism risk compared to their younger counterparts, given that this defendant was convicted of his first sex offense after the age of 50 suggests that this generalization may not apply to him.

Overall, Mr. Doe was viewed as posing a low to moderate long-term risk for sexual and general violent re-offense. He was viewed as an appropriate candidate for community-based sex offender treatment. Such treatment would need to take into account his intellectual capabilities, which appear to be limited based on IQ screening test results and clinical observations. It is possible that completing sex offender treatment may reduce his level of risk, although the literature in the area of sex offender treatment effectiveness is controversial and unsettled. While the defendant is on probation, it is also recommended that he participate in a structured chemical dependency treatment and aftercare program in order to support his abstinence from chemicals. Substance abuse was viewed as a significant dynamic risk factor that would likely impact his risk for future violent and sexual re-offense.

_____

Licensed Psychologist
Board Certified in Forensic Psychology
American Board of Professional Psychology

PSYCHOLOGICAL EVALUATION

This sample report was provided by Mary Alice Conroy, PhD, ABPP. The attorney for the offender requested a risk assessment in preparation for presenting his client's case to the parole board. Such evaluations are frequently requested in this jurisdiction and are often accompanied by videotaped testimony. In this case, the imposition of specific risk management (release conditions) is the province of the parole board.

Name: McDee, Bruce
Prison #:
Date of Birth: 00/00/1963
Date of Report: 00/00/2005

Identification and Reason for Referral

Bruce McDee is a 46-year-old man currently serving a 35-year sentence in the state prison system for two counts of Solicitation of Capital Murder. He was convicted of trying to solicit a murder contract on his wife in 1997. This evaluation was requested by his attorney for use in presenting his case before the parole board. Specifically, the attorney requested an assessment of future risk were he to be released.

Procedures

Clinical interview of approximately three hours conducted at a prison unit on November 16, 2005.

Completion of the Psychopathy Checklist-Revised (PCL-R) and the Violence Risk Appraisal Guide (VRAG). Documents provided by Mr. McDee's attorney were reviewed:

- Judgment on Jury Verdict of Guilty, dated 3/18/1999
- Synopsis of Reporter's Record prepared by Mr. McDee's Attorney
- Final Decree of Divorce, dated 8/13/1999
- Prison certificates awarded to Mr. McDee
- Transcript from Michigan State University, dated 1978–1985
- Resume by Bruce B. McDee
- Transcripts of Mr. McDee's trial

Prior to the clinical interview, Mr. McDee was informed of the nature of the evaluation and the limits of confidentiality inherent therein. He then signed a consent form.

Background Information

Bruce McDee was born in Michigan on 01/17/1959 and raised by his natural parents. He had one brother and one sister, both older. He said his father was a sales manager who worked constantly and drank heavily. During childhood, he had a much closer relationship with his mother. He described the family as very traditional and denied ever experiencing any type of abuse.

Mr. McDee described his school years as very ordinary. He said he was never a significant behavior problem either at home or at school. He worked delivering newspapers to earn some extra money.

In 1977, Mr. McDee graduated from high school. On impulse, he enlisted in the U.S. Army's delayed entry program; however, he thought the better of that decision and was never required to serve. He worked for about 18 months before enrolling at Michigan State University in the fall of 1978. His first semester proved to be rather disastrous. He discovered that he hated chemistry (his declared major) and failed almost all of his classes, resulting in his exit from the university. During this same period his parents divorced and his grandparents died. After working for another year, he re-enrolled at Michigan State. This time he studied electronics, made good grades, and graduated with a degree in Industrial Technology.

Mr. McDee married for the first time during his college years. This marriage ended in divorce after about 4 years. The couple had no children. As college came to a close and his marriage dissolved, Mr. McDee found himself in dire financial straits. He had significant credit card debt, was unable to keep up the mortgage on his house, and eventually filed for bankruptcy.

Despite intermittent financial difficulties, Mr. McDee remained gainfully employed throughout his adult life up until his incarceration. He was never terminated and worked for one company for as long as 8 years. He appears to have been particularly successful in sales positions.

Mr. McDee was married for the second time at the age of 30. Two daughters (currently ages 11 and 13) were born to this union. The marriage was apparently conflicted from the beginning. The couple separated for 4 months before the first child was born, and the marriage was ending in divorce at the time of the current offense. Mr. McDee described the final separation and divorce from his second wife as a very tumultuous period. Although not usually a heavy drinker, he received three charges for Public Intoxication during this time. Despite problems in the marriage, Mr. McDee described being very close to his daughters during their early years. He remembered the exact date and time at which he was officially served with the divorce papers.

Mr. McDee was eventually arrested and charged with attempting to so-licit an undercover operative to murder his wife. Before his subsequent trial and conviction, he was on bond for approximately 2 years. There were no bond violations, and he remained gainfully employed. He also en-tered into another romantic relationship and was living with this woman up until his incarceration. She has recently re-established contact.

During his time in prison, Mr. McDee has received one minor discipli-nary case for violating rules surrounding commissary privileges. Records indicate that he has taken advantage of programming offered in the prison system. He has been able to secure a job assignment that allows him to use his technology skills as well as teaching a class.

Mr. McDee's plans and expectations for the future appeared quite real-istic. He expects to be on parole until the age of 75. He has strong support from his parents and siblings. When released, he said he initially plans to take any job available. Eventual career goals include starting a small tech-nology support and training company. He is aware that his second wife has remarried and speaks highly of her husband. He fully understands that his parental rights have been terminated and that he is not likely to have any further contact with his daughters.

Mental Health History

Mr. McDee had no contact with mental health professionals during childhood or adolescence. The only family problem he described was his father's alco-hol abuse. He apparently became quite distraught over his second divorce and was treated for depression. He received several individual psychotherapy sessions and then entered a support group for people experiencing divorce. He was also prescribed antidepressant medication, but took it for only a very brief period. He said he has occasionally seen mental health staff when hav-ing difficult times in prison but has never received ongoing treatment.

Mental Status Examination

Mr. McDee appeared for the interview well groomed, polite, and coopera-tive. Rapport was easily established. No unusual movements or manner-isms were noted. His speech was spontaneous, articulate, and normal in rate and tone.

Mr. McDee was well oriented to time, place, person, and situation. There was no evidence of thought disorder, such as confusion or disor-ganization. There were no indications of hallucinations or bizarre ideation of any kind. Based upon his vocabulary and level of abstract thinking, he would be estimated to have above average intelligence. Both recent and remote memory seemed to be intact.

Throughout the interview, Mr. McDee's affect was flexible and appropriate to the content of the discussion. There was no current evidence of depression or indications of significant mood swings. He denied any past suicidal behavior or current intent.

Psychological Testing

The only psychometric instrument completed during the evaluation was the Psychopathy Checklist-Revised (PCL-R). This requires both a structured interview and the review of available records to assess for the presence of psychopathic traits. Persons who score high on this instrument often have a personality structure characterized by an extreme disregard for the rights of others, an inability to empathize with the pain experienced by others, a propensity to view others as objects to be manipulated, and a total lack of remorse for any harm inflicted upon other people. The PCL-R is one of the only psychometric instruments shown to have strong positive predictive power for future violence when persons score in the psychopathic range (generally over 30). However, Mr. McDee's PCL-R score is very low (less than 5). Psychopathy is one risk factor he clearly does not have.

Diagnostic Impressions

Axis I: 309.0   Adjustment Disorder with Depressed Mood, by history

Axis II: V71.09 No diagnosis

Mr. McDee apparently became quite depressed as his second marriage was dissolving. He also admits to being very briefly depressed a few times in prison. However, these episodes appear to be situational rather than a true clinical depression.

Risk Assessment

Mr. McDee's crime was very serious and could have resulted in severe violence toward another person. However, along with his episodes of public intoxication, it appears to have been circumscribed to a specific time in his life and a particular situation. He had no criminal offense record until well into adulthood, so it does not represent an established pattern of behavior. In fact, judging from his career records, his life before the crime appears to have been decidedly pro-social. He takes full responsibility for the crime and now classifies it as the "stupidest thing" he has ever done. He does not seem to be harboring any residual negative emotions toward the victim or unrealistic expectations about reuniting with his children, but rather is concentrating his energy on developing a positive plan for his life once released.

In a final effort to apply all available psychological research to an analysis of risk posed by Bruce McDee if released, the Violence Risk Appraisal Guide (VRAG) was completed. This is an actuarial instrument that has been widely tested on violent populations in an effort to provide risk assessments for future violent behavior. It is not a test administered to the offender, but rather a set of statistically weighted factors gleaned primarily from past records. It includes such things as overall violent and non-violent criminal record, history of substance abuse, early behavioral problems, psychopathic or anti-social traits, and personality abnormalities or disorders. Mr. McDee's score of −11 places him within the third lowest of the nine risk categories, suggesting that the probability of any violent behavior in the next 7 years in the community would be less than 15%.

Taking into consideration all of the available information, it is my professional opinion that Bruce McDee would present a low risk for violent behavior if released to the community.

Diplomate in Forensic Psychology,
American Board of Professional Psychology

RISK ASSESSMENT REPORT

This report sample was provided by David F. Mrad, PhD, ABPP. The individual was found Not Guilty by Reason of Insanity. This evaluation was conducted to determine if he met the criteria for continued commitment due to risk of bodily harm to another person or serious damage to the property of another as a result of severe mental disease or defect. The facility utilizes a risk assessment panel composed of three clinicians, who are not directly providing treatment to the subject of the assessment, to make the recommendation to the court. A formal risk management plan would be included only if a conditional release were being recommended.

Name: Smith, George
Criminal Number: CR-00-xxxxx
Date of Birth: 00/00/1951
Date of Report: October 19, 2001

Introduction

George Smith is a 50-year-old White male who was referred to the Maximum Security Forensic Hospital by the District Court. Mr. Smith had been found not guilty only by reason of insanity for Making a Threat Against a Public Official. Following that verdict, the Court referred him to the forensic hospital requesting an opinion concerning whether Mr. Smith's release would present a substantial risk to the persons and property of others.

A Risk Assessment Panel was convened on October 16, 2001, in order to render an opinion concerning whether the release of Mr. Smith would present a substantial risk of bodily injury to others or serious damage to the property of others due to a present mental disease or defect. This was Mr. Smith's first risk assessment at the forensic hospital. The Panel was composed of the Chief of Psychology, the Chief of Psychiatry, and a Staff Psychologist. Mr. Smith's records were reviewed, and he was interviewed by the Panel. Prior to the Panel interview, Mr. Smith had been observed on his ward of residence by both clinical and correctional staff. He had been clinically interviewed by his psychologist, the preparer of this report, and additional information was obtained by telephonic interviews with Sergeant Fred Jones of the Police Department in Mr. Smith's hometown, Dave Roberts of the V.A. Medical Center where Mr. Smith had been treated, and Mr. Smith's parents.

The Risk Assessment Panel considered a variety of factors relevant to their predictive effort. These factors are divided into two broad categories of historical issues and treatment issues. Historical issues concern static personal characteristics and previously exhibited behaviors that are relevant to the individual's overall level of risk. Treatment issues concern personal characteristics and situational factors that are deemed amenable to change over time and through various treatment modalities.

Historical Considerations

Psychiatric History. Mr. Smith has an extensive psychiatric history, which is detailed in the reports of the doctors who evaluated him prior to the adjudication of his case. Since those reports are available to the Court, Mr. Smith's psychiatric history will only be summarized here. Mr. Smith was first admitted for psychiatric treatment to an inpatient setting on an involuntary commitment at age 21 after being found not guilty by reason of insanity for Sending Threatening Letters. Since that time, Mr. Smith has had 23 admissions to Central State Hospital, 10 of which involved civil commitments. Those commitments often involved threatening statements made by Mr. Smith. Mr. Smith, who was initially diagnosed as suffering from schizophrenia, paranoid type, was later diagnosed as suffering from schizoaffective disorder. He was often psychotic, with grandiose, persecutory, and erotomanic delusional beliefs. Mr. Smith has also had two inpatient admissions to the V.A. Medical Center in his hometown. He has most recently received psychiatric treatment from that facility on an outpatient basis.

Antisocial Behavior/Characteristics. Most of the following information is also documented in the previous forensic reports available to the Court and will be stated here only in summary form. Since the onset of his mental illness, Mr. Smith has often been involved in problematic behaviors in the community which have led to a number of arrests and psychiatric commitments. Most frequently, these behaviors have involved threatening or harassing others, either public figures or private individuals in his community on whom Mr. Smith became fixated. Some of the incidents, however, in his earlier years, involved more serious behavior with a greater potential for injury to others or to Mr. Smith. In 1975, Mr. Smith was arrested on the grounds of the County Court House carrying a concealed weapon, a 9 mm pistol. That incident resulted in a commitment to the state hospital.

In 1977, Mr. Smith was arrested for Unlawful Imprisonment and Third Degree Assault. This involved an incident in which Mr. Smith barricaded himself and his sister in his house with a number of weapons. Mr. Smith was again committed to Central State Hospital, where the commitment continued with sporadic conditional releases for a 5-year period.

In 1986, Mr. Smith allegedly threatened to assault an employee at a store. In 1987, he was hospitalized after an episode of agitation and threats. He allegedly assaulted a female staff member during the admission process. The subsequent incidents, though numerous, have all involved various threats (such as the instant offense) or harassment of specific individuals. Mr. Smith has denied possessing any firearms for several years, claiming that he was aware he was not allowed to possess them. He acknowledged possessing a straight edged razor for protection until a few years ago, when he also learned that was also illegal.

Mr. Smith has acknowledged a history of alcohol abuse in his early 20s. He denied any abuse of alcohol from his 1973 Central State Hospital discharge until 2000. It does not appear that Mr. Smith has been given any substance abuse diagnoses during his numerous hospitalizations at Central State Hospital.

Treatment Review

Hospital Course and Treatment during Current Hospitalization.   Mr. Smith was admitted to the forensic hospital on September 20, 2000. He initially remained on a locked ward for close observation until we could obtain sufficient information about him. On September 25, he was moved to an open ward, where he stayed throughout the remainder of his evaluation period. He did not display any bizarre behavior. He did not receive any incident reports for infractions of institutional rules.

After an initial period of restriction to the ward, Mr. Smith was placed on open status, allowing him to go to the main institution dining hall and recreation areas. Mr. Smith had been receiving psychiatric medication at the time of his admission. He continued to receive those medications throughout this evaluation period. At the completion of his evaluation, he was receiving Depakene (500 mg in the morning and 1,000 mg in the evening) and Risperdal (6 mg once daily).

Community Impressions/Resources.   Mr. Smith's parents were interviewed over the telephone by a staff social worker. They indicated that they live five miles from Central State Hospital, and Mr. Smith lives with them when he is not an inpatient at the hospital. His parents indicated that he was previously eligible for Social Security income. They did not believe Mr. Smith was dangerous, and they would welcome him back into their home. Mr. Smith's parents also recommended contacting Dave Roberts, his case manager at the V.A. Medical Center in his hometown.

Mr. Roberts was contacted telephonically by Mr. Smith's evaluating psychologist. He indicated that he had known Mr. Smith since 1988. In recent years, Mr. Roberts believed Mr. Smith was generally willing to take his medication. He also indicated that Mr. Smith's parents helped assure that he took his medication. Mr. Roberts reported that he was not aware of any violent behavior by Mr. Smith. He believed, apparently because of the intensive case management, that the parents would generally react and get Mr. Smith back into inpatient status before his behavior could become too problematic. Mr. Roberts indicated that the staff at the V.A. Medical Center had been considering trying to place Mr. Smith in an assisted living situation, which would provide a more structured environment with assurance that his medication was regularly given. Mr. Smith, however, had been resistant to that idea. Mr. Roberts indicated that Mr. Smith would be welcome to return to the V.A. Medical Center for continued treatment.

Interview Impressions

Mr. Smith gave a very detailed and accurate explanation of the possible alternatives available to the Court in his case. He also gave an explanation of his behavior at the time of the offense, explaining that he had a belief that there was a national emergency, and he was attempting to prevent the threatened public official from declaring himself "Governor for life, like an American Marcos." He explained that, at that time, he believed he had a special mission and was in the "vanguard" to participate in a trial that would lead to media exposure. He denied any intent to individually try to harm the official. When questioned concerning this set of delusional beliefs, which also included ideas about the militia, 9–11, and certain elements of state law, Mr. Smith stated that he "can't afford to believe it anymore." It did not appear he had completely given up his delusional beliefs, but rather recognized the problems they caused him and presently had sufficient control not to be preoccupied with them or publicly endorse them.

Mr. Smith was aware of his current psychiatric medications. He expressed the belief that he needed these medications and functioned better when he was taking them. Mr. Smith was questioned concerning weapon possession. He denied having any weapon at the time of the offense. He denied ever using a weapon against anyone. He acknowledged times in the past when he had felt he needed a weapon to protect himself. He denied any current feelings that others would harm him and verbalized recognition that he could not legally carry a weapon at this time. Mr. Smith was questioned concerning the fixations he has apparently had with women in his community, leading to some harassment and possibly stalking. He reported that he has poor social skills, especially with females. He described himself as having "imaginary relationships" which he does not know how to handle properly.

Diagnostic Impressions

According to the criteria set forth in the *Diagnostic and Statistical Manual of Mental Disorders, Fourth Edition,* of the American Psychiatric Association, Mr. Smith is diagnosed as follows:

Axis I: Schizoaffective disorder, bipolar type Alcohol abuse (by history)

Axis II: No diagnosis.

Opinions and Recommendations

It is the opinion of the Panel that Mr. Smith continues to suffer from a major mental disorder, schizoaffective disorder, bipolar type. At the present time, he appears stable in this structured setting with consistent medication. His mood presently appears adequately controlled. There are some indications that he continues to experience delusional ideas but, with the control of his medication, is able to avoid dwelling or acting on them. He at least had some recognition that his ideas are not socially acceptable and lead to problems with his environment.

While Mr. Smith clearly appears to be suffering from a mental disorder, predictions concerning future risk of violent behavior are more complex. Such predictions have been shown to be of limited reliability, which tends to diminish even more over extended periods of time. In general, such predictions tend to be of little value beyond a 6-month period. Given that qualification, the Panel undertook the difficult task of offering such an opinion. In Mr. Smith's case, there are a number of factors that create concern about potential risk to others. He has had periods in the past in which he has carried or brandished weapons apparently in response to his delusional ideas. He continues to have episodes of delusional ideas when not consistently medicated. Even at the present time, there are indications that he continues to hold some of those delusional beliefs. Nevertheless, there are also a number of factors that mitigate Mr. Smith's potential for violence. First, he is at an age at which the base rate for violence is lower. Secondly, he has a good support system of parents, mental health professionals, and even law enforcement officials who know him well and encourage his continued treatment. His most recent case manager believes he has been attempting to comply with medications in recent years, although he may have occasionally failed due to some confusion. Mr. Smith has had some episodes in his past during which there was apparently a potential for harm to others. It does not appear, however, that he has actually ever seriously harmed anyone. Additionally, looking at the overall pattern of his behavior, it appears that the severity of his actions and potential risk to others has been diminishing over time rather than increasing.

Given these observations, it is our opinion that Mr. Smith is a chronically mentally ill individual whose symptoms and behavior are likely to continue, causing some nuisance offenses for his community. We anticipate he will continue to have occasional problems with legal authorities. Nevertheless, his pattern of behavior does not suggest that even with his mental illness he currently presents a substantial risk to others. Therefore, based on all of this information, it is our opinion that Mr. Smith's release would not present a substantial risk of bodily injury to others or serious damage to the property of others due to present mental disease or defect. The Panel would strongly recommend Mr. Smith continue to receive psychiatric treatment and regular monitoring. It appears likely that his current treating agency will recommend a more structured environment. We would not disagree with that recommendation. We, of course, cannot state that Mr. Smith presents absolutely no risk to others, and it is reasonable to conclude that whatever level of risk he might pose would be further diminished by that level of structure and treatment.

Diplomate in Forensic Psychology   Chief of Psychiatry
Chief of Psychology   Panel Member
Chairperson

Diplomate in Forensic Psychology
Staff Psychologist
Panel Member

Preparer of Report

This report sample was provided by Mark D. Cunningham, PhD, ABPP. It is a risk assessment provided in a federal capital sentencing case. It is not unusual for attorneys to request that no report be prepared in these cases. The following is a letter to the attorney summarizing the data and proposed testimony.

02/06/2006

John Cane, Esq.
Attorney at Law
2027 Maple
Midville, USA

Re: *State v. Franklin Ross*

Dear Mr. Cane:

You have requested that I summarize my findings and opinions to date regarding my capital sentencing evaluation of Mr. Franklin Ross relative to his risk of perpetrating serious violence in prison if confined for a capital life term. These findings and opinions are based on an interview of Mr. Ross, a review of records, and a review of scholarly literature. These sources are of a sort that are customarily relied upon by clinical and forensic psychologists in coming to expert opinions. My findings and conclusions may be modified by additional information that may be made known to me.

Analysis of a defendant's past behavior pattern (in a similar setting) and the application of group statistical data are the two approaches that are most reliable in assessing likelihood of violent behavior in a prison context. Behavior pattern analysis that is specific to context is critically important because prison represents a fundamentally different context from the community—and prison violence does not predictably follow from pre-confinement violence or the capital offense of conviction.

There are a number of factors pointing to Mr. Ross adjusting to a capital life term in the state Department of Corrections without serious violence. These include the following:

1. Mr. Ross was confined in the Department of Corrections from May 1999 until he transferred to the County Jail for a new sentencing

trial. His adjustment in the Department of Corrections was with infrequent disciplinary misconduct and was without serious violence towards inmates or staff.

2. Mr. Ross is 40 years old. Increasing age is strongly associated with steadily decreasing likelihood of involvement in prison misconduct and violence. This has been demonstrated in analysis of inmate misconduct data in New York, Missouri, Florida, and from nationwide samples (see Cunningham & Reidy, 1998, 2002; Cunningham & Sorensen, 2006a; Cunningham, Sorensen, & Reidy, 2005).

3. Institutional Risk Appraisals performed by the Department of Corrections reflect a rating of "minimal or no risk" since January 2001.

4. Mr. Ross has a GED as well as a history of employment in the community. Such a history is associated with an increased likelihood that an inmate will constructively occupy himself in confinement (Cunningham, Sorensen, & Reidy, 2005).

5. Mr. Ross will be serving a capital life sentence. Multiple group statistical studies indicate that the majority of individuals convicted of capital murder are not cited for violent misconduct in prison. Similarly, group statistical data point to capital offenders representing better institutional assault risks than inmates serving shorter sentences. Utilizing a sample of all inmates confined in a maximum security prison from 1991 to 2002, Cunningham, Sorensen, and Reidy (2005) found that life-without-parole inmates were half as likely to be cited for assaultive misconduct as the parole-eligible prisoners they were side by side with in the same facility. Subsequent large-scale research by Cunningham and Sorensen (2006b) found that life-without-parole inmates did not represent a disproportionate risk of assaultive infractions in prison.

6. Rates of violent misconduct among inmates in the Department of Corrections are relatively low. The rate of inmate and staff assaults among DOC inmates as a whole in fiscal year 2003 was 3.26 per 100 inmates (DOC, 2003). Data from other large correctional samples has identified that assaults resulting in serious injury represent a very small fraction of total institutional assaults.

There are two factors in Mr. Ross's case that would be associated with a heightened risk of violent prison misconduct:

1. Mr. Ross was implicated in and pled to an offense involving the group assault of another inmate in the County Jail in 1999. The risk implications of this assault are ambiguous, however. The assault oc-

curred in a county jail group tank context that is quite distinct from the celling, security, and supervision procedures Mr. Ross would reasonably encounter in the Department of Corrections. Mr. Ross's role and relative culpability in this group assault are disputed. Finally, Mr. Ross is now 7 years older than he was at the time of this incident.

2. Mr. Ross was convicted of a murder in the course of a burglary. This is a modest risk-enhancing factor.

Utilizing studies of death-commuted and life-sentenced capital offenders as anchors regarding the probability of a serious act of prison violence from a capital offender, there is a 20–30% prevalence rate of an act of assaultive violence at some time across a capital prison term among capital offenders (see Cunningham & Reidy, 1998, 2002). There is an approximately 8–10% prevalence rate of more chronic institutional offending among capital offenders. Applying group statistical data from an exceptionally large ($N = 6,390$) study of assaultive conduct by convicted murderers in state prison (Sorensen & Pilgrim, 2000), offenders matching the offense characteristics, demographic features, and incarceration history of Mr. Ross were projected as having the following probabilities of serious institutional violence across a capital life term: 9.4% any serious assault, less than 1% aggravated assault on staff, and less than .2% homicide of an inmate. The likelihood of homicide of a state correctional staff member is 1 per 1,000,000 inmates annually.

As risk of violence is always a function of context, these estimates of the risk of serious violence could be markedly reduced by ultra-secure confinement. Should the Department of Corrections determine that Mr. Ross is disproportionately likely to perpetrate serious institutional violence, there are mechanisms to confine him under heightened security procedures such as those available on a Secure Management Unit that involve single-celling, application of restraints with any movement, solitary recreation, and other security measures. Under such conditions, any opportunity to engage in serious violence is substantially negated.

I anticipate that my testimony will be accompanied by numerous PowerPoint digital demonstrative text and graphic model exhibits to assist the jury's understanding of this complex, statistically oriented testimony regarding violence risk assessment. This testimony will also include discussion of essential questions and various models of violence risk assessment, illustrative follow-up studies of institutional assault rates of capital offenders and other inmate groups, and explanatory models.

Please advise me if additional information is desired. Thank you for your consideration.

Sincerely,

References

Cunningham, M. D., & Reidy, T. J. (1998). Integrating base rate data in violence risk assessments at capital sentencing. *Behavioral Sciences and the Law, 16,* 71–95.

Cunningham, M. D., & Reidy, T. J. (2002). Violence risk assessment at federal capital sentencing: Individualization, generalization, relevance, and scientific standards. *Criminal Justice and Behavior, 29,* 512–537.

Cunningham, M. D., & Sorensen, J. R. (2006a). Actuarial models for assessment of prison violence risk: Revisions and extensions of the Risk Assessment Scale for Prison (RASP). *Assessment, 13,* 253–265.

Cunningham, M. D., & Sorensen, J. R. (2006b). Nothing to lose? A comparative examination of prison misconduct rates among life-without-parole and other long-term high security inmates. *Criminal Justice and Behavior, 33,* 683–705.

Cunningham, M. D., Sorensen, J. R., & Reidy, T. J. (2005). An actuarial model for assessment of prison violence risk among maximum security inmates. *Assessment, 12,* 40–49.

Sorensen, J. R., & Pilgrim, R. L. (2000). An actuarial risk assessment of violence posed by capital murder defendants. *Journal of Criminal Law and Criminology, 90,* 1251–1270.

RISK ASSESSMENT

This is a sample report provided by Mary Alice Conroy, PhD, ABPP. The purpose of this type of report is to assist in the selection of offenders who will be put forth for commitment under the state's Sexually Violent Predator Law. Each year the state selects between 100 and 200 offenders considered to be of particularly high risk from a pool of over 900 sex offenders scheduled for release. Expert assessment is then requested to determine the 15 to 20 of these offenders who would be at the highest risk and against whom petitions for commitment will be filed. It should be noted that virtually all offenders assessed by experts already have high scores on the STATIC-99 and MnSOST-R, so details of these instruments are not discussed. State law does require testing for psychopathy.

Name: Caren, James
Prison #:
Date of Birth: April 10, 1962
Discharge Date: 00/00/2006
Date of Evaluation: 00/00/2006

Identification and Reason for Referral

James Caren is a 44-year-old Caucasian male referred for assessment to assist in determining his level of risk and possible need for civil commitment. The purpose of the evaluation was to assist in determining whether Mr. Caren suffers from a behavioral abnormality making him likely to engage in acts of predatory sexual violence when released from incarceration.

Evaluation Procedures

Prior to the interview, Mr. Caren was informed of the nature of the assessment and possible outcomes. He was given an opportunity to ask questions of the evaluators. He stated that he understood the purpose of the interview, agreed to participate, and signed the evaluation disclosure statement.

As part of the process, Mr. Caren was interviewed and the Hare Psychopathy Checklist-Revised (PCL-R), second edition, was completed. All official records provided by the state were reviewed. These included results of a STATIC-99 and MnSOST-R.

Background Information

Mr. Caren, the first of five children, was born in a small town in Kansas. His paternal grandparents raised him until he was 8 years old, at which time his biological parents became his primary caregivers. Mr. Caren described his childhood as very chaotic because his parents were physically and emotionally abusive. In addition, Mr. Caren reported a history of sexual abuse beginning at age 9, when he was raped by a stranger at a local park. He continued to be sexually molested on a regular basis by neighbors and his scout master. As a result, Mr. Caren attempted to commit suicide on more than one occasion during his childhood. He stated that his most serious attempt occurred at age 9, when he consumed half a bottle of his mother's prescription antihistamines.

Mr. Caren reported getting into trouble nearly every day for various acts of misbehavior, including running away from home, lying to his parents, stealing from neighbors, and general combativeness. At the age of seven, Mr. Caren began participating in criminal activity when he destroyed ¼ acre of corn. When Mr. Caren was 10 years old he hung his neighbor's dog out of anger. He reported breaking his sister's leg as the result of his violent temper. Mr. Caren also demonstrated insubordinate behavior at school, as evidenced by his proclivity to disrupt class, destroy property, and skip class regularly. In junior high school, he was suspended for fighting with another student after he tied a rope around his peer's neck and sat on top of him.

Mr. Caren evidenced an extensive substance abuse history beginning at age 10, when older cousins provided him with gin. By the age of twelve he was drinking straight vodka on a daily basis. During that year, Mr. Caren willingly engaged in sexual intercourse for the first time. Mr. Caren continued to run away from home, met some older men who took advantage of him sexually, and began posing nude for financial gain. During his teenage years, Mr. Caren prostituted himself regularly.

Mr. Caren was labeled a chronic runaway and was sent to a youth reformatory for 1 year. He continued to rebel by disobeying the rules and initiating fights. The offender was conditionally released to the custody of his paternal aunt, where he resided for 1 month. Upon his return home, he attended individual and family therapy for 1 year. Information obtained from records mention another suicide attempt by prescription overdose at age 14.

Mr. Caren did not graduate from high school. He quit school during his sophomore year due to racial tension. At this time he began experimenting with various illicit drugs. He reported using LSD up to twice a week and using speed and barbiturates when available, although his preference was to drink a quart of liquor everyday.

The offender has held hundreds of jobs in a variety of fields, including construction, security, restaurants, and property management. However, he stated that his longest place of employment was the military. In 1976, Mr. Caren enlisted in the U.S. Navy. He did not complete basic training and received an honorable discharge for medical reasons. Shortly after his discharge, Mr. Caren started selling Quaaludes and was arrested for prostitution, although the charges were dismissed. In 1980, Mr. Caren enlisted in the U.S. Army because he was looking for a career. During his military service, Mr. Caren was charged with Theft by Check and Drunkenness. Subsequently, he spent 1 year at a retraining base in Georgia. He was also court ordered to be confined in a detention center in West Germany for 6 months, where he discontinued his alcohol abuse. Mr. Caren obtained his GED while in the military before receiving a bad conduct discharge in 1985. The offender experienced several periods of unemployment during the late 1980s and early 1990s. During this time, he received welfare checks and sometimes lived on the street.

Mr. Caren has been in three serious romantic relationships, two of which resulted in marriage. Mr. Caren was married for 7 years, during which time he and his wife had three children. The offender admitted that his first marriage was abusive, and the offender reported an incident in which he assaulted his wife during her pregnancy. Shortly after the marriage was dissolved, the children were given up for adoption. Mr. Caren has not had any contact with his children since they were adopted. In 1989, while separated from his first wife, Mr. Caren began a relationship that would eventually result in his second marriage. The offender described taunting and teasing his obese wife about her weight problem. The couple was divorced after 3 years of marriage. His most recent relationship began as a friendship in 1991 and continues to date. Mr. Caren explained that his partner is 22 years his senior and is more of a parent figure than a romantic partner.

On January 20, 1994, while working as the manager of an apartment complex, Mr. Caren lured three young boys, ages 6, 9, and 10, into his office. Mr. Caren reported that he had observed the boys experimenting with their sexuality a few days prior to the offense. He knew when they would be playing in the area and made sure that he would be alone in the office. The offender proceeded to approach the children and manip-ulate them into believing that sexual acts with adults are appropriate. Records indicate that he exposed himself to the boys, forced the 9-year-old boy into oral sodomy as the active and passive partner, masturbated in front of them, and encouraged two of the children to perform anal sodomy on each other while he masturbated the third boy. He also showed them pictures of adult males engaged in intercourse. The of-fender warned the children to keep the incident a secret. He was subse-quently charged with three counts of Aggravated Sexual Assault of a Child. Currently, Mr. Caren is serving two 12-year sentences and a 10-year term of probation to run concurrently. He has received several minor disciplinary infractions.

Mental Health History

Mr. Caren attempted to commit suicide on more than one occasion during his childhood due to the stress associated with living in an abusive family. He attended individual and family counseling for 1 year when he was 15 years old, following his release from the youth reformatory. Although he has sought out individual therapy numerous times, the offender reported that he "never got past the initial interview." Mr. Caren identifies his alco-hol abuse as a problem in the past.

Diagnostic Impressions

Axis I: 305.00 Alcohol Abuse

Axis II: 301.7   Antisocial Personality Disorder

Mr. Caren has a long history of abusing alcohol beginning at age 10. His substance abuse significantly affected his ability to succeed in the mil-itary and other occupations. He reported going to work intoxicated almost every day.

A personality disorder is a cluster of aberrant personality traits that tend to be socially maladaptive. Antisocial personality disorder is defined by a pervasive pattern of disregard for, and violation of, the rights of others that begins in childhood or early adolescence and continues into adulthood. As currently defined, it can be broadly applied to almost anyone who has a history of illegal activities that started during adolescence. In general, it describes someone who has behaved irresponsibly, had difficulty dealing with authority, and often ignored the rules and mores of the larger society. File information and information obtained during Mr. Caren's interview are consistent with this diagnosis.

A diagnosis of pedophilia cannot currently be given in this case because there is insufficient evidence that Mr. Caren was engaging in inappropriate sexual behavior with children for more than 6 months. The offender denied any additional sexual contact with the current victims or other children.

Risk Factors

This offender demonstrated several risk factors associated with sexual recidivism. First, previous sexual offending is one of the strongest predictors of future sexual offending. Therefore, the prior sexual offense record raises his risk of future sexual offending. Second, Mr. Caren demonstrated deviant sexual interests, as evidenced by his choice of young children as victims of sexual assault. A preference for young, male children is also associated with a higher risk of sexual recidivism. Third, early onset of sexual misconduct is a robust predictor of sexual recidivism. The offender began posing naked and participating in pornographic movies at the age of eleven. He continued to profit from these encounters until he was 14 years old, at which time he began working as a prostitute. Fourth, the predatory nature of the Aggravated Sexual Assault of Child offenses is evident. None of the victims were members of Mr. Caren's immediate family; however, he appears to have groomed the children at the pool, and a degree of planning went into the sexual assault. The offender took precautions so that no adults would be present during the offense.

Mr. Caren has a lengthy history of general offending beginning at the age of seven. He reported several juvenile arrests for running away. Mr. Caren was discharged from the Army for passing bad checks, and he reported arrests for possession of an illicit drug and prostitution, although these charges were dropped. The offender admitted to several crimes for which he was not arrested, including driving while intoxicated and selling Quaaludes. A history of nonsexual offenses increases Mr. Caren's risk of future offending, generally. Mr. Caren's substance abuse history increases risk of recidivism. However, he denies that alcohol played any part in his sexual offenses.

Mr. Caren received a score of 26 on the PCL-R, which currently is the most accurate measure of psychopathy. Research indicates that a score above 30 is a strong predictor of violent recidivism and represents a personality structure characterized by an extreme disregard for the rights of others, an inability to empathize with pain experienced by others, a propensity to view others as objects to be manipulated, and a lack of remorse for one's destructive behaviors. Although this offender did not score in the psychopathic range, he demonstrated strong psychopathic tendencies. He is conning and manipulative, as evidenced by his exploitation of children and history of scams, such as passing bad checks. Mr. Caren freely admitted that he can be manipulative. The offender's irresponsibility is reflected in his history of defaulting on personal loans, driving while intoxicated, and inability to maintain steady employment.

There are some important risk factors that this offender does not exhibit. Mr. Caren has demonstrated an ability to maintain sexual relationships with an appropriate adult partner. There is no evidence that Mr. Caren has been in violation of conditional release, and he is past the age of highest risk, both of which reduce his risk for sexual recidivism.

Conclusions

In our professional opinion, based on the information available to us and given the risk factors identified above, James Caren would be described most appropriately as being at a high risk for general recidivism, although his re-offending may not necessarily be sexual in nature.

_____   _____
Clinical Psychology Student   Diplomate in Forensic Psychology
                                         American Board of Professional
                                         Psychology

Risk Assessment Review Report

This report sample was provided by Chad Brinkley, PhD. The individual was coming due for release from a federal prison facility. This evaluation was conducted to determine if he met the criteria for continued commitment due to risk of bodily harm to another person or serious damage to the property of another as a result of mental disease or defect. The facility utilizes a risk assessment panel composed of three clinicians, who are not directly providing treatment to the subject of the assessment, to make the recommendation to the court. The report is of special interest because three risk assessment instruments were included in the evaluation.

It should be noted that opinions expressed in this report are those of the author and do not necessarily represent the position of the Federal Bureau of Prisons or the U.S. Department of Justice.

Name:
Registration number:

Mr. X is a 58-year-old African American male. He was initially charged with Armed Robbery, Assault With Intent to Kill While Armed, and Attempted Robbery. He was sentenced to 30 years to life for these crimes. Over the years, efforts have been made to designate the inmate to a mainline institution. He has, however, experienced significant mental health problems, which limited his ability to function in non-clinical settings.

Mr. X was seen by the parole board recently and received a recommendation for supervised release. Due to his mental health history, the inmate was subsequently referred for a mental health evaluation to determine if he may be substantially dangerous due to a mental illness if released to the community.

This writer met with Mr. X on (date). This writer reviewed the nature and purpose of the risk assessment with the inmate. This writer explained that any information provided by the inmate would not be confidential, could be included in this report, and would be provided to the risk assessment panel. The inmate was also informed that a copy of the final risk assessment report would be presented to the parole board and may also be seen by a judge, lawyers, and any outside mental health experts should his release become contested. Mr. X indicated that he understood this information and demonstrated this understanding in discussions with this writer. He indicated that he was willing to cooperate with the evaluation and agreed to proceed.

Mr. X was interviewed and his available records were reviewed. These records included prior psychological reports as well as the inmate's central file, medical chart, and his notes in the electronic Psychological Data System (PDS). His behavior was observed on his ward of residence by both clinical and correctional staff.

A Risk Assessment Panel was convened on (date) to review Mr. X's assessment, interview the inmate, and render an opinion concerning whether the release of the inmate would present a substantial risk of bodily injury to others or serious damage to the property of others due to a mental illness.

Historic Considerations

Prior Psychiatric History. According to the available records, Mr. X does not appear to have a history of mental health treatment prior to his incarceration. The inmate reported that he was first evaluated for mental illness at a mental health hospital in (year). He said he began hearing voices talking to him shortly after he was arrested for the index offenses. Records indicate that he was initially diagnosed with schizophrenia.

Since that time, Mr. X has consistently presented with a variety of psychotic symptoms. These have included auditory hallucinations, increased irritability/aggression, rambling/incoherent speech, and disorganized behavior (such as pacing naked in his cell). He has also displayed significant delusional ideation, as indicated by his prior claims that he worked for the military and/or the secret service, despite there being no collateral evidence to support this.

Collateral records indicate that Mr. X has been hospitalized on at least seven occasions. He has been treated with a variety of psychiatric medications, including anti-psychotics, mood stabilizers, anti-depressants, and anti-anxiety medication. He has a history of stabilizing well on medication while in clinical settings. He has, however, routinely refused to continue taking psychiatric medication when returned to mainline facilities, which has consistently resulted in a return of florid psychotic symptoms. Prior treatment records suggest that the inmate has a pattern of becoming very anxious when his psychotic symptoms are well managed by medications.

Antisocial Behavior/Characteristics. Mr. X reported that he began having problems around the age of 14, when he began drinking alcohol and lying to his parents to get out of trouble. He noted that he was involved in several fights around the age of 15, and this was confirmed by records that indicated he left school in the 9th grade due to difficulties getting along with peers.

According to the pre-sentence investigation, Mr. X had a variety of problems while he was out in the community. His sister-in-law described him as irritable, aggressive, and intimidating during a prior interview. She noted during that same interview that she believed Mr. X would be capable of killing someone if the circumstances were correct. The pre-sentence investigation noted that Mr. X was apparently abusive to his wife and lost custody of his children due to neglect.

Mr. X has a variety of charges on his juvenile record beginning at age 16. These include Disorderly Conduct, Simple Assault, Unlawful Entry, Unauthorized Use of a Vehicle, and Tampering with an Automobile. According to his pre-sentence investigation, most of these charges were dismissed, settled, or resolved informally.

Mr. X has a history of adult offenses beginning at age 18. These include Disorderly Conduct, Petty Larceny, Larceny from DC Government, Interstate Transport of a Stolen Vehicle and Possession of an Unregistered Firearm. His records indicate that he completed at least one period of supervised release without difficulty. He appears to have no history of revocations of conditional release.

As noted previously, Mr. X's index offense involves three charges— Armed Robbery, Attempted Robbery, and Assault With Intent to Kill While Armed. These charges resulted from a series of robberies in which Mr. X entered a restaurant with his co-defendants. The three were apparently armed with sawed off shotguns, which they used to threaten security guards and store managers. According to the pre-sentence investigation, they shot at least one store manager who was attempting to comply with their demands for money. Mr. X admitted to the offense when caught, but made several excuses for his behavior, including blaming his actions on drug use and claiming that he was only doing it to get money for his kids (despite the fact they were removed from his custody due to neglect).

Mr. X has a lengthy history of incident reports. Records indicate that he has been charged with a variety of different kinds of misconduct, including Refusing Drug Test, Threats, Refusing an Order, Insolence, Assault Without Serious Injury, Disorderly Conduct, Destruction of Property (more than $100), Unsanitary, Fighting, and Assaulting a Correctional Officer. A review of these incident reports indicates that Mr. X has an established pattern of becoming irritable and aggressive when he is not taking medication.

Reports from the United States Penitentiary indicate that Mr. X was routinely combative, struck a physician's assistant making rounds in segregation, flooded his cell so severely that sand bags were required, and attempted to spit on staff through the crack in his cell door. The inmate has been found responsible for some of these incidents, but most were dismissed after psychology staff determined the inmate was too mentally ill to understand the nature or consequences of his actions. Staff from USP indicated that they believed much of his aggression was directly related to his mental deterioration after medication was discontinued.

Mr. X reported that he began drinking alcohol at age 14 and began using street drugs at age 17. Mr. X said he tried a variety of drugs, including Heroin, THC, LSD, and PCP. At the time of the offense, he blamed his actions on drug use, and he has since admitted that he experienced blackouts in the past because of substance use. He denied, however, having a drug or alcohol problem and never sought treatment for substance abuse. Collateral information indicates that the inmate came into conflict with his parents when he was 19 because he used their money to support his drug habit. Information from the pre-sentence investigation suggests that Mr. X's drug and/or alcohol use may also have been responsible for his difficulties getting to work on time and maintaining steady employment.

Treatment Review

Hospital Course.   Mr. X discontinued his medication each time he was transferred to a regular prison facility. When he refused medication the third time, the inmate was transferred to the hospital to serve the remainder of his sentence in inpatient treatment.

Mr. X was admitted to the Mental Health Treatment Unit at this hospital on (date) under the care of Dr. Goodcare, a Psychiatrist. He was started on quetiapine (an anti-psychotic medication), which was started at 200 mg orally twice per day and increased to 400 mg orally twice per day. He was initially on a locked unit, and medication compliance was only about 50%.

After admission Mr. X remained irritable and agitated with evidence of psychosis for several weeks. There were some periods of medication refusal. On one occasion, Mr. X rushed the cell door and yelled at staff in an attempt to demonstrate his level of agitation. In August he was moved to another locked unit. He improved enough to be transferred to a semi open transitional unit later in the year. During that same year, he began focusing upon the likelihood of having a parole hearing within the coming weeks. His psychotic symptoms improved due to medication, but evidence of anxiety and significant cognitive worry about such issues as his parole and relationships with other inmates moved to the forefront. As a result, it was decided to begin buspirone, a non-addicting anti-anxiety medication. The following January he was transferred to an open unit and began attending group therapy.

Nine months later, the inmate began refusing psychiatric medication, and his mental status declined significantly. He became increasingly agitated, disorganized, aggressive, threatening, and uncooperative. He was placed back in a locked unit. On one occasion, he was observed engaging in fecal play and spit at a staff member. At that time, psychiatric staff determined that the inmate's condition had deteriorated to the point where he was a danger to himself and others. Emergency medication was administered, and a due process hearing was conducted. After stabilizing, the inmate was able to recognize that he needed to be on medication and agreed to take them without incident.

Within the next several months, however, the inmate appeared to be delusional, disorganized, and disruptive despite his continued compliance with psychiatric medication. He was transferred back to a locked unit as he became more agitated and irritable.

Four months later, Mr. X's strange behaviors ceased and his mental status appeared to stabilize. He was transferred back to an open unit, where he has remained since that time. Since then, the inmate has remained compliant with psychiatric medications and has displayed no significant side effects. His psychotic symptoms appear to be in remission. Although he displays some signs of residual thought disorder, his thought process is significantly better organized and he has demonstrated the ability to function on a daily basis without incident.

Community Impressions/Resources. Mr. X was raised by both his parents. He described his parents' relationship as good and denied experiencing any abuse as a child.

Mr. X reported that he was married and had three children with his wife. He claimed that he was married for 5 years but became divorced at some point after he was arrested for the current offenses. Collateral information indicates that he was abusive to his wife and lost custody of his children after he neglected to care for them.

Mr. X said he has not had contact with his wife for several years. He said he has had no contact with his other children since (date).

Mr. X indicated that the only family member he remains in contact with is his cousin. He does not appear to have any other source of social support in the community.

Mr. X reported that he completed the 10th grade when he was in school, but dropped out to get a job. He said he completed a GED.

Collateral information indicates that Mr. X has a history of short term, low skilled labor jobs. The inmate admitted having been fired from at least one job. He claims that he would like to obtain a low skilled labor job upon his release to support himself in the community.

Interview Impressions

When the risk assessment panel asked Mr. X about his mental health problem, he reported that he has a history of hearing voices and "trembles," which he identified as being nervous. He stated that he is not currently hearing voices because he is taking medication, has matured with age, and has been working with people, including the treatment staff.

Mr. X said he realizes he will need to take medication in the community.

Risk Assessment Measures

Psychopathy Checklist Revised, Second Edition. The PCL-R is a 20-item instrument designed to measure negative interpersonal style, limited affect, deviant lifestyle, and antisocial behavior. Scores are determined based on information obtained from both clinical interviews and review of collateral file information.

Scores range from 0 to 40. Scores below 20 are generally considered indicative of a distinct lack of psychopathic traits. Scores of 30 or more are generally considered indicative of the presence of significant psychopathic traits. Higher scores on this instrument have been found to be associated with higher risk for revocation of parole, revocation of mandatory supervision, being unlawfully at large, and general recidivism. There are also studies linking higher PCL-R scores to higher risk for acting violently when released from prison.

Mr. X's total PCL-R score was 18. Research with this instrument has found that individuals with similar scores are at reduced risk for recidivism compared to people with higher scores. The PCL-R has four facets that make up two larger factors. The first factor is made up of interpersonal and affective facets, which measure selfish, callous, remorseless use of others. Factor one is positively correlated with measures of narcissism, Machiavellianism, and dominance. It is negatively correlated with measures of empathy and state/trait anxiety. Mr. X's factor one score was 7. Based on a normative sample of 5,408 male prison inmates, this score is higher than 45% of inmates'. Based on a normative sample of 1,246 male forensic patients, this score is higher than 46% of patients'. In other words, Mr. X's PCL-R factor one score is just below average compared to a sample of his peers.

The second factor is made up of lifestyle and antisocial facets, which measure chronic, unstable, antisocial behavior. It is positively correlated with measures of sensation seeking, substance abuse, and impulsivity. It is negatively correlated with measures of empathy and dependency. Mr. X's factor two score was 10. Based on a normative sample of 5,408 male prison inmates, this score is higher than 46% of inmates'. Based on a normative sample of 1,246 male forensic patients, this score is higher than 44% of patients'. In other words, Mr. X's factor two score is also slightly below average compared to his peers.

Summary Scores

PCL-R Total Score: 18
PCL-R Factor One Score: 7
PCL-R Factor Two Score: 10

Violence Risk Assessment Guide. The VRAG is a 12-item instrument used to assess an offender's risk to commit a violent crime within 10 years of returning to the community. Each item represents a different historical risk factor that has been demonstrated by research to predict future violent behavior. These twelve risk factors include PCL-R psychopathy, elementary school maladjustment, age at index offense, *DSM* diagnosis of personality disorder, *DSM* diagnosis of schizophrenia, being separated from one's biological parents before age 16, criminal history of non-violent offenses, severity of victim injury in the index offense, failure on prior conditional release, history of alcohol abuse, marital status, and male victim for the index offense. These risk factors are considered static in that each is highly unlikely to change over time.

Each item is weighted based on how predictive of future violence it is. Scores range from −11 to +32, with higher scores indicating a higher risk of violent recidivism. The developers divided VRAG scores into nine categories, each associated with a different risk for future violence. It has been found to be a reliable means of assessing risk for violent recidivism. It should be noted, however, that some researchers have questioned the validity of making risk predictions for individuals by comparing them to a standardization sample of only 600 criminal offenders. These predictions should, therefore, be considered estimates with room for error.

Mr. X's VRAG score was −4, placing him in the fourth of nine risk categories. Based on the observed rates of re-offense within the standardization sample of 600 criminal offenders, inmates with scores in this category are estimated to have between 11% and 24.8% chance of committing a violent offense within 7 years of release and between 22% and 39.2% chance of committing a violent offense within 10 years of release (once error estimates have been considered).

Specific factors indicating that Mr. X may be at higher risk for future violence include his criminal history, his young age at the time of the index offense, the nature of the index offense, and some history of alcohol use. Possible protective factors for Mr. X include having been raised by his family, his success on a past conditional release, having few problems in elementary school, and having a low PCL-R score.

Historical/Clinical/Risk Scheme. The HCR-20 is an instrument developed in Canada as a way of formalizing risk assessment decisions and generating risk management plans for correctional systems.

The HCR-20 has 10 items that measure historical or static risk factors, including prior acts of violence, substance abuse, major mental illness, psychopathy, and early adjustment problems. It has five items that measure current, dynamic, clinical factors, such as level of insight, negative attitudes, active mental health symptoms, impulsivity, and responsivity to treatment. Finally, the measure uses five risk items to examine specifically how the person may react to a specific setting. These items examine future plans, exposure to destabilizers, lack of personal support, compliance with remediation attempts, and anticipated stressors.

Scores on the HCR-20 range from 0 to 40 and are based on data collected during clinical interviews as well as collateral information from other data sources, such as files. The authors of the instrument recommend against using simple cutoff scores to determine if someone is at high or low risk. They emphasize that the instrument is designed to provide a guide for thinking about how to weight risk factors rather than a formalized test.

The authors also note that the instrument is still in the process of being validated, but note that the preliminary data support the HCR-20's usefulness in risk prediction.

Mr. X had several historical factors that may place him at risk for future violence. These include a history of previous violence beginning at a relatively young age (as documented in file information and prior reports), his abusive relationship with his ex-wife, his history of employment problems, his history of untreated substance abuse, and his record of significant juvenile offenses. Historical factors that may protect Mr. X against future risk include his low score on the PCL-R, his lack of a diagnosable personality disorder, and his apparent success on a prior period of supervised release.

The clinical scales suggest the presence of both risk and protective factors that might impact Mr. X's risk for reoffense. The primary protective factor is the inmate's current compliance with medication and the impact of medication on his mental illness. There is significant evidence that the inmate's thinking is more organized and rational when he is taking medication. He also demonstrates better self-care skills, reality testing, and temper control. Although records indicate that he has demonstrated the ability to be callous and violent, he endorsed no pro-criminal thinking during the interview. He showed no signs of a hostile attributional bias and seems to have good relationships with both staff and peers at this facility.

Mr. X claims he now understands how his medications help him remain stable, but his actual commitment to continue taking them in less supervised settings remains unclear. He has made promises to remain on medications before but has a long history of stopping medications as soon as he is able to. Although he is currently friendly, cooperative, and motivated to participate in treatment, he continues to minimize his responsibility for offenses and has not sought treatment for substance abuse problems. He also continues to show signs of restlessness and agitation that might make it difficult for him to maintain sustained attention.

When assessing the risk management items for Mr. X, he expressed a desire to be released to a group home. He stated that he wanted to get a low-skilled labor job like working as a clerk in order to support himself. He claimed he has friends in the community, but his only contact with anyone on the outside is his cousin. Most of his current friends appear to be other inmates he has met over the years while he was incarcerated.

Mr. X has made no specific plans for mental health aftercare, but said that he needs it and is willing to work with staff at this facility to make proper arrangements for mental health aftercare. He said his case manager is the one helping him arrange for his release. Collateral information indicates that Mr. X has been successful on a period of supervised release in the past. As noted, however, his past compliance with psychiatric medication after being discharged from inpatient settings has been poor.

If he returns to the community, Mr. X would likely be exposed to several potential destabilizers and stressors. The inmate has a history of untreated substance abuse problems and will once again have access to alcohol and/or drugs. Mr. X said that his son is a convicted felon, and at least one of his other relatives was arrested as well. The inmate has been incarcerated since (date) and is likely to be unprepared for how much the outside world has changed in that time. He does not have a GED, he has limited job skills, and his sources of social support are limited. For the first time in over 20 years, he will need to resume responsibility for keeping a residence, cooking, cleaning, etc.

In summary, Mr. X's release plan currently appears to be lacking. He is aware, however, that he will need to complete release preparation classes and knows which staff members he needs to work with to develop a better release plan. Although he is currently very stable on psychiatric medication, his insight into his need for ongoing need for mental health treatment remains questionable, and he will be exposed to significant stresses and temptations when released to the community. To the extent that these concerns could be addressed, the inmate's risk for future problems could be reduced.

Based on the HCR-20, as well as the specific risk and protective factors that were considered, it was concluded that the inmate appears to be at low to moderate risk to engage in future violence were he returned to the community within the next 12 months.

Diagnostic Impression

Axis I: Schizophrenia (paranoid type)

Axis II: None noted

Axis III: History of positive PPD

Axis IV: Incarceration

Axis V: Global Assessment of Functioning (Current) = 55 (Most symptoms under control via medications; Signs of residual thought disorder remain, including mild disorganization, restlessness, and social difficulties)

Opinions and Recommendations

It should be noted that the prediction of dangerousness is of limited accuracy at the time of formulation, and the accuracy of a prediction diminishes over time. The Risk Assessment Panel generated an opinion on whether Mr. X is presently suffering from a mental disease or defect as the result of which his release would create a substantial risk of bodily injury to another person or serious damage to property of another. Factors not related to mental illness may contribute to the individual's being at greater risk for violent, criminal, or nuisance behavior. The present evaluation identified several historical factors that may place the inmate at risk, and those factors were addressed earlier in this report. In accordance with the statute, however, our prediction specifically concerns the risk of violent behavior that results from mental illness.

Mr. X has consistently been diagnosed with schizophrenia (paranoid type) since he was initially incarcerated on (date). When unmedicated, he displays significant psychotic symptoms, including hallucinations, delusions, and disorganized behavior. As such, he appears to meet the first criterion, in that he has a mental illness. The question remains, however, as to whether he is dangerous because of the mental illness.

Mr. X has a pattern of becoming irritable, aggressive, and belligerent when he is not taking psychiatric medication. The inmate would engage in a variety of disruptive and dangerous behaviors while he was off medications, including assaulting staff, spitting at staff, flooding his cell, and making unprovoked threats. In contrast, Mr. X presents as friendly and cooperative when he is taking psychiatric medication and has received few, if any, incident reports while he has been actively engaged in treatment. This suggests that the inmate's mental illness makes it more difficult to regulate his emotions, utilize good reality testing, and control his behavior. As such, he is more likely to see others as threats and act out violently when he is actively psychotic. Based on these observations, the inmate's mental illness appears to place him at increased risk of acting dangerously. At the moment, however, Mr. X is taking psychiatric medication as prescribed and has been functioning well on an open unit for several months. Given the inmate's response to treatment, it is likely that his mental illness can be effectively managed in the community as long as he remains compliant with medication and mental health aftercare.

In forming their final opinion, the risk assessment panel considered several factors that may impact Mr. X's ability to succeed on a conditional release. Specific factors that were reviewed included his diagnosis of schizophrenia, history of violence, his current compliance with psychiatric medication, his institutional adjustment, his substance abuse history, his sources of social support, and his plans for returning to the community. The panel also noted Mr. X's low PCL-R score, low VRAG score, as well as the risk and protective factors identified by the HCR-20. The panel noted that Mr. X is currently functioning at a high level within the institution and noted his preliminary approval for supervised release by the DC parole commission.

After interviewing the inmate and considering these factors, the opinion of the Risk Assessment Panel was that Mr. X currently suffers from a mental illness (paranoid schizophrenia) that places him at risk of harming others, or the property of others, if he is untreated when released. They clarified, however, that they believed that he is currently functioning at a high enough level that the risk can be managed in a community setting provided Mr. X receives significant supervision and aftercare treatment. The panel suggested that the inmate may do better in a setting where his medication compliance can be closely monitored. They also recommended that the inmate may benefit from other kinds of programming including GED classes, job training, and substance abuse treatment. The panel expressed the belief that the inmate is ready for conditional release to a community setting under appropriate supervision.

References

Abel, G. G., Becker, J. V., Mittelman, M. S., Cunningham-Rathner, J., Rouleau, J. L., & Murphy, W. D. (1987). Self-reported sex crimes of nonincarcerated paraphiliacs. *Journal of Interpersonal Violence, 2,* 3–25.

Abel, G. G., Huffman, J., Warberg, B. W., & Holland, R. (1998). Visual reaction time and plethysmography as measures of sexual interest in child molesters. *Sexual Abuse: A Journal of Research and Treatment, 10,* 317–335.

Abel, G. G., & Rouleau, J. L. (1990). The nature and extent of sexual assault. In W. L. Marshall, D. R. Laws, & H. E. Barbaree (Eds.), *Handbook of sexual assault* (pp. 9–21). New York: Plenum Press.

Abushualeh, K., & Abu-Akel, A. (2006). Association of psychopathic traits and symptomatology with violence in patients with schizophrenia. *Psychiatry Research, 143,* 205–211.

Addington v. Texas, 441 U.S. 418 (1979).

Ahmeyer, S., Heil, P., McKee, B., & English, K. (2000). The impact of polygraph on admissions of victims and offenses in adult sexual offenders. *Sexual Abuse: A Journal of Research and Treatment, 12,* 123–138.

Ake v. Oklahoma, 470 U.S. 68 (1985).

Alexander, J., & Austin, J. (1992). *Handbook for evaluating objective prison classification systems.* Washington, DC: NIC.

Amenta, A. E. (2005). The assessment of sex-offender for civil commitment proceedings: An analysis of report content (Doctoral dissertation, Sam Houston State University, 2005). *Dissertation Abstracts International, 67,* 528.

American Psychiatric Association. (1974). *Clinical aspects of the violent individual.* Washington, DC: Author.

American Psychiatric Association. (1983). Brief for the American Psychiatric Association as *amicus curiae* in Support of Petitioner, in *Barefoot v. Estelle,* No. 82-6080, 463 U.S. 880 (1983). Retrieved July 1, 2007 from www.psych.org/edu/other_res/lib_archives/archives/amicus/82-6080.pdf.

American Psychiatric Association. (1994). *Diagnostic and statistical manual of mental disorders* (4th ed.). Washington, DC: Author.

American Psychiatric Association. (2000). *Diagnostic and statistical manual of mental disorders* (4th ed., text rev.). Washington, DC: Author.

American Psychological Association. (1978). Report of the taskforce on the role of psychology in the criminal justice system. *American Psychologist, 33,* 1099–1113.

American Psychological Association. (2002). *Ethical principles of psychologists and code of conduct.* Washington, DC: Author.

American Psychological Association. (2003). Guidelines on multicultural education, training, research, practice, and organizational change for psychologists. *American Psychologist, 58,* 377–402.

American Psychological Association. (2005). *Brief of amicus curiae in support of defendant-appellant in the case of U.S. v. Fields* (Docket No. 04-50393, filed April 2005). Retrieved February 22, 2007, from www.apa.org/psyclaw /us-v-fields.pdf.

American Psychological Association. (2006). Presidential task force on evidence-based practice. *American Psychologist, 61,* 271–285.

Americans with Disabilities Act, 2 U.S.C.S. §1331.

Andrews, D. A., & Bonta, J. (1995). *LSI-R: The Level of Service Inventory-Revised.* Toronto: Multi-Health Systems.

Andrews, D. A., & Bonta, J. (2003). *The psychology of criminal conduct* (3rd ed.). Cincinnati, OH: Anderson Press.

Andrews, D. A., Bonta, J., & Hoge, R. D. (1990). Classification for effective rehabilitation: Rediscovering psychology. *Criminal Justice and Behavior, 17,* 19–52.

Andrews, D. A., Bonta, J., & Wormith, J. S. (2006). The recent past and near future of risk and/or need assessment. *Crime and Delinquency, 52,* 7–27.

Andrews, D. A., Bonta, J., & Wormith, J. S. (in press). *Manual for the Level of Service/Case Management Inventory* (LS/CMI). Toronto: Multi-Health Systems.

Appelbaum, P. S., Robbins, P. C., & Monahan, J. (2000). Violence and delusions: Data from the MacArthur Violence Risk Assessment Study. *American Journal of Psychiatry, 157,* 566–572.

Archer, R. P. (Ed.). (2006). *Forensic uses of clinical assessment instruments.* Mahwah, NJ: Erlbaum.

Archer, R. P., Buffington-Vollum, J. K., Stredny, R. V., & Handel, R. W. (2006). A survey of psychological test use patterns among forensic psychologists. *Journal of Personality Assessment, 87,* 84–94.

Arkes, H. R. (1989). Principles in judgment/decision-making research pertinent to legal proceedings. *Behavioral Sciences and the Law, 7,* 429–456.

Atkinson, D. R., Morten, G., & Sue, D. W. (1998). *Counseling American minorities* (5th ed.). New York: McGraw-Hill.

Augimeri, L. K., Koegl, C. J., Levene, K. S., & Webster, C. D. (2005). Early assessment risk lists for boys and girls. In T. Grisso, G. Vincent, & D. Seagrave (Eds.), *Mental health screening and assessment in juvenile justice* (pp. 295–310). New York: Guilford Press.

Augimeri, L. K., Koegl, C. J., Webster, C. D., & Levene, K. S. (2001). *Early Assessment Risk List for Boys: EARL-20B, version 2.* Toronto: Earlscourt Child and Family Centre.

Baird, S. C. (1984). *Classification of juveniles in corrections: A model systems approach.* Madison, WI: National Council on Crime and Delinquency.

Barbaree, H. E., & Marshall, W. L. (1988). Deviant sexual arousal, demographic features, and offense history variables as predictors of re-offense among untreated child molesters and incest offenders. *Behavioral Sciences and the Law, 6,* 257–280.

Barbaree, H. E., & Marshall, W. L. (1998). Treatment of the sexual offender. In R. M. Wettstein (Ed.), *Treatment of offenders with mental disorders* (pp. 265–328). New York: Guilford Press.

Barbaree, H. E., Seto, M. C., Langton, C. M., & Peacock, E. J. (2001). Evaluating the predictive accuracy of six risk assessment instruments for adult sexual offenders. *Criminal Justice and Behavior, 28,* 490–521.

Barefoot v. Estelle, 463 U.S. 880, 103 S. Ct. 3383 (1983).

Bar-Hillel, M. (1990). Back to base rates. In R. M. Hogarth (Ed.), *Insights in decision making: A tribute to Hillel J. Einhorn* (pp. 200–216). Chicago: University of Chicago Press.

Barrowcliff, A. L., & Haddock, G. (2006). The relationship between command hallucinations and factors of compliance: A critical review of the literature. *Journal of Forensic Psychiatry and Psychology, 17,* 266–298.

Barry, C. T., Frick, P. J., DeShazo, T. M., McCoy, M. G., Ellis, M., & Loney, B. R. (2000). The importance of callous-unemotional traits for extending the concept of psychopathy to children. *Journal of Abnormal Psychology, 109,* 335–340.

Bartosh, D. L., Garby, T., Lewis, D., & Gray, S. (2003). Differences in predictive validity of actuarial risk assessments in relation to sex offender type. *International Journal of Offender Therapy and Comparative Criminology, 47,* 422–438.

Battin, S., Hill, K., Abbott, R., Catalano, R., & Hawkins, J. (1998). The contribution of gang membership to delinquency beyond delinquent friends. *Criminology, 36,* 93–115.

Baxstrom v. Herald, 383 U.S. 107 (1966).

Beasley v. Molett, 95 S.W.3d 590 (2002).

Bechara, A., Damasio, H., & Damasio, A. R. (2000). Emotion, decision-making, and the orbitofrontal cortex. *Cerebral Cortex, 10,* 295–307.

Beech, A. R., Fisher, D. D., & Thornton, D. (2003). Risk assessment of sex offenders. *Professional Psychology: Research and Practice, 34,* 339–352.

Benedek, E., & Cornell, D. G. (1989). *Juvenile homicide.* Washington, DC: American Psychiatric Press.

Berlin, F. S., Galbreath, N. W., Geary, B., & McGlone, G. (2003). The use of actuarials at civil commitment hearings to predict the likelihood of future sexual violence. *Sexual Abuse: A Journal of Research and Treatment, 15,* 377–382.

Bersoff, D. N., & Glass, D. J. (1995). The not-so Weisman: The Supreme Court's continuing misuse of social science research. *University of Chicago Law School Roundtable, 2,* 279–302.

Bjorkly, S. (2002). Psychotic symptoms and violence toward others: A literature review of some preliminary findings. *Aggression and Violent Behavior, 7,* 605–615.

Blair, P. R. (2005). *Actuarial risk assessment instruments: A quantitative review.* Unpublished master's thesis, Sam Houston State University, Huntsville, TX.

Blair, R. J. R., & Ciplotti, L. (2000). Impaired social response reversal: A case of acquired sociopathy. *Brain, 123,* 1122–1141.

Blau, T. (Ed.). (1998). *The psychologist as expert witness.* New York: Wiley.

Boccaccini, M. T., & Brodsky, S. L. (2002). Believability of expert and law witnesses: Implications for trial consultation. *Professional Psychology: Research and Practice, 33,* 384–388.

Boer, D. P., Hart, S. D., Kropp, P. R., & Webster, C. D. (1997). *Manual for the Sexual Violence Risk-20: Professional guidelines for assessing risk of sexual violence.* Vancouver, Canada: British Columbia Institute Against Family Violence.

Boer, D. P., Tough, S., & Haaven, H. (2004). Assessment of risk manageability of intellectually disabled sex offenders. *Journal of Applied Research in Intellectual Disabilities, 17,* 272–283.

Boer, D. P., Wilson, R. J., Gauthier, C. M., & Hart, S. D. (1997). Assessing risk of sexual violence: Guidelines for clinical practice. In C. D. Webster & M. A. Jackson (Eds.), *Impulsivity: Theory, assessment, and treatment* (pp. 326–342). New York: Guilford Press.

Bolt, D. M., Hare, R. D., & Neumann, C. S. (2007). Score metric equivalence of the Psychopathy Checklist-Revised (PCL-R) across criminal offenders in North America and the United Kingdom. *Assessment, 14,* 44–57.

Bonta, J., Harman, W. G., Hann, R. G., & Cormier, R. B. (1996). The prediction of recidivism among federally sentenced offenders: A re-validation of the SIR scale. *Canadian Journal of Criminology, 38,* 61–79.

Bonta, J., Law, M., & Hanson, R. K. (1998). The prediction of criminal and violent recidivism among mentally disordered offenders: A meta-analysis. *Psychological Bulletin, 123,* 123–142.

Bonta, J., Wallace-Capretta, S., & Rooney, J. (2000). A quasi-experimental evaluation of an intensive rehabilitation program. *Criminal Justice and Behavior, 27,* 312–329.

Bornstein, B. H. (1999). The ecological validity of jury simulations: Is the jury still out? *Law and Human Behavior, 23,* 75–91.

Borum, R. (1996). Improving the clinical practice of violence risk assessment: Technology, guidelines, and training. *American Psychologist, 51,* 945–956.

Borum, R. (2000). Assessing violence risk among youth. *Journal of Clinical Psychology, 56,* 1263–1288.

Borum, R. (2003). Managing at-risk juvenile offenders in the community: Putting evidence-based principles into practice. *Journal of Contemporary Criminal Justice, 19,* 114–137.

Borum, R. (2006). Assessing risk for violence among juvenile offenders. In S. N. Sparta & G. P. Koocher (Eds.), *Forensic mental health assessment of children and adolescents* (pp. 190–202). Oxford: Oxford University Press.

Borum, R., Bartel, P., & Forth, A. (2001). *Manual for the Structured Assessment for Violence Risk in Youth (SAVRY): Consultation Edition*. Tampa, FL: Louis de la Parte Florida Mental Health Institute, University of South Florida.

Borum, R., Bartel, P., & Forth, A. (2005). Structured Assessment of Violence Risk in Youth. In T. Grisso, G. Vincent, & D. Seagrave (Eds.), *Mental health screening and assessment in juvenile justice* (pp. 311–323). New York: Guilford Press.

Borum, R., Bartel, P., & Forth, A. (2006). *Manual for the Structured Assessment for Violence Risk in Youth (SAVRY)*. Odessa, FL: Psychological Assessment Resources.

Borum, R., Fein, R., Vossekuil, B., & Berglund, J. (1999). Threat assessment: Defining an approach for evaluating risk of targeted violence. *Behavioral Sciences and the Law, 17*, 323–337.

Borum, R., & Grisso, T. (1995). Psychological test use in criminal forensic evaluations. *Professional Psychology: Research and Practice, 26*, 465–473.

Borum, R., & Grisso, T. (2007). Developmental considerations for forensic assessment in delinquency cases. In A. Goldstein (Ed.), *Forensic psychology: Advanced topics for forensic mental health experts and attorneys* (pp. 553–570). Hoboken, NJ: Wiley.

Borum, R., Otto, R., & Golding, S. (1993). Improving clinical judgment and decision making in forensic evaluation. *Journal of Psychiatry and Law, 21*, 35–76.

Borum, R., & Reddy, M. (2001). Assessing violence risk in Tarasoff situations: A fact-based model of inquiry. *Behavioral Sciences and the Law, 19*, 373–385.

Borum, R., & Verhaagen, D. (2006). *Assessing and managing violence risk in juveniles*. New York: Guilford Press.

Brakel, S. J., & Cavanaugh, J. L. (2000). Of psychopaths and pendulums: Legal and psychiatric treatment of sex offenders in the United States. *New Mexico Law Review, 30*, 69–94.

Brame, R., Mulvey, E. P., & Piquero, A. (2001). On the development of different kinds of criminal activity. *Sociological Methods and Research, 29*, 319–342.

Brandt, J. R., Kennedy, W. A., Patrick, C. J., & Curtain, J. J. (1997). Assessment of psychopathy in a population of incarcerated adolescent offenders. *Psychological Assessment, 9*, 429–435.

Braun, H. I., & Zwick, R. (1993). Empirical Bayes analysis of families of survival curves: Applications to the analysis of degree attainment. *Journal of Educational Statistics, 18*, 285–303.

Brennan, P. A., Mednick, B. R., & Mednick, S. A. (1993). Parental psychopathology, congenital factors, and violence. In S. Hodgins (Ed.), *Mental disorder and crime* (pp. 244–261). Newbury Park, CA: Sage.

Brenner, E. (2003). Consumer-focused psychological assessment. *Professional Psychology: Research and Practice, 34*, 240–247.

Brewster, M. P. (2000). Stalking by former intimates: Verbal threats and other predictors of physical violence. *Violence and Victims, 15*, 41–54.

Brodsky, S. L. (1991). *Testifying in court: Guidelines and maxims for the expert witness.* Washington, DC: American Psychological Association.

Brodsky, S. L. (1999). *The expert expert witness.* Washington, DC: American Psychological Association.

Buchanan, A. (1999). Risk and dangerousness. *Psychological Medicine, 29*, 465–473.

Buffington-Vollum, J. K., Edens, J. F., & Keilen, A. (2006, March). *Predicting violence among death row inmates: The utility of the Sorensen and Pilgrim actuarial model.* Paper presented at the annual meeting of the American Psychology-Law Society, St. Petersburg, FL.

Bureau of Justice Statistics. (2006). Retrieved December 10, 2006, from www.ojp.usdoj.gov/bjs/.

Burgess, E. (1928). Factors determining success or failure on parole. In A. A. Bruce, E. W. Burgess, & A. J. Harno (Eds.), *The workings of the indeterminate sentence law and the parole system in Illinois* (pp. 205–249). Springfield: Illinois State Board of Parole.

Burgess, E. (1936). Protecting the public by parole and by parole prediction. *Journal of Criminal Law and Criminology, 27*, 491–502.

Burns, J. M., & Swerdlow, R. H. (2003). Right orbitofrontal tumor with pedophilia symptom and constructional apraxia sign. *Archives of Neurology, 60*, 437–440.

Cale, E. M., & Lilienfeld, S. O. (2002). Sex differences in psychopathy and antisocial personality disorder: A review and integration. *Clinical Psychology Review, 22*, 1179–1207.

Callahan, L. A., & Silver, E. (1998). Factors associated with the conditional release of persons acquitted by reason of insanity: A decision tree approach. *Law and Human Behavior, 22*, 147–163.

Campbell, T. W. (2004). *Assessing sex offenders: Problems and pitfalls.* Springfield, IL: Charles C. Thomas.

Caperton, J. D. (2005). *Predicting recidivism among sex offenders: Utility of the STATIC-99, the MnSOST-R, and the PCL-R.* Unpublished doctoral dissertation, Sam Houston State University, Huntsville, TX.

Carroll, J. S. (1977). Judgments of recidivism risk: Conflicts between clinical strategies and base-rate information. *Law and Human Behavior, 1*, 191–198.

Centers for Disease Control and Prevention. (2006, June). Morbidity and mortality weekly report. *Surveillance Summaries, 55*, No. SS-5.

Cheung, P., Schweitzer, I., Crowley, K., & Tuckwell, V. (1997). Violence in schizophrenia: Role of hallucinations and delusions. *Schizophrenia Research, 26*, 181–190.

Cicchetti, D., & Rogosch, F. A. (1996). Equifinality and multifinality in developmental psychopathology. *Development and Psychopathology, 8,* 597–600.

Cleckley, H. (1941). *The mask of sanity.* St. Louis, MO: Mosby.

Cocozza, J., & Steadman, H. (1976). The failure of psychiatric predictions of dangerousness: Clear and convincing evidence. *Rutgers Law Review, 29,* 1012–1020.

Coie, J. D., & Dodge, K. A. (1998). Aggression and antisocial behavior. In W. Damon & N. Eisenberg (Eds.), *Handbook of child psychology: Vol. 3. Social, emotional, and personality development* (5th ed., pp. 779–862). New York: Wiley.

Colorado v. Parrish, 879 P.2d 453 (1994).

Commitment of Sexually Violent Predators Act, Kan. Stat. Ann. §59–29a02 (2002).

Committee on Ethical Guidelines for Forensic Psychologists. (1991). Specialty guidelines for forensic psychologists. *Law and Human Behavior, 15,* 655–665.

Conroy, M. A. (2003). Evaluation of sexual predators. In A. Goldstein (Ed.), *Handbook of psychology: Vol. 11. Forensic psychology* (pp. 463–484). Hoboken, NJ: Wiley.

Conroy, M. A. (2006). Risk management of sexual offenders: A model for community intervention. *Journal of Psychiatry and Law, 34,* 5–23.

Constantine, M. G. (1998). Developing competence in multicultural assessment: Implications for counseling psychology training and practice. *Counseling Psychologist, 26,* 922–929.

Cooke, D. J., Forth, A. E., & Hare, R. D. (Eds.). (1998). *Psychopathy: Theory, research, and implications for society.* Dordrecht, The Netherlands: Kluwer Academic.

Cooke, D. J., Michie, C., Hart, S. D., & Clark, D. (2005a). Assessing psychopathy in the UK: Concerns about cross-cultural generalisability. *British Journal of Psychiatry, 186,* 335–341.

Cooke, D. J., Michie, C., Hart, S. D., & Clark, D. (2005b). Searching for the pan-cultural core pf psychopathic personality disorder. *Personality and Individual Differences, 39,* 283–295.

Cooper, J., Bennett, E., & Sukel, H. (1996). Complex scientific testimony: How do jurors make decisions? *Law and Human Behavior, 20,* 379–395.

Cooper, J., & Neuhas, I. M. (2000). The "hired gun" effect: Assessing the effect of pay, frequency of testifying, and credentials on the perception of expert testimony. *Law and Human Behavior, 24,* 149–171.

Cooper, R., & Werner, P. T. (1990). Predicting violence in newly admitted inmates: A lens model of staff decision making. *Criminal Justice and Behavior, 17,* 431–447.

Cornell, D. (2002). Teaching point: What training and experience in forensic and mental health areas are needed for juvenile forensic practice. In K. Heilbrun, G. R. Marczyk, & D. DeMatteo (Eds.), *Forensic mental health assessment: A casebook* (pp. 186–187). New York: Oxford University Press.

Cornell, D. (2004). Student threat assessment. In E. Gerler (Ed.), *Handbook of school violence* (pp. 115–136). Binghamton, NY: Haworth Press.

Cornell, D. (2005). School violence: Fears versus facts. In K. Heilbrun, N. Goldstein, & R. Redding (Eds.), *Juvenile delinquency: Prevention, assessment, and intervention* (pp. 45–66). New York: Oxford University Press.

Cornell, D. (2006). *School violence: Fears versus facts.* Mahwah, NJ: Erlbaum.

Cornell, D., Peterson, C., & Richards, H. (1999). Anger as a predictor of aggression among incarcerated adolescents. *Journal of Consulting and Clinical Psychology, 67,* 108–115.

Cornell, D., & Sheras, P. (2005). *Guidelines for responding to student threats of violence.* Longmont, CO: Sopris West.

Cornell, D., Sheras, P., Kaplan, S., McConville, D., Douglass, J., Elkon, A., et al. (2004). Guidelines for student threat assessment: Field-test findings. *School Psychology Review, 33,* 527–546.

Corrigan, P. W., & Watson, A. C. (2005). Findings from the National Comorbidity Survey on the frequency of violent behavior in individuals with psychiatric disorders. *Psychiatry Research, 136,* 153–162.

Cottle, C. C., Lee, R. J., & Heilbrun, K. (2001). The prediction of criminal recidivism by juveniles: A meta-analysis. *Criminal Justice and Behavior, 28,* 367–394.

Crick, N. R., & Dodge, K. A. (1994). A review and reformulation of social information processing mechanisms in children's social adjustment. *Psychological Bulletin, 115,* 74–101.

Crocker, A. E., Mueser, K. T., Drake, R. E., Clark, R. E., McHugo, G. J., Ackerson, T. H., et al. (2005). Antisocial personality, psychopathy, and violence in persons with dual disorders: A longitudinal analysis. *Criminal Justice and Behavior, 32,* 452–476.

Cunningham, M. D. (2006a). Dangerousness and death: A nexus in search of science and reason. *American Psychologist, 61,* 827–839.

Cunningham, M. D. (2006b). Informed consent in capital sentencing evaluations: Targets and content. *Professional Psychology: Research and Practice, 37,* 452–459.

Cunningham, M. D. (in press). Institutional misconduct among capital murders. In M. DeLisi & P. J. Conis (Eds.), *Violent offenders: Theory, research, public policy, and practice.* Boston: Jones & Barlett Publishers.

Cunningham, M. D., & Goldstein, A. M. (2003). Sentencing determinations in death penalty cases. In A. Goldstein (Ed.), *Handbook of psychology: Vol. 11. Forensic psychology* (pp. 407–436). Hoboken, NJ: Wiley.

Cunningham, M. D., & Reidy, T. J. (1998a). Antisocial personality disorder and psychopathy: Diagnostic dilemmas in classifying patterns of antisocial behavior in sentencing evaluations. *Behavioral Sciences and the Law, 16,* 331–351.

Cunningham, M. D., & Reidy, T. J. (1998b). Integrating base rate data in violence risk assessments at capital sentencing. *Behavioral Sciences and the Law, 16,* 71–95.

Cunningham, M. D., & Reidy, T. J. (1999). Don't confuse me with the facts: Common errors in violence risk assessment at capital sentencing. *Criminal Justice and Behavior, 26,* 20–43.

Cunningham, M. D., & Reidy, T. J. (2001). A matter of life and death: Special considerations and heightened practice standards in capital sentencing evaluations. *Behavioral Sciences and the Law, 19,* 473–490.

Cunningham, M. D., & Reidy, T. J. (2002). Violence risk assessment at federal capital sentencing: Individuation, generalization, relevance, and scientific standards. *Criminal Justice and Behavior, 29,* 512–527.

Cunningham, M D., Reidy, T. J., & Sorensen, J. R. (2005). Is death row obsolete? A decade of mainstreaming death-sentenced inmates in Missouri. *Behavioral Sciences and the Law, 23,* 307–320.

Cunningham, M. D., & Sorensen, J. R. (2006a). Actuarial models for assessing prison violence risk: Revisions and extensions of the Risk Assessment Scale for Prison (RASP). *Assessment, 13,* 253–265.

Cunningham, M. D., & Sorensen, J. R. (2006b). Nothing to lose? A comparative examination of prison misconduct rates among life-without-parole and other long-term high security inmates. *Criminal Justice and Behavior, 33,* 683–705.

Cunningham, M. D., Sorensen, J. R., & Reidy, T. J. (2005). An actuarial model for assessment of prison violence among maximum security inmates. *Assessment, 12,* 40–49.

Cunningham, M. D., & Vigen, M. P. (2002). Death row inmate characteristics, adjustment, and confinement: A critical review of the literature. *Behavioral Sciences and the Law, 20,* 191–210.

Daicoff, S., & Wexler, D. B. (2003). Therapeutic jurisprudence. In A. Goldstein (Ed.), *Handbook of psychology: Vol. 11. Forensic psychology* (pp. 561–580). Hoboken, NJ: Wiley.

Dana, R. H. (2005). *Multicultural assessment: Principles, applications, and examples.* Mahwah, NJ: Erlbaum.

Daubert v. Merrell Dow Pharmaceuticals, Inc., 509 U.S. 579, 113 S.Ct. 2786 (1993).

Death Penalty Information Center. (2007, January). Available from www.deathpenaltyinfo.org.

DeMatteo, D., & Edens, J. F. (2006). The role and relevance of the Psychopathy Checklist-Revised in court: A case law survey of U.S. Courts (1991–2004). *Psychology, Public Policy, and Law, 12,* 214–241.

DeMatteo, D., & Marczyk, G. (2005). Risk factors, protective factors, and the prevention of antisocial behavior among juveniles. In K. Heilbrun, N. Goldstein, & R. Redding (Eds.), *Juvenile delinquency: Prevention, assessment, and intervention* (pp. 19–44). New York: Oxford University Press.

Dershowitz, A. (1969). Psychiatrists' power in civil commitments. *Psychology Today, 2,* 43–47.

de Vogel, V., de Ruiter, C., Hildebrand, M., Bos, B., & van de Ven, P. (2004). Type of discharge and risk of recidivism measured by the HCR-20: A retrospective study in a Dutch sample of treated forensic psychiatric patients. *International Journal of Forensic Mental Health, 3,* 149–165.

de Vogel, V., de Ruiter, C., van Beek, D., & Mead, G. (2004). Predictive validity of the SVR-20 and Static-99 in a Dutch sample of treated sex offenders. *Law and Human Behavior, 28,* 235–251.

Diamond, S. S. (1997). Illuminations and shadows from jury simulations. *Law and Human Behavior, 21,* 561–571.

Dishion, T. J., & Patterson, G. (2006). The development and ecology of antisocial behavior in children and adolescents. In D. Cicchetti & D. J. Cohen (Eds.), *Developmental psychopathology* (2nd ed., pp. 503–541). Hoboken, NJ: Wiley.

Dix, G. (1977). The death penalty, "dangerousness," psychiatric testimony, and professional ethics. *American Journal of Criminal Law, 5,* 151–204.

Dixon v. Attorney General of the Commonwealth of Pennsylvania, 325 F. Supp. 966 (1971).

Dolan, M., & Doyle, M. (2000). Violence risk prediction: Clinical and actuarial measures and the role of the Psychopathy Checklist. *British Journal of Psychiatry, 177,* 303–311.

Doren, D. M. (1998). Recidivism base rates, predictions of sex offender recidivism, and the "sexual predator" commitment laws. *Behavioral Sciences and the Law, 16,* 97–114.

Doren, D. M. (2001). Analyzing the analysis: A response to Wollert. *Behavioral Sciences and the Law, 19,* 185–196.

Doren, D. M. (2002). *Evaluating sex offenders: A manual for civil commitments and beyond.* Thousand Oaks, CA: Sage.

Doren, D. M., & Epperson, D. L. (2001). Great analysis, but problematic assumptions: A critique of Janus and Meehl (1997). *Sexual Abuse: A Journal of Research and Treatment, 13*(1), 45–51.

Douglas, K. S., Guy, L. S., & Weir, J. (2005). *HCR-20 violence risk assessment scheme: Overview and annotated bibliography.* Burnaby, British Columbia, Canada: Simon Fraser University, Department of Psychology.

Douglas, K. S., & Ogloff, J. (2003). Violence by psychiatric patients: The impact of archival measurement source on violence base rates and risk assessment accuracy. *Canadian Journal of Psychiatry, 48,* 734–739.

Douglas, K. S., & Skeem, J. L. (2005). Violence risk assessment: Getting specific about being dynamic. *Psychology, Public Policy, and Law, 11,* 347–383.

Douglas, K. S., Vincent, G. M., & Edens, J. F. (2006). Risk for criminal recidivism: The role of psychopathy. In C. Patrick (Ed.), *Handbook of psychopathy* (pp. 533–554). New York: Guilford Press.

Douglas, K. S., & Webster, C. D. (1999). Predicting violence in mentally and personality disordered individuals. In R. Roesch, S. D. Hart, & J. R. P.

Ogloff (Eds.), *Psychology and law: The state of the discipline* (pp. 175–239). New York: Kluwer Academic/Plenum Press.

Douglas, K. S., Webster, C. D., Hart, S. D., Eaves, D., & Ogloff, J. R. P. (2001). *HCR-20 violence risk management companion guide*. Burnaby, British Columbia, Canada: Simon Fraser University, Mental Health, Law, and Policy Institute.

Douglas, K. S., Yeomans, M., & Boer, D. P. (2005). Comparative validity analysis of multiple measures of violence risk in a sample of criminal offenders. *Criminal Justice and Behavior, 32,* 479–510.

Dowden, C., & Andrews, D. (1999). What works in young offender treatment: A meta-analysis. *FORUM on Corrections Research, 11,* 21–24.

Dowden, C., & Brown, S. L. (2002). The role of substance abuse factors in predicting recidivism: A meta-analysis. *Psychology, Crime, and Law, 8,* 243–264.

Doyle, M., Dolan, M., & McGovern, J. (2002). The validity of North American risk assessment tools in predicting inpatient violent behavior in England. *Legal and Criminological Psychology, 7,* 141–154.

D'Silva, K., Duggan, C., & McCarthy, L. (2004). Does treatment really make psychopaths worse? A review of the evidence. *Journal of Personality Disorders, 18,* 163–177.

Dvoskin, J., & Heilbrun, K. (2001). Risk assessment and release decision-making: Toward resolving the great debate. *Journal of the American Academy of Psychiatry and the Law, 29,* 6–10.

Edens, J. F., Buffington-Vollum, J. K., Keilen, A., Roskamp, P., & Anthony, C. (2005). Predictions of future dangerousness in capital murder trials: Is it time to "disinvent the wheel"? *Law and Human Behavior, 29,* 55–86.

Edens, J. F., & Cahill, M. A. (2007). Psychopathy in adolescence and criminal recidivism in young adulthood: Longitudinal results from a multiethnic sample of youthful offenders. *Assessment, 14,* 57–65.

Edens, J. F., Campbell, J. S., & Weir, J. M. (2007). Youth psychopathy and criminal recidivism: A meta-analysis of the Psychopathy Checklist measures. *Law and Human Behavior, 31,* 53–75 .

Edens, J. F., Colwell, L. H., Desforges, D. M., & Fernandez, K. (2005). The impact of mental health evidence on support for capital punishment: Are defendants labeled psychopathic considered more deserving of death? *Behavioral Sciences and the Law, 23,* 603–625.

Edens, J. F., Desforges, D. M., Fernandez, K., & Palac, C. A. (2004). Effects of psychopathy and violence risk testimony on mock juror perceptions of dangerousness in a capital murder trial. *Psychology, Crime, and Law, 10,* 393–412.

Edens, J. F., Marcus, D. K., Lilienfeld, S. O., & Poythress, N. G. (2006). Psychopathic, not psychopath: Taxometric evidence for the dimensional structure of psychopathy. *Journal of Abnormal Psychology, 115,* 131–144.

Edens, J. F., Petrila, J., & Buffington-Vollum, J. K. (2001). Psychopathy and the death penalty: Can the Psychopathy Checklist-Revised identify offenders who represent "a continuing threat to society"? *Journal of Psychiatry and Law, 29,* 433–481.

Edens, J. F., Poythress, N. G., & Watkins, M. M. (2001). Further validation of the Psychopathic Personality Inventory among offenders: Personality and behavioral correlates. *Journal of Personality Disorders, 15,* 403–415.

Edens, J. F., Skeem, J. L., Cruise, K. R., & Cauffman, E. (2001). Assessment of "juvenile psychopathy" and its association with violence: A critical review. *Behavioral Sciences and the Law, 19,* 53–80.

Edens, J. F., Skeem, J. L., & Douglas, K. S. (2006). Incremental validity analyses of the Violence Risk Appraisal Guide and the Psychopathy Checklist: Screening version in a civil psychiatric sample. *Assessment, 13,* 368–374.

Elbogen, E. B., Calkins Mercado, C. C., Scalora, M. J., & Tomkins, A. J. (2002). Perceived relevance of factors for violence risk assessment: A survey of clinicians. *International Journal of Forensic Mental Health, 1,* 37–47.

Elbogen, E. B., Williams, A. L., Kim, D., Tomkins, A. J., & Scalora, M. J. (2001). Gender and perceptions of dangerousness in civil psychiatric patients. *Legal and Criminological Psychology, 6,* 215–228.

Elliott, D. S. (1994). Serious violent offenders: Onset, developmental course, and termination (The American Society of Criminology 1993 presidential address). *Criminology, 32,* 1–21.

Elliott, D. S., Hamburg, B. A., & Williams, K. R. (1998). Violence in American schools: An overview. In D. S. Elliott, B. A. Hamburg, & K. R. Williams (Eds.), *Violence in American schools* (pp. 3–28). Cambridge: Cambridge University Press.

Elliott, D. S., Huizinga, D., & Morse, B. (1986). Self-reported violent offending: An analysis of juvenile violent offenders and their offending careers. *Journal of Interpersonal Violence, 1,* 472–513.

Elliott, D. S., & Menard, S. (1996). Delinquent friends and delinquent behavior: Temporal and developmental patterns. In J. D. Hawkins (Ed.), *Delinquency and crime: Current theories* (pp. 28–67). Cambridge: Cambridge University Press.

English, K., Pullen, S., & Jones, L. (Eds.). (1996). *Managing adult sexual offenders: A containment approach.* Lexington, KY: American Probation and Parole Association.

Epperson, D. L., Kaul, J. D., & Hesselton, D. (1998a, October). *Final report of the development of the Minnesota Sex Offender Screening Tool-Revised (MnSOST-R).* Presentation at the 17th annual Research and Treatment Conference of the Association for the Treatment of Sexual Abusers, Vancouver, British Columbia, Canada.

Epperson, D. L., Kaul, J. D., & Hesselton, D. (1998b). *Minnesota Sex Offender Screening Tool-Revised (MnSOST-R): Development, performance and recommended risk cut scores.* Iowa State University and Minnesota Department of Corrections.

Epstein, S. (1994). Integration of the cognitive and the psychodynamic unconscious. *American Psychologist, 49,* 709–724.

Estroff, S. E., & Zimmer, C. (1994). Social networks, social support, and violence among persons with severe, persistent mental illness. In J. Monahan & H. J. Steadman (Eds.), *Violence and mental disorder: Developments in risk assessment* (pp. 259–295). Chicago: University of Chicago Press.

Falshaw, L., Bates, A., Patel, V., Corbett, C., & Friendship, C. (2003). Assessing reconviction, reoffending, and recidivism in a sample of U.K. sexual offenders. *Legal and Criminological Psychology, 8,* 207–215.

Farrington, D. (1989). Early predictors of adolescent aggression and adult violence. *Violence and Victims, 4,* 79–100.

Fein, R. A., Vossekuil, F., & Holden, G. A. (1995). *Threat assessment: An approach to prevent targeted violence.* National Institute of Justice: Research in Action, 1–7 (NCJ 155000). Available from www.secretservice.gov/ntac.htm.

Firestone, P., Bradford, J. M., Greenberg, D. M., & Serran, G. A. (2000). The relationship between deviant sexual arousal and psychopathy in incest offenders, extrafamilial child molesters, and rapists. *Journal of the American Academy of Psychiatry and the Law, 28,* 303–308.

Flanagan, T. J. (1980). Time served and institutional misconduct: Patterns of involvement in disciplinary infractions among long-term and short-term inmates. *Journal of Criminal Justice, 8,* 357–367.

Forth, A. E., Kosson, D. S., & Hare, R. D. (2003). *Hare Psychopathy Checklist: Youth version manual.* Toronto: Multi-Health Systems.

Forth, A. E., & Mailloux, D. L. (2000). Psychopathy in youth: What do we know? In C. Gacono (Ed), *The clinical and forensic assessment of psychopathy* (pp. 25–53). New Jersey: Lawrence Earlbaum.

Foucha v. Louisiana, 112 S. Ct. 1780 (1992).

Fradella, H. F., Fogarty, A., & O'Neill, L. (2003). The impact of Daubert on the admissibility of behavioral science testimony. *Pepperdine Law Review, 30,* 403–444.

Frick, P. J., Bodin, S. D., & Barry, C. T. (2000). Psychopathic traits and conduct problems in community and clinic-referred samples of children: Further development of the Psychopathy Screening Device. *Psychological Assessment, 12,* 382–393.

Frick, P. J., & Ellis, M. L. (1999). Callous-unemotional traits and subtypes of conduct disorder. *Clinical Child and Family Psychology Review, 2,* 149–168.

Frick, P. J., & Hare, R. D. (2001). *The Antisocial Process Screening Device (APSD).* Toronto: Multi-Health Systems.

Frick, P. J., Kimonis, E. R., Dandreaux, D. M., & Farrell, J. M. (2003). The four-year stability of psychopathic traits in non-referred youth. *Behavioral Sciences and the Law, 21,* 713–736.

Frick, P. J., Lilienfeld, S. O., Ellis, M L., Loney, B. R., & Silverthorn, P. (1999). The association between anxiety and psychopathy dimensions in children. *Journal of Abnormal Child Psychology, 27,* 381–390.

Frick, P. J., & Marsee, M. A. (2006). Psychopathy and developmental pathways to antisocial behavior in youth. In C.J. Patrick (Eds.), *Handbook of psychopathy* (pp. 355–374). New York: Guilford Press.

Frick, P. J., O'Brien, B. S., Wootton, J. M., & McBurnett, K. (1994). Psychopathy and conduct problems in children. *Journal of Abnormal Psychology, 103*, 700–707.

Frick, P. J., Stickle, T. R., Dandreaux, D. M., Farrell, J. M., & Kimonis, E. R. (2005). Callous-unemotional traits in predicting the severity and stability of conduct problems and delinquency. *Journal of Abnormal Child Psychology, 33*, 471–487.

Frye v. United States, 293 F. 1013 (D.C. Cir. 1923).

Fukuyama, M. A., & Ferguson, A. D. (2000). Lesbian, gay, and bisexual people of color: Understanding cultural complexity and managing multiple oppressions. In R. M. Perez, K. A. DeBord, & K. J. Bieschke (Eds.), *Handbook of counseling and psychotherapy with lesbian, gay, and bisexual clients* (pp. 81–106). Washington, DC: American Psychological Association.

Fulero, S. M., & Finkel, N. J. (1991). Barring ultimate issue testimony: An "insane" rule? *Law and Human Behavior, 15*, 495–507.

Fuller, J., & Cowan, J. (1999). Risk assessment in a multidisciplinary forensic setting: Clinical judgment revisited. *Journal of Forensic Psychiatry, 10*, 276–289.

Furby, L., Weinrott, M. R., & Blackshaw, L. (1989). Sex offender recidivism: A review. *Psychological Bulletin, 105*, 3–30.

Furman v. Georgia, 408 U.S. 238 (1972).

Gacono, C., Nieberding, R., Owen, A., Rubel, J., & Bodholdt, R. (2001). Treating conduct disorder, antisocial, and psychopathic personalities. In J. Ashford, B. Sales, & W. Reid (Eds.), *Treating adult and juvenile offenders with special needs* (pp. 99–129). Washington, DC: American Psychological Association.

Gagliardi, G. J., Lovell, D., Peterson, P. D., & Jemelka, R. (2004). Forecasting recidivism in mentally ill offenders released from prison. *Law and Human Behavior, 28*, 133–155.

Gendreau, P., Goggin, C., & Law, M. A. (1997). Predicting prison misconduct. *Criminal Justice and Behavior, 24*, 414–431.

Gendreau, P., Goggin, C., & Smith, P. (2002). Is the PCL-R really the unparalleled measure of offender risk? A lesson in knowledge cumulation. *Criminal Justice and Behavior, 29*, 397–426.

Gendreau, P., Little, T., & Goggin, C. (1996). A meta-analysis of the predictors of adult recidivism: What works? *Criminology, 34*, 575–607.

Gigerenzer, G. (1996). The psychology of good judgment: Frequency formats and simple algorithms. *Journal of Medical Decision Making, 16*, 273–280.

Glancy, G. D., & Chaimowitz, G. (2005). The clinical use of risk assessment. *Canadian Journal of Psychiatry, 50*, 12–17.

Goodwin, D. W., Alderson, P., & Rosenthal, R. (1971). Clinical significance of hallucinations in psychiatric disorders: A study of 116 hallucinatory patients. *Archives of General Psychiatry, 24*, 76–80.

Gorman-Smith, D., Henry, D. B., & Tolan, P. H. (2004). Exposure to community violence perpetration: The protective effects of family functioning. *Journal of Clinical Child and Adolescent Psychology, 33,* 439–449.

Greenberg, S. A., & Shuman, D. W. (1997). Irreconcilable conflict between therapeutic and forensic roles. *Professional Psychology: Research and Practice, 28,* 50–57.

Greenhouse, J. B., Stangl, D., & Bromberg, J. (1989). An introduction to survival analysis: Statistical methods for analysis of clinical trial data. *Journal of Consulting and Clinical Psychology, 57,* 536–544.

Gretton, H. M., Hare, R. D., & Catchpole, R. (2004). Psychopathy and offending from adolescence to adulthood: A 10-year follow up. *Journal of Consulting and Clinical Psychology, 72,* 636–645.

Gretton, H. M., McBride, M., Hare, R. D., O'Shaughnessy, R., & Kumka, G. (2001). Psychopathy and recidivism in adolescent sex offenders. *Criminal Justice and Behavior, 28,* 427–449.

Grisso, T. (1987). The economic and scientific future of forensic psychological assessment. *American Psychologist, 42,* 831–839.

Grisso, T. (1996). Society's retributive response to juvenile violence: A developmental perspective. *Law and Human Behavior, 20,* 229–247.

Grisso, T. (1998). *Forensic evaluation of juveniles.* Sarasota, FL: Professional Resource Press.

Grisso, T. (2003). *Evaluating competencies: Forensic assessments and instruments* (2nd ed.). New York: Kluwer Academic/Plenum Press.

Grisso, T. (2004). *Double jeopardy: Adolescent offenders with mental disorders.* Chicago: University of Chicago Press.

Grisso, T., & Schwartz, R. (2000). *Youth on trial.* Chicago: University of Chicago Press.

Grisso, T., & Tomkins, A. J. (1996). Communicating violence risk assessments. *American Psychologist, 51,* 928–930.

Groth-Marnat, G. (2003). *Handbook of psychological assessment* (4th ed.). Hoboken, NJ: Wiley.

Grove, W. M., & Meehl, P. E. (1996). Comparative efficiency of informal (subjective impressionistic) and formal (mechanical, algorithmic) prediction procedures: The clinical-statistical controversy. *Psychology, Public Policy, and Law, 2,* 293–323.

Grubin, D. (1998). *Sex offending against children: Understanding the risk* (Police Research Series Paper 99). London: Home Office.

Gurmankin, A. D., Baron, J., & Armstrong, K. (2004). The effect of numerical statements of risk on trust and comfort with hypothetical physician risk communication. *Medical Decision Making, 24,* 265–271.

Guy, L. S., Edens, J. F., Anthony, C., & Douglas, K. S. (2005). Does psychopathy predict institutional misconduct among adults? A meta-analytic investigation. *Journal of Consulting and Clinical Psychology, 73,* 1056–1064.

Hagen, M. A. (1997). *Whores of the court: The fraud of psychiatric testimony and the rape of American justice.* New York: Harper-Collins.

Halikias, W. (2004). School-based risk assessments: A conceptual framework and model for professional practice. *Professional Psychology: Research and Practice, 35,* 598–607.

Hall, G. C. N. (1995). Sexual offender recidivism revisited: A meta-analysis of recent treatment studies. *Journal of Consulting and Clinical Psychology, 63,* 802–809.

Hamberger, L. K., Lohr, J. M., Bonge, D., & Tolin, D. F. (1996). A large sample empirical typology of male spouse abusers and its relationship to dimensions of abuse. *Violence and Victims, 11,* 277–292.

Hans, V. P. (1986). An analysis of public attitudes toward the insanity defense. *Criminology, 24,* 393–414.

Hanson, R. K. (1997). *The development of a brief actuarial risk scale for sex offender recidivism* (User Report 97–04). Ottawa, Ontario, Canada: Department of the Solicitor General.

Hanson, R. K. (1998). What do we know about sex offender risk assessment? *Psychology, Public Policy, and Law, 4,* 50–72.

Hanson, R. K. (2002). Recidivism and age: Follow-up data from 4,673 sexual offenders. *Journal of Interpersonal Violence, 17,* 1046–1062.

Hanson, R. K. (2005). Twenty years of progress in violence risk assessment. *Journal of Interpersonal Violence, 20,* 212–217.

Hanson, R. K., Broom, I., & Stephenson, M. (2004). Evaluating community sex offender treatment programs: A 12-year follow-up of 724 offenders. *Canadian Journal of Behavioral Science, 36,* 97–96.

Hanson, R. K., & Bussiere, M. T. (1998). Predicting relapse: A meta-analysis of sexual recidivism studies. *Journal of Consulting and Clinical Psychology, 66,* 348–362.

Hanson, R. K., Gordon, A., Harris, A. J. R., Marques, J. K., Murphy, W., Quinsey, V. L., et al. (2002). First report of the collaborative outcome data project on the effectiveness of psychological treatment for sex offenders. *Sexual Abuse: A Journal of Research and Treatment, 14,* 169–194.

Hanson, R. K., & Harris, A. J. R. (1998). *Dynamic predictors of sexual recidivism* (User Report 97–04). Ottawa, Ontario, Canada: Department of the Solicitor General.

Hanson, R. K., & Harris, A. J. R. (2000). Where should we intervene? Dynamic predictors of sex offense recidivism. *Criminal Justice and Behavior, 27,* 6–35.

Hanson, R. K., & Harris, A. J. R. (2001). A structured approach to evaluating change among sexual offenders. *Sexual Abuse: A Journal of Research and Treatment, 13,* 105–122.

Hanson, R. K., Morton, K. E., & Harris, A. J. R. (2003). Sexual offender recidivism risk: What we know and what we need to know. In R. A. Prentky, E. S. Janus, & M. C. Seto (Eds.), *Annals of the New York Academy of Sci-*

ences: Vol. 989. *Sexually coercive behavior: Understanding and management* (pp. 154–166). New York: New York Academy of Sciences.

Hanson, R. K., & Morton-Bourgon, K. (2004). *Predictors of sexual recidivism: An updated meta-analysis* (Public Safety and Emergency Preparedness). Canada: Public Works and Government Services Canada.

Hanson, R. K., & Morton-Bourgon, K. (2005). The characteristics of persistent sexual offenders: A meta-analysis of recidivism studies. *Journal of Consulting and Clinical Psychology, 73*, 1154–1163.

Hanson, R. K., Steffey, R. A., & Gauthier, R. (1993). Long-term recidivism of child molesters. *Journal of Consulting and Clinical Psychology, 61*, 646–652.

Hanson, R. K., & Thornton, D. (1999). *Static-99: Improving actuarial risk assessments for sex offenders* (User Report 99–02). Ottawa, Ontario, Canada: Department of the Solicitor General.

Hardyck, C., & Petrinovich, L. F. (1977). Left-handedness. *Psychological Bulletin, 84*, 385–404.

Hare, R. D. (1991). *Hare Psychopathy Checklist-Revised manual.* Toronto: Multi-Health Systems.

Hare, R. D. (2003). *Hare Psychopathy Checklist-Revised (PCL-R): Technical manual* (2nd ed.). Toronto: Multi-Health Systems.

Hare, R. D., Clark, D., Grann, M., & Thornton, D. (2000). Psychopathy and the predictive validity of the PCL-R: An international perspective. *Behavioral Sciences and the Law, 18*, 623–645.

Hare, R. D., & Hart, S. D. (1993). Psychopathy, mental disorder, and crime. In S. Hodgkins (Ed.), *Mental disorder and crime* (pp. 104–115). Newbury Park, CA: Sage.

Hare, R. D., & McPherson, L. D. (1984). Violent and aggressive behavior by criminal psychopaths. *International Journal of Law and Psychiatry, 7*, 35–50.

Harris, A., Phenix, A., Hanson, R. K., & Thornton, D. (2003). *STATIC-99 coding rules revised—2003* (Solicitor General of Canada). Retrieved July 14, 2007, from www.sgc.gc.ca.

Harris, G. T., & Rice, M. E. (2007). Adjusting actuarial violence risk assessments based on aging or the passage of time. *Criminal Justice and Behavior, 34*, 297–313.

Harris, G. T., Rice, M. E., & Camilleri, J. A. (2004). Applying a forensic actuarial assessment (the Violence Risk Appraisal Guide) to nonforensic patients. *Journal of Interpersonal Violence, 19*, 1063–1074.

Harris, G. T., Rice, M. E., & Cornier, C. A. (1991). Psychopathy and violent recidivism. *Law and Human Behavior, 15*, 625–637.

Harris, G. T., Rice, M. E., & Quinsey, V. L. (1993). Violent recidivism of mentally disordered offenders: The development of a statistical prediction instrument. *Criminal Justice and Behavior, 20*, 315–335.

Harris, G. T., Rice, M. E., & Quinsey, V. L. (1998). Appraisal and management of risk in sexual aggressors: Implications for criminal justice policy. *Psychology, Public Policy, and Law, 4*, 73–115.

Harris, G. T., Rice, M. E., Quinsey, V. L., Lalumiere, M. L., Boer, D., & Lang, C. (2003). A multi-site comparison of actuarial risk instruments for sex offenders. *Psychological Assessment: A Journal of Consulting and Clinical Psychology, 15*, 413–425.

Hart, S. D. (1998a). Psychopathy and risk for violence. In D. Cooke, A. E. Forth, & R. D. Hare (Eds.), *Psychopathy: Theory, research, and implications for society* (pp. 355–375). Dordrecht, The Netherlands: Kluwer Press.

Hart, S. D. (1998b). The role of psychopathy in assessing risk for violence: Conceptual and methodological issues. *Legal and Criminological Psychology, 3*, 121–137.

Hart, S. D. (2001). Assessing and managing violence risk. In K. S. Douglas, C. D. Webster, S. D. Hart, D. Eaves, & J. R. P. Ogloff (Eds.), *HCR-20 violence risk management guide* (pp. 27–40). Burnaby, British Columbia, Canada: Simon Fraser University.

Hart, S. D., Watt, K. A., & Vincent, G. M. (2002). Commentary on Seagrave and Grisso: Impressions of the state of the art. *Law and Human Behavior, 26*, 241–245.

Hart, S. D., Webster, C. D., & Douglas, K. S. (2001). Risk management using the HCR-20: A general overview focusing on historical factors. In K. S. Douglas, C. D. Webster, S. D. Hart, D. Eaves, & J. R. P. Ogloff (Eds.), *HCR-20 violence risk management guide* (pp. 27–40). Burnaby, British Columbia, Canada: Simon Fraser University.

Harvey, V. S. (1997). Improving readability of psychological reports. *Professional Psychology: Research and Practice, 28*(3), 271–274.

Hawkins, J. D., Herrenkohl, T., Farrington, D. P., Brewer, D., Catalano, R. F., & Harachi, T. W. (1998). A review of predictors of youth violence. In R. Loeber & D. P. Farrington (Eds.), *Serious and violent juvenile offenders: Risk factors and successful interventions* (pp. 106–146). Thousand Oaks, CA: Sage.

Hawkins, J. D., Herrenkohl, T., Farrington, D. P., Brewer, D., Catalano, R. F., & Harachi, T. W. (2000). *Predictors of youth violence* (Juvenile Justice Bulletin). Washington, DC: U.S. Department of Justice, Office of Justice Programs, Office of Juvenile Justice and Delinquency Prevention.

Hazler, R. J., & Carney, J. V. (2000). When victims turn aggressors: Factors in the development of deadly school violence. *Professional School Counseling, 4*, 105–112.

Heilbrun, K. (1992). The role of psychological testing in forensic assessment. *Law and Human Behavior, 16*, 257–272.

Heilbrun, K. (1997). Prediction versus management models relevant to risk assessment: The importance of legal decision-making context. *Law and Human Behavior, 21*, 347–359.

Heilbrun, K. (2001). *Principles of forensic mental health assessment.* New York: Kluwer Academic/Plenum Press.

Heilbrun, K., & Collins, S. (1995). Evaluations of trial competency and mental state at the time of the offense: Report characteristics. *Professional Psychology: Research and Practice, 26*, 61–67.

Heilbrun, K., Dvoskin, J., Hart, S. D., & McNeil, D. (1999). Violence risk communication: Implications for research, policy, and practice. *Health, Risk, and Society, 1*, 91–106.

Heilbrun, K., Leheny, C., Thomas, L., & Huneycutt, D. (1997). A national survey of U.S. statutes of juvenile transfer: Implications for policy and practice. *Behavioral Sciences and the Law, 15*, 125–149.

Heilbrun, K., Marczyk, G. R., & DeMatteo, D. (2002). *Forensic mental health assessment: A casebook*. New York: Oxford University Press.

Heilbrun, K., Nezu, C. M., Keeney, M., Chung, S., & Wasserman, A. L. (1998). Sexual offending: Linking assessment, intervention, and decision making. *Psychology, Public Policy, and Law, 4*, 138–174.

Heilbrun, K., O'Neill, M. L., Stevens, T. N., Strohman, L. K., Bowman, Q., & Lo, Y. (2004). Assessing normative approaches to communicating violence risk: A national survey of psychologists. *Behavioral Sciences and the Law, 22*, 187–196.

Heilbrun, K., O'Neill, M. L., Strohman, L. K., Bowman, Q., & Philipson, J. (2000). Expert approaches to communicating violence risk. *Law and Human Behavior, 24*, 137–148.

Heilbrun, K., Phillipson, J., Berman, L., & Warren, J. (1999). Risk communication: Clinicians reported approaches and perceived values. *Journal of the American Academy of Psychiatry and the Law, 27*, 397–406.

Heilbrun, K., Warren, J., & Picarello, K. (2003). Use of third-party information in forensic assessment. In I. Weiner (Series Ed.) & A. Goldstein (Vol. Ed.), *Comprehensive handbook of psychology: Vol. 11. Forensic psychology* (pp. 69–86). Hoboken, NJ: Wiley.

Hemphill, J. F., Hare, R. D., & Wong, S. (1998). Psychopathy and recidivism: A review. *Legal and Criminological Psychology, 3*, 139–170.

Henderson, C. E., Marvel, F., & Liddle, H. A. (in press). Multidimensional family therapy: An evidence-based treatment for juvenile justice involved and substance abusing adolescents. In N. Jainchill (Ed.), *Understanding and treating adolescent substance use disorders*. Kingston, NJ: Civic Research Institute.

Henggeler, S. W., Schoenwald, S. S., Bourdin, C. M., Rowland, M. D., & Cunningham, P. B. (1998). *Multisystemic treatment of antisocial behavior in children and adolescents*. New York: Guilford Press.

Hess, A. K. (2006). Serving as an expert witness. In I. B. Weiner & K. Hess (Eds.), *Handbook of forensic psychology* (3rd ed., pp. 487–533). Hoboken, NJ: Wiley.

Hiday, V. A. (1990). The dangerousness of civil commitment candidates: A 6-month follow-up. *Law and Human Behavior, 14*, 551–567.

Hiday, V. A. (2006). Putting community risk in perspective: A look at correlations, causes and controls. *International Journal of Law and Psychiatry, 29*, 316–331.

Hiday, V. A., Swartz, M. S., Swanson, J. W., Borum, R., & Wagner, H. R. (1998). Male-female differences in the setting and construction of violence among people with severe mental illness. *Social Psychiatry and Psychiatric Epidemiology, 33*, S68–S74.

Hildebrand, M., de Ruiter, C., & de Vogel, V. (2004). Psychopathy and sexual deviance in treated rapists: Association with sexual and non-sexual recidivism. *Sexual Abuse: A Journal of Research and Treatment, 16*, 1–24.

Hill, R. W., Langevin, R., Paitich, D., Handy, L. Russon, A., & Wilkinson, L. (1982). Is arson an aggressive act or a property offense? A controlled study of psychiatric referrals, assaultive offenders and property offenders. *Canadian Journal of Psychiatry, 27*, 648–654.

Hilton, Z., Harris, G. T., & Rice, M. E. (2006). Sixty-six years of research on the clinical versus actuarial prediction of violence. *Counseling Psychologist, 34*, 400–409.

Hinckley v. U.S., 140 F. 3d 277 (1998).

Hinshaw, S. P., & Lee, S. (2003). Conduct and oppositional defiant disorders. In E. Mash & R. Barkley (Eds.), *Child psychopathology* (2nd ed., pp. 144–199). New York: Guilford Press.

Hirschi, T., & Gottfredson, M. (1983). Age and the explanation of crime. *American Journal of Sociology, 89*, 552–584.

Hodgins, S. (2001). The major mental disorders and crime: Stop debating and start treating and preventing. *International Journal of Law and Psychiatry, 24*, 427–446.

Hoffrage, U., & Gigerenzer, G. (1998). Using natural frequencies to improve diagnostic influences. *Academic Medicine, 73*, 538–540.

Hoge, R. D. (2005). Youth Level of Service/Case Management Inventory. In T. Grisso, G. Vincent, & D. Seagrave (Eds.), *Mental health screening and assessment in juvenile justice* (pp. 283–294). New York: Guilford Press.

Hoge, R. D., & Andrews, D. A. (1994). *Youth Level of Service/Case Management Inventory and manual.* Ottawa, Canada: Carleton University, Department of Psychology.

Hoge, R., & Andrews, D. (1996). *Assessing the youthful offender.* New York: Plenum Press.

Hoge, R. D., & Andrews, D. A. (2002). *The Youth Level of Service/Case Management Inventory manual and scoring key.* Toronto: Multi-Health Systems.

Hoge, R. D., Andrews, D. A., & Leschied, A. W. (1996). An investigation of risk and protective factors in a sample of youthful offenders. *Journal of Child Psychology and Psychiatry, 37*, 419–424.

Holtzworth-Munroe, A., & Stuart, G. L. (1994). Typologies of male batterers: Three subtypes and the differences among them. *Psychological Bulletin, 116,* 476–494.

Hoptman, M. J., Yates, K. F., Patanlinjug, M. B., Wack, R. C., Convit, A. (1999). Clinical prediction of assaultive behavior among male psychiatric patients at a maximum-security forensic facility. *Psychiatric Services, 50,* 1461–1466.

Howell, J. C. (1995). *Guide for implementing the comprehensive strategy for serious, violent, and chronic juvenile offenders.* Washington, DC: Office of Juvenile Justice and Delinquency Prevention.

Howell, J. C. (1999). Promising programs for youth gang violence prevention and intervention. In R. Loeber & D. P. Farrington (Eds.), *Serious and violent juvenile offenders* (pp. 284–312). Thousand Oaks, CA: Sage.

Howell, J. C. (2003). *Preventing and reducing juvenile delinquency: A comprehensive framework.* Thousand Oaks, CA: Sage.

Howell, J. C., Krisberg, B., Hawkins, J., & Wilson, J. (1995). *Serious, violent, and chronic juvenile offenders.* Thousand Oaks, CA: Sage.

Ingoldsby, E., & Shaw, D. (2002). Neighborhood contextual factors and the onset and progression of early-starting antisocial pathways. *Clinical Child and Family Psychology Review, 5,* 21–55.

In re Branch, 890 So. 2d 322 (2004).

In re commitment of Dennis H., 647 N.W. 2d 851 (2002).

In re David B., 97 N.Y. 2d 267 (2002).

In re Fisher, 164 S.W. 3d 637 (2005).

In re Gault, 387 U.S. 1 (1967).

In re K. L., 806 N.E. 2d 480 (2004).

In re Mark, N.W. 2d 90 (2006).

In re Winship, 397 U.S. 358 (1970).

Insanity Defense Reform Act, 18 U.S.C.S. §§4243, 4246 (1984).

Janus, E. S., & Prentky, R. A. (2003). Forensic use of actuarial risk assessment with sex offenders: Accuracy, admissibility and accountability. *American Criminal Law Review, 40,* 1443–1499.

Jensen, E. (1993). When "hired guns" backfire: The witness immunity doctrine and the negligent expert witness. *University of Missouri at Kansas City Law Review, 62,* 185–207.

Jones v. U.S., 463 U.S. 354 (1983).

Junginger, J. (1995). Command hallucinations and the prediction of dangerousness. *Psychiatric Services, 46,* 911–914.

Jurek v. Texas, 96 S. Ct. 2950 (1976).

Kahneman, D., Slovic, P., & Tversky, A. (Eds.). (1982). *Judgments under uncertainty: Heuristics and biases.* Cambridge: Cambridge University Press.

Kahneman, D., & Tversky, A. (1973). On the psychology of prediction. *Psychological Review, 80,* 237–251.

Kamphaus, R. W., & Frick, P. (1996). *Clinical assessment of children's personality and behavior.* New York: Allyn & Bacon.

Kansas v. Crane, 534 U.S. 407 (2002).

Kansas v. Hendricks, 117 S. Ct. 2072 (1997).

Kashini, J., & Allan, W. (1998). *The impact of family violence on children and adolescents.* Thousand Oaks, CA: Sage.

Kasturirangan, A., Krishnan, S., & Riger, S. (2004). The impact of culture and minority status on women's experience of domestic violence. *Trauma, Violence, and Abuse, 5*, 318–332.

Kazdin, A. (2005). *Parent management training: Treatment for oppositional, aggressive, and antisocial behavior in children and adolescents.* New York: Oxford University Press.

Kenny, D. T., & Press, A. L. (2006). Violence classifications and their impact on observed relationships with key factors in young offenders. *Psychology, Public Policy, and Law, 12*, 86–105.

Kent v. United States, 383 U.S. 541 (1966).

Kienlen, K. K., Birmingham, D. L., Solberg, K. B., O'Regan, J. T., & Meloy, J. R. (1997). A comparative study of psychotic and nonpsychotic stalking. *Journal of the American Academy of Psychiatry and Law, 25*, 317–335.

Kimmel, M. S., & Mahler, M. (2003). Adolescent masculinity, homophobia, and violence: Random school shootings, 1982–2001. *American Behavioral Scientist, 46*, 1439–1458.

Klassen, D., & O'Connor, W. A. (1988). A prospective study of predictors of violence in adult male mental health admissions. *Law and Human Behavior, 12*, 143–158.

Klassen, D., & O'Connor, W. A. (1990). Assessing the risk of violence in released mental patients: A cross-validation study. *Psychological Assessment: A Journal of Consulting and Clinical Psychology, 1*, 75–81.

Klassen, D., & O'Connor, W. A. (1994). Demographic and case history variables in risk assessment. In J. Monahan & H. J. Steadman (Eds.), *Violence and mental disorder: Developments in risk assessment* (pp. 229–258). Chicago: University of Chicago Press.

Klein, J. (2006). Culture capital and high school bullies: How social inequality impacts school violence. *Men and Masculinities, 9*, 53–75.

Koehler, J. J. (1996). The base rate fallacy reconsidered: Descriptive, normative, and methodological challenges. *Behavioral and Brain Sciences, 19*, 1–53.

Koehler, J. J. (2002). When do courts think base rate statistics are relevant? *Jurimetrics Journal, 42*, 373–402.

Kozol, H., Boucher, R., & Garofolo, R. (1972). The diagnosis and treatment of dangerousness. *Crime and Delinquency, 18*, 371–392.

Krakowski, M. I., Czobor, P., Citrome, L., Bank, N., & Cooper, T. B. (2006). Atypical antipsychotic agents in the treatment of violent patients with schizophrenia and schizoaffective disorder. *Archives of General Psychiatry, 63*, 622–629.

Krauss, D. A., & Lee, D. (2003). Deliberating on dangerousness and death: Jurors' ability to differentiate between expert actuarial and clinical predictions of dangerousness. *International Journal of Law and Psychiatry, 26,* 113–137.

Krauss, D. A., Lieberman, J. D., & Olson, J. (2004). The effects of rational and experiential information processing of expert testimony in death penalty cases. *Behavioral Sciences and the Law, 22,* 801–822.

Krauss, D. A., & Sales, B. D. (2001). The effects of clinical and scientific expert testimony on juror decision making in capital sentencing. *Psychology, Public Policy, and Law, 7,* 267–310.

Kravitz, H. M., Haywood, T. W., Kelly, J., Wahlstrom, C., Liles, S., & Cavanaugh, J. L. (1995). Medroxyprogesterone treatment for paraphilics. *Bulletin of the American Academy of Psychiatry and the Law, 23,* 19–33.

Krisberg, B. (2005). *Juvenile justice: Redeeming our children.* Thousand Oaks, CA: Sage.

Kropp, P. R., & Hart, S. D. (1997). Assessing risk of violence in wife assaulters: The Spousal Assault Risk Assessment Guide. In C. D. Webster & M. A. Jackson (Eds.), *Impulsivity: Theory, assessment, and treatment* (pp. 302–325). New York: Guilford Press.

Kropp, P. R., Hart, S. D., Webster, C. D., & Eaves, D. (1995). *Manual for the Spousal Assault Risk Assessment Guide* (2nd ed.). Vancouver, British Columbia, Canada: British Columbia Institute on Family Violence.

Krysik, J., & LeCroy, C. W. (2002). The empirical validation of an instrument to predict risk of recidivism among juvenile offenders. *Research on Social Work Practice, 12,* 71–81.

Kumho v. Carmichael, 526 U.S. 137 (S. Ct., 1999).

Kwartner, P. K., & Boccaccini, M. T. (in press). Testifying in court: Evidence-based recommendations for expert-witness testimony. In R. Jackson (Ed.), *Learning forensic assessment.* Mahwah, NJ: Erlbaum.

Kwartner, P. K., Lyons, P. M., & Boccaccini, M. T. (2006). Judges' risk communication preferences in risk for future violence cases. *International Journal of Forensic Mental Health, 5,* 185–194.

LaFond, J. Q. (2003). The costs of enacting a sexual predator law and recommendations for keeping them from skyrocketing. In B. J. Winick & J. Q. LaFond (Eds.), *Protecting society from sexually dangerous offenders* (pp. 283–300). Washington, DC: American Psychological Association.

LaFond, J. Q. (2005). *Preventing sexual violence: How society should cope with sex offenders.* Washington, DC: American Psychological Association.

Lally, S. J. (2003). What tests are acceptable for use in forensic evaluations? A survey of experts. *Professional Psychology: Research and Practice, 5,* 491–498.

Lalumiere, M. L., Harris, G. T., Quinsey, V. L., & Rice, M. E. (2005). *The causes of rape: Understanding individual differences in male propensity for sexual aggression.* Washington, DC: American Psychological Association.

Langevin, R., Curnoe, S., Federoff, P., Bennett, R., Langevin, M., Peever, C., et al. (2004). Lifetime sex offender recidivism: A 25-year follow-up study. *Canadian Journal of Criminology and Criminal Justice, 46*, 531–552.

Langstrom, N. (2004). Accuracy of actuarial procedures for assessment of sexual offender recidivism risk may vary across ethnicity. *Sexual Abuse: A Journal of Research and Treatment, 16*, 107–120.

Langton, C. M., Barbaree, H. E., Harkins, L., & Peacock, E. J. (2006). Sex offenders' response to treatment and its association with recidivism as a function of psychopathy. *Sexual Abuse: A Journal of Research and Treatment.* Retrieved July 14, 2007, from www.springerlink.com/media /012c8x61qp7rtm8arvv3/contributions/.

Lattimore, P. K., Visher, C. A., & Linster, R. L. (1995). Predicting rearrest for violence among serious youthful offenders. *Journal of Research in Crime and Delinquency, 32*, 54–83.

Leary, M. R., Kowalski, R. M., Smith, L., & Phillips, S. (2003). Teasing, rejection, and violence: Case studies of the school shootings. *Aggressive Behavior, 29*, 202–214.

Lessard v. Schmidt, 349 F. Supp. 1078 (1972).

Lidz, C. W., & Mulvey, E. P. (1995). Dangerousness: From legal definition to theoretical research. *Law and Human Behavior, 19*, 41–48.

Lidz, C. W., Mulvey, E. P., & Gardner, W. (1993). The accuracy of predictions of violence to others. *Journal of the American Medical Association, 269*, 1007–1011.

Lieb, R., Quinsey, V. L., & Berliner, L. (1998). Sexual predators and social policy. In M. Tonry (Ed.), *Crime and justice: Vol. 23. A review of research* (pp. 42–114). Chicago: University of Chicago Press.

Lilienfeld, S. O., & Andrews, B. P. (1996). Development and preliminary validation of a self-report measure of psychopathic personality traits in noncriminal populations. *Journal of Personality Assessment, 66*, 488–524.

Lindqvist, P. (1991). Homicides committed by abusers of alcohol and illicit drugs. *British Journal of Addiction, 86*, 321–326.

Link, B. G., Andrews, H., & Cullen, F. T. (1992). The violent and illegal behavior of mental patients reconsidered. *American Sociological Review, 57*, 575–592.

Link, B. G., Monahan, J., Stueve, A., & Cullen, F. T. (1999). Real in their consequences: A sociological approach to understanding the association between psychotic symptoms and violence. *American Sociological Review, 64*, 316–332.

Link, B. G., & Stueve, A. (1994). Psychotic symptoms and the violent/illegal behavior of mental patients compared to community controls. In J. Monahan & H. J. Steadman (Eds.), *Violence and mental disorder: Developments in risk assessment* (pp. 137–159). Chicago: University of Chicago Press.

Lipsey, M. W. (1992). Juvenile delinquency treatment: A meta-analytic inquiry into the variability of effects. In T. D. Cook, H. Cooper, D. S.

Cordray, H. Hartmann, L. V. Hedges, R. J. Light, et al. (Eds.), *Meta-analysis for explanation: A casebook* (pp. 83–127). New York: Russell Sage Foundation.

Lipsey, M. W. (1995). What do we learn from 400 research studies on the effectiveness of treatment with juvenile delinquents? In J. McGuire (Ed.), *What works? Reducing reoffending* (pp. 63–78). New York: Wiley.

Lipsey, M. W., & Derzon, J. H. (1998). Predictors of violent or serious delinquency in adolescence and early adulthood. In R. Loeber & D. P. Farrington (Eds.), *Serious and violent juvenile offenders* (pp. 86–105). Thousand Oaks, CA: Sage.

Litwack, T. R. (2001). Actuarial versus clinical assessments of dangerousness. *Psychology, Public Policy, and Law, 7,* 409–443.

Litwack, T. R. (2002). Some questions for the field of violence risk assessment and forensic mental health: Or, back to basics revisited. *International Journal of Forensic Mental Health, 1,* 171–178.

Litwack, T. R., & Schlesinger, L. B. (1999). Dangerousness risk assessments: Research, legal, and clinical considerations. In A. K. Hess & I. B. Weiner (Eds.), *The handbook of forensic psychology* (2nd ed., pp. 171–217). New York: Wiley.

Litwack, T. R., Zapf, P. A., Groscup, J. L., & Hart, S. D. (2006). Violence risk assessment: Research, legal, and clinical considerations. In I. B. Weiner & K. Hess (Eds.), *The handbook of forensic psychology* (3rd ed., pp. 487–533). Hoboken, NJ: Wiley.

Lochman, J. E., & Dodge, K. A. (1994). Social-cognitive processes of severely violent, moderately aggressive, and nonaggressive boys. *Journal of Consulting and Clinical Psychology, 62,* 366–374.

Lockett v. Ohio, 438 U.S. 586, 604 (1978).

Loeber, R., & Farrington, D. P. (1998). *Serious and violent juvenile offenders: Risk factors and successful interventions.* Thousand Oaks, CA: Sage.

Loeber, R., Farrington, D. P., Stouthamer-Loeber, M., Moffit, T. E., & Caspi, A. (2001). The development of male offending: Key findings from the first decade of the Pittsburgh Youth Study. In R. Bull (Ed.), *Children and the law: The essential readings—Essential readings in developmental psychology* (pp. 336–378). Malden, MA: Blackwell.

Loeber, R., Farrington, D. P., & Waschbusch, D. A. (1998). Serious and violent juvenile offenders. In R. Loeber & D. P. Farrington (Eds.), *Serious and violent juvenile offenders: Risk factors and successful interventions* (pp. 13–29). Thousand Oaks, CA: Sage.

Loeber, R., Pardini, D., Homish, D. L., Wei, E., Crawford, A., Farrington, D. P., et al. (2005). The prediction of violence and homicide in young men. *Journal of Consulting and Clinical Psychology, 73,* 1074–1088.

Looman, J. (2006). Comparison of two risk assessment instruments for sexual offenders. *Sexual Abuse: A Journal of Research and Treatment, 18,* 193–206.

Looman, J., Abracen, J., Serin, R., & Marquis, P. (2005). Psychopathy, treatment change, and recidivism in high-risk, high-need sexual offenders. *Journal of Interpersonal Violence, 20,* 549–568.

Ludwig, J., Duncan, G., & Hirschfield, P. (2001). Urban poverty and juvenile crime: Evidence form a randomized housing-mobility experiment. *Quarterly Journal of Economics, 116,* 665–679.

Luthar, S. S. (2006). Resilience in development: A synthesis of research across 5 decades. In D. Cicchetti & D. J. Cohen (Eds.), *Developmental psychopathology* (2nd ed., pp. 739–796). Hoboken, NJ: Wiley.

Lynam, D. R. (1996). The early identification of chronic offenders: Who is the fledgling psychopath? *Psychological Bulletin, 120,* 209–234.

Lynam, D. R. (1997). Pursuing the psychopath: Capturing the fledgling psychopath in a nomological net. *Journal of Abnormal Psychology, 106,* 425–438.

Lyon, D., & Slovic, P. (1976). Dominance of accuracy information and neglect of base rates in probability estimation. *Acta Psychologica, 40,* 287–298.

Malinosky-Rummell, R., & Hansen, D. J. (1993). Long term consequences of childhood physical abuse. *Psychological Bulletin, 114,* 68–79.

Marquart, J. W., Ekland-Olson, S., & Sorensen, J. (1989). Gazing into the crystal ball: Can jurors accurately predict future dangerousness in capital cases? *Law and Society Review, 23,* 449–468.

Marquart, J. W., Ekland-Olson, S., & Sorensen, J. (1994). *The rope, the chair, and the needle: Capital punishment in Texas, 1923–1990.* Austin: University of Texas Press.

Marquart, J. W., & Sorensen, J. (1988). Institutional and postrelease behavior of *Furman*-commuted inmates in Texas. *Criminology, 26,* 677–693.

Marques, J. K., Wiederanders, M., Day, D. M., Nelson, C., & van Ommeren, A. (2005). Effects of a relapse prevention program on sexual recidivism: Final results from California's Sex Offender Treatment and Evaluation Project (SOTEP). *Sexual Abuse: A Journal of Research and Treatment, 17,* 79–107.

Marshall, W. L., & Anderson, D. (1996). An evaluation of the benefits of relapse prevention programs with sex offenders. *Sexual Abuse: A Journal of Research and Treatment, 3,* 499–511.

Marshall, W. L., & Barbaree, H. E. (1988). The long-term evaluation of a behavioral treatment program for child molesters. *Behavior Research and Therapy, 26,* 499–511.

Marshall, W. L., & Fernandez, Y. M. (2000). Phallometric testing with sexual offenders: Limits to its value. *Clinical Psychology Review, 20,* 807–822.

Mash, E., & Dozois, D. (2003). Child psychopathology: A developmental systems perspective. In E. Mash & R. Barkley (Eds.), *Child psychopathology* (2nd ed., pp. 3–71). New York: Guilford Press.

Maxfield, M. G., & Widom, C. S. (1996). The cycle of violence revisited 6 years later. *Archives of Pediatrics and Adolescent Medicine, 150,* 390–395.

McConaghy, N. (1999). Methodological issues concerning evaluation of treatment for sexual offenders: Randomization, treatment dropouts, untreated controls, and within-treatment studies. *Sexual Abuse: A Journal of Research and Treatment, 11*, 183–194.

McCord, J. (1979). Some child-rearing antecedents of criminal behavior in adult men. *Journal of Personality and Social Psychology, 37*, 1477–1486.

McNeil, D. E. (1994). Hallucinations and violence. In J. Monahan & H. J. Steadman (Eds.), *Violence and mental disorder: Developments in risk assessment* (pp. 183–202). Chicago: University of Chicago Press.

McNeil, D. E., Borum, R., Douglas, K. S., Hart, S. D., Lyon, D. R., Sullivan, L. E., et al. (2002). Risk assessment. In J. R. Ogloff (Ed.), *Taking psychology and law into the twenty-first century: Vol. 14. Perspectives in law and psychology* (pp. 147–170). New York: Kluwer Academic/Plenum Press.

McNeil, D. E., Eisner, J. P., & Binder, R. L. (2000). The relationship between command hallucinations and violence. *Psychiatric Services, 51*, 1288–1293.

Meehl, P. (1954). *Clinical versus statistical prediction: A theoretical analysis and a review of the evidence.* Minneapolis: University of Minnesota Press.

Meehl, P., & Rosen, A. (1955). Antecedent probability and the efficiency of psychometric signs, patterns, or cutting scores. *Psychological Bulletin, 52*, 194–216.

Megargee, E. I. (1981). Methodological problems in the prediction of violence. In J. R. Hays, T. K. Roberts, & K. S. Solway (Eds.), *Violence and the violent individual* (pp. 179–191). New York: Spectrum.

Meloy, J. R. (1999). Stalking: An old behavior, a new crime. *Psychiatric Clinics of North America, 22*, 85–99.

Meloy, J. R., Hempel, A. G., Gray, B. T., Mohandie, K., Shiva, A., & Richards, T. C. (2004). A comparative analysis of North American adolescent and adult mass murderers. *Behavioral Sciences and the Law, 22*, 291–309.

Melton, G. B., Petrila, J., Poythress, N. G., & Slobogin, C. (1997). *Psychological evaluations for the courts: A handbook for mental health professionals and lawyers* (2nd ed.). New York: Guilford Press.

Menzies, R., & Webster, C. D. (1995). Construction and validation of risk assessments in a 6-year follow-up of forensic patients: A tridimensional analysis. *Journal of Consulting and Clinical Psychology, 63*, 766–778.

Mercado, C. C., Bornstein, B. H., & Schopp, R. F. (2006). Decision-making about volitional impairment in sexually violent predators. *Law and Human Behavior, 30*, 587–602.

Mercado, C. C., Schopp, R. F., & Bornstein, B. H. (2003). Evaluating sex offenders under sexually violent predator laws: How might mental health professionals conceptualize the notion of volitional impairment? *Aggression and Violent Behavior, 10*, 289–309.

Mercy, J. A., & O'Carroll, P. W. (1988). New directions in violence prediction: The public health arena. *Violence and Victims, 3*, 285–301.

Meyer, W. J., Molett, M., Richards, C. D., Arnold, L., & Latham, J. (2003). Outpatient civil commitment in Texas for management and treatment of sexually violent predators: A preliminary report. *International Journal of Offender Therapy and Comparative Criminology, 47*, 396–406.

Meyers, W. C., Scott, K., Burgess, A. W., & Burgess, A. G. (1995). Psycho-pathology, psychosocial factors, crime characteristics, and classification of 25 homicidal youth. *Journal of the American Academy of Child and Adolescent Psychiatry, 34,* 1483–1489.

Miller, H. A., Amenta, A. E., & Conroy, M. A. (2005). Sexually violent predator evaluations: Empirical limitations, strategies for professionals, and research directions. *Law and Human Behavior, 29,* 29–54.

Miller, R. D. (1998). Forced administration of sex drive reducing medication to sex offenders: Treatment or punishment? *Psychology, Public Policy, and Law, 4,* 175–199.

Moffitt, T. (1993). Adolescence-limited and life-course-persistent antisocial behavior: A developmental taxonomy. *Psychological Review, 100,* 674–701.

Moffitt, T. (2002). Males on the life-course-persistent and adolescence-limited antisocial pathways: Follow-up at age 26 years. *Development and Psychopathology, 14,* 179–207.

Moffitt, T. (2006). Adolescence limited antisocial behavior. In D. Cicchetti & D. J. Cohen (Eds.), *Developmental psychopathology* (2nd ed., pp. 570–598). Hoboken, NJ: Wiley.

Monahan, J. (1981). *Predicting violent behavior: An assessment of clinical techniques.* Beverly Hills, CA: Sage.

Monahan, J. (1984). The prediction of violent behavior: Toward a second generation of theory and policy. *American Journal of Psychiatry, 141,* 10–15.

Monahan, J. (1992). Mental disorder and violent behavior: Perceptions and evidence. *American Psychologist, 47,* 511–521.

Monahan, J. (1993). Mental disorder and violence: Another look. In S. Hodgins (Ed.), *Mental disorder and crime* (pp. 287–302). Thousand Oaks, CA: Sage.

Monahan, J. (1996). Violence prediction: The past 20 and the next 20 years. *Criminal Justice and Behavior, 23*(1), 107–120.

Monahan, J. (2003). Violence risk assessment. In A. M. Goldstein (Ed.), *Handbook of psychology: Vol. 11. Forensic psychology* (pp. 527–540). Hoboken, NJ: Wiley.

Monahan, J., Heilbrun, K., Silver, E., Nabors, E., Bone, J., & Slovic, P. (2002). Communicating violence risk: Frequency formats, vivid outcomes, and forensic settings. *International Journal of Forensic Mental Health, 1,* 121–126.

Monahan, J., & Silver, E. (2003). Judicial decision thresholds for violence risk management. *International Journal of Forensic Mental Health, 2,* 1–6.

Monahan, J., & Steadman, H. J. (Eds.). (1994). *Violence and mental disorder: Developments in risk assessment.* Chicago: University of Chicago Press.

Monahan, J., & Steadman, H. J. (1996). Violent storms and violent people: How meteorology can inform risk communication in mental health law. *American Psychologist, 51,* 931–938.

Monahan, J., Steadman, H., Appelbaum, P., Grisso, T., Mulvey, E., Roth, L., et al. (2005). *The Classification of Violence Risk.* Lutz, FL: Psychological Assessment Resources.

Monahan, J., Steadman, H., Appelbaum, P., Grisso, T., Mulvey, E., Roth, L., et al. (2006). The Classification of Violence Risk. *Behavioral Sciences and the Law, 24,* 721–730.

Monahan, J., Steadman, H. J., Robbins, P. C., Appelbaum, P. S., Banks, S., Grisso, T., et al. (2005). An actuarial model of violence risk assessment for persons with mental disorders. *Psychiatric Services, 56,* 810–815.

Monahan, J., Steadman, H. J., Silver, E., Appelbaum, P. S., Robbins, P. C., Mulvey, E. P., et al. (2001). *Rethinking risk assessment: The MacArthur Study of Mental Disorder and Violence.* Oxford: Oxford University Press.

Monahan, J., & Walker, L. (1998). *Social science in the law* (4th ed.). Westbury, NY: Foundation Press.

Morse, S. J. (1998). Fear of danger, flight from culpability. *Psychology, Public Policy, and Law, 4,* 250–267.

Mossman, D. (1994). Assessing predictions of violence: Being accurate about accuracy. *Journal of Consulting and Clinical Psychology, 62,* 783–792.

Mrad, D. F., & Nabors, E. (2007). The role of the psychologist in civil commitment. In A. M. Goldstein (Ed.), *Forensic psychology: Emerging topics and expanding roles* (pp. 232–259). Hoboken, NJ: Wiley.

Mulvey, E. P. (2005). Risk assessment in juvenile justice policy and practice. In K. Heilbrun, N. Goldstein, & R. Redding (Eds.), *Juvenile delinquency: Prevention, assessment, and intervention* (pp. 209–231). New York: Oxford University Press.

Mulvey, E. P., & Caufman, E. (2001). The inherent limits of predicting school violence. *American Psychologist, 56,* 797–802.

Mulvey, E. P., & Lidz, C. (1988, March). *What clinicians talk about when assessing dangerousness.* Paper presented at the meeting of the American Psychology Law Society, Miami, FL.

Mulvey, E. P., & Lidz, C. W. (1995). Conditional prediction: A model for research on dangerousness to others in a new era. *International Journal of Law and Psychiatry, 18,* 129–143.

Mulvey, E. P., Odgers, C., Skeem, J., Gardner, W., Schubert, C., & Lidz, C. (2006). Substance use and community violence among high risk psychiatric patients: A test of the relationship at the daily level. *Journal of Consulting and Clinical Psychology, 74,* 743–754.

Mulvey, E. P., Shaw, E., & Lidz, C. (1994). Why use multiple sources in research on patient violence in the community? *Criminal Behavior and Mental Health, 4,* 253–258.

Murrie, D. C., & Balusek, K. (in press). Forensic assessment of violence risk in adversarial proceedings: Pursuing objectivity and avoiding bias. *Journal of Forensic Psychology Practice.*

Murrie, D. C., Boccaccini, M., Johnson, J., & Jahnke, C. (in press). Does interrater (dis)agreement on Psychopathy Checklist scores in Sexually Violent Predator trials suggest partisan allegiance in forensic evaluation? *Law and Human Behavior.*

Murrie, D. C., Boccaccini, M. T., McCoy, W., & Cornell, D. G. (2007). Diagnostic labels in juvenile court: How do descriptions of psychopathy and conduct disorder influence judges? *Journal of Clinical Child and Adolescent Psychology, 36, 228–241.*

Murrie, D. C., Cornell, D. G., Kaplan, S., McConville, D., & Levy-Elkon, A. (2004). Psychopathy scores and violence among juvenile offenders: A multi-measure study. *Behavioral Sciences and the Law, 22, 49–67.*

Murrie, D. C., Cornell, D. G., & McCoy, W. (2005). Psychopathy, conduct disorder, and stigma: Does diagnostic language affect juvenile probation officer recommendations? *Law and Human Behavior, 29, 323–342.*

Murrie, D. C., Marcus, D. K., Douglas, K. S., Salekin, R. T., Lee, Z., & Vincent, G. (2007). Youth with psychopathy features are not a discrete class: A taxometric analysis. *Journal of Child Psychology and Psychiatry, 48, 714–723.*

Murrie, D. C., & Warren, J. I. (2005). Clinician variation in rates of legal sanity opinions: Implications for self-monitoring. *Professional Psychology: Research and Practice, 36, 519–524.*

Navaco, R. W. (1994). Anger as a risk factor for violence among the mentally disordered. In J. Monahan & H. J. Steadman (Eds.), *Violence and mental disorder: Developments in risk assessment* (pp. 21–59). Chicago: University of Chicago Press.

Newhill, C. E., Mulvey, E. P., & Lidz, C. W. (1995). Characteristics of violence in the community by female patients seen in a psychiatric emergency service. *Psychiatric Services, 46, 785–789.*

New York Mental Hygiene Law, §9.60.

Nicholls, T. L., Ogloff, J. R. P., & Douglas, K. S. (2004). Assessing risk for violence among male and female civil psychiatric patients. *Behavioral Sciences and the Law, 22, 127–158.*

Norko, M. A., & Baranoski, M. V. (2005). The state of contemporary risk assessment research. *Canadian Journal of Psychiatry, 50, 18–26.*

O'Connor v. Donaldson, 422 U.S. 563 (1975).

Odeh, M. S., Zeiss, R. A., & Huss, M. T. (2006). Cues they use: Clinicians' endorsement of risk cues in predictions of dangerousness. *Behavioral Science and the Law, 24, 147–156.*

Odgers, C. L., Moretti, M. M., & Reppucci, N. D. (2005). Examining the science and practice of violence risk assessment with female adolescents. *Law and Human Behavior, 29, 7–27.*

Odgers, C. L., Reppucci, N. D., & Moretti, M. M. (2005). Nipping psychopathy in the bud: An examination of the convergent, predictive, and theoretical utility of the PCL:YV among adolescent girls. *Behavioral Sciences and the Law, 23, 743–763.*

Ogloff, J. R. P. (2001). Professional, legal, and ethical issues in violence risk management. In K. S. Douglas, C. D. Webster, S. D. Hart, D. Eaves, & J. R. P. Ogloff (Eds.), *HCR-20 violence risk management guide* (pp. 59–71). Burnaby, British Columbia, Canada: Simon Fraser University Press.

O'Keefe, D. (1990) *Persuasion theory and research*. London: Sage.

Olmstead v. Zimring, 119 S. Ct. 2176 (1999).

O'Toole, M. E. (2000). *The school shooter: A threat assessment perspective*. Quantico, VA: National Center for the Analysis of Violent Crime, Federal Bureau of Investigation.

Otto, R. K. (1989). Bias and expert testimony of mental health professionals in adversarial proceedings: A preliminary investigation. *Behavioral Sciences and the Law, 7*, 267–273.

Otto, R. K. (1992). Prediction of dangerous behavior: A review and analysis of "second generation" research. *Forensic Reports, 5*, 103–133.

Otto, R. K. (2000). Assessing and managing violence risk in outpatient settings. *Journal of Clinical Psychology, 56*, 1239–1262.

Otto, R. K. (2006, March). *Discussion of the Forensic Specialty Guidelines*. Panel discussion presented at the annual meeting of the American Psychology-Law Society, St. Petersburg, FL.

Otto, R. K., & Heilbrun, K. (2002). The practice of forensic psychology: A look toward the future in light of the past. *American Psychologist, 57*, 5–18.

Otto, R. K., Slobogin, C., & Greenberg, S. A. (2007). Legal and ethical issues in accessing third-party information. In A. M. Goldstein (Ed.), *Forensic psychology: Emerging topics and expanding roles* (pp. 190–205). Hoboken, NJ: Wiley.

Pardini, D. A., Lochman, J. E., & Frick, P. J. (2003). Callous-unemotional traits and social cognitive processes in adjudicated youth: Exploring the schema of juveniles with psychopathic traits. *Journal of the American Academy of Child and Adolescent Psychiatry, 42*, 364–371.

Patrick, C. J., Edens, J. F., & Poythress, N. G. (2006). Construct validity of the Psychopathic Personality Inventory two-factor model with offenders. *Psychological Assessment, 18*, 204–208.

Patterson, G. R., Capaldi, D., & Bank, L. (1991). An early starter model for predicting delinquency. In D. J. Pepler & K. H. Rubin (Eds.), *The development and treatment of childhood aggression* (pp. 139–168). Hillsdale, NJ: Erlbaum.

Penney, S. R., & Moretti, M. M. (2007). The relation of psychopathy to concurrent aggression and antisocial behavior in high risk boys and girls. *Behavioral Sciences and the Law, 25*, 21–41.

Perlin, M. L. (2003). Therapeutic jurisprudence and outpatient commitment law: Kendra's Law as case study. *Psychology, Public Policy, and Law, 9*, 183–208.

Petrila, J. (2004). Emerging issues in forensic mental health. *Psychiatric Quarterly, 75*, 3–19.

Petrila, J. (2007). Recent civil decisions: Implications for forensic mental health experts. In A. M. Goldstein (Ed.), *Forensic psychology: Emerging topics and expanding roles* (pp. 209–231). Hoboken, NJ: Wiley.

Petrila, J., Ridgely, M. S., & Borum, R. (2003). Debating outpatient commitment: Controversy, trends, and empirical data. *Crime and Delinquency, 49*, 157–172.

Petrila, J., & Skeem, J. L. (2003). Juvenile psychopathy: The debate. *Behavioral Sciences and the Law, 21*, 689–694.

Pfohl, S. (1978). *Predicting dangerousness.* Lexington, MA: Lexington Books/Heath.

Philipse, M. W. G., Koeter, M. W. J., van der Staak, C. P. F., & van den Brink, W. (2006). Static and dynamic patient characteristics as predictors of criminal recidivism: A prospective study in a Dutch forensic psychiatric sample. *Law and Human Behavior, 30*, 309–327.

Phillips, H. K., Gray, N. S., MacCulloch, S. I., Taylor, J., Moore, S. C., Huckle, P., et al. (2005). Risk assessment in offenders with mental disorders: Relative efficacy of personal demographic, criminal history, and clinical variables. *Journal of Interpersonal Violence, 20*, 833–847.

Pihl, R. O., & Peterson, J. B. (1993). Alcohol/drug use and aggressive behavior. In S. Hodgins (Ed.), *Mental disorder and crime* (pp. 263–283). Newbury Park, CA: Sage.

Piquero, A. R., Farrington, D. P., & Blumstein, A. (2003). The criminal career paradigm. In M. Tonry (Ed.), *Crime and justice: A review of research* (Vol. 30, pp. 359–506). Chicago: University of Chicago Press.

Ponterotto, J. G., Gretchen, D., & Chauhan, R. V. (2001). Cultural identity and multicultural assessment: Quantitative and qualitative tools for the clinician. In L. A. Suzuki, J. G. Ponterotto, & P. J. Meller (Eds.), *Handbook of multicultural assessment: Clinical, psychological, and educational practices* (2nd ed., pp. 67–99). San Francisco: Jossey-Bass.

Porter, S., Fairweather, D., Drugge, J., Herve, H., Birt, A., & Boer, D. P. (2000). Profiles of psychopathy in incarcerated sexual offenders. *Criminal Justice and Behavior, 27*, 216–233.

Prentky, R. A., & Burgess, A. W. (2000). *Forensic management of sexual offenders.* New York: Kluwer Academic/Plenum Press.

Prentky, R. A., Harris, B., Frizzell, K., & Righthand, S. (2000). An actuarial procedure for assessing risk with juvenile sex offenders. *Sexual Abuse: A Journal of Research and Treatment, 12*, 71–93.

Prentky, R. A., Knight, R. A., & Lee, A. F. S. (1997). Risk factors associated with recidivism among extrafamilial child molesters. *Journal of Consulting and Clinical Psychology, 65*, 141–149.

Prentky, R. A., Lee, A. F. S., Knight, R. A., & Cerce, D. (1997). Recidivism rates among child molesters and rapists: A methodological analysis. *Law and Human Behavior, 21*, 635–659.

Proulx, J., Pellerin, B., Paradis, Y., McKibben, A., Aubut, J., & Ouimet, M. (1997). Static and dynamic predictors of recidivism in sexual aggressors. *Sexual Abuse: A Journal of Research and Treatment, 9*, 7–27.

Quinsey, V. L. (1986). Men who have sex with children. In D. N. Weisstub (Ed.), *Law and mental health: Vol. 2. International perspectives* (pp. 140–172). New York: Pergamon Press.

Quinsey, V. L., Harris, G. T., Rice, M. E., & Cormier, C. A. (1998). *Violent offenders: Appraising and managing risk.* Washington, DC: American Psychological Association.

Quinsey, V. L., Harris, G. T., Rice, M. E., & Cormier, C. A. (2006). *Violent offenders: Appraising and managing risk* (2nd ed.). Washington, DC: American Psychological Association.

Quinsey, V. L., Khanna, A., & Malcolm, B. (1998). A retrospective evaluation of the Regional Treatment Centre Sex Offender Treatment Program. *Journal of Interpersonal Violence, 13,* 621–644.

Quinsey, V. L., Rice, M. E., & Harris, G. T. (1995). Actuarial prediction of sexual recidivism. *Journal of Interpersonal Violence, 10,* 85–105.

Quinsey, V. L., Warneford, A. A., Pruesse, M. G., & Link, N. (1975). Released Oak Ridge patients: A follow-up of review board discharges. *British Journal of Criminology, 15,* 264–270.

Redding, R. E. (1998). How common sense psychology can inform law and psycholegal research. *University of Chicago Law School Roundtable, 5,* 107–142.

Redding, R. E. (2003). The effects of adjudicating and sentencing juveniles as adults: Research and policy implications. *Youth Violence and Juvenile Justice, 1,* 128–155.

Redding, R. E., Floyd, M. Y., & Hawk, G. L. (2001). What judges and lawyers think about the testimony of mental health experts: A survey of the courts and bar. *Behavioral Sciences and the Law, 19,* 583–594.

Redding, R. E., & Murrie, D. (2007). Judicial decision making about forensic mental health evidence. In A. Goldstein (Ed.), *Forensic psychology: Advanced topics for forensic mental health experts and attorneys* (pp. 683–707). Hoboken, NJ: Wiley.

Redding, R. E., & Reppucci, N. D. (1999). Effects of lawyers' sociopolitical attitudes on their judgments of social science in legal decision making. *Law and Human Behavior, 23,* 31–54.

Redding, R. E., Sevin Goldstein, N., & Heilbrun, K. (2005). Juvenile delinquency: Past and present. In K. Heilbrun, N. Goldstein, & R. Redding (Eds.), *Juvenile delinquency: Prevention, assessment, and intervention* (pp. 3–18). New York: Oxford University Press.

Reddy, M., Borum, R., Berglund, J., Vossekuil, B., Fein, R., & Modzeleski, W. (2001). Evaluating risk for targeted violence in schools: Comparing risk assessment, threat assessment, and other approaches. *Psychology in the Schools, 38,* 157–172.

Reidy, T. J., Cunningham, M., & Sorensen, J. R. (2001). From death to life: Prison behavior of former death row inmates. *Criminal Justice and Behavior, 28,* 67–82.

Reisner, R., & Slobogin, C. (1990). *Law and the mental health system: Civil and criminal aspects* (2nd ed.). St. Paul, MN: West Group.

Rennie v. Klein, 653 F. 2d 836 (1981).

Rev. Code Wash. (ARCW) §71.09.010 (2007).

Rice, M. E. (1997). Violent offender research and implications for the criminal justice system. *American Psychologist, 52*, 414–423.

Rice, M. E., & Harris, G. T. (1995). Violent recidivism: Assessing predictive validity. *Journal of Consulting and Clinical Psychology, 63*, 737–748.

Rice, M. E., & Harris, G. T. (1996). Predicting the recidivism of mentally disordered fire setters. *Journal of Interpersonal Violence, 11*, 364–375.

Rice, M. E., & Harris, G. T. (1997). Cross validation and extension of the Violence Risk Appraisal Guide for child molesters and rapists. *Law and Human Behavior, 21*, 231–241.

Rice, M. E., Harris, G. T., & Cormier, C. A. (1992). Evaluation of a maximum security therapeutic community for psychopaths and other mentally disordered offenders. *Law and Human Behavior, 16*, 399–412.

Rice, M. E., Harris, G. T., Lang, C., & Cormier, C. A. (2006). Violent sex offenses: How are they best measured from official records? *Law and Human Behavior, 30*, 525–541.

Rice, M. E., Harris, G. T., & Quinsey, V. L. (1990). A follow-up of rapists assessed in a maximum security psychiatric facility. *Journal of Interpersonal Violence, 5*, 435–448.

Rice, M. E., Harris, G. T., & Quinsey, V. L. (1991). Sexual recidivism among child molesters released from a maximum security psychiatric institution. *Journal of Consulting and Clinical Psychology, 59*, 381–386.

Ridley, C. R., Hill, C. L., Thompson, C. E., & Omerod, A. J. (2001). Clinical practice guidelines in assessment: Toward an idiographic perspective. In D. Pope-Davis & H. Coleman (Eds.), *The intersection of race, class, and gender: Implications for multicultural counseling* (pp. 191–211). Thousand Oaks, CA: Sage.

Rivers v. Katz, 495 N.E. 2d 337 (1986).

Robbins, P. C., Monahan, J., & Silver, E. (2003). Mental disorder, violence, and gender. *Law and Human Behavior, 27*, 561–571.

Rockett, J., Murrie, D. C., & Boccaccini, M. T. (2007). Diagnostic labeling in juvenile justice settings: Do psychopathy and conduct disorder findings influence clinicians? *Psychological Services, 4*, 107–122.

Rodney, L. W., Johnson, D. L., & Srivastava, R. P. (2005). The impact of culturally relevant violence prevention models on school-age youth. *Journal of Primary Prevention, 26*, 439–454.

Rogers v. Okin, 634 F. 2d 650 (1980).

Rogers, R. (1987). Ethical dilemmas in forensic evaluations. *Behavioral Sciences and the Law, 5*, 149–160.

Rogers, R. (2000). The uncritical acceptance of risk assessment in forensic practice. *Law and Human Behavior, 24*, 595–605.

Rogers, R., & Ewing, C. P. (2003). The prohibition of ultimate opinions: A misguided enterprise. *Journal of Forensic Psychology Practice, 3*, 65–75.

Rosenberg, M. L., & Fenley, M. A. (1991). *Violence in America: A public health approach.* New York: Oxford University Press.

Rosenfeld, B. (1999). Risk assessment in the wake of *Hendricks.* In American Psychological Association (Ed.), *Psychological expertise and criminal justice* (pp. 451–464). Washington, DC: American Psychological Association.

Rosenfeld, B. (2004). Violence risk factors in stalking and obsessional harassment: A review and preliminary meta-analysis. *Criminal Justice and Behavior, 31,* 9–36.

Rosler, A., & Witztum, E. (2000). Pharmacology of paraphilias in the next millennium. *Behavioral Sciences and the Law, 18,* 43–56.

Russell, D. E. (1982). The prevalence and incidence of forcible rape and attempted rape of females. *Victimology, 7,* 81–93.

Salekin, R. T. (2002). Psychopathy and therapeutic pessimism: Clinical lore or clinical reality? *Clinical Psychology Review, 22,* 79–112.

Salekin, R. T. (2006). Psychopathy in children and adolescents: Key issues in conceptualization and assessment. In C. J. Patrick (Ed.), *Handbook of psychopathy* (pp. 389–414). New York: Guilford Press.

Salekin, R. T., Rogers, R., & Sewell, K. W. (1996). A review and meta-analysis of the Psychopathy Checklist and Psychopathy Checklist—Revised: Predictive validity of dangerousness. *Clinical Psychology: Science and Practice, 3,* 203–215.

Salekin, R. T., Yff, R. M. A., Neumann, C. S., Leistico, A. R., & Zalot, A. A. (2002). Juvenile transfer to adult courts: A look at the prototypes for dangerousness, sophistication-maturity, and amenability to treatment through a legal lens. *Psychology, Public Policy, and Law, 8,* 373–410.

Sameroff, A. J. (2000). Developmental systems and psychopathology. *Development and Psychopathology, 12,* 297–312.

Sampson, R., Raudenbush, S., & Earls, F. (1997). Neighborhoods and violent crime: A multilevel study of collective efficacy. *Science, 277,* 918–924.

Schall v. Martin, 104 S. Ct. 2403 (1984).

Schopp, R. F. (1996). Communicating risk assessments: Accuracy, efficacy, and responsibility. *American Psychologist, 51,* 939–944.

Schopp, R. F., Scalora, M. J., & Pearce, M. (1999). Expert testimony and professional judgment: Psychological expertise and commitment as a sexual predator after *Hendricks. Psychology, Public Policy, and Law, 5,* 120–174.

Schwalbe, C. S. (in press). Risk assessment for juvenile justice: A meta-analysis. *Law and Human Behavior.*

Schwalbe, C. S., Fraser, M. W., Day, S. H., & Arnold, E. M. (2004). North Carolina Assessment of Risk (NCAR): Reliability and predictive validity with juvenile offenders. *Journal of Offender Rehabilitation, 40,* 1–22.

Schwalbe, C. S., Fraser, M. W., Day, S. H., & Cooley, V. (2006). Classifying juvenile offenders according to risk of recidivism: Predictive validity, race/ethnicity, and gender. *Criminal Justice and Behavior, 33,* 305–324.

Schwarz, N. (1990). Assessing frequency reports of mundane behaviors: Contributions of cognitive psychology to questionnaire construction. In C. Hendrick & M. S. Clark (Eds.), *Research methods in personality and social psychology* (pp. 98–119). Beverly Hills, CA: Sage.

Scott, E. S. (2000). The legal construction of adolescence. *Hofstra Law Review, 29,* 547–598.

Seagrave, D., & Grisso, T. (2002). Adolescent development and the measurement of juvenile psychopathy. *Law and Human Behavior, 26,* 219–239.

Sell v. U.S., 282 F.3d 560 (2003).

Serin, R. C., & Amos, N. L. (1995). The role of psychopathy in the assessment of dangerousness. *International Journal of Law and Psychiatry, 18,* 231–238.

Serin, R. C., Mailloux, D. L., & Malcolm, P. B. (2001). Psychopathy, deviant sexual arousal, and recidivism among sexual offenders: A psycho-culturally determined group offense. *Journal of Interpersonal Violence, 16,* 234–246.

Seto, M. C., & Barbaree, H. E. (1999). Psychopathy, treatment behavior, and sex offender recidivism. *Journal of Interpersonal Violence, 14,* 1235–1248.

Seto, M. C., Harris, G. T., Rice, M. E., & Barbaree, H. E. (2004). The Screening Scale for Pedophilic Interests predicts recidivism among adult sex offenders with child victims. *Archives of Sexual Behavior, 33,* 455–466.

Shah, S. (1975). Dangerousness and civil commitment of the mentally ill: Some public policy considerations. *American Journal of Psychiatry, 132,* 501–505.

Shah, S. (1981). Dangerousness: Conceptual, prediction, and public policy issues. In J. R. Hays, T. K. Robert, & K. S. Solway (Eds.), *Violence and the violent individual* (pp. 151–178). New York: SP Medical and Scientific.

Shah, S. (1993). Some research on crime and mental disorder: Some implications for programs and policies. In S. Hodgins (Ed.), *Mental disorder and crime* (pp. 303–316). Thousand Oaks, CA: Sage.

Shuman, D. W., & Greenberg, S. A. (2003). The expert witness, the adversary system, and the voice of reason: Reconciling impartiality and advocacy. *Professional Psychology: Research and Practice, 34,* 219–224.

Silver, E. (2000a). Extending social disorganization theory: A multilevel approach to the study of violence among persons with mental illnesses. *Criminology, 38,* 1043–1074.

Silver, E. (2000b). Race, neighborhood disadvantage, and violence among persons with mental disorders: The importance of contextual measurement. *Law and Human Behavior, 24,* 449–456.

Silver, E. (2006). Understanding the relationship between mental disorder and violence: The need for a criminological perspective. *Law and Human Behavior, 30,* 685–706.

Silver, E., Cirincione, C., & Steadman, H. (1994). Demythologizing inaccurate perceptions of the insanity defense. *Law and Human Behavior, 18,* 63–70.

Silver, E., Mulvey, E. P., & Monahan, J. (1999). Assessing violence risk among discharged psychiatric patients: Toward an ecological approach. *Law and Human Behavior, 23,* 237–255.

Silver, E., & Teasdale, B. (2005). Mental disorder and violence: An examination of stressful life events and impaired social support. *Social Problems, 52*, 62–78.

Simon, J. (2005). Reversal of fortune: The resurgence of individualized risk assessment in criminal justice. *Annual Review of Law and Social Science, 1*, 397–421.

Skeem, J. L., & Golding, S. L. (1998). Community examiners' evaluations of competence to stand trial: Common problems and suggestions for improvement. *Professional Psychology: Research and Practice, 29*, 357–367.

Skeem, J. L., Golding, S., Cohn, N., & Berge, G. (1998). The logic and reliability of expert opinion on competence to stand trial. *Law and Human Behavior, 22*, 519–547.

Skeem, J. L., Monahan, J., & Mulvey, E. P. (2002). Psychopathy, treatment involvement, and subsequent violence among civil psychiatric patients. *Law and Human Behavior, 26*, 577–603.

Skeem, J. L., & Mulvey, E. P. (2001). Psychopathy and community violence among civil psychiatric patients: Results from the MacArthur Violence Risk Assessment Study. *Journal of Consulting and Clinical Psychology, 69*, 358–374.

Skeem, J. L., Mulvey, E. P., & Lidz, C. W. (2000). Building mental health professionals' decisional models into tests of predictive validity: The accuracy of contextualized predictions of violence. *Law and Human Behavior, 24*, 607–628.

Skeem, J. L., Schubert, C., Odgers, C., Mulvey, E., Gardner, W., & Lidz, C. (2006). Psychiatric symptoms and community violence among high-risk patients: A test of the relationship at the weekly level. *Journal of Consulting and Clinical Psychology, 74*, 976–979.

Skeem, J. L., Schubert, C., Stowman, S., Beeson, S., Mulvey, E., Gardner, W., et al. (2005). Gender and risk assessment accuracy: Underestimating women's violent potential. *Law and Human Behavior, 29*, 173–186.

Skipper v. South Carolina, 461 U.S. 1 (1986).

Slobogin, C. (1989). The "ultimate issue" issue. *Behavioral Sciences and the Law, 7*, 259–266.

Slobogin, C. (1998). Psychiatric evidence in criminal trials: To junk or not to junk? *William and Mary Law Review, 40*, 1–56.

Slovic, P., & Monahan, J. (1995). Danger and coercion: A study of risk perception and decision making in mental health law. *Law and Human Behavior, 19*, 49–65.

Slovic, P., Monahan, J., & MacGregor, D. G. (2000). Violence risk assessment and risk communication: The effects of using actual cases, providing instruction, and employing probability versus frequency formats. *Law and Human Behavior, 24*, 271–296.

Smith, C. A., & Thornberry, T. P. (1995). The relationship between childhood maltreatment and adolescent involvement in delinquency. *Criminology, 33*, 451–481.

Snyder, H. N., & Sickmund, M. (1999). *Juvenile offenders and victims: 1999 national report*. Washington, DC: U.S. Department of Justice, Office of Justice Programs, Office of Juvenile Justice and Delinquency Prevention.

Snyder, H. N., & Sickmund, M. (2006). *Juvenile offenders and victims: 2006 national report*. Washington, DC: U.S. Department of Justice, Office of Justice Programs, Office of Juvenile Justice and Delinquency Prevention.

Sorensen, J. R., & Pilgrim, R. L. (2000). An actuarial risk assessment of violence posed by capital murder defendants. *Journal of Criminal Law and Criminology, 90*, 1251–1270.

Sorensen, J. R., & Wrinkle, R. D. (1996). No hope for parole: Disciplinary infractions among death-sentenced and life-without-parole inmates. *Criminal Justice and Behavior, 23*, 542–552.

Stadtland, C., Hollweg, M., Kleindienst, N., Dietl, J., Reich, U., & Nedopil, N. (2005). Risk assessment and prediction of violent and sexual recidivism in sex offenders: Long-term predictive validity of four risk assessment instruments. *Journal of Forensic Psychiatry and Psychology, 16*, 92–108.

Stafford, E., & Cornell, D. (2003). Psychopathy scores predict adolescent inpatient aggression. *Assessment, 10*, 102–112.

Stahl, A. L., Puzzanchera, C., Sladky, A., Finnegan, T. A., Tierny, N., & Snyder, H. N. (2005). *Juvenile court statistics, 2001–2002*. Pittsburgh, PA: National Center for Juvenile Justice.

Stalans, L. J. (2004). Adult sex offenders on community supervision: A review of recent assessment strategies and treatment. *Criminal Justice and Behavior, 31*, 564–608.

Steadman, H. J. (1977). A new look at recidivism among Patuxent inmates. *Bulletin of the American Academy of Psychiatry and Law, 5*, 200–209.

Steadman, H. J., & Cocozza, J. J. (1974). *Careers of the criminally insane*. Lexington, MA: Lexington Books.

Steadman, H. J., Fabisiak, S., Dvoskin, J., & Holohean, E. (1987). A survey of mental disability among state prison inmates. *Hospital and Community Psychiatry, 38*, 1086–1090.

Steadman, H. J., & Felson, R. (1984). Self-reports of violence: Ex-mental patients, ex-offenders, and the general population. *Criminology, 22*, 321–342.

Steadman, H. J., Monahan, J. J., Appelbaum, P. S., Grisso, T., Mulvey, E. P., Roth, L. H., et al. (1994). Designing a new generation of risk assessment research. In J. Monahan & H. J. Steadman (Eds.), *Violence and mental disorder: Developments in risk assessment* (pp. 297–318). Chicago: University of Chicago Press.

Steadman, H. J., Monahan, J. J., Robbins, P. C., Appelbaum, P., Grisso, T., Klassen, D., et al. (1993). From dangerousness to risk assessment: Implications for appropriate research strategies. In S. Hodgins (Ed.), *Mental disorder and crime* (pp. 39–62). Newbury Park, CA: Sage.

Steadman, H. J., Mulvey, E. P., Monahan, J., Robbins, P. C., Appelbaum, P. S., Grisso, T., et al. (1998). Violence by people discharged from acute psychiatric inpatient facilities and by others in the same neighborhoods. *Archives of General Psychiatry, 55*, 393–401.

Steadman, H. J., Silver, E., Monahan, J., Appelbaum, P. S., Robbins, P. C., Mulvey, E. P., et al. (2000). A classification tree approach to the development of violence risk assessment tools. *Law and Human Behavior, 24*, 83–100.

Steinberg, L. (2002). The juvenile psychopath: Fads, fictions, and facts. *National Institutes of Justice Perspectives on Crime and Justice: 2001 Lecture Series, 5*, 35–64.

Steinke, P. (1991). Using situational factors to predict types of prison violence. *Journal of Offender Rehabilitation, 17*, 119–132.

Stephan, J. (1989). *Prison rule violators* (BJS Special Report NCJ-120344). Washington, DC: U.S. Department of Justice, Bureau of Justice Statistics.

Stompe, T., Ortwein-Swoboda, G., & Schanda, H. (2004). Schizophrenia, delusional symptoms, and violence: The threat/control-override concept reexamined. *Schizophrenia Bulletin, 30*, 31–44.

Sue, D. W., & Sue, D. (2003). *Counseling the culturally diverse: Theory and practice* (4th ed.). Hoboken, NJ: Wiley.

Swanson, J. W. (1994). Mental disorder, substance abuse, and community violence: An epidemiological approach. In J. Monahan & H. J. Steadman (Eds.), *Violence and mental disorder: Developments in risk assessment* (pp. 101–136). Chicago: University of Chicago Press.

Swanson, J. W., Borum, R., Swartz, M. S., Hiday, V. A., Wagner, H. R., & Burns, B. J. (2001). Can involuntary outpatient commitment reduce arrests among persons with severe mental illness? *Criminal Justice and Behavior, 28*, 156–189.

Swanson, J. W., Borum, R., Swartz, M., & Monahan, J. (1996). Psychotic symptoms and disorders and the risk of violent behavior in the community. *Criminal Behavior and Mental Health, 6*, 317–338.

Swanson, J. W., Holtzer, III, C. E., Granju, V. K., & Jono, R. T. (1990). Violence and psychiatric disorder in the community: Evidence from the Epidemiological Catchment Area surveys. *Hospital and Community Psychiatry, 41*, 761–770.

Swanson, J. W., Swartz, M. S., Borum, R., Hiday, V. A., Wagner, H. R., & Burns, B. J. (2000). Involuntary out-patient commitment and the reduction of violent behavior in persons with severe mental illness. *British Journal of Psychiatry, 176*, 324–331.

Swanson, J. W., Swartz, M. S., & Elbogen, E. B. (2004). Effectiveness of atypical antipsychotic medications in reducing violent behavior among persons with schizophrenia in community-based treatment. *Schizophrenia Bulletin, 30*, 3–20.

Swanson, J. W., Swartz, M. S., Elbogen, E. B., & Van Dorn, R. A. (2004). Reducing violence risk in persons with schizophrenia: Olanzapine versus risperidone. *Journal of Clinical Psychiatry, 65*, 1666–1673.

Swanson, J. W., Swartz, M. S., Essock, S. M., Wagner, H. R., Goodman, L. A., Rosenberg, S. D., et al. (2002). The social-environmental context of violent behavior in persons treated for severe mental illness. *American Journal of Public Health, 92,* 1523–1531.

Swanson, J. W., Swartz, M. S., Estroff, S. E., Borum, R., Wagner, R., & Hiday, V. (1998). Psychiatric impairment, social contact, and violent behavior: Evidence from a study of outpatient-committed persons with severe mental disorder. *Social Psychiatry and Psychiatric Epidemiology, 33,* S86–S94.

Swanson, J. W., Swartz, M. S., Van Dorn, R. A., Elbogen, E. B., Wagner, H. R., Rosenheck, R. A., et al. (2006). A national study of violent behavior in persons with schizophrenia. *Archives of General Psychiatry, 63,* 490–499.

Swartz, M. S., Swanson, J. W., Hiday, V. A., Wagner, H. R., Burns, B. J., & Borum, R. (2001). A randomized controlled trial of outpatient commitment in North Carolina. *Psychiatric Services, 52,* 325–329.

Szasz, T. (1963). *Law, liberty, and psychiatry.* New York: Macmillan.

Tanford, J. A. (1990). The limits of a scientific jurisprudence: The Supreme Court and psychology. *Indiana Law Journal, 66,* 137–173.

Tarasoff v. The Regents of the University of California, 551 P.2d 334 (1976).

Taylor, K. W., & Kliewer, W. (2006). Violence exposure and early adolescent alcohol use: An exploratory study of family risk and protective factors. *Journal of Child and Family Studies, 15,* 201–215.

Taylor, P. J. (1985). Motives for offending among violent and psychotic men. *British Journal of Psychiatry, 147,* 491–498.

Teasdale, B., Silver, E., & Monahan, J. (2006). Gender, threat/control-override delusions and violence. *Law and Human Behavior, 30,* 649–657.

Tengström, A., Grann, M., Långström, N., & Kullgren, G. (2000). Psychopathy (PCL-R) as a predictor of violent recidivism among criminal offenders with schizophrenia. *Law and Human Behavior, 24,* 45–58.

Tengström, A., Hodgins, S., Grann, M., Långström, N., & Kullgren, G. (2004). Schizophrenia and criminal offending: The role of psychopathy and substance use disorders. *Criminal Justice and Behavior, 31,* 367–391.

Teplin, L. A., Abram, K. M., McClelland, G. M., Dulcan, M. K., & Mericle, A. A. (2002). Psychiatric disorders in youth in juvenile detention. *Archives of General Psychiatry, 59,* 1133–1143.

Texas Code of Criminal Procedures, Article 37.071.2 (1996).

Texas Code of Criminal Procedure Annotated, art. 37.071 §2(b)(1) (Vernon Supp. 2002).

Texas Code of Criminal Procedure Annotated, art. 37.071 §2(c) (Vernon Supp. 2002).

Texas Department of Criminal Justice Programs and Services Division. (2002, September). *Civil commitment.* Austin, TX: Author.

Texas Health & Safety Code §841.000 (2000).

Thornberry, T., Huizinga, D., & Loeber, R. (1995). The prevention of serious delinquency and violence: Implications from the program of research on the causes and correlates of delinquency. In J. Howell, B. Krisberg, J. Hawkins, & J. Wilson (Eds.), *Sourcebook on serious, violent, and chronic juvenile offenders* (pp. 213–237). Thousand Oaks, CA: Sage.

Thornberry, T., & Jacoby, J. (1979). *The criminally insane: A community follow-up of mentally ill offenders.* Chicago: University of Chicago Press.

Thornton, D. (2006). Age and sexual recidivism: A variable connection. *Sexual Abuse: A Journal of Research and Treatment, 18,* 123–135.

Tillbrook, C., Mumley, D., & Grisso, T. (2003). Avoiding expert opinions on the ultimate legal question: The case for integrity. *Journal of Forensic Psychology Practice, 3,* 77–87.

Toch, H., & Adams, K. (1986). Pathology and disruptiveness among prison inmates. *Journal of Research in Crime and Delinquency, 23,* 7–21.

Tolan, P. H., & Gorman-Smith, D. (1998). Development of serious and violent offending careers. In R. Loeber & D. P. Farrington (Eds.), *Serious and violent juvenile offenders: Risk factors and successful interventions* (pp. 68–85). Thousand Oaks, CA: Sage.

Tolman, A. O., & Mullendore, K. B. (2003). Risk evaluations for the courts: Is service quality a function of specialization? *Professional Psychology: Research and Practice, 34,* 225–232.

U.S. Department of Health and Human Services. (1986). *Surgeon general's workshop on violence and public health: Leesburg, Virginia, October 27–29, 1985.* Rockville, MD: Author.

U.S. Department of Health and Human Services (2001). *Youth violence: A report of the Surgeon General.* Rockville, MD. U.S. Department of Health and Human Services, Substance Abuse and Mental Health Services Administration, Center for Mental Health Services, National Institutes of Mental Health, National Institutes of Health.

U.S. Department of Justice (1995, June). *Guide for implementing the comprehensive strategy for serious, violent, and chronic juvenile offenders* (Juvenile Justice Bulletin: OJJDP Update on Programs, NCJ 153571). Washington, DC: U.S. Department of Justice, Office of Justice Programs, Office of Juvenile Justice and Delinquency Prevention.

U.S. v. Bilyk, 29 F. 3d 459 (1994).

U.S. v. Henley, 8 F. Supp. 2d 503 (1998).

U.S. v. Horowitz, 360 F. Supp. 772 (1973).

U.S. v. Lee, 89 F. Supp. 2d 1017 (E.D. Ark. 2000).

U.S. v. Lyons, 731 F. 2d 243 (1984).

U.S. v. Murdoch, 98 F. 3d 472 (1996).

U.S. v. Sahhar, 917 F. 2d 1197 (1990).

U.S. v. Salerno, 481 U.S. 739 (1987).

U.S. v. Taylor, 320 F. Supp. 2d 790 (N.D. Ind. 2004).

U.S. v. Weed, 389 F. 3d 1060 (2004).

Velasquez, R. J., Castellanos, J., Garrido, M., Maness, P., & Anderson, U. (2006). Interpreting forensic interview and test data of Latino children:

Recommendations for culturally competent evaluations. In S. N. Sparta & G. P. Koocher (Eds.), *Forensic mental health assessment of children and adolescents* (pp. 97–112). Oxford: Oxford University Press.

Vincent, G., & Grisso, T. (2005). A developmental perspective on adolescent personality, psychopathology, and delinquency. In T. Grisso, G. Vincent, & D. Seagrave (Eds.), *Mental health screening and assessment in juvenile justice* (p. 22–43). New York: Guilford Press.

Vincent, G. M., & Hart, S. D. (2002). Psychopathy in childhood and adolescence: Implications for the assessment and management of multiproblem youths. In R. R. Corrado et al. (Eds.), *Multi-problem violent youth: A foundation for comparative research on needs, interventions, and outcomes.* Amsterdam: IOS Press.

Vitacco, M. J., & Vincent, G. M. (2006). Understanding the downward extension of psychopathy to youth: Implications for risk assessment and juvenile justice. *International Journal of Forensic Mental Health, 5,* 29–38.

Vossekuil, B., Reddy, M., Fein, R., Borum, R., & Modzeleski, W. (2002). *The final report of the Safe School Initiative: Implications for the prevention of school attacks in the United States.* Washington, DC: U.S. Secret Service, National Threat Assessment Center.

Wallsten, T. S., Budescu, D. V., Zwick, R., & Kemp, S. M. (1993). Preferences and reasons for communicating probabilistic information in verbal or numerical terms. *Bulletin of the Psychonomic Society, 31,* 135–138.

Walters, G. D. (2003). Predicting criminal justice outcomes with the Psychopathy Checklist and Lifestyle Criminality Screening Form: A meta-analytic comparison. *Behavioral Sciences and the Law, 21,* 89–102.

Webster, C. D., Douglas, K. S., Eaves, D., & Hart, S. D. (1997a). Assessing risk of violence to others. In C. D. Webster & M. A. Jackson (Eds.), *Impulsivity: Theory, assessment, and treatment* (pp. 251–277). New York: Guilford Press.

Webster, C. D., Douglas, K. S., Eaves, D., & Hart, S. D. (1997b). *HCR-20: Assessing risk for violence* (Version 2). Burnaby, British Columbia, Canada: Simon Fraser University, Mental Health, Law, and Policy Institute.

Webster, C. D., Harris, G. T., Rice, M. E., Cormier, C., & Quinsey, V. L. (1994). *The violence prediction scheme: Assessing dangerousness in high risk men.* Toronto: University of Toronto, Centre of Criminology.

Webster, C. D., & Jackson, M. A. (1997). *Impulsivity: Theory, assessment, and treatment.* New York: Guilford Press.

Webster, C. D., Muller-Isberner, R., & Fransson, G. (2002). Violence risk assessment: Using structured clinical guides professionally. *International Journal of Forensic Mental Health, 1,* 185–193.

Weibush, R., Baird, C., Krisberg, B., & Onek, D. (1995). Risk assessment and classification for serious, violent, and chronic juvenile offenders. In R. Loeber & D. Farrinton (Eds.), *Serious and violent juvenile offenders: Risk factors and successful interventions* (pp. 68–85). Thousand Oaks, CA: Sage.

Weiner, I. B. (2006). Writing forensic reports. In I. B. Weiner & A. K. Hess (Eds.), *Handbook of forensic psychology* (3rd ed., pp. 631–651). Hoboken, NJ: Wiley.

Werner, E. E. (2000). Protective factors and individual resilience. In R. Meisells & J. Shonkoff (Eds.), *Handbook of early intervention* (pp. 115–132). Cambridge: Cambridge University Press.

Werner, P. T., Rose, T. L., Yesavage, J. A., & Seeman, K. (1984). Psychiatrists' judgments of dangerousness in patients on an acute care unit. *American Journal of Psychiatry, 141,* 263–266.

Westen, D., & Weinberger, J. (2004). When clinical description becomes statistical prediction. *American Psychologist, 59,* 595–613.

Wexler, D. (1992). Putting mental health into mental health law. *Law and Human Behavior, 16,* 27–38.

White, J. L., Moffitt, T. E., Caspi, A., Bartusch, D. J., Needles, D. J., & Stouthamer-Loeber, M. (1994). Measuring impulsivity and examining its relationship to delinquency. *Journal of Abnormal Psychology, 103,* 192–205.

Widiger, T. A., & Corbitt, E. (1995). Antisocial personality disorder. In W. J. Livesley (Ed.), *DSM-IV personality disorders* (pp. 103–134). New York: Guilford Press.

Widom, C. S. (1989). The cycle of violence. *Science, 244,* 160–166.

Widom, C. S. (1994). Childhood victimization and adolescent problem behaviors. In R. D. Ketterlinus & M. E. Lamb (Eds.), *Adolescent problem behaviors* (pp. 127–164). Hillsdale, NJ: Erlbaum.

Willie, C. V., Rieker, P. P., Kramer, B. M., & Brown, B. S. (Eds.). (1995). *Mental health, racism, and sexism.* Pittsburgh, PA: University of Pittsburgh Press.

Winick, B. J. (1998). Sex offender law in the 1990s: A therapeutic jurisprudence analysis. *Psychology, Public Policy, and Law, 4,* 505–570.

Winick, B. J., & Kress, K. (Eds.). (2003). Preventive outpatient commitment for persons with serious mental illness [Special issue]. *Psychology, Public Policy, and Law, 9*(1/2).

Wollert, R. (2001). An analysis of the argument that clinicians under-predict sexual violence in civil commitment cases. *Behavioral Sciences and the Law, 19,* 171–184.

Wollert, R. (2006). Low base rates limit certainty when current actuarials are used to identify sexually violent predators: An application of Bayes's theorem. *Psychology, Public Policy, and Law, 12,* 56–85.

Wong, S., & Hare, R. D. (2005). *Guidelines for a psychopathy treatment program.* North Tonawanda, NY: Multi-Health Systems.

Woodson v. North Carolina, 428 U.S. 280, 305 (1976).

Worling, J. (2004). The Estimate of Risk of Adolescent Sexual Offense Recidivism (ERASOR): Preliminary psychometric data. *Sexual Abuse: A Journal of Research and Treatment, 16,* 235–254.

Wright, K. R., Clear, T. R., & Dickson, P. (1984). Universal applicability of probation risk assessment instruments. *Criminology, 22,* 113–133.

Wyatt v. Stickney, 344 F. Supp. 373 (1972).

Yamagishi, K. (1997). When a 12.86% mortality is more dangerous than 24.14%: Implications for risk communication. *Applied Cognitive Psychology, 11,* 495–506.

Zisook, S., Byrd, D., Kuck, J., & Jeste, D. V. (1995). Command hallucinations in outpatients with schizophrenia. *Journal of Clinical Psychology, 56,* 462–465.

Index

A

Academic performance, 75
Actuarial versus clinical debate,
    8–9, 67, 115
Addington v. Texas, 156
Adjustment Disorder with
    Depressed Mood, in sample
    report, 279
Adolescent offenders. *See* Juvenile
    offenders
Adult court, transfer to, 233–234
Adult relationships:
    juvenile offenders, and loss of,
        227
    sexual offenders, and romantic
        relationships, 193–194
Adversarial nature of legal
    proceedings, 30
Adversity in early home life,
    220–221
Affect, negative, 74
Age:
    death penalty case and, 246
    as risk factor, 70–71
    sexual offenders and, 188–189,
        194
Alcoholism. *See* Substance
    abuse/alcoholism
Americans with Disabilities Act
    (1990), Title II, 158
Anamnestic approach, 94–98, 177

Anger as risk factor, 73
Antisocial attitudes, 74
Antisocial lifestyle, sexual
    offenders, 188
Antisocial personality disorder
    (APD):
    Foucha v. Louisiana, 42, 43, 159
    gender differences, 73
    pervasiveness in prison,
        242–243
    predictive value of, 70, 242
    in sample reports, 274, 294
    sexual offenders and, 43–44,
        188
Archival sources versus self-
    report, base rate variation,
    50–51
Arrest rates, 52
Arson, 37
Attachment, 75
Authority, positive response to, 75

B

Barefoot v. Estelle, 5–6, 7, 115,
    237, 251–252
Base rate(s), 21, 22–23, 45–66
    actuarial instruments for
        identifying/estimating:
    described, 62–64
    generalizability, 64–65

Base rate(s)(*Continued*)
    limitations to the use of,
        64–65
    scope of inquiry, 65–66
  death penalty cases, 238–241
  defined, 45
  illustration of, 54–55
  importance of to violence risk
    assessments, 46–48
  juvenile offenders, 208–209
  key factors, 59
  local, 60–62
  model for risk assessment,
    overview, 21, 22–23
  overview table, base rates of
    violence or reoffense across
    studies and populations,
    56–58
  as point of reference, 126–127
  sample/examinee characteristics
    and, 59
  serious mental illness, 161–163
  setting/context characteristics
    and, 59
  sexual offenders, 183–185
  time-frame characteristics and,
    54, 59
  trickiness of for violence risk
    assessment, 48–54
  undetected information, 53–54
  using, 55–60
  varying:
    by method of detection,
      50–53
    by type of violence, 49–50
    over time, 54
  violence characteristics and, 37,
    59
Base rate fallacy, 48
Base rate neglect, 48
Baxstrom v. Herald, 3

Beasley v. Molett, 183
Berberoglu, Linda (sample risk
    assessment report), 270–275
Borum, R., 47–48, 207, 218, 231
Brinkley, Chad (sample risk
    assessment report), 297–307
Burgess, A. W., 185

C

Capital cases. *See* Death penalty
    defendants
Categorical estimates of risk,
    102–106
Childhood sexual abuse, 190–191
Child molesters. *See* Sexual
    offenders
Civil commitment, 2, 19, 35–36,
    54, 132–133, 155–156, 291
Classification of Violence Risk,
    11–12, 259–260
Cleckley, Hervey (*The Mask of
    Sanity*), 2
Clinical assessment versus forensic
    evaluation, 77
Clinical judgment, 9, 67–68, 84,
    115
Clinical versus actuarial debate,
    8–9
Coercion, impact of on treatment,
    176
Cognitive-behavioral approach,
    sexual offenders, 200
Cognitive-experiential self theory,
    116
Colorado v. Parrish, 43
Commitment:
  civil, 2, 19, 35–36, 132–133,
    155–156, 291
  criminal justice system, 157–158

Communication:
  of risk assessment results (*see*
    Risk communication)
  risk management planning, and
    clear channels for, 148
Competence:
  evaluator, 17–20, 203–204
  legal determination of, 183
Compliance, treatment, 38,
    39–40, 74, 88
Conditional model of risk, 13
Confidentiality, 150–151
Conroy, Mary Alice (sample risk
    assessment reports),
    276–280, 291–296
Containment approach, sexual
    offenders, 200–201
Contexts:
  base rates and, 59
  defining the question, 40–42
  emphasizing, in risk
    communication, 128–131
  juvenile offenders, 220–222,
    226, 227–228
  neighborhood, 167, 221–222
  risk management, 13–14
  serious mental illness, 167,
    172–173
Continuum, dichotomy versus, 7, 9
Cormier, C. A., 8
Cornell, D., 203–204
Counsel, right to, 183
Court preferences:
  case-specific/idiographic data
    versus base rate data, 61
  risk communication strategies,
    112–117
Cultural variability, 75, 84, 89–92
Cunningham, M. D., 244, 250–251
  sample risk assessment report,
    287–290

D

Dangerousness, defined, 35
*Daubert v. Merrell Dow
    Pharmaceuticals, Inc.*, 27, 76
Death penalty defendants,
    235–253
  base rates and normative data,
    238–241
  bifurcated trials, 237
  defining the question, 236–237
  gang membership, 248, 253
  idiographic risk factors and
      individualized assessment,
      247–248
  instruments for assessing risk
      factors, 244–247
  legal context, 236–237
  risk communication, 248–252,
      287–290
    consultant's roles, 249
    context, 128–129
    initial negotiation, 248–249
    role as evaluator, 249–250
    role as teaching witness,
      249
    sample report, 287–290
    to trier of fact, 250–252
  risk factors, empirically
      supported, 241–244
  risk management, 252–253
Decision thresholds, 112
Decision tree methodology:
  Classification of Violence Risk,
    11–12, 259–260
  Iterative Classification Tree
    (ICT), 69, 169–170
Defining the question, 21–22,
    34–44
  cause, 42–44
  context/contexts, 40–42

Defining the question (*Continued*)
  death penalty cases, 236–237
  defining terms:
    dangerousness, 35
    predatory, 36
    violence, 35
  juvenile offenders, 205–207
  model for risk assessment,
    overview, 21–22, 99
  serious mental illness, 154–161
  sexual offenders, 179–183
  time periods covered, 38–40
  violence types, 35–37
Delinquent peer affiliation, 221.
  See also Juvenile offenders;
  Peer relationships
Delusional beliefs, 83, 95, 96,
  164, 196
Deviant sexual interests,
  186–187
*Diagnostic and Statistical Manual
  of Mental Disorders (DSM)*,
  43, 159, 198
Diplomate status, 19
Discharge statutes, 175
Disposition proceedings, juvenile
  offenders, 232
*Dixon v. Attorney General of the
  Commonwealth of Pennsylvania*,
  4
Doctrine of least restrictive
  alternative, 138, 158
Domestic violence, 36–37
Doren, D. M., 132–133
"Dr. Death," 251–252
Dual roles, 151
Due process protections, 42, 204
Duty to warn, 5
Dvoskin, J., 99
Dynamic risk factors, 13, 73–74,
  111, 189–190

E

Early Assessment Risk Lists
  (EARL-20B/EARL-21G),
  225, 266
Early-onset violence, juvenile
  offenders, 214
Education as protective factor,
  244
Empirically supported
  risk/protective factors.
  See Risk/protective factors,
  empirically supported
Employment instability, 190
Estimate of Risk of Adolescent
  Sexual Offense Recidivism
  (ERASOR), 11, 266–267
Estimating risk. *See* Risk estimates
Ethical Guidelines for Forensic
  Psychologists, 32, 34–35
*Ethical Principles of Psychologists
  and Code of Conduct*, 23,
  76–77, 120
Evaluator competence, 17–20,
  203–204
Evidence-based practice,
  comparison of models, 26

F

Family:
  abuse within, 36–37
  as risk/protective factor, 75,
  220–221, 227
Female gender as protective factor,
  75. *See also* Gender
Fifth Amendment rights, 183,
  250
Financial cost, relative, 137–138
Fire setting, 37

Flexibility in risk management planning, 148–149
Florida, 183, 239, 247
Foucha v. Louisiana, 42, 43, 159
Frequency versus probability estimates of risk, 102, 106–109
Frye rule (*Frye v. United States*), 27, 76
Furman v. Georgia, 236, 238

G

Gang affiliation:
   death penalty cases, 244, 246, 248, 253
   juvenile offenders, 221
Gender, 72–73, 74, 75
"Gravely disabled" construct, 156
Grigson, James ("Dr. Death"), 251–252
Grisso, T., 33, 205–206, 228

H

Hallucinations, 164, 166
Hanson, R. K., 47
Hare, R. D., 20, 90. *See also* Psychopathy Checklist-Revised (PCL-R)
Harris, A. J. R., 47
Harris, G. T., 8
Hart, S. D., 65
HCR-20. *See* Historical, Clinical, Risk Scheme (HCR-20)
Heilbrun, K., 99
Hendricks case. *See Kansas v. Hendricks*
Hinckley v. U.S., 38

Hinshaw, S. P., 215
Historical, Clinical, Risk Scheme (HCR-20):
   categorical estimates of risk, 102
   described, 14–15, 24, 79–80, 224, 225, 261
   gender and, 73
   historical perspective on development of instruments, 11, 14–15
   idiographic information and, 93
   mock death penalty sentencing phase, used in, 116
   nomothetic base, 93
   overview, 261
   PCL-R and cultural bias and, 91
   predictive value of, 246
   reference, 261
   role in assessment process, 30, 80
   in sample risk assessment report, 304–306, 307
   serious mental illness and, 169
   supervision violations and, 72
   web sites, 261
Historical perspective. *See* Risk assessment in historical perspective
Hormone compounds for sex drive reduction, 200

I

ICT. *See* Iterative classification tree decision model
Idiographic factors and individualized assessment, 21, 24–26, 83–98
   anamnestic approach, 94–98
   death penalty defendants, 247–248

Idiographic factors and
  individualized assessment
  (*Continued*)
  dynamic factors, 84, 87
    mental illness, 87–88
    stressors, 89
    substance abuse, 88–89
  face validity and legal relevance
    of risk assessment process,
    84, 93–94
  juvenile offenders, 225–227
  model for risk assessment,
    overview, 21, 24–26
  multicultural variability, 84,
    89–92
  nomothetic data and, 97
  overview/introduction, 83–84
  risk management, 84, 92–93
  seriously mentally ill patients,
    170–174
  sexual offenders, 193–196
  unique risk/protective factors,
    25, 84, 85–87
  vignettes, 94–98, 170–171
"Imminently dangerous" construct,
  54
Impulse control, 198
Impulsivity, 73–74, 215
In re Branch, 183
In re commitment of Dennis H., 159
In re David B., 40
In re Fisher, 183
In re Gault, 205
In re K. L., 160
In re Mark, 136
In re Winship, 205
Insanity defense:
  Not Guilty By Reason of
    Insanity (NGRI), 153, 164,
    165, 175
  in sample report, 281–286

in sample risk management
    plan, 142–145
  in vignette, 95
Insanity Defense Reform Act
  (1984), 157, 169
Institution versus community, 13
Instruments. *See also specific
    instruments*:
  death penalty cases, 244–247
  historical perspective on
    development of, 10–12
  juveniles, 224–225, 266–268
  overviews of, 259–268
  risk factors, 75–81
    admission as evidence, 76
    appropriateness to task, 76–77
    pure actuarial approach, 79
    selection, 80–81
    standard psychological test
      batteries, 78–79
    structured guide to risk
      assessment, 79–80
  serious mental illness, 169–170
  sexual offenders, 191–193, 263,
    265
  specialty, 169–170
  testing, role of, 28–30
Intelligence, 75
Iterative classification tree
  decision model:
  Classification of Violence Risk,
    11–12, 259–260
  Iterative Classification Tree
    (ICT), 69, 169–170

J

Jones v. U.S., 36
JSOAP. *See* Juvenile Sex Offender
  Assessment Protocol II
  (JSOAP)

Judges, 20, 112–117, 126, 176
Jurek v. Texas, 5, 6, 237
Jurisprudence, therapeutic,
    136–138
Juvenile offenders, 202–234
    base rates and nomothetic data,
        50, 208–209, 210–211
    changes in juvenile court,
        204–208
    defining the question, 205–207
    evaluator competence, 203–204
    idiographic risks factors and
        individualized assessment,
        225–227
        adult relationship, loss of,
            227
        context, 226
        family, 227
        peer group, 226
    instruments, 11, 212, 224–225,
        266–268
    labels, 229–230
    life-course persistent offenders,
        39
    parens patriae model of juvenile
        justice, 2, 204
    risk assessment statistics, 18
    risk communication, 227–230
    risk factors, 212–223
        caveats about, 222–223
        contextual, 220–222
        delinquent peer affiliation,
            221
        early-onset violence, 214
        family variables, 220–221
        gang affiliation, 221
        impulsivity, 215
        individual and historical,
            213–220
        neighborhood context,
            221–222
        peer relationships, 221
        predictive value, near versus
            distant future, 222
        prior violence, 213
        psychiatric illness, 216
        psychopathic personality
            features, 216–220
        social information
            processing, 215–216
        substance abuse, 214–215,
            223
        total number of risk factors,
            223
    risk management, 230–232
    threat assessment versus risk
        assessment, 207–208
    time frames, importance of, 39
    types of juvenile proceedings:
        disposition, 232
        pretrial proceedings, 232
        transfer to adult court,
            233–234
    varied operational definitions of
        violence, 50
Juvenile Sex Offender Assessment
    Protocol II (JSOAP), 11, 267

K

Kansas v. Crane, 198
Kansas v. Hendricks, 6, 43,
    181–182, 197
Kendra's Law, 158–159, 160
Kent v. United States, 205, 233
Kumho v. Carmichael, 27

L

Labels, diagnostic, 229–230
Least restrictive alternative,
    doctrine of, 138, 158

Lee, S., 215
Legal context:
  adversarial nature of legal
    proceedings, 30
  confidentiality, 150–151
  death penalty, 236–237
  serious mental illness, 155–161
  sexually violent predator risk
    assessments, 180–183
Legal statute, example in risk
  communication, 118
Leisure activities, organized, 75
Lessard v. Schmidt, 156, 158
Level of Service Inventory-
  Revised, 11, 15, 80, 246,
  260
Life without parole (LWOP), 237,
  239–240
Litwack, T. R., 8
Local base rates, 60–62
Lockett v. Ohio, 235
Lombroso, Cesare, 1
Loss of significant adult, 227

M

MacArthur Risk Study, 7, 11, 50,
  54, 114, 162, 164, 166, 169
Management-oriented
  communication, 100–102,
  111
Marriage as protective factor, 74
McNeil, D. E., 23–24
Measuring risk, 8–10
Medication:
  serious mental illness, 130,
    160–161, 176–177
  sexual offenders, 200
"Mental disorders," defined, 44,
  159–160

Mental illness, serious, 153–178
  anamnestic assessment, 171
  base rates and nomothetic data,
    161–163
  civil commitment, 155–156
  coercion, impact of on
    treatment, 176
  commitment, 157–159, 176
  defining the question,
    154–161
  doctrine of least restrict
    alternative, 158
  idiographic risk and
    individualized assessment,
    87–88, 170–174
  insanity defense (*see* Insanity
    defense)
  juvenile offenders and, 216
  legal context, 155–161
  medication, 160–161,
    176–177
  mental disorder defined,
    159–160, 162
  psychopathy, 177
  risk communication, 174–176,
    281–286
  risk factors, 163–170
    comorbid substance abuse,
      166
    context of problem behavior,
      172–173
    current mental status,
      168–169
    delusions/hallucinations,
      164
    dynamic, 87–88
    hallucinations, 166
    instruments for assessing,
      169–170
    neighborhood context, 167
    past violence, 168

pattern of mental illness, 172
pattern of violent or
    potentially violent
    behavior, 173–174
problematic relationships,
    167–168
specific to mental disorder,
    163–167, 171–174
threat/control override
    delusions (TCOs),
    164–165
treatment response, 173
risk management, 176–178
sample report, 281–286
vignette, 170–171
Meta-analytic techniques, 12
Methodology:
advances in, 12–13
methodological flaws in early
    studies, 4–5
rigor/objectivity, 30
Millon Clinical Multiaxial
    Inventory-III, 78
Minnesota Multiphasic
    Personality Inventory
    (MMPI-2), 78, 271, 273
Minnesota Sex Offender
    Screening Tool-Revised
    (MnSOST-R), 11, 72, 191,
    262, 292
Minority status and oppression,
    91–92. *See also* Cultural
    variability
Misleading risk factors, 190–191
Model. *See* Risk assessment model
Monahan, J., 65–66, 103, 107–108,
    154
Mood, as risk factor, 73
Mood disorder, 162, 279
Moral insanity, 1–2
Morton, K. E., 47

Mrad, David F. (sample risk
    assessment report), 281–286
"Multiple pathways/dimensions to
    recidivism," metaphor offered
    for, 133

N

Neighborhood context:
    juvenile offenders, 221–222
    serious mental illness, 167
Normative data, 21, 22–23. *See
    also* Base rate(s)
Not Guilty By Reason of Insanity
    (NGRI), 153, 164, 165, 175
    in sample report, 281–286
    in sample risk management
        plan, 142–145
    in vignette, 95
Numerical estimates of risk, 102,
    106–109

O

Objectivity in risk assessments,
    30–33
O'Connor v. Donaldson, 3, 156
Olmstead v. Zimring, 158
Oppression, 91–92
Organized leisure activities, 75
Outpatient commitment,
    158–159, 176

P

Parens patriae model of juvenile
    justice, 2, 204
Partisan bias, 30–33

Past history of violent/offending behavior:
death penalty cases, 243
empirically supported risk factor, 68–69
juvenile offenders, 213
serious mental illness, 168
sexual offenders, 194
Patient's Bill of Rights, 156
Pattern of offending behavior:
serious mental illness, 173–174
sexual offenders, 195
Peer relationships, 75, 221, 226
Personality Assessment Inventory, 78
Personality disorder, 42, 43, 166
Personality trait, dangerousness as, 41
Phallometric testing, 186
Physical injury/disability, 25, 83, 86, 97
Plethysmograph, 187
Polygraph, 187
Predatory, defined, 36
Prentky, R. A., 185
Pretrial proceedings, juvenile offenders, 232
Pritchard, James, 1–2
Probability versus frequency estimates of risk, 102, 106–109
Progestronal hormone compounds for sex drive reduction, 200
Protection of society, 149–150
Protective factors, 75
Psychiatric illness. See Mental illness, serious
Psychopathic Personality Inventory, 70
Psychopathy:
gender, 73
juvenile offenders, 216–220

label of, 229–230
as risk factor, 69
serious mental illness and, 177
sexual offenders and, 187–188
Psychopathy Checklist (PCL):
historical perspective on risk assessment, 10
Screening Version, 73
Youth Version (PCL:YV), 11, 217, 220
Psychopathy Checklist-Revised (PCL-R):
capital sentencing evaluations and, 244–246
cultural issues, 90, 91
decision tree methodology and, 11
description/overview, 261
extent of use of, 80–81
historical perspective on development of, 10–11, 77
nomothetic base, 93
predictive value of (correlation of scores with violent behavior), 69–70, 74, 166–167, 187–188
reference, 261
risk assessment and, 77, 177–178
in sample risk assessment reports, 276, 279, 291, 302–303, 307
in sample risk communication message, 123, 124, 127
self-report versus, 166–167
study comparing scores in, 31–32
in vignettes, 93, 95, 97, 171

VRAG and, 69, 70, 91, 246
web sites, 261
Psychosis/psychotic state, 74, 196.
See also Mental illness,
serious; Schizophrenia
Psychotropic medication, 130,
160–161, 176–177

Q

Quinsey, V. L., 8, 162–163

R

Rapid Risk Assessment for Sexual
Offense Recidivism
(RRASOR), 11, 262, 265
Receiver operating characteristic
(ROC) analysis, 12, 93
Redding, R. E., 112–113
Rehabilitative/incapacitation
model, 1
Reidy, T. J., 244, 250–251
Reisner, R., 251–252
Relationships:
peers, 75, 221, 226
problematic interpersonal, 74,
167–168
Rennie v. Klein, 160
Reports/testimony. *See* Risk
communication
Research driven normative data,
83
Research methodology, strives in
improving, 15
Resilient temperament as
protective factor, 75
Responsivity principle, 141, 231
Rice, M. E., 8

Risk assessment in historical
perspective, 1–15
advances in methodology and
analysis, 12–13
meta-analytic techniques, 12
receiver operating
characteristic (ROC)
analysis, 12
survival curve analysis, 13
clinical versus actuarial debate,
8–9, 67
court opinions, 5–6
development of instruments,
10–12
dichotomy versus continuum,
dangerousness prediction,
7, 9
first-generation research, 2–5
learning to measure risk, 8–10
risk management, 13–15
shift in paradigm, 6–8
Risk assessment model, 16–33
competence issue, 17–20
components of evidence-based
practice model compared
to, 26
components/stages:
overviews, 20–28
stage 1: defining the question
(*see* Defining the
question)
stage 2: considering
normative data and
population base rates
(*see* Base rate(s))
stage 3: considering
empirically supported
risk and protective
factors (*see* Risk/
protective factors,
empirically supported)

Risk assessment model
(*Continued*)
    stage 4: considering
        idiographic risk factors
        (*see* Idiographic factors
        and individualized
        assessment)
    stage 5: communicating risk
        assessment results (*see*
        Risk communication)
    stage 6: linking risk
        assessment to risk
        management (*see* Risk
        management)
    key task of risk assessment,
        17
    nonclinicians, note for, 20
    rationale, 16–17
    testing, role of, 28–30
Risk assessment reports, sample,
    269–307
Risk Assessment Scale for Prison,
    247
Risk communication, 21, 26–27,
    99–134
    case-specific testimony, 120
    death penalty cases, 248–252
    ethical standards, 27
    juvenile offenders, 227–230
    legal criteria for admission, 27
    model for risk assessment,
        overview, 21, 26–27
    options, 100–109
        risk estimates (categorical
            versus numerical),
            102–109
        style (descriptive versus
            prediction-oriented
            versus management-
            oriented), 100–102

    practical guidance, 117–133
        acknowledging limits,
            131–132
        articulating clearly reasoning
            behind conclusions,
            123–124
        assuming role of educator,
            119–120
        avoiding red herring data,
            121–122
        delineating procedure used to
            arrive at risk opinion,
            120
        emphasizing context,
            128–131
        knowing your audience,
            133
        multiple formats, 124–126
        point of reference, 126–128
        presenting relevant data
            clearly, 120
        reiterating referral question
            and evaluation
            boundaries, 117–119
        tests and test results, 123
        using clear, simple, and
            precise language, 132
    preferences:
        clinician, 109–112
        court, 112–117
        judges, 112–114
        laypersons and mock jurors,
            114–117
    research on, 100–117
    resources, 133–134
        court testimony guides, 134
        report writing generally,
            134
    serious mental illness, 174–176
    sexual offenders, 196–199

Risk estimates, 102–109
  categorical, 102–106
  clinician practices/preferences,
      109–112
  numerical (probability or
      frequency), 102,
      106–109
Risk management, 13–15, 21,
      27–28, 135–152
  common errors, 138–140
  conditional model of risk, 13
  context, importance of, 13, 14
  death penalty cases, 252–253
      gang association, 253
      levels of custody available,
          253
      limiting telephone usage and
          visitation privileges,
          253
  doctrine of least restrictive
      alternative, 138
  dynamic risk factors, 13
  financial costs, relative,
      137–138
  formulating plan for, 138–142
      planning process, 140–142
      responsivity principle, 141
      risk factors, analysis of, 141
  historical perspective on,
      13–15
  juvenile offenders, 230–232
  model for risk management,
      overview, 21, 27–28
  principles, 145–152
      clarification on
          confidentiality and legal
          reporting, 150–151
      clear channels of
          communication
          identified, 148

clearly identified centralized
    entity monitoring plan,
    146–147
identified risk factors directly
    linked to management
    strategies, 146
immediate intervention and
    graduated response,
    149–150
maximum energy/resources
    devoted to individuals at
    highest risk for violent
    behavior, 145–146
regular reassessment and
    modification, 151–152
specificity and flexibility,
    148–149
tailoring plans to situational
    realities, 147–148
thinking beyond
    conventional treatments,
    147
risk status versus risk state, 13
sample plan for, 142–145
serious mental illness, 176–178
  coercion, and impact on
      treatment, 176
  outpatient commitment,
      176
  psychopathy, 177
  psychotropic medication,
      176–177
sexual offenders, 199–201
  cognitive behavioral
      approach, 200
  containment approach,
      200–201
  medication, 200
therapeutic jurisprudence,
    136–138

Risk/protective factors,
  empirically supported, 21,
    23–24, 67–82
  death penalty defendants,
    241–244
  instruments, 75–81
    admission as evidence, 76
    appropriateness to task,
      76–77
    pure actuarial approach, 79
    selection, 80–81
    standard psychological test
      batteries, 78–79
    structured guide to risk
      assessment, 79–80
  juvenile offenders, 212–223
  metaphor offered for,
    132–133
  model for risk assessment,
    overview, 21, 23–24
  protective factors, 74–75
  risk factors, 68–74
    age, 70–71
    anger, 73
    antisocial attitudes, 74
    dynamic factors, 73–74
    gender, 72–73
    impulsiveness, 74
    impulsivity, 73–74
    mood, 73
    negative affect, 74
    past history of violent
      behavior, 68–69
    poor treatment compliance,
      74
    problems in interpersonal
      relationships, 74
    psychopathy, 69
    psychosis, 74
    static factors, 68–72

    substance abuse, 71, 73, 74
    supervision violation, 71–72
  risk management and, 80, 141,
    146
  scientific literature on risk
    assessment, 82
  serious mental illness, 163–170
  sexual offenders, 185–191
  third party information,
    81–82
Risk status versus risk state, 13
Rivers v. Katz, 160
ROC curves. See Receiver
    operating characteristic
    (ROC) analysis
Rogers v. Okin, 160
Romantic relationships as
    protective factor, 193
RRASOR. See Rapid Risk
    Assessment for Sexual
    Offense Recidivism
    (RRASOR)
Ryce Act, 183

S

SARA. See Spousal Assault Risk
    Assessment Guide (SARA)
Schall v. Martin, 6
Schizoaffective disorder (in
    sample risk assessment
    report), 285
Schizophrenia. See also Mental
    illness, serious:
  sample risk assessment reports,
    281–286, 298, 306
  sample risk management plan,
    142
  violence and, 88

School(s):
  academic performance as
    protective factor, 75
  threats/incidents of violence in,
    18, 87, 92
Schopp, R. F., 104
Screening Scale for Pedophilic
  Interests (SSPI), 263
Self-mutilation, 156
"Serious bodily harm," 156
Serious mental illness. *See* Mental
  illness, serious
Sex Offender Need Assessment
  Rating, 190
Sex Offender Risk Appraisal
  Guide (SORAG), 11, 72, 91,
  106, 263
Sexual abuse in childhood,
  190–191
Sexually violent predator (SVP)
  statutes, 36–37, 192
Sexual offenders, 179–201
  access to victims, 41
  base rates, 51–52, 183–185
  context, 25, 40
  defining the question, 179–183
  historical perspective, sexual
    psychopath laws, 2
  instruments, 11, 191–193
  legal competence issue, 183
  legal context, 180–183
    Hendricks case, 6, 43,
      181–182, 197
    "predatory," 36
    proceedings as civil not
      criminal, 182
    sexually violent predator
      (SVP) statutes, 36–37,
      192
  red herring data, 121

  risk communication, 196–199
    examples, 124, 130
    sample reports, 270–275,
      291–296
  risk management, 199–201
    cognitive behavioral
      approach, 200
    containment approach,
      200–201
    medication/hormones, 200
  risk/protective factors,
    185–191
    adult romantic relationships,
      193–194
    age, 188–189, 194
    antisocial lifestyle, 188
    atypical, 195–196
    delusional beliefs, 196
    detailed functional analysis
      of past offenses, 196
    deviant sexual interests,
      186–187
    dynamic factors, 189–190
    idiographic, 193–196
    misleading risk factors,
      190–191
    past failures in cooperating
      with treatment
      providers, 189
    past history of sexual
      offending, 194
    pattern of offending, 195
    prior sexual offenses, 186
    psychopathology, severe
      Axis I, 196
    psychopathy, 187–188
    psychotic state, 196
    substance abuse, 194–195
    victim's sex and relationship,
      189

Sexual offenders (Continued)
  therapeutic jurisprudence, 136
  ultimate legal issue
    opinion/testimony, 199
  unusual circumstances (blinded
    prisoner), 25
  in vignette, 96–97
  violence risk, sexual versus
    general, 50
Sexual/Violence/Risk (SVR-20),
  11, 72, 191, 265
Shah, Saleem, 3
Shift in paradigm, 6–8
Situational realities, risk
  management plan and,
  147–148
Situational variability, complexity
  of, 13
Skipper v. South Carolina, 237
Slobogin, C., 251–252
Slovic, P., 107–108
Social bonding to positive role
  models, 75
Social information processing,
  violence-conducive, juvenile
  offenders, 215–216
Social orientation, positive, 75
Social support, 75, 190
SORAG. See Sex Offender Risk
  Appraisal Guide (SORAG)
Specialty Guidelines for Forensic
  Psychologists, 32, 81, 122
Specialty instruments, 169–170
Spiritual values, 75
Spousal Assault Risk Assessment
  Guide (SARA), 11, 37, 93,
  264
SSPI. See Screening Scale for
  Pedophilic Interests (SSPI)
Stalkers, 36
State/status, risk, 13

STATIC-99:
  described, 17, 29, 191, 265
  historical perspective, 11
  reference, 265
  role in risk assessment, 17, 192
  in sample reports, 125, 126,
    273, 292
  STATIC-2002 in final research
    stages, 265
  in vignette, 97
  web site, 265
Static factors, 68–72
Steadman, H. J., 103
Stressors, 89
Structured Anchored Clinical
  Judgment (SACJ-Min; "the
  Thornton"), 264, 265
Structured Assessment of
  Violence Risk in Youth
  (SAVRY), 102, 224, 267–268
Substance abuse/alcoholism:
  child molester, paradoxical
    case, 89
  as dynamic factor, in
    individualized assessment,
    88–89, 190
  intentional intoxication by
    rapists, 93
  juvenile offenders, 214–215,
    223
  mental illness and, 166
  as risk factor, 71, 73, 74, 242
  risk management, 141–142,
    150
  in sample reports, 272, 274,
    285, 293, 294, 298–299
  schizoaffective disorder and,
    285
  sexual offenders, 89, 194–195
  in vignette, 95
Suicidal behavior, 156, 294

Supervision:
   inclusion of special conditions,
      41–42
   poor cooperation with, 190
   violation of probation, 71–72
Survival curve analysis, 13
SVP. *See* Sexually violent predator
   (SVP) statutes
SVR-20. *See* Sexual/Violence/
   Risk (SVR-20)
Szasz, Thomas, 2
Szell v. U.S., 160

T

*Tarasoff v. The Regents of the
   University of California*, 5,
   87
Teaching witness, 249
Temperament as protective factor,
   75
Testing. *See also* Instruments:
   risk communication and, 123
   role of, 28–30
Testimony/reports. *See* Risk
   communication
Texas:
   death penalty proceedings,
      128–129, 236–237, 238,
      252
   outpatient commitment, 182,
      199
   sexual offenders, 137, 182
Therapeutic jurisprudence,
   136–138
Thornton. *See* Structured
   Anchored Clinical Judgment
   (SACJ-Min; "the Thornton")
Threat assessment, versus risk
   assessment, 86–87, 207–208

Threat/control override delusions
   (TCOs), 164–165
Time frame(s):
   base rates, 54, 59
   disposition phase versus pretrial
      phase, 233
   juvenile offenders, 38–40, 233
Trait, dangerousness as, 41
Transfer to adult court, 233–234
Treatment:
   compliance, 38, 39–40, 74, 88
   planning (*see* Risk
      management)
   response history, in serious
      mental illness, 173
Typographical errors, 82

U

Ultimate issue opinions/decisions,
   105–106, 174, 199
Urinalysis, 141–142
U.S. v. Bilyk, 43
U.S. v. Henley, 43
U.S. v. Murdoch, 43
U.S. v. Sahhar, 40
U.S. v. Salerno, 6, 38
U.S. v. Weed, 159

V

Verhaagen, D., 218
Violence:
   defined, 35
   frequency and severity, 36
   model for assessing risk of (*see*
      Risk assessment model)
   prevention (*see* Risk
      management)

Violence *(Continued)*
  social information processing
    conducive to, 215–216
  types of, 35–37
Violence Prediction Scheme, 11
Violence prevention versus
  violence prediction, 92–93.
  See also Risk management
VRAG (Violence Risk Appraisal
  Guide):
  description/overview, 266
  historical perspective on
    development of
    instruments, 11
  juvenile instruments and, 212
  PCL-R and, 69, 70, 91, 246
  probability estimates, 106
  reference, 266
  in sample risk assessment
    reports, 276, 280,
    303–304, 307
  schizophrenia and, 88

  supervision failure, items
    related to, 72
  testimony based on, 115
  value of, 17
  in vignettes, 93, 95, 171
  web site, 266

W

Webster, C. D., 79
Woodson v. North Carolina, 235
Wyatt v. Stickney, 156

Y

Youth Level of Service/Case
  Management Inventory
  (YLS/CMI), 11, 224–225,
  268